A SARAH ORNE JEWETT
COMPANION

A SARAH ORNE JEWETT COMPANION

Robert L. Gale

GREENWOOD PRESS
Westport, Connecticut • London

Library of Congress Cataloging-in-Publication Data

Gale, Robert L., 1919–
    A Sarah Orne Jewett companion / Robert L. Gale.
    p.   cm.
    Includes bibliographical references (p.) and index.
    ISBN 0–313–30757–1 (alk. paper)
    1. Jewett, Sarah Orne, 1849–1909—Encyclopedias.   2. Women and
literature—Maine—History—19th century—Encyclopedias.   3. Women
authors, American—19th century—Biography—Encyclopedias.   4.
Maine—In literature—Encyclopedias. I. Title.
    PS2133.A3   1999
    813'.4—dc21   98–46814
    [b]

British Library Cataloguing in Publication Data is available.

Library of Congress Catalog Card Number: 98–46814
ISBN: 0–313–30757–1

First published in 1999

Greenwood Press, 88 Post Road West, Westport, CT 06881
An imprint of Greenwood Publishing Group, Inc.
www.greenwood.com

Printed in the United States of America

The paper used in this book complies with the
Permanent Paper Standard issued by the National
Information Standards Organization (Z39.48–1984).

10 9 8 7 6 5 4 3 2 1

For Maureen and our family

CONTENTS

PREFACE

For too long, Sarah Orne Jewett was dismissed as a timid New England local colorist. In 1940, Van Wyck Brooks, the distinguished cultural historian who, despite his unquestioned significance, got into a little trouble with his curious theories concerning Mark Twain and Henry James, dismissed Jewett with similar misguided one-sidedness. After recognizing her stylistic excellence, Brooks felt compelled to add this: "Her vision was certainly limited. It scarcely embraced the world of men, and the vigorous, masculine life of towns like Gloucester, astir with Yankee enterprise and bustle, lay quite outside her province and point of view" (*New England: Indian Summer*, pp. 347–48). Brooks must have been insufficiently impressed by the fact that F. O. Matthiessen, one of America's greatest literary critics, had published a pioneering study of Jewett in 1929 or that a French student, Jean Sougnac, had published his dissertation on Jewett in 1937. She was obviously respected by the knowledgeable both here and abroad.

Then came Richard Cary, Jewett's most devoted, pioneering critic. He skillfully edited a selection of Jewett's letters in 1956, published several apt essays on her then and later, and quickly followed John Eldridge Frost's 1960 study of Jewett with a vista-opening 1962 monograph and an expanded selection of Jewett's letters in 1967. During these years, numerous short biographical and critical pieces appeared. And with the advent of the women's movement came what must be called a Jewett renaissance. Contemporary critics, and innumerable purchasers and readers of popular reprints of Jewett as well, now recognize her as a uniquely sharp, compassionate observer of women and their lot in the New England of her era. Brooks wrongly implies that "masculine . . . bustle" was about nine-tenths of what was important in that region, though accomplished by only about 40 percent of its population. Jewett's New England had tragically lost many of its men—in the Civil War to her south, to the sea to her east, and out to the receding frontiers to her west. So Jewett focused her attention largely on New England women—generous, stingy, "hard-worked" (to use her term), aristocratic, attractive, wizened, but mostly toughing it out. More often than not, Jewett's male characters have retired from gnarling sea or farm work, and they talk of the good-to-fair old days; other Jewett men are still working but without much talk, or are so effete that their female associates run tactful rings around them.

The best recent critics of Jewett are women. Helpful introductory studies are by Margaret Ferrand Thorp (1966) and Josephine Donovan (1980). Following their monographs have been four longer, more intricate probings by Sarah Way Sherman (1989), Margaret Roman (1992), Elizabeth Silverthorne (1993), and Paula Blanchard (1994). Sherman is concerned with the mother-daughter myth in Jewett's fiction; Roman theorizes that Jewett wrote to rebuke the patriarchical norms that assume male superiority; and Silverthorne and Blanchard combine rich biographical detail and apt textual interpretation.

With or without too much critical aid, however, rank-and-file readers can appreciate Jewett quite nicely. Professional interpreters may examine, analyze, and help explicate her subtleties, but for decades Jewett's message has come through loud and clear. She celebrates the ordinary person's loyalty to family and adoration of nature—forests, rivers and the sea, farms and hills, and gardens—and she endorses the commitment by the lowly to the old-fashioned work ethic and the beneficence of solitude managed and life's inevitable strictures endured. Readers often leave their time under Jewett's spell challenged by her powers of observation and recording, to look afresh at their own patch of place with sharpened vision and to laugh a little, with her, in the face of problems. As the United States enters a new century ever more distressed by the gap between the "successful" and those left in the wake of "progress," Jewett and her message will become more important. She and Robert Frost, a New Englander whom she would have admired in the main, both advocate building soil, making much of diminished things, and seeing the all in the each. There is nothing hurtful in a good-sized dose of the old-fashioned.

A Sarah Orne Jewett Companion is informational rather than critical. It aims to cover all plots, situations, scenes, and characters in the twenty books Jewett published in her lifetime, plus *Verses* (Boston: privately printed, 1916) and *The Uncollected Short Stories of Sarah Orne Jewett* (ed. Richard Cary, Waterville Me.: Colby College Press, 1971). *Verses* collects nineteen poems; *Uncollected Short Stories* reprints forty-four stories first appearing in periodicals. The *Companion* also identifies Jewett's main family members and personal and professional friends, provides minibiographies of them, and indicates her relationship to them. Because of limitations of space, I ignore Jewett's trivial tales for children, insignificant poems, and ephemeral short stories and essays never reappearing in book form. A comparison of my index with that of Clara Carter

Weber and Carl J. Weber's Jewett bibliography (1949) will quickly help the curious identify the fugitive items I have omitted. Judicious use of my general bibliography and individual end-of-entry bibliographies, as well as my cross-referencing by asterisks, should enable readers to move from my work to Jewett's with both profit and fun. My hope here is to assist young readers just beginning to study Jewett, to aid more experienced readers eager to compare aspects of her diverse works, and to help graduate students, teachers, and publishing scholars locate primary and secondary data or merely refresh their memories of earlier readings. My intention has never been to eclipse Sarah's rich expressions by any clipped words of mine. My visit in June 1997 to the Sarah Orne Jewett House and the nearby Hamilton House in South Berwick, Maine, was a delight, made me at least minimally acquainted with the spirit of these places, and has given me the right—I think—to call their presiding genius "Sarah."

I offer thanks to my many colleagues in the Department of English of the University of Pittsburgh (my home away from home for four decades now) for making my retirement professionally congenial, to the reference librarians and interlibrary-loan personnel at Pitt for their unfailing cooperation, to the good people at and near Greenwood Press (especially Dr. George F. Butler, Betty C. Pessagno, and Diana Drew), and to my family for love that surpasses understanding.

CHRONOLOGY

1815	Theodore Herman Jewett* (1815–1878), Sarah Orne Jewett's father, is born.
1820	Caroline Frances Perry Jewett* (1820–1891), Sarah Jewett's mother, is born.
1842	Jewett's parents marry.
1847	Mary Rice Jewett* (1847–1930), Jewett's sister, is born.
1849	(Theodora) Sarah Orne Jewett is born 3 September in South Berwick, Maine, where physician father practices medicine.
1850	Jewett's first name, Theodora, is dropped.
1855	Jewett begins to attend local school.
1855	Caroline Augusta Eastman* (1855–1897), sister, is born.
1858	Jewett spends summer with maternal grandparents in Exeter and attends local school, hears yarns by retired sea captains when they visit her grandfather.
1861	Attends Berwick Academy in class of twelve children, begins to suffer lifelong attacks of arthritis, often joins father on rounds of rural practice, begins to read voraciously.
1866	Graduates from Berwick Academy, decides against becoming a physician for health reasons; continues habit of visiting relatives and friends in shore homes, New York City, and Boston.

1868   Publishes "Jenny Garrow's Lovers," her first short story, in *The Flag of Our Union* (Boston).

1868–69   Visits relatives in Cincinnati, Ohio, studies painting and attends dancing classes there.

1869   "Mr. Bruce" (under the pseudonym A. C. Eliot) accepted by William Dean Howells* for publication in *Atlantic Monthly*; begins publishing stories for children (under the pseudonyms Alice Eliot and A. C. Eliot) in several magazines; expands range of reading.

1870   Baptized and confirmed in St. John's Episcopal Church, Portsmouth, New Hampshire; attends and teaches Sunday school in South Berwick Congregational church.

1871   Meets and is guest of Howells and family.

1872   Expands circle of friends in Boston, Cambridge, and Newport; tries to translate a French novel.

1873   Studies German, determines to be professional writer.

1874–75   Visits Chicago and Indian reservation in Wisconsin.

1876   Visits Centennial Exposition in Philadelphia.

1877   Publishes *Deephaven*, her first book; visits Orrs Island; meets John Greenleaf Whittier,* in Amesbury, Massachusetts.

1878   Spends two months in Washington, D.C., as guest of Mary Bucklin Davenport Claflin* and William Claflin;* meets Abraham Lincoln's son, Robert Todd Lincoln, and President Rutherford B. Hayes; publishes *Play Days*, first book for children.

1879   Attends birthday party for Oliver Wendell Holmes* in Cambridge; other guests include Ralph Waldo Emerson, Annie Adams Fields* and James T. Fields, Julia Ward Howe,* Harriet Beecher Stowe,* Mark Twain,* and Charles Dudley Warner.*

1880   Though often ill, travels widely in New England.

1881   Visits New York with Fieldses; meets Henry Wadsworth Longfellow in Cambridge.

1882   Travels to Europe with the widowed Annie Fields, meets several British writers, including Alfred, Lord Tennyson;* begins pattern of living with Annie Fields in Boston during summer and winter months.

1883   Develops routine of writing letters in mornings and creative work in afternoons.

1884   Visits Moravians in Bethlehem, Pennsylvania, and the Howellses in Kennebunkport, Maine; begins habit of reading published letters of eminent persons.

1885	Begins correspondence with Marie Thérèse de Solms Blanc;* vacations on Isles of Shoals.
1886	Seeks treatment for rheumatism in spa at Richfield Springs, New York; meets James Russell Lowell* in Boston.
1887	Helps raise money for Walt Whitman and for Longfellow Memorial Fund.
1888	Is first impressed by works of Leo Tolstoy; travels with Annie Fields to South Carolina, Georgia, and Florida.
1889	Visits Longfellow's daughter, Alice Longfellow,* at Boothbay Harbor, Maine (later known as "the country of the pointed firs").
1891	Is impressed by Gustave Flaubert's *Madame Bovary*.
1892	Travels with Annie Fields and Katharine and Robert Underwood Johnson to Europe; meets Madame Blanc in Paris, and sees Mark Twain in Venice.
1893	Attends World's Columbian Exposition in Chicago.
1894	With Annie Fields, entertains Holmes and Twain.
1895	Recurrently ill.
1896	Sails with Annie Fields and Lilian and Thomas Bailey Aldrich* to the Caribbean; publishes *The Country of the Pointed Firs*.
1897	Attends William James's speech at unveiling of Augustus Saint-Gauden's Robert Gould Shaw relief; travels with Madame Blanc to Shaker settlement at Alfred, Maine.
1898	Vacations with Annie Fields in England, meeting Henry James,* and on Continent.
1899	Summers with relatives and friends in Maine and Massachusetts.
1900	Vacations with Annie Fields in Italy, Greece, Turkey, and France; begins serializing *The Tory Lover* (to 1901).
1901	Publishes *The Tory Lover* in book form; awarded honorary Litt.D. degree by Bowdoin College.
1902	Suffers severe spinal injury in carriage accident (3 September), causing permanent debility and greatly diminishing her writing.
1908	Stays most of year with Annie Fields, meets Willa Cather* in Boston.
1909	Confined to wheelchair by stroke; dies from cerebral hemorrhage, 24 June, in South Berwick home.

ABBREVIATIONS

Blanchard

Paula Blanchard, *Sarah Orne Jewett: Her World and Her Work* (Reading, Mass.: Addison-Wesley, 1994).

Cary, *Jewett*

Richard Cary, *Sarah Orne Jewett* (New York: Twayne, 1962).

Cary, *Letters*

Richard Cary, ed., *Sarah Orne Jewett Letters* (Waterville, Maine: Colby College Press, 1956; enl., rev. ed.; Waterville, Maine: Colby College Press, 1967).

Donovan

Josephine Donovan, *Sarah Orne Jewett* (New York: Frederick Ungar, 1980).

Fields

Annie Fields, ed., *Letters of Sarah Orne Jewett* (Boston and New York: Houghton Mifflin, 1911).

Frost

John Eldridge Frost, *Sarah Orne Jewett* (Kittery Point, Maine: Gundalow Club, 1960).

Matthiessen

Francis Otto Matthiessen, *Sarah Orne Jewett* (Boston and New York: Houghton Mifflin, 1929).

Morgan and Renza

Jack Morgan and Louis A. Renza, eds., *The Irish Stories of Sarah Orne Jewett* (Carbondale and Edwardsville: Southern Illinois University Press, 1996).

Nagel

Gwen L. Nagel, ed., *Critical Essays on Sarah Orne Jewett* (Boston: G. K. Hall, 1984).

Renza

Louis A. Renza, *"A White Heron" and the Question of Minor Literature* (Madison: University of Wisconsin Press, 1984).

Roman   Margaret Roman, *Sarah Orne Jewett: Reconstructing Gender*
                 (Tuscaloosa and London: University of Alabama Press, 1992).

Sherman   Sarah Way Sherman, *Sarah Orne Jewett, An American Perseph-
                 one* (Hanover, N.H., and London: University Press of New Eng-
                 land, 1989).

Silverthorne   Elizabeth Silverthorne, *Sarah Orne Jewett: A Writer's Life*
                 (Woodstock, N.Y.: Overlook Press, 1993).

Thorp   Margaret Ferrand Thorp, *Sarah Orne Jewett* (Minneapolis: Uni-
                 versity of Minnesota Press, 1966).

A SARAH ORNE JEWETT
COMPANION

A

ABBOTT, JOHN. In "An Every-Day Girl," he is the sweetheart, nineteen, of Mary Fleming. Orphaned and hard-working, he has a job on a farm near Dolton, and they will soon get married.

ABEL. In *The Country of the Pointed Firs*, he is a "self-contained" old fisherman.

ABEL. In "Fame's Little Day," he is the schoolboy son of Sarah, the widowed daughter of Mary Ann Pinkham and her husband, Abel Pinkham.

ADAMS, ADALINE. In "An Autumn Holiday," she is a woman who stages "dying spells" for attention and sympathy. She is catered to by her family but gossiped about by Miss Polly Marsh. Mary Susan Ash is Adaline's genuinely sick sister.

ADAMS, CLORINTHY. In *Deephaven*, this is the maiden name of the wife of Mrs. Tom Kew's brother.

ADAMS, JOE. In "An Autumn Holiday," he is Adaline Adams's kind husband.

ADAMS, JOHN (1735–1826). American Revolutionary figure and later second president of the United States. In *The Tory Lover*, he is in communication with Benjamin Franklin.

ADAMS, SAMUEL (1722–1803). American Revolutionary patriot. In *The Tory Lover*, he is mentioned as seeking funds in Exeter for the war.

ADDICKS. In *The Country of the Pointed Firs*, he is a fisherman Elijah Tilley knows. He has a store through which Tilley and other old sailors sell items they have knitted.

ADDICKS, MRS. In *The Country of the Pointed Firs*, she is Mrs. Blackett's neighbor from White Island Landing.

ADELINE ("AD'LINE"). In "A Winter Courtship," she is one of two evidently married daughters of Fanny Tobin. The other is Susan Ellen.

AGASSIZ, LOUIS (1807–1873). Naturalist, geologist, and educator. Born in Switzerland, educated in Europe, and widely traveled, he lectured in the Boston area from 1846, including at Harvard. Jewett wrote Agassiz's daughter, Ida Agassiz Higginson, the wife of Henry Lee Higginson (2 June 1877), to thank her for praising *Deephaven*. Jewett was occasionally a guest of the Higginsons in their summer home at West Manchester, Massachusetts. In *Betty Leicester*, Thomas Leicester mentions Agassiz as an inspiration to him in college. *Bibliography*: Cary, *Letters*.

AGNES. In "Lady Ferry," she is the wife of Matthew, a cousin of Marcia's parents. She welcomes Marcia to the house by the ferry and is genuinely affectionate and maternal.

AHERN. In "The Gray Mills of Farley," he is a worker at the mills. Dan, the mill agent, tells Ellen Carroll he will help Ahern.

AINSLIE, HELEN. In "A Sorrowful Guest," she, the narrator, is the bachelor John Ainslie's unmarried sister. She returns to live with him in Boston after the death of their Aunt Alice, with whom Helen has lived in Florence, Italy. When he brings Whiston home for dinner, she is intrigued by his story of being followed by the ghost of his cousin Henry Dunster, allegedly killed in the Civil War.

AINSLIE, JOHN ("JACK"). In "A Sorrowful Guest," he is Helen Ainslie's brother. Neither has ever married. He is a Civil War veteran, a semiretired surgeon, and the friend of and would-be comfort to Whiston. John diagnoses Whiston as suffering from the monomania of fancying he is haunted by Henry Dunster, Whiston's cousin allegedly killed in the Civil War. After Whiston's death, John chances to find Dunster in a marine hospital. Dunster confesses he did "haunt" Whiston a time or two.

AJAX. In *The Tory Lover*, he is Judge Chadbourne's black servant.

ALDIS. In "The Life of Nancy," he is Tom Aldis's father. He bought land at East Rodney, Maine, for possible real-estate development.

ALDIS, MRS. TOM. In "The Life of Nancy," she is Tom Aldis's understanding wife. When he brings Nancy Gale to their summer house at East Rodney, Mrs. Aldis leaves the room so the two can talk more amiably.

ALDIS, TOM. In "The Life of Nancy," he is a Harvard graduate, twenty-two, from Boston. When he vacationed at East Rodney, Maine, he met and danced with Nancy Gale and admired her fresh innocence. Seeing her in Boston, Tom escorts her around the city, takes her to Papanti's dancing school, and introduces her to Mrs. Annesley, his aunt. Tom is relieved when Nancy tells him Addie Porter, an East Rodney flirt with whom he also danced, perhaps too amiably, is marrying elsewhere. Tom marries, has children, and after seventeen or so years goes to East Rodney to consider land development started there by his father. He sees Nancy, crippled by rheumatism but courageous. A year later Tom and his family return to a summer home he has built there, and he tells Nancy he will not exploit the region's beautiful environment.

ALDIS, TOM. In "The Life of Nancy," he is Tom Aldis's young son.

ALDRICH, THOMAS BAILEY (1836–1907). Author and editor. Born in Portsmouth, New Hampshire, he lived in New Orleans (1846–1849) with his father, whose death prevented Aldrich's attending college. After clerking for a merchant uncle in New York, Aldrich became a reporter, critic, freelance writer, and editor there (1855–1864) and from 1866 in Boston, where he called himself not Bostonian but "Boston-plated." Among his extensive publications, best remembered is *The Story of a Bad Boy* (1870), an autobiographical novel set in Rivermouth (Portsmouth). *The Stillwater Tragedy* (1880) is an anti-union, anti-immigrant novel. "Anti-immigrant" also is the title poem of *Unguarded Gates and Other Poems* (1895). In 1881 Aldrich succeeded William Dean Howells* as editor of the *Atlantic Monthly*. After retiring in 1890, Aldrich traveled extensively with his wife, Lilian, and continued for almost a decade to capitalize on his popularity. Howells and Mark Twain* praised *The Story of a Bad Boy* for innovatively describing what boys really do, not what they should do. Aldrich's short story, "Marjorie Daw" (1873), was sensational because of its clever surprise ending—a new device when it appeared.

Jewett met Aldrich and his wife in the 1870s. Over the years he accepted twenty of her stories for the *Atlantic*. She socialized with the Aldriches through her friendship with Annie Adams Fields,* visited their summer homes in Ponkapog, Massachusetts, and Tenants Harbor, Maine, appreciated Aldrich's editorial advice, but overvalued his poetry. He wrote her to praise "The Dulham

Ladies'' as superior to anything in that vein by Nathaniel Hawthorne. The depth of her friendship with Aldrich, perhaps her closest male friend, is indicated by her tender letter to him (now lost) concerning the death of their mothers. She approved of his love of Portsmouth as expressed in his novel, *An Old Town by the Sea* (1893). She accompanied the Aldriches on a two-month Caribbean cruise (1899). Strangely, in her book of reminiscences, titled *Crowding Memories* (1920), Lilian Woodman Aldrich does not mention Jewett. *Bibliography*: Blanchard; Frost; Matthiessen; Sherman; Silverthorne.

ALEXIS. In "Little French Mary," he is Marie's French-Canadian husband and French Mary's father. They come to Dulham, where he is a handyman, but soon leaves to live with and care for an aunt in Canada.

ALICE. In "Good Luck," she is the aunt of Mary Leslie, Parkhurst Leslie, and Tom Leslie. Alice's imminent visit is the indirect cause of Tom's finding the secret closet in the Leslies' summer home.

ALICE, AUNT. In "A Sorrowful Guest," she is the aunt of Helen Ainslie and John Ainslie. Helen has been living with her in Florence. When Alice dies, Helen returns to live in Boston with John.

ALISON, BESSIE. In "A Dark Carpet," she is a friend of Mary Weston. Mary patterns the colors of her sofa pillow on those of one of Bessie Alison's.

ALLEN. In "A Landless Farmer," she is the little daughter of Ezra Allen, who smiles when he sees her doll on his wagon.

ALLEN. In *A Marsh Island*, he is a man who occasionally works as a farmhand for Israel Owen.

ALLEN, EZRA. In "A Landless Farmer," he is a farmer-wheelwright, rosy faced, pleasant, and about forty. He is Susan's husband, a father, and Jerry Jenkins's nephew. Ezra is sympathetic toward Jerry, whose daughters are mistreating him.

ALLEN, SERENA ("FARMER ALLEN"). In "Farmer Finch," she was a cousin of Mrs. Wall, who tells Polly Finch that when Serena's husband was killed in the war she learned to farm and successfully supported herself and her two children.

ALLEN, SUSAN. In "A Landless Farmer," she is Ezra Allen's timid wife.

ALLEN, SUSAN. In "Miss Manning's Minister," she is the housekeeper for the Reverend Edward Taylor, until he suffers a stroke.

ALLISON. In "A Village Patriot," he is one of the six shinglers of the house owned by the Bostonian. Allison is "sober-looking."

ALLISTER, CAPTAIN. In "The Taking of Captain Ball," he is a friend of Captain Asaph Ball, who invites him and Captain Dunn to dinner. Allister annoys Ball by asking about Mrs. Ann French, Ball's housekeeper.

"ALL MY SAD CAPTAINS" (1895). Short story. (Characters: Captain Crowe, Eliza Crowe, Miss Crowe, Decket, Dimmett, the Reverend Mr. Farley, Mrs. Hicks, Captain Peter Lunn, Maria Lunn, Captain Eli Proudfit, Captain Asa Shaw, Deacon Torby, Captain John Witherspoon.) Toward summer's end in Longport, Maria Lunn, Captain Peter Lunn's second wife and a widow for four years, secretly seeks advice on repairing shingles on her attractive house from each of three old captains. Each former shipmaster would like to marry her. And each combines advantages and disadvantages: Huge, clumsy Captain Crowe owns the best house in town but provides a home for two unpleasant maiden sisters; rich Captain Asa Shaw, the least old, owns a tugboat, but is a widower with four unruly children; and tiny Captain John Witherspoon is a gallant bachelor but has little money and lives with a deaf, widowed cousin. One evening, Shaw calls on Mrs. Lunn at her front door, Crowe raps at the side door, and Witherspoon, with a nice mackerel, enters from the rear. After vying with each other before Mrs. Lunn by boasts and criticism, they leave—first peppy Witherspoon, then rich Shaw, and finally big Crowe. That night each talks to himself about desirable Maria. At his idle warehouse, Witherspoon chances to meet Crowe, and they gripe about Longport's ruined economy, Shaw's money, and the new minister, a bachelor named the Reverend Mr. Farley. In September Mrs. Lunn returns from visiting her dying cousin, Mrs. Hicks, attends church, and sees Farley, whom she knows because he has come from her cousin's parish and whom she lets room and board with her. Ensuing gossip alarms the three captains into pressing forward. Shaw visits Maria, proposes, boasts of his $40,000, but is coolly rejected. Crowe arrives with a mackerel, proposes, but is gently rejected. As Witherspoon walks by, Maria invites him in and is accepted almost wordlessly. They wed and let Farley, harmless bookworm, remain as a paying boarder. Maria inherits her cousin's property. In the spring, when Crowe asks Witherspoon about house repairs, he says their shingles will last some years yet. Rudyard Kipling* liked the title of "All My Sad Captains." Modern readers find it amusing that Jewett calls the three footdraggingly inarticulate captains "lovers," while feminists deplore old New England mores requiring Maria Lunn to have "lovers" call on her instead of going right after her preference. *Bibliography*: Roman.

AMANDY. In "Marsh Rosemary," she is the Walpole minister's sister, who keeps house for him.

AMES. In "The Parshley Celebration," this is the name of a family for the boys of which Martha Binney plans to sew some clothes. She tells Mary Ann Winn that the boys' grandmother is a soldier's widow.

ANDERSON, MRS. In "Good Luck," she was a friend of Mrs. Leslie's mother. At her death in Baltimore, Mrs. Anderson leaves Mrs. Leslie a large sum of money.

ANDREW. In *Deephaven*, he is a poor coastal farmer. After his wife's death, he drank excessively, died, and left his children to be scattered.

ANDREW. In "A Lost Lover," he is Horatia Dane's stubborn old servant.

"ANDREW'S FORTUNE" (1881). Short story. (Characters: Ann, Mrs. Ash, Beedle, Jonas Beedle, Mrs. Jonas Beedle, Dennett, Jonas Dennett, Lysander Dennett, Mrs. Lysander Dennett, Mrs. Stephen Dennett, Stephen Dennett, Tim Dennett, Dunning, Estes, Mrs. Goodsoe, Mrs. Haynes, Aunt Hitty, Joseph, Kimball, Nathan Martin, Mathes, Mrs. Mathes, Susan Mathes, Betsey Morris, Otis, Andrew Phillips, Mrs. Andrew Phillips, Jim Pierce, Shepley, Mrs. Thompson, Mrs. Towner.) One December evening Mrs. Haynes enters the farmhome of Stephen Dennett, a respected, well-to-do farmer dying upstairs. His housekeeper, Betsey Morris, is busy caring for several contentious neighbors preparing to watch at his deathbed. Andrew Phillips, Dennett's ineffectual nephew who lives with him, is sorrowful but also counts on inheriting Dennett's estate. Dennett dies. His will, known to be a single sheet of blue paper naming Andrew as heir, cannot be found. Dunning, a successful friend of Dennett's, comes from Boston and with a crowd attends the home funeral. As the minister reads from Dennett's Bible, a piece of blue paper floats to the floor. Old Mrs. Towner picks it up. After the funeral, Andrew learns Mrs. Towner has just died of a heart attack and the will is missing. A search turns up nothing. Susan, Andrew's girlfriend, seems angry about his lost inheritance. Dunning likes Andrew, wishes him well, and returns to Boston. Lysander Dennett, the deceased man's cousin several miles distant, arrives by sleigh, makes excuses for not attending the funeral, and says so be it if Providence has arranged for him instead of Andrew to inherit. He offers to "share even" with Andrew, who refuses but persuades him to give Betsey the $500 his uncle promised her. Susan regards Andrew as "noble" but too idealistic and decides to dump him before spring. Betsey goes to her sister's home. In January, Andrew gets a job in Boston through Dunning, does well, and is only momentarily sad when Susan dissolves their relationship. He rises to a prominent position with a tea-importing firm, marries, and is happy. Years later he revisits the old Dennett house. Lysander is dead, but his two sons are pleasantly established and have families. Andrew happens to look at his uncle's undisturbed little library and finds his will. Weak-sighted Mrs. Towner innocently put it in a religious book resembling the Bible. Andrew secretly burns the will, feels he has his own fortune now, and determines to help one of

Lysander's grandsons get ahead in Boston. "Andrew's Fortune" is not a typical Jewett story. In it, she suggests that commercial life is better for the hero than farm work. In sardonic tones, she depicts most of Stephen Dennett's rural neighbors as petty backbiters.

ANGELO. In "The Hare and the Tortoise," he is named as a "rapacious" courier. According to Mary Chester, her great-aunt, Sophia Duncan, was uniquely afraid of him when they toured in Europe.

ANN. In "Andrew's Fortune," she is a person Mrs. Haynes mentions having visited. She may be Joseph's wife.

ANN. In *Deephaven*, she is a Lancaster family servant in Boston, as is Maggie. Both are from Deephaven and accompany Kate Lancaster and Helen Denis there.

ANN. In "Mr. Bruce," she is Mrs. Tennant's Irish maid and is away during the Easter season.

ANNA. In *Deephaven*, she is Kate Lancaster's aunt, who will take title to the Newport house and go there.

ANNESLEY, MRS. In "The Life of Nancy," she is Tom Aldis's aristocratic aunt, living in Boston. He introduces Nancy Gale to her. The two like each other, and Nancy always remembers her advice about finding happiness through being "self-forgetful."

ANNIS, DANIEL. In "Miss Becky's Pilgrimage," he is a Brookfield farmer living with his sister, Julia Downs, and his niece, Annie Downs.

ANNIS, SOPHIA ("SOPHY"). In "Miss Becky's Pilgrimage," she is Becky Parson's cousin, Julia Downs's mother, and Annie Downs's grandmother. They live in Brookfield. Sophia is five years older than Becky. It is indirectly through her visit to Sophia that Becky meets Beacham, the widowed minister.

APOLLO (" 'POLLO"). In *The Tory Lover*, he is one of the black servants of Major Tilly Haggens.

ARLEY, MARY. In "An Every-Day Girl," she is a friend of Mary Fleming and quits her job in the Dolton shoe factory to get a job with Mary Fleming in a nearby summer hotel. Mary Arley, one of seven somewhat neglected children, is so happy-go-lucky that only Mary Fleming takes advantage of the possibility of job advancement by hard work.

ASA. In *The Country of the Pointed Firs*, he is a critic of Almira Todd's handling of her boat. She rebukes him by saying he is from "upcountry."

ASA. In "The Lost Turkey," he is the hired man working for Grandpa Jones. Asa was given time off around Thanksgiving.

ASH, MARY SUSAN. In "An Autumn Holiday," she was a hard-working woman who became sick. She is Adaline Adams's sister.

ASH, MRS. In "Andrew's Fortune," she is mentioned as one who will help with funeral arrangements, following Mrs. Towner's sudden death.

ASH, MRS. In "A Winter Courtship," she is a person whose husband was a deacon; Jefferson Briley says she would like to marry him.

ASHBY. In "Miss Debby's Neighbors," he is Joseph Ashby's and Susan Ellen Ashby's son. He goes to sea and dies.

ASHBY. In "A New Parishioner," he is mentioned as the owner of a place on the way to Knowles's mills.

ASHBY, JOHN. In "Miss Debby's Neighbors," he is the son of Mrs. Ashby, the brother of Marilla Ashby, and the father of John Ashby and Joseph Ashby. He eggs his son, John, to tease Joseph. Old John, who drinks excessively, eventually dies.

ASHBY, JOHN. In "Miss Debby's Neighbors," he is the son of John Ashby and the brother of Joseph Ashby. Their father encourages John to tease Joseph. John gets John Jacobs to help him drag Joseph's house down the road. John marries a woman named Miss Pecker (*see* Ashby, Mrs. John). When he dies, she remarries.

ASHBY, JOSEPH ("JOE"). In "Miss Debby's Neighbors," he is the son of John Ashby and the brother of young John Ashby. Joseph, good at carpentry, marries Susan Ellen (*see* Ashby, Sue Ellen). The two Johns tease Joseph, once even hauling down the road the farmhouse he built. Joseph's and Susan's son is lost at sea. When Joseph dies, Susan remarries.

ASHBY, MARILLA ("MARILLY"). In "Miss Debby's Neighbors," she is the daughter of Mrs. Ashby, the sister of John Ashby, and the aunt of his sons, John Ashby and Joseph Ashby. The quarrelsomeness of the three men evidently contributes to her death soon after her mother's death.

ASHBY, MRS. In "Miss Debby's Neighbors," she is the mother of John Ashby and Marilla Ashby, and the grandmother of John's sons, John Ashby and Joseph Ashby. The quarrelsomeness of the three men worsens her health to a fatal degree.

ASHBY, MRS. JOHN. In "Miss Debby's Neighbors," formerly Miss Pecker, she makes John leave the farm and work in the city briefly.

ASHBY, SUSAN ELLEN. In "Miss Debby's Neighbors," she is Joseph Ashby's stupid wife. Seven years his senior, she brought money to the marriage. Their son is lost at sea. When Joseph dies, she and her estate are snapped up by "a roving preacher," and the two sell out and move "up country" to where he came from.

ASHER. In *A Marsh Island*, this is mentioned as the name of folks Israel Owen knows along the road leading away from Sussex.

ASHTON. In "An Empty Purse," this is the name of a family to whose country house the granddaughters of Mrs. Wallis go to skate, dine, and dance on Christmas Day.

ASHTON, ALICE WILSON. In "Tom's Husband," she is Tom Wilson's sister and Captain Ashton's wife. Entertaining expensively in Japan, she complains to Tom about insufficient family money until his wife, Mary Dunn Wilson, manages the family mill profitably.

ASHTON, CAPTAIN. In "Tom's Husband," he is an American naval officer living with his wife, Alice Wilson Ashton, and their two sons in Nagasaki, Japan.

ASHTON, MISS. In "A Late Supper," she is a well-to-do invalid traveling with her niece Alice West. The two meet Miss Catherine Spring on the train and fortuitously decide to rent rooms from her.

ASHTON, MRS. In "The Spur of the Moment," she is the daughter of Walton. At his funeral she sees Miss Peet, takes pity on her, and resolves to continue his habit of regularly sending her money.

ASHURST. In "Good Luck," he is a minister whose visit delays Tom Leslie's finding the secret closet in the Leslies' summer home.

ASHURST, DR. In "In a Country Practice," he was the father, now deceased, of Dr. John Ashurst. The older physician practiced medicine in Alton, to which his son returns to practice.

ASHURST, DR. JOHN. In "In a Country Practice," he is a self-sacrificing physician. After medical school, he practices in Alton, his small hometown, instead of accepting the offer of Dr. Best to join him in a lucrative practice in New York. Dr. John Ashurst gets married, has two daughters, Lizzie Ashurst and Nelly Ashurst, and happens to befriend an unnamed businessman working in Cuba. At his death, Ashurst's estate is worth almost nothing, owing to a bank failure and his generosity to patients. His family receives a providential bequest of $50,000 from the businessman's estate. Ashurst is patterned to a degree on Jewett's beloved father, Theodore Herman Jewett.*

ASHURST, LIZZIE. In "In a Country Practice," she is the schoolteacher daughter of Dr. John Ashurst and his wife. Lizzie's young sister is Nelly Ashurst.

ASHURST, MRS. In "In a Country Practice," she is Dr. John Ashurst's mother. His return to Alton is partly motivated by his desire to be near and care for her.

ASHURST, MRS. In "In a Country Practice," she is Dr. John Ashurst's wife. Described as frail and little, she is the mother of Lizzie Ashurst and Nelly Ashurst. After her husband's death, she fears poverty until a bequest of $50,000 comes from an unnamed businessman whose life her husband saved.

ASHURST, MRS. In "Paper Roses," she is the woman Kate accompanies on a visit to the poor. While doing so, Kate meets the old woman who made the paper roses.

ASHURST, NELLY. In "In a Country Practice," she is the daughter of Dr. John Ashurst and his wife and is Lizzie Ashurst's young sister.

ATHERTON. In "A Sorrowful Guest," this is the name of the family that rented John Ainslie's house in Boston. The lease now "out," he moves back in and welcomes his sister, Helen Ainslie, there.

AULEY, TOM. In "The Luck of the Bogans," he is a person down whose well some boys, perhaps including Dan Bogan, throw a cat.

"AUNT CYNTHY DALLETT" (1899). Short story. (Characters: Aunt Cynthy Dallett, Nathan Dunn, Johnny Foss, Mrs. Eben Fulham, Mrs. Hand, Jabez Hooper, Abby Pendexter, Miss Abby Pendexter.) Mrs. Hand visits Miss Abby Pendexter, who has limited means. The two recall that Abby's aunt, Aunt Cynthy Dallett, who lives on a mountain side, likes to celebrate New Year's Day. On January 1 the two trudge up to visit her. Fussing happily, she prepares a meal including items brought by her guests. When Abby hints that Cynthy should live with her, she pleads being set in her ways, suggests that Abby should come to her, and vows to bequeath everything to her. The great question is nicely settled. "Aunt Cynthy Dallett" is unified by a sequence of three visits, with Mrs. Hand telling Abby about calling on grateful Mrs. Eben Fulham earlier.

The story is divided into two parts, when the point of view shifts from Mrs. Hand and Abby to old Aunt Cynthy, in the act of hoping Abby will visit. *Bibliography*: Cary, *Jewett*.

AUSTIN. In "An Only Son," he is the son of Jacob Austin, a neighbor of Deacon John Price. The son would use part of Price's farmland, if purchased, to become a truck farmer.

AUSTIN, JACOB. In "An Only Son," he is a neighbor of Deacon John Price and wishes to buy part of his farmland.

"AN AUTUMN HOLIDAY" (1880). Short story. (Characters: Adaline Adams, Joe Adams, Mary Susan Ash, Miss Becket, Nathan Becket, Parson Croden, Elizabeth, Captain Daniel Gunn, Jacob Gunn, Patience Gunn, Miss Polly Marsh, Miss Martin, Deacon Abel Pinkham, Ichabod Pinkham, Parson Ridley, Mrs. Ridley, Mrs. William Sands, Mrs. Snow, Cousin Statiry, Miss West.) Elizabeth, the narrator, takes an October walk across the fields, observing birds, apples, and vegetation with delight. She happens on a child's abandoned grave and imagines family details. She sees her physician father driving on his rounds. She pays a visit to two sisters who live together. They are Miss Polly Marsh, a nurse, and the widowed Mrs. Snow. They stop spinning yarn, start knitting it, and gossip with their guest in their kitchen over gingerbread and milk. They chat about Adams and Ash family members. Polly concentrates on Captain Daniel Gunn. Fifty years earlier, after his sister, Patience Gunn, died, he became feeble-minded and took to wearing her clothes—usually in the afternoons but once to church and later to a female missionary society meeting in Mrs. William Sands's home. As Elizabeth's father approaches to take her home, Mrs. Snow whispers to her that Polly declined Gunn's nephew Jacob Gunn's proposal. "An Autumn Holiday" seems so autobiographical that some critics name the narrator and her father Jewett. *Bibliography*: Roman; Sherman.

B

BALFOUR, JOHN. In "A Little Captive Maid," widowered and childless, he is a retired sea captain and a wealthy businessman. His servants include Mrs. Nash and James Reilly. When Nora Connelly becomes his "little maid," he gains temporary strength from her kindness but within three years weakens and dies. He wills his house to a nephew, money to his servants, and $500 and passage money to Nora to return to Ireland and her faithful lover, John Morris.

BALL, ANN. In "The Taking of Captain Ball," she is Captain Asaph Ball's older sister and his adoring, frugal housekeeper until her death.

BALL, ANN. In "The Taking of Captain Ball." *See* French, Ann.

BALL, ASA. In "An Only Son," he is a Dalton shoemaker with whom the selectman, Deacon John Price, talks laconically about town business.

BALL, CAPTAIN ASAPH. In "The Taking of Captain Ball," he is a retired old bachelor shipmaster with a nice house on tidewater land. After the death of Ann Ball, his sister and housekeeper, he hires Mrs. Ann French instead of asking his unseen great-niece to come from New York state and take over. When Mrs. French turns out to be his great-niece, all is well.

BANFIELD. In *Betty Leicester's English Xmas*, he is a witty, popular lawyer from New York. He and his daughter, Miss Edith Banfield, are Lady Mary Danesley's guests.

BANFIELD, MISS EDITH. In *Betty Leicester's English Xmas*, she is Lady Mary Danesley's guest, sixteen. Pretentious and critical at first, she becomes more pleasant because of Betty Leicester's kindnesses.

BANGS. In *A Marsh Island*, he is the owner of the new schooner on which Dan Lester plans to sail out of Westmarket.

BANGS, DR. In "The Passing of Sister Barsett," he is the physician who has cared for Sister Barsett.

BANGS, MISS LYDDY. In "Law Lane," she is the skinny little friend of Mrs. Harriet Powder. The gossip of the two women about the love affair of Ezra Barnet and Ruth Crosby sets off a chain of unhappy events, which, however, ends with their marriage.

BANGS, MRS. In "A New Parishioner," she is mentioned as friendly with a deacon in Walton. She may be his wife.

BANKS, DR. In "A Landless Farmer," he is the physician who pronounces Jerry Jenkins's illness likely to be fatal. Jerry recovers.

BANKS, JOE. In "A Neighbor's Landmark," he is a young fisherman who loves and is loved by Lizzie Packer. He is unnecessarily afraid that his signing the petition to try to save the landmark trees of her father, John Packer, will jeopardize their romance. It turns out that Packer finally saves the trees himself.

BAPTIST. In "Peg's Little Chair," he was a Frenchman (undoubtedly named Baptiste) who fought alongside General Lafayette, was wounded in the head and rendered somewhat deranged, and was thought dead by Lafayette. Margaret Benning, the mother of Margaret ("Peg") Benning, fed and cared for him. When Lafayette arrived at the public house of Peg's mother and saw Baptist, he gave the man money and promised to see whether any relatives of Baptist were alive back in France.

BAREBONES, PRAISE-GOD. In *The Tory Lover*, he is one of the neighbors of Major Tilly Haggens. He undoubtedly took his name from that of Praise-God Barbon (c. 1596–1680), the paedobaptist who opposed the restoration of King Charles II of England.

BARLOW. In "The Guests of Mrs. Timms," he is Mrs. Timms's parish minister. Mrs. Timms says his salary may be raised soon.

BARLOW, HATTIE. In *A Country Doctor*, she is a person who, according to Nancy Prince, is getting married only because she cannot support herself.

BARNARD. In "Miss Esther's Guest," this may be the name of a family having rowdy boys, mentioned by Miss Esther Porley.

BARNES. In "Going to Shrewsbury," he is a neighbor lad who wrote Isabella that Mrs. Peet was coming to Shrewsbury to stay with her.

BARNET, EZRA. In "Law Lane," he is Jane Barnet's husband and young Ezra Barnet's father. His obduracy regarding the ownership of land between his farm and Crosby's delays the marriage of young Ezra and Ruth Crosby next door.

BARNET, EZRA ("EZRY"). In "Law Lane," he is the son of Ezra Barnet and Jane Barnet. His love for their next-door neighbor, Ruth Crosby, is frustrated by a longstanding land dispute. The cleverness of Mrs. Harriet Powder, another neighbor, enables the lovers to get married.

BARNET, GRANDSIRE. In "Law Lane," he is mentioned as old Ezra Barnet's father and an instigator of the land feud between the Barnets and their neighbors, the Crosbys.

BARNET, JANE. In "Law Lane," she is Ezra Barnet's wife and young Ezra Barnet's mother. Her maiden name was Sands. She is largely responsible for keeping up the feud between her family and that of their neighbors, Crosby and his wife, Abby Crosby. This feud stands in the way of a romance between young Ezra and Ruth Crosby, who love each other. When Jane hurts herself in a barn fall, her clever neighbor, Mrs. Harriet Powder, makes Jane think she is so near dying that she repents and relents. The lovers can then wed.

BARNWELL. In "The Mistress of Sydenham Plantation," he was the owner of a summer home Mistress Sydenham thinks about. His family was ruined during the Civil War.

BARRINGTON, WILLIAM WILDMAN SHUTE (1717–1793). British secretary of war early in the American Revolution. In *The Tory Lover*, Lord Newburgh says Lord Mount Edgecumbe can influence Barrington.

BARRY. In *Betty Leicester*, this is the name of a family visited by Betty Leicester on the Isle of Wight.

BARSETT, SISTER. In "The Passing of Sister Barsett," she is the person Dr. Bangs tended when she may have had "new" maladies. Sister Barsett was cared for by Sarah Ellen Dow and was wrongly pronounced dead by Sister Barsett's sisters, Nancy Deckett and Mrs. Peak. Sister Barsett is one of Jewett's most "meeching" characters, whose neighbors say little nice about her, even after her "death." *Bibliography*: Blanchard.

BARSTOW. In "Miss Esther's Guest," he is a lawyer in Daleham whose handsome house Miss Esther Porley proudly points out to Mr. Rill.

BARSTOW, DR. In "The Hiltons' Holiday," he is a minister whose former preaching John Hilton mentions to his daughters, Susan Ellen Hilton and Katy Hilton, as they pass the North Meeting-house in Topham Corners.

BARSTOW, GENERAL. In "The Failure of David Berry," he is a customer whose best boots David Berry makes for a while.

BARTON. In "Decoration Day," he is the owner of the Barlow Plains store, where the veterans meet and plan their parade.

BARTON. In "A Little Captive Maid," he is the lawyer working for John Balfour. He prepares Balfour's "memorandum" leaving money to Nora Connelly.

BARTON. In "The Lost Turkey," he is a store owner in the village and doubles as postmaster. He gives Grandpa Jones a bundle of mail to deliver to John Jones, the old man's grandson.

BARTON, GENERAL. In "The First Sunday in June," he was the father, now deceased, of Harriet Barton and Susan Barton. Miss Lydia Bent went to school with the general's wife.

BARTON, HARRIET. In "The First Sunday in June," she is the gentle person whom Miss Lydia Bent, older than she, urges to attend church the following Sunday. Harriet Barton's sister is Susan Barton.

BARTON, MRS. In "The First Sunday in June," she is or was the wife of General Barton and the mother of Harriet Barton and Susan Barton. Miss Lydia Bent went to school with Mrs. Barton.

BARTON, SUSAN. In "The First Sunday in June," she is the tall, serious person whom Miss Lydia Bent, older than she, urges to attend church the following Sunday. Susan Barton's sister is Harriet Barton.

BASCOM, ANN. In "Fair Day," she is the wife of the younger Tobias Bascom, the mother of Johnny Bascom and other children as well, and the daughter-in-law of Mercy Bascom. Mercy likes Ann well enough but regards her as uppity and lazy. Her maiden name was probably Bassett.

BASCOM, CYNTHIA ("CYNTHI"). In "A Change of Heart," she is the daughter of David Bascom and his wife, Mrs. Bascom. Cynthia tells Sally Martin of the fall Isaac Bolton has suffered.

BASCOM, DAVID. In "A Change of Heart," he is Cynthia Bascom's father. He and his wife married too late to have a comfortable life. They have debts on their farm.

BASCOM, JOHNNY. In "Fair Day," he is the son of Tobias Bascom and Ann Bascom. This friendly boy is the favorite grandchild of Mercy Bascom.

BASCOM, 'LIZA. In "Fair Day," she is the last of the three daughters of Mercy Bascom to marry and move away.

BASCOM, MERCY. In "Fair Day," she is the hard-working, tired, but spry widow, seventy-seven, of shiftless, drunken Tobias Bascom, who died when she was twenty-eight and left her with three daughters, including 'Liza Bascom, and one son, also named Tobias Bascom. Mercy raised them well and now lives with her son and his family. Her main regret in life is an argument of forty years' standing with her sister-in-law, Ruth Bascom Parlet. At the end, the two women will make up. Mercy Bascom is a prime example of a Jewett wife infinitely stronger than her husband. *Bibliography*: Roman.

BASCOM, MRS. In "A Change of Heart," she is the aging, lame wife of David Bascom and the mother of their daughter, Cynthia Bascom. Mrs. Bascom gently warns her young friend, Sally Martin, of the dangers of self-indulgence instead of frankness with respect to Isaac Bolton, Sally's would-be suitor.

BASCOM, THE REVEREND MR. In "The Foreigner," he was the Protestant minister who conducted the French-Catholic Mrs. John Tolland's funeral and said that, though "reared among the heathen," she might well get to "the New Jerusalem."

BASCOM, TOBIAS. In "Fair Day," he was the shiftless, alcoholic husband of Mercy Bascom. When he died, he left his widow with four children, including 'Liza Bascom and young Tobias Bascom.

BASCOM, TOBIAS ("T'BIAS"). In "Fair Day," he is the son of Mercy Bascom and Tobias Bascom. The younger Tobias married Ann (*see* Bascom, Ann), sold his farm home, moved into Ann's better one, and took his unhappy mother along. He and Ann are now raising several children, including Johnny Bascom. Tobias returns from the county fair and tells his mother that her sister-in-law, Ruth Bascom Parlet, would like to let bygones be bygones. Mercy is willing.

BASCOMS. In "The Guests of Mrs. Timms," this, says Persis Flagg, is the name of the aunt whose house Mrs. Timms remodeled and lives in.

BASSETT. In "Fair Day," this is the name of the owner or owners of the farm property to which Tobias Bascom and his wife, Ann Bascom, move. Since Ann is the owner of the property, it is likely that her maiden name was Bassett.

BEACHAM. In "Miss Becky's Pilgrimage," he is a Brookfield Congregationalist minister, widowered some seven years before he meets Becky Parsons at Phebe Littlefield's tea party. He and Becky meet again while separately visiting a sick person named Mary Ann Dean. He and Becky seem compatible almost at once and soon get married.

BEAN, JOHN. In "Told in the Tavern," he is the cynical, "cross-grained" town clerk. He gossips about Abby Sands in Timothy Hall's Byfleet tavern. Bean tells about Abby buying a headstone for Parkins.

BEAN, MRS. In "An Empty Purse," she is a poorhouse inmate to whom Miss Debby Gaines gives her own warm, mended petticoat on Christmas Day.

BEAUMONT, ABBÉ DE. In *The Tory Lover*, he is a person with whom the teacher Sullivan vacationed in France and whose memory he reveres.

BECK, CAPTAIN. In *Betty Leicester*, he is a packet captain and Mary Beck's grandfather.

BECK, JIM. In *Betty Leicester*, he is Mary Beck's cousin.

BECK, MARY ("BECKY"). (Full name: Mary Elizabeth Beck.) In *Betty Leicester*, she is a Tideshead friend, initially suspicious, of Betty Leicester. Gloomy Becky's mother cannot afford singing lessons for her gifted daughter. In *Betty Leicester's English Xmas*, Betty remembers her fondly.

BECK, MRS. In *Betty Leicester*, she is Mary ("Becky") Beck's mother, widowed and plaintive.

BECKER, MRS. In "The Hiltons' Holiday," she may be the person with whom the woman lives who teaches in the school attended by Susan Ellen Hilton and Katy Hilton. The girls visit her house and are pleasantly treated.

BECKET. In "The Hare and the Tortoise," he is the melancholy servant in the household of Mary Chester and her family.

BECKET, ANN. In "The Becket Girls' Tree," she is the older Becket "girl." Lydia Becket is her sister. Reclusive but kind, they are both in their seventies. Their neighbors, John Parsons and his sister, Jess Parsons, give "the Becket girls" the first Christmas tree they have ever seen.

BECKET, LYDIA. In "The Becket Girls' Tree," she is the younger Becket "girl." Ann Becket is her sister. In return for the kindness of John Parsons and Jess Parsons in giving the "girls" a Christmas tree with presents, they give the children small but treasured possessions of their own.

BECKET, MISS. In "An Autumn Holiday," she was a pretty girl adopted by Nathan Becket after her parents were lost at sea. Miss Polly Marsh says the girl has "property."

BECKET, NATHAN. In "An Autumn Holiday," he is the man who provided a home for little Miss Becket, whose parents died at sea.

"THE BECKET GIRLS' TREE" (1884). Short story. (Characters: Ann Becket, Lydia Becket, Ann Donnell, Aaron Ellis, Henry, Lawton, Parsons, Jess Parsons, John Parsons, Mrs. Parsons, Mrs. Peters, John Sands, Sarah Ann, Miss Thomas, Mr. Willis.) The Parsonses live on a farm four miles from the fishing village of Eastport. John ("Johnny") Parsons and his younger sister, Jess ("Jessie") Parsons, plan to surprise their parents by rigging up a Christmas tree and putting presents underneath it. The children saw the only such tree in the whole region at Sunday School the year before. Johnny has saved money from fishing and from taking passengers out boating. Jessie sells berries to nearby boardinghouses for a little cash. Two days before Christmas, the family receives word that Sarah Ann, the wife of Henry, Mrs. Parsons' brother, may be dying in Gloucester. Both parents leave for Gloucester. For their meals, Jessie bakes some mince pieces, with Johnny's help. They decide to take their tree to Ann Becket and Lydia Becket, their reclusive neighbors, now in their seventies. "The Becket girls," as they are called, have never seen a Christmas tree. The children have sold milk and berries to the kind old women, who seem to like them. Next day, the children trudge through the snow into town to buy some presents and tree decorations for the old girls. On Christmas Day Johnny milks the family cow and Jessie takes a pail to the Beckets. That night they bring over the tree—a little spruce from the woods nearby. They are invited to a supper of tea, preserved plums, and cake, and set the tree up—candles and all—in the Beckets' parlor. They give the old girls a work basket, a shoulder shawl, and handkerchiefs with George Washington depicted on them. The old girls, who rummaged upstairs while the children were preparing the tree, give their guests 50¢ each, plus Lafayette handkerchiefs—in Salem, Ann once saw the Marquis de Lafayette,* who patted her cheek. To Johnny they also give their long-gone brother's many-bladed pocket knife; to Jessie they give a worn purse with a small silver thimble in it. When Johnny and Jessie return home, they find their parents. Sarah Ann, their aunt, is reported recovering.

BECKETT. In "A New Parishioner," he is the owner of a quarry. Henry Stroud arranges to have stones from it delivered to build the new Walton vestry but leaves a worthless note as payment.

BECKETT, EZRA. In "The Guests of Mrs. Timms," he was the nephew of Susan Beckett, who willed him her home at Beckett's Corner. He died and left it to his wife.

BECKETT, HATE-EVIL. In *Deephaven*, he is Samanthy Barnes Beckett's husband. They are Mrs. Bonny's neighbors and shop in town for her.

BECKETT, JUDITH. In *Deephaven*, she is the child, ten, who made a sampler for Mrs. Patton.

BECKETT, MRS. EZRA. In "The Guests of Mrs. Timms," she is a widow living at Beckett's Corner. She proves hospitable to the Freewill woman she met at a state conference when that woman pays her a surprise visit.

BECKETT, SAMANTHY BARNES. In *Deephaven*, she is Hate-evil Beckett's wife. The two shop for Mrs. Bonny, their neighbor.

BECKETT, SUSAN. In "The Guests of Mrs. Timms," she was an unmarried woman who willed her home in Beckett's Corner to her nephew, Ezra Beckett. He died and left it to his wife.

BECKETT, SUSAN. In "Miss Becky's Pilgrimage," she is Mary Ann Dean's mother and knew Becky Parsons's aunt in Brookfield decades earlier.

BECKLEY, JOHN. In "A Born Farmer," he and his family, called "country people," go to Boston to see the sights but stay in the old Fitchburg depot and then return home.

BECKY. In "The White Rose Road," this may be the name of the thin little girl who tends a sage-bordered rural garden. She may also be called Katy.

BEEDLE. In "Andrew's Fortune," she is the daughter of Jonas Beedle and his wife, and once thought Andrew Phillips would be a good catch.

BEEDLE, JONAS. In "Andrew's Fortune," he is one of Stephen Dennett's neighbors.

BEEDLE, MRS. JONAS. In "Andrew's Fortune," she is a close friend of Betsey Morris and is a back-biting, hypocritical gossip. Her verbosity closely resembles that of non sequitur talkers in works by Mark Twain.*

BEGG. In *The Country of the Pointed Firs*, she was a thrice-married woman from out of town. The narrator attends her funeral.

BEGG, SAM. In *The Country of the Pointed Firs*, he is a person who inherited money on condition that he and not his family spend it. Mrs. Blackett, Almira Todd, and the narrator travel by his ''high wagon'' to the Bowden reunion.

BEGGS, MRS. In ''The Foreigner,'' she was an experienced old woman who, with Almira Todd, helped out during Mrs. John Tolland's final illness. In ''William's Wedding,'' Mrs. Beggs visits friendly Almira Todd to gain news of Almira's brother William Blackett's wedding.

BELLAMY, COLONEL. In ''A War Debt,'' he is the old Confederate Army veteran who offers Thomas Burton hospitality and is delighted to receive from him the family cup that Burton's father pilfered from the Bellamy estate in Virginia during the Civil War.

BELLAMY, MADAM. In ''A War Debt,'' she is Colonel Bellamy's old wife, and is frail and a little deaf. She is happy to receive the family cup from Thomas Burton. She tells Burton the girl he saw and admired on the train is her granddaughter.

BELLAMY, MISS. In ''A War Debt,'' she is the attractive daughter of Colonel Bellamy and Madam Bellamy. Thomas Burton sees her fleetingly on the train and admires her so much that he promises her father to return for some hunting at Christmastime.

BELTON, MRS. In ''Miss Esther's Guest,'' she is the chairman of the Committee for the Country Week, in Boston. She sends Mr. Rill to Miss Esther Porley's home for his week's vacation.

BENNET. In *A Marsh Island*, he is a hay-farmer neighbor of Israel Owen. He visits the Owen family for a Sunday social. He makes cider.

BENNET, MRS. In *A Marsh Island*, she is the gossipy wife of Israel Owen's hay-farmer neighbor.

BENNETT, DR. In *The Country of the Pointed Firs*, he calls on some of his patients by sailboat, according to Almira Todd.

BENNING. In ''Peg's Little Chair,'' he was Margaret Benning's husband and Margaret (''Peg'') Benning's father. He was lost at sea, and Peg never saw him.

BENNING, HANNAH. In "Peg's Little Chair," she was an older sister of Margaret ("Peg") Benning. Both girls helped wait on tables for their mother, also named Margaret Benning.

BENNING, JONAS. In "Peg's Little Chair," he was a brother of Margaret ("Peg") Benning. Jonas Benning was lost at sea.

BENNING, MARGARET. In "Peg's Little Chair," she was the mother of five children, including Hannah Benning, Jonas Benning, and Margaret ("Peg") Benning. Her husband was lost at sea while sailing with her father, Henderson. Margaret Benning established a public house, was famous as a fine hostess, and once entertained General Lafayette.

BENNING, MARGARET ("PEG"). In "Peg's Little Chair," she is a bright-eyed, peppy old lady, seventy. She tells the narrator how, as a child, she used to drag her little chair around, was often criticized for being in the way, but once placed the chair for General Lafayette to use as a step to help him descend from his carriage. Peg reveres the silver coin he gave her and remembers that he patted, kissed, and blessed her.

BENT. In "The Green Bonnet," he owns a store in Walsingham. The township post office is located in it.

BENT, DR. In *A Country Doctor*, he is a rural, upriver physician.

BENT, MISS LYDIA. In "The First Sunday in June," she is a timid parishioner who faithfully attends the First Parish church of Dalton. The minister is Dr. Joe Darley. Miss Lydia, described as little and old, is so distressed at the steadily dwindling attendance that she successfully urges numerous slackers to attend the first Sunday in June.

BENTZON, THÉRÈSE. *See* Blanc, Marie-Thérèse de Solms.

BERRY, DAVID. In "The Failure of David Berry," he is a skillful old shoe-maker living in a village near Lynn. He is enticed into expanding his business by his wife's social-climbing ways and a loan of $50 from Sam Wescott, who also gives him some poor advice. David's business fails, and he contracts pneumonia and dies.

BERRY, FOX'L. In "A Neighbor's Landmark," he is the owner of the store at the Cove where people are signing the petition to try to keep John Packer from selling his landmark trees.

BERRY, MRS. DAVID. In "The Failure of David Berry," she is the pleasant but complaining wife of the village shoemaker. She encourages him to expand his business because she wants a better social position she thinks money can buy. When she falls ill, David loses income by caring for her and then hiring a servant. When David dies, she must auction their furniture and move upcountry to live with a cousin. Jewett demeans this selfish woman by denying her a first name.

BESSIE. In *Deephaven*, she is named by a friend of Helen Denis as a person grateful for small favors.

BEST, DR. In "In a Country Practice," he is a distinguished physician and medical-school professor. He praises Dr. John Ashurst as his finest student but cannot persuade him to join his lucrative New York practice.

BETSEY. In "A Dark Night," she is an evil innkeeper near Bristol. She tries to rob Weymouth, goes to America, becomes ill, and dies. Her evil husband, unnamed, also goes to America, and is soon is jailed for theft.

BETSEY. In *The Tory Lover*, she is the aunt of a child. While both visit the home of Jonathan Hamilton, the child asks Peggy for some cake.

BETSY. In "The Passing of Sister Barsett," she is mentioned by Sarah Ellen Dow as her sister who had consumption, but " 't wa'n't an expensive sickness."

BETTY. In "A Village Shop," she is the servant in the home of Esther Jaffrey and Leonard Jaffrey. Betty admires Leonard more than she should and Esther less than she should.

BETTY LEICESTER (1890). (Full title: *Betty Leicester: A Story for Girls.*) (Characters: Louis Agassiz, Barry, Captain Beck, Jim Beck, Mary Beck, Mrs. Beck, Buckland, Asa Chick, Clinturn, Frank Crane, Cynthy, Drummond, Miss Marcia Drummond, Duff, Duncan, Ada Duncan, Bessie Duncan, Mary Duncan, Lizzie Edwards, Edwards, Miss Fedge, Jim Foss, Foster, Henry Foster, Mrs. Foster, Nelly Foster, Lizzie French, Georgie, Ellen Grant, Mary Grant, Mr. Grant, Mrs. Grant, Mrs. Grimshaw, Jake Hallett, Ida, Jimmy, Jonathan, Barbara Leicester, Betty Leicester, Madam Leicester, Mary Leicester, Thomas Leicester, Letty, 'Liza Loomis, Marie, Marsh, George Max, Mrs. Max, Miss Murdon, Pepper, Picknell, Julia Picknell, Mary Picknell, Mrs. Picknell, Plunkett, Mrs. Pond, Seth Pond, Dr. Prince, Sarah, Serena, Ann Sparks, Standish, Miss Winter.)

Tom Leicester, a widowered naturalist, and Betty Leicester, his peppy daughter, fifteen, are in Boston. He leaves for an expedition in Alaska. She goes by train to Riverport and by packet, with Captain Beck, to Tideshead, to summer with her affectionate grand-aunts, Barbara Leicester, who is older and fun, and

Mary Leicester, a hypochondriac. She plays with her friend Mary ("Becky") Beck, the captain's granddaughter. Betty gives a garden party for ten friends, including Harry Foster. One day three girlfriends persuade her to join their Sin Book Club but will not admit Becky. The four try to say nothing bad about anyone and record their failures. The club soon becomes inactive. Betty receives letters from her father and from friends in Switzerland. She likes the trees and houses in Tideshead, argues with Aunt Mary about her torn underwear, and resolves to behave better. She goes to a mill with Seth Pond, a servant ambitious to play the violin, and enjoys the rural scene. She accompanies Jonathan and Serena—two servants—upcountry by wagon; Jonathan gets firewood and Serena visits her sister, a lame rag-rug maker. Betty and Becky please the minister by asking him to explain a certain parable, then are shocked by news that Harry's father, jailed for fraud, has escaped. To comfort Nelly Foster, his sad daughter, Betty walks in the woods with her. They find Foster, injured from a fall, and bring him home, where he dies. When Betty establishes an Out-of-Door Club, some fourteen people, including Aunt Barbara, visit the Picknell family farm, near which a French and Indian War battle was fought. In August Betty is delighted when her father appears. He chats with his aunts, rents a boat, and he, Betty, Barbara, Seth, Harry, and Becky sail down to Riverport and camp overnight under the pines ashore. Betty's father promises to help Harry with schooling and promises Betty that they will return from Europe next summer and make a permanent home in Tideshead.

Jewett expanded "A Bit of Color," published in *St. Nicholas* (1889), into *Betty Leicester*. Tideshead somewhat resembles South Berwick. Considered a children's classic when first published, this novel paved the way for *Betty Leicester's English Xmas: A New Chapter of an Old Story*. Yet *Betty Leicester: A Story for Children* is too sweetly sentimental for modern taste. Offputting too are these awkward Jewett constructions: "the fire was not unwelcome," "not unmixed with enjoyment," and others not unduly different. Also, why does Jewett have five Marys, three Jims, and two Lizzies in this story? *Bibliography*: Blanchard; Roman.

BETTY LEICESTER'S ENGLISH XMAS (1894). (Full title: *Betty Leicester's English Xmas: A New Chapter of an Old Story*.) (Characters: Banfield, Miss Edith Banfield, Mary Beck, Bond, Lady Mary Danesley, Miss Day, Lady Dimdale, Mrs. Drum, Mary Duncan, Lord Dunwater, Harry Foster, Frame, Barbara Leicester, Betty Leicester, Mary Leicester, Thomas Leicester, Letty, Mr. Macalister, the Honorable Miss Northumberland, Pagot, Mrs. Procter, the Earl of Seacliffe, Serena, Toby, Warford.)

Betty Leicester left Tideshead in September and is in London with her father, who is doing research at the British Museum on American Indians. She receives a telegram from their friend, Lady Mary Danesley, inviting them to visit at Danesley House, near the Scottish border. They go, and Lady Danesley is most hospitable, especially to Betty. The first night, from the musicians' gallery, Betty and Pagot, her maid, spy on the dinner for eighteen glittering guests. Next morning, Banfield, a witty, popular American lawyer, and his daughter, Miss Edith Banfield, arrive. Betty tries to be helpful to Edith, who, however, seems pretentious and critical—but only at first. In comes Lady Danesley's nephew, Warford, fifteen, a pupil at Eton and heir to Danesley House. He, Betty, and Edith get along amiably at once, and time passes pleasantly until the day of Christmas Eve. Betty plans and participates with Warford, Edith, and a few adults in a pageant of costumed musicians, to the delight of the surprised dinner guests. Afterwards, childless Lady Danesley warmly embraces Betty, who treasures her friendship with this brilliant, lonely English lady. The popularity of *Betty Leicester: A Story for Girls* encouraged Jewett to write this follow-up story about Betty, which was republished as *Betty Leicester's Christmas* (1899).

"BETWEEN MASS AND VESPERS" (1893). Short story. (Characters: Braley, Dennis Call, Mag Call, Mrs. Dennis Call, Mrs. Dillon, Patrick Finn, John Finnerty, Katy Finnerty, Mary Finnerty, Fletcher, Jerry Hannan, John Mulligan, Dan Nolan, Tom Nolan, Johnny O'Donnell, Mary O'Donnell, Mrs. O'Flaherty, Father Ryan, Mary Sullivan.) Several Irish worshippers emerge from the mass conducted by Father Ryan in a prosperous little New England village one sunny day in May. Dennis Call, a sturdy teamster, is inviting his widowed niece, Mary O'Donnell, home for dinner when Father Ryan interrupts by requesting his presence. Telling Mary to explain the delay to his wife, Dennis bolts down a hasty meal at Father Ryan's rectory and then drives a borrowed horse and buggy with Father Ryan into the woods, up a hill, and toward an abandoned house. Father Ryan has learned that Dan Nolan, an altar boy who went wrong long ago, has returned from the West and is hiding there. Dan swindled some families, including that of his girlfriend, Katy Finnerty, out of money on the pretext of investing it in a gold mine. When the priest enters, Dan hits him, whereupon Dennis knocks Dan down and holds him. Father Ryan orders Dan to empty his pockets. Counterfeit bills pour out. Dan explains that he was cheated and is almost penniless. Father Ryan burns the bills; then in a gentle, forgiving manner, he offers Dan, blubbering and vowing to reform, a second chance. Dennis takes the priest back to vespers, which, though bruised and a little late, he conducts well. Under cover of darkness Dan sneaks into the rectory for his first meal in days. Father Ryan sees in the youth's eyes those of his brother, drowned decades ago back in Ireland. In this story Jewett shows that neither Father Ryan's preaching nor Dennis Call's fists bring about repentance here, but forgiveness and a second chance can. *Bibliography*: Cary, *Jewett*.

BICKERS, ELDER. In "A Winter Courtship," he is an East Sanscrit church official who, Fanny Tobin says, " 's been and got married again," this time to a girl four years younger than his oldest daughter.

BICKFORD. In "The Only Rose," he is the deceased third husband of Mrs. Bickford, who describes him as dignified but uninteresting. She feels indebted to him because he left her in comfortable circumstances.

BICKFORD, MRS. In "The Only Rose," she is a widow with a problem: how to decorate the graves of her three husbands with three pots of flowers. The solitary rose should go to her favorite. Bickford, her third husband, was dignified and dull but left her well off. Wallis, her second husband, was a good conversationalist, a clever inventor, but an impractical businessman. Albert Fraley, her first husband, a mere boy when they wed, was handsome and loving. She and Albert were "dreadful happy," but he died in debt. Albert, the only one she was "in love" with, would be her choice for the rose; but fate decrees that John Parsons, a nephew who escorts her to the cemetery, keeps it for his fiancée— which suits Mrs. Bickford. She is fussy about her house, complains too much, dislikes sunlight and fresh air, is offputting with others, and remembers her husbands' flaws; however, she is portrayed with great sympathy. *Bibliography*: Roman.

BINET, MARIE. In "Mère Pochette," she is one of Mère Pochette's gossiping neighbors, described as a thief and a liar.

BINNEY. In "The Parshley Celebration," he is Asa Binney's son by his first marriage. The young man helps on the farm.

BINNEY, ASA. In "The Parshley Celebration," he is a farmer living with his second wife, Martha Binney, on their farm near Parshley, the village in which he is a selectman. Asa Binney participates in the Decoration Day celebration.

BINNEY, DAVID. In "The Parshley Celebration," he was Asa Binney's brother. Mary Ann Win loved David Binney and would have married him but for his being killed during the Civil War.

BINNEY, MARTHA. In "The Parshley Celebration," she is Asa Binney's second wife, described as big and strong. She suggests the Decoration Day parade to honor the soldiers from Parshley who served during the Civil War.

BINNEY, MRS. In "The Parshley Celebration," she was Asa Binney's first wife, now deceased. She was frail, ailing, and sad.

BINSON, SARAH ANN. In "Miss Tempy's Watchers," she is an unmarried farm woman who works hard to support her inefficient, widowed sister-in-law and her six whining children. Watching with Mrs. Daniel Crowe, a former schoolmate, over Temperance Dent's body the night before the funeral makes

Sarah Ann, described as "too sharp-set," more sympathetic toward Mrs. Crowe. Miss Tempy may well have planned everything this way.

BIRNEY. In "Good Luck," he is Mrs. Birney's son and plans to go fishing with Tom Leslie.

BIRNEY, ANNIE. In "Good Luck," she is Mrs. Birney's orphaned niece. She has been studying in a seminary and plans to teach school.

BIRNEY, MRS. In "Good Luck," she is the hospitable neighbor of the Leslies and lives near their summer home.

"A BIT OF COLOR" (1889). See *Betty Leicester: A Story for Girls.*

"A BIT OF SHORE LIFE" (1879). Short story. (Characters: Captain Donnell, Mrs. 'Lisha Downs, Skipper 'Lisha Downs, Captain Abiah Lane, Mrs. Walton Peters, Mrs. Sands, Stiles, Wallis, John Wallis, Miranda Wallis, Mrs. John Wallis, Mrs. Wallis, West, Andrew West, Cynthy West, Georgie West, Hannah West, Mrs. West, Mrs. West.) During her summer vacation by the shore, the narrator goes fishing with a local boy named Georgie West, who is serious, wizened, and only about twelve, and with his widowered father, Andrew. She gives her catch to Andrew's delighted sister, Hannah West, who is visiting and who invites her to come see her at the little farm she shares with her sister, Cynthia West, six miles inland. Going one day by horse and wagon, the narrator and Georgie stop on the way at an auction of household effects by the widowed Mrs. Wallis, who is going to live with her successful son John Wallis in Boston. The narrator and Georgie go on to Hannah's and Cynthia's house, with three lordly pines near the road and four apple trees positioned like dancers in front of the place. While Georgie manfully chops kindling and Hannah is busy in the kitchen, Cynthia shows the narrator their peaceful woods and her garden and beehives. Tea includes biscuits, gingerbread, preserves, honey, and pie, along with lobsters and fish Georgie brought. Georgie takes the reins as he and the narrator return home. She sees him set out to fish that night at eight. She prays that her "little fisherman" will find Christ, as others have, and in time "make the harbor of heaven by and by. . . ." "A Bit of Shore Life" contains subtle contrasts between old and new, rural and city, shore and farm. The dour depictions of rural New England life in it have been compared to those in Mary E. Wilkins Freeman's similar stories. *Bibliography*: Blanchard; Cary, *Jewett.*

BLACK, JOE. In "Jim's Little Woman," he is a drunken sailor whom Martha drives away from her house. He then falls over the sea wall and drowns.

BLACKETT, CAPTAIN. In *The Country of the Pointed Firs*, he is the deceased sea captain whose daguerreotype, taken in Portland, his daughter, Almira

Todd, shows the narrator. In "The Foreigner," he was a sea captain who with three other captains, according to his daughter, Almira Todd, rescued the French singer and dancer from rowdies in Kingston, Jamaica. Captain John Tolland, one of the other captains, took the woman to Maine and married her.

BLACKETT, MRS. In *The Country of the Pointed Firs*, she is Almira Todd's mother, eighty-six. She lives on Green Island, about five miles off shore from Dunnet Landing. She is the exemplar of hospitality when Mrs. Todd and the narrator visit her. She delights in attending the Bowden reunion. In "The Queen's Twin," Almira Todd says her mother will enjoy hearing about her visiting Abby Martin with the narrator. In "The Dunnet Shepherdess," William Blackett says his mother will enjoy having word of Thankful Hight's folks. In "The Foreigner," she defends Mrs. John Tolland against villagers' animosity and practically orders Almira Todd to befriend the lonely stranger. In "William's Wedding," Almira says her mother will be happy to have William come home with his bride, the former Esther Hight. Mrs. Blackett is manifestly of good French blood, of which her daughter is justly proud.

BLACKETT, SARAH JANE. In *The Country of the Pointed Firs*, she is Nathan Blackett's cousin. Almira Todd, Nathan's widow, endured her for his sake. Nathan did not like Sarah either. Almira tells the narrator she hates Sarah, whom they meet at the Bowden reunion.

BLACKETT, MRS. WILLIAM. In "William's Wedding." *See* Hight, Esther.

BLACKETT, WILLIAM. In *The Country of the Pointed Firs*, he is Mrs. Blackett's son and Almira Todd's brother, about sixty and a little deaf. Almira describes him as never ambitious and now a contented failure. Out of shyness, he does not attend the Bowden reunion, which saddens his mother. In "The Queen's Twin," Almira Todd says men fishing for mackerel will "detain" William Blackett. In "The Dunnet Shepherdess," William fishes with the narrator and takes her to meet Mrs. Thankful Hight and Esther Hight. He goes off with the latter for his brief annual rendezvous. In "The Foreigner," Almira Todd fears William may get caught in the storm. In "William's Wedding," he bravely sails across the bay to Dunnet Landing, reports to the minister's home, is married to Esther Hight, and calls with her at his sister Almira's house, where they have cakes and wine. They sail to his island home.

BLAKE, EZRA. In "The Night before Thanksgiving," he was a poor, deaf lad Mary Ann Robb helped long ago.

BLAKE, MARGERY ("MAGGY," "MARGY"). In "Jenny Garrow's Lovers," she is Jenny Garrow's close friend. She likes Richard Tyler, visits him in prison, and reveals Jenny's death to him. As the never-married narrator, she tells the tragic story forty years later.

BLAKE, MRS. In "Jenny Garrow's Lovers," she is the mother of Margery Blake and Tim Blake. Mrs. Blake does not question Richard Tyler's guilt.

BLAKE, TIM. In "Jenny Garrow's Lovers," he is Margery Blake's older brother. He takes her to the prison to visit Richard Tyler.

BLANC, MADAME. In "A Business Man," she is a person for whom one of the customers of William Chellis sews.

BLANC, MARIE-THÉRÈSE DE SOLMS (1840–1907). Author and translator. Born in Seine-Port, France, into an aristocratic family, Thérèse de Solms used Bentzon, her mother's maiden name, as part of "Th. Bentzon," her pen name. She was educated by her mother and an English governess. She married Alexandre Blanc (a man selected by her father) at sixteen, bore a son at seventeen, and divorced at nineteen. Her stepfather introduced her to George Sand, through whose influence she began publishing translations, critical pieces on foreign authors, travel essays, and novels in the *Revue des Deux Mondes* and elsewhere. In 1893 Blanc visited the United States, traveling to Chicago and New Orleans. In *Les Américaines chez elles* (1895), she expresses admiration for the independence of many American women. She revisited the United States in 1897 and also made literary use of visits to Canada, England, Germany, and Russia. She produced almost a novel a year from 1868 to 1902, the best being *Un divorce* (1872), the prize-winning *Un remords* ("Remorse," 1878), and *Tony* (1885). She published four additional books on American writers and social conditions. She helped familiarize the French reading public with the works of Thomas Bailey Aldrich,* Edward Bellamy, George Washington Cable, Hamlin Garland, Bret Harte, William Dean Howells,* Henry James,* Sidney Lanier, Thomas Nelson Page, Charles Warren Stoddard, Mark Twain,* Walt Whitman, and Jewett. A conservative Catholic, liberal feminist, and adviser to young French girls, Blanc was admitted to the Legion d'Honneur of France shortly before she died in Paris.

Blanc reviewed *A Country Doctor* in *Deux Mondes* (February 1885), began corresponding with Jewett in 1885, entertained Jewett and Annie Adams Fields* in Paris and its environs (1892, 1898, 1900), was grateful when Jewett got some of Blanc's work translated and published in the United States (1896), published her translations of *A Country Doctor* and nine Jewett stories (1900), was Annie Fields's guest (1893) and Jewett's guest (1897, 1898), and conferred with Jewett (1903) about the French translation of *The Tory Lover*. Shortly after Blanc's death, Jewett corresponded poignantly about her with Violet Paget,* their mutual friend. Jewett and Blanc had in common a love of nature (especially flowers) and the past, and a desire to see improvements evolve in women's living conditions. *Bibliography*: Blanchard; Cary, *Letters*; Silverthorne.

BLAND, MRS. In "The Flight of Betsey Lane," she is a well-to-do person mentioned as saving her good clothes too long.

BLAND, NANCY. In "The New Methuselah," she is Masters's housekeeper. She is ungrateful for food received from Dr. Asa Potterby. At one point she tells Mrs. Yard, Potterby's housekeeper, she "don't want no more o' that salt beef."

BLUNT. In *The Tory Lover*, this is the family name of "pretty" guests from Newcastle at Mary Hamilton's wedding.

BOB. In *A Country Doctor*, he was an English protégé of Dr. Ferris, who aided him in Bombay and Japan. Ferris says he gave Bob money to get married in England and quit wandering.

BOB. In "The Green Bowl," he is Katie Montague's faithful horse. He takes Katie and Frances Kent to the empty church.

BOB. In "The Two Browns," he is Lucy Brown's brother. He is an accountant. Lucy tells her husband, John Benedict Brown, to ask Bob about his wife's health.

BOGAN, ANN. In "Bold Words at the Bridge," she is a person whom the strange woman from Lawrence met years ago at Honora Flaherty's home. Biddy Connelly recalls that Ann Bogan and her mother—also named Ann Bogan—died thirty years earlier.

BOGAN, BIDDY FLAHERTY. In "The Luck of the Bogans," she is Mike Bogan's wife, from Glengariff. She gets him to leave Bantry for America with her and their son, Dan Bogan. She complains briefly; has three daughters, including Mary Ellen Bogan, in the New World; is religious, and respects Father Miles.

BOGAN, DAN ("DANNY"). In "The Luck of the Bogans," he is the son of Mike Bogan and Biddy Flaherty Bogan. They go to America, where he learns arithmetic, is spoiled, abuses his sisters, feels superior, associates with riffraff, and embarrasses his father by boasting, conniving, and drinking excessively. He is stabbed to death in a fight.

BOGAN, JERRY. In "The Luck of the Bogans," he is a retired sailor who drinks in the saloon of Mike Bogan (no relation). Jerry is poor and crippled, considerate and witty, and "full of Irish lore and legend." His close friend is Corny Sullivan. Jerry thinks Mike's son, Dan Bogan, might be improved if he went to sea.

BOGAN, MARY ELLEN. In "The Luck of the Bogans," she is the oldest of the three daughters of Mike Bogan and Biddy Flaherty Bogan. Biddy keeps Mary Ellen out of school to tend to her sisters.

BOGAN, MIKE ("MICKY"). In "The Luck of the Bogans," he is the husband, from Bantry, of Biddy Flaherty Bogan, from Glengariff. Together with their son, Dan Bogan, they leave for America, where Mike works in a carriage-shop forge, saves money, buys a saloon, and becomes a decent dispenser of liquor. He favors Dan over his three daughters, including Mary Ellen Bogan, and is fatally sorrowful when Dan is stabbed to death.

"BOLD WORDS AT THE BRIDGE" (1899). Short story. (Characters: Ann Bogan, Father Brady, Biddy Connelly, Mary Dunleavy, Honora Flaherty.) Two old neighbors, Biddy Connelly and Mary Dunleavy, are arguing on a bridge in the mill town. Biddy contends that Mary's pumpkin vines are running into her melons and stunting their growth. After harsh words and fist shakings, Mary vows never to speak to Biddy again. One day weeks later, in late summer, a strange woman walks up the hill and asks Mary for directions to the home of Ann Bogan. Mary does not know, and the woman leaves. Biddy, who overheard, courteously tells Mary she remembers a mother and a daughter, both named Ann Bogan and both dead these thirty years, who lived near Biddy's cousins the Flahertys, gone to Lawrence twelve years earlier. Mary answers gently, and their foolish quarrel quietly ends. The two are having tea at Biddy's house when the strange woman returns, disappointed in her search. They invite her in and learn she worked in Lawrence and visited her friend Honora Flaherty seventeen years ago, just before returning to Ireland to care for her mother. After that old woman's death she came back here, only to find everything changed. She is grateful for this warm welcome from such pleasant neighbor ladies, who explain that they had "bold words" they can now laugh about. Biddy offers a luscious melon, while Mary says her worthless pumpkins briefly threatened Biddy's nice cabbages. That evening the three women walk over the bridge together into town. Jewett's handling of the neighbors' rapprochement is brilliantly delicate. The story has folk-tale elements: isolation versus community, bridge and gardens, archetypal stranger, and ritual drink. *Bibliography*: Morgan and Renza.

BOLTON, ISAAC. In "A Change of Heart," he is the would-be suitor of Sally Martin, who has rebuffed him through a misunderstanding. Orphaned as a child, he was raised by an aunt and an uncle, and has prospered as a farmer. When he falls while building a new house, Sally forgets her pride and rushes to him. All will be well.

BOND. In *Betty Leicester's English Xmas*, he is Lady Mary Danesley's old butler.

BOND, PEGGY. In "The Flight of Betsey Lane," she is a Byfleet Poorhouse resident. Her two closest friends are Lavina Dow and Betsey Lane. Miss Bond is small, feisty looking but meek, and suffers because of "upsighted" vision. When in Philadelphia, Betsey chances to consult Dunster, who promises to treat what he diagnoses as Peggy's cataracts. She is a character of a sort frequently found in Jewett's writing; she is handled in a way combining pathos and comedy.

BONNY, MRS. In *Deephaven*, she is the widow of a charcoal burner and basket maker. She lives twelve miles from Deephaven in a two-room house with chickens inside. She reveres Deephaven's Parson Lorimer. She is a fund of wood lore.

"A BORN FARMER" (1901). Short story. (Characters: John Beckley, Fanny, Adeline Gaines, Jacob Gaines, Jacob "Jakey" Gaines, Mary Ellen Gaines, Dr. Marsh, Nat, Abel Potter, Hiram Ray, John Ray, Mrs. Ray, Tiger.) A big change occurs in the life of Jacob Gaines, forty-nine, a hard-working farmer on Pine Hill near Upton Corners. His cousin, Nat, died rich in Minnesota and willed Jacob $50,000 in November. His wife, Adeline Gaines, who never especially liked farming, and their children, Jacob ("Jakey") Gaines, eighteen, and Mary Ellen Gaines, are pleased. In January they move to Boston, where Jacob, reluctant to bid his unproductive farm a permanent goodbye, is persuaded by his wife's brother to invest substantially in his lumber business, so that it can expand. By April, Jacob is shuffling papers in the lumber company office, while Adeline, feeling like a stranger in the neighborhood of their rented house and also at church, becomes ill. In bed one night she complains so much that Jacob pretends to be asleep. A young doctor's ministrations only make the lonely woman more nervous. One mild spring day Jacob thinks of farm work neglected back home and that night dreams he is being rebuked by neighbors. He walks Jakey, a happy worker at the lumber company but worried about his father, to the railroad train, which he takes on a business trip to New Hampshire. Jacob ambles into the market district and feels comfortably at home when he smells a load of "earthy" potatoes. Late in April, Mary Ellen, happily home on Pine Hill ahead of her parents, welcomes them back to their farm. Jacob notes to Adeline that "home's home," as she starts to prepare supper. Jacob explains to John Ray, a neighbor lad who wagoned them from the station, that only Jakey, who "ain't no farmer," likes Boston. Jacob adds that the lumber company can keep his money, which is helping to earn everyone a good profit. By May, Jacob and Adeline observe that Mary Ellen and young John seem happy together too.

BOUFFLERS, DUKE DE. In *The Tory Lover*, he was a friend of the teacher Sullivan during their school days in France.

BOUTINEAU. In *The Tory Lover*, this is the name of a family of Loyalists who are now refugees in Bristol.

BOWDEN. In "The Dunnet Shepherdess," he is the owner of the place past which Almira Todd says her brother William Blackett goes trout fishing once a year.

BOWDEN, ALICK. In "The Foreigner," he is mentioned by Almira Todd as her mother Mrs. Blackett's beloved nephew.

BOWDEN, ASA. In "The Queen's Twin," he is mentioned by Almira Todd as having family members who went berrying in the woods one afternoon, were lost overnight, and were dreadfully frightened when rescued.

BOWDEN, CAPTAIN. In *The Country of the Pointed Firs*, he is a sea captain with whom the narrator visits Shell-heap Island, where Joanna Todd lived, died, and is buried. He may be Jonathan Bowden. *See also* Bowden, Captain Jonathan.

BOWDEN, CAPTAIN JONATHAN. In *The Country of the Pointed Firs*, he is a "self-contained" old fisherman with a distinctive boat. In "The Foreigner," Jonathan Bowden is a sea captain the narrator says is safe on Green Island during the storm. He was one of the four captains who rescued the French-born singer and dancer from rowdies in Kingston, Jamaica. When it fell to him to take her to New England, he said his wife would make trouble. So Captain John Tolland sailed with her and later married her. *See also* Bowden, Captain.

BOWDEN, CAPTAIN LORENZO. In "The Foreigner," he was Almira Todd's uncle and an enterprising sea captain. He handled the will of Mrs. John Tolland, told Almira she had inherited the woman's estate, and accepted payment from Almira for his legal work. Lorenzo unsuccessfully sought Captain Jonathan Tolland's sea "chist" in the old house and accidentally burned the place down.

BOWDEN, JOHNNY. In *The Country of the Pointed Firs*, he is the son of Almira Todd's cousin and works around the Dunnet Landing wharf. In "The Foreigner," he is a person the narrator says is safe on Green Island during the storm. In "William's Wedding," he helps the narrator from the Dunnet Landing dock to Almira Todd's house and later escorts Esther Hight to her wedding.

BOWDEN, MRS. In *The Country of the Pointed Firs*, she is Almira Todd's cousin and Johnny Bowden's mother. In "William's Wedding," she is young

Johnny Bowden's mother. She visits friendly Almira Todd to gain news of the wedding of Almira's brother, William Blackett.

BOWDEN, MRS. JONATHAN. In "The Foreigner," she is the jealous wife of the sea captain who was reluctant to have the French singer board his vessel in Kingston.

BOWDEN, MRS. PETER. In *The Country of the Pointed Firs*, she attends the Bowden reunion and participates in the hymn singing—"far out o' tune," according to Almira Todd.

BOWDEN, PA'LINA. In *The Country of the Pointed Firs*, she is a person Almira Todd only briefly thinks resembles the farm woman who served Almira, Mrs. Blackett, and the narrator doughnuts on their way to the Bowden reunion. That woman turns out not to be a Bowden.

BOWDEN, SANTIN ("SANT"). In *The Country of the Pointed Firs*, he is a shoemaker, is not of sound mind, would have wished for a military career, and may be partly of French extraction. He drinks when gloomy. He seats participants in the Bowden reunion in a regimented fashion.

BOWLER. In "Mr. Bruce," he is a guest at the dinner party given by Miss Alice Thornton's father. When he and Philip Bruce, also a guest, discuss John Keith's marrying his mother's nursemaid, Bowler speaks approvingly of the maid as "remarkably ladylike," whereas Bruce smugly judges her to be wrongly elevated to an undeserved social class.

BRADISH. In *A Marsh Island*, he is Richard Dale's inepcunious artist friend who shares Dale's studio. Flippant Bradish causes humor to emerge in others.

BRADY, FATHER. In "Bold Words at the Bridge," he urges Biddy Connelly and Mary Dunleavy to stop arguing. For too long they ignore his suggestion.

BRALEY. In "Between Mass and Vespers," he is mentioned as a person with whom Patrick Finn missed getting a ride home because he paused to talk to friends after mass.

BRANDON, CHANTREY. In *Deephaven*, he was Hathaway Brandon's brother and fished with Captain Jacob Lant.

BRANDON, HATHAWAY. In *Deephaven*, he was Kate Lancaster's grandfather.

BRANDON, HENRY. In *Deephaven*, he was Katharine Brandon's youngest brother. He turned Catholic while studying in Europe. Captain Jacob Lant liked him.

BRANDON, MISS KATHARINE ("KITTEN"). In *Deephaven*, she was Kate Lancaster's great-aunt, recently deceased. She evidently loved a sailor lost at sea and thereafter never married. She never liked Rebecca Lorimer. Katharine willed the Deephaven mansion to the Lancasters, which enables Kate and Helen Denis to stay there through the summer.

BRANDON, MRS. CHANTREY. In *Deephaven*, she obtained a recipe for spice cake in England and gave it to Mrs. Patton.

BRAY, DEACON. In "The Town Poor," he is the deceased father of Ann and Mandana Bray. Rumor says he had a misspent youth. Later he was so generous to the church that he left his daughters in poverty.

BRAY, MANDANA ("MANDANY," "MANDY"). In "The Town Poor," she is Miss Ann Bray's younger sister. Mandana has weakened eyesight and complains more than Ann does.

BRAY, MISS ANN. In "The Town Poor," she is Mandana Bray's older sister. They were both left in poverty by their father, Deacon Bray. Ann has a lame wrist but is cheerful. The Hampton selectmen have placed the two sisters in the cramped home of Abel Janes and his family. Mrs. William Trimble vows to improve the Bray sisters' lot.

BRAYTON. In "A Pinch of Salt," he is John Brayton's deaf, old father. John returns home to be of support to his father and mother.

BRAYTON, JOHN. In "A Pinch of Salt," he was the especially remembered schoolmate of Hannah Dalton, now a teacher in that same school. John Brayton is the uncle of Nelly Catesby, one of Hannah's pupils. Hannah has not seen John for ten years. During this time he went to Florida and then the west, made money in mining, and returned to Winfield to help his aging parents. He meets Hannah by the spring in fulfillment of her Halloween legend about a pinch of salt and a drink of spring water. The two get married.

BRAYTON, MRS. In *The Country of the Pointed Firs*, she is a person Susan Fosdick says she stayed with. The two knitted and reminisced. Her husband may be Nahum Brayton.

BRAYTON, MRS. In "A Pinch of Salt," she is John Brayton's aging mother. John returns home to help both of his parents.

BRAYTON, NAHUM. In *The Country of the Pointed Firs*, since Susan Fosdick says she rode over from his house to Dunnet Landing, he is probably Mrs. Brayton's husband.

BRENT, ELIZABETH ("LIZZIE"). In "A Dark Night," she is the young woman Weymouth loves. She is part of a group of robbers. She helps Weymouth escape from Rogers and his thugs at an inn near Bristol. When she goes to America, Weymouth follows, and they get married.

BRENTON. In "The Orchard's Grandmother," he is mentioned as Colonel Brenton's brother.

BRENTON, COLONEL ("SQUIRE BRENTON"). In "The Orchard's Grandmother," he is the royalist father of Mary ("Polly") Brenton. When Oliver Cromwell's soldiers pursue him, he escapes with his family to America for a year.

BRENTON, MARY. In "The Orchard's Grandmother," she is the grandmother of Mary ("Polly") Brenton. She gives Polly an apple, a seed from which the little girl successfully plants. When Polly and her parents escape for a time to America, the old woman remains in England.

BRENTON, MARY ("POLLY"). In "The Orchard's Grandmother," she is the little daughter of Colonel Brenton and Mrs. Brenton. Her grandmother gives her an apple and encourages her to plant its seeds. Polly takes a sapling from one seed to America with her, and it grows into a tree alive two hundred years later.

BRENTON, MRS. In "The Orchard's Grandmother," she is the wife of Colonel Brenton and the mother of Mary ("Polly") Brenton. The Brenton family escapes Oliver Cromwell's men by going to America.

BRIDGET. In *Deephaven*, she was a person in Katharine Brandon's home when Kate Lancaster was there at age seven. She criticized Kate's uncle, Jack Lancaster, for smoking in Kate's room.

BRIEN, MRS. In "A Visit Next Door," she does the washing for Mrs. Filmore and her family on Tuesdays.

BRIGGS, ASA. In "The Quest of Mr. Teaby," he is the East Wilby depot master. Sister Hannah Jane Pinkham asks him to tell Teaby she has his forgotten umbrella and will hold it for him.

BRILEY, JEFFERSON. In "A Winter Courtship," he is a bachelor who, for eighteen years, has driven a mail and passenger wagon between North Kilby and Sanscrit Pond. He has some savings, reads Western fiction, sees himself as a resolute stage driver, and carries a pistol—unloaded. He imagines that Mrs. Ash and Mrs. Peak would like to capture him. But Fanny Tobin, an old widow, drives with him to North Kilby, plays up to his boastful nature, and maneuvers him into a proposal, which she accepts. She calls him "Jeff'son."

BRIMBLECOM, MRS. SILAS. In "The Courting of Sister Wisby," she was, according to Mrs. Goodsoe, the long-suffering first wife of Silas Brimblecom, a hypocritical "deacon," and the mother of his four children. He briefly left her. Not long after he returned home, she died.

BRIMBLECOM, PHEBE. In "The Courting of Sister Wisby," she was one of Silas Brimblecom's four children, according to Mrs. Goodsoe. When Brimblecom, widowered, married Eliza Wisby, Phebe happily lived with the couple. When Eliza died, she left most of her property to Phebe.

BRIMBLECOM, SILAS ("BRIMFUL," "DEACON"). In "The Courting of Sister Wisby," he was a footloose sort of revivalist preacher, according to Mrs. Goodsoe. He temporarily left his wife and children for a "spirit bride" but soon returned home; after his wife died, he courted and was courted by Eliza Wisby. They eventually married, got along reasonably well, but were both selfish. He grew too fond of cider.

BRINDLE. In *A Country Doctor*, she is Mrs. Thacher's old cow, which she sells.

BROCK, PHEBE ANN. In *The Country of the Pointed Firs*, she is a person who, according to Mrs. Blackett, will probably attend the Bowden reunion, although she is "slow."

BROOKS, MISS. In "A Business Man." *See* Chellis, Mrs. William.

BROOKS, PHILLIPS (1835–1893). Episcopal clergyman. Born in Boston, he graduated from Harvard (1855) and was rector at Holy Trinity, Philadelphia (1859–1869), and at wealthy Trinity Church, Boston (1869–1891). He was an influential minister and spiritual leader, becoming Bishop of Massachusetts in 1891. He often visited England, where he preached once before Queen Victoria and several times at Oxford and Cambridge. Though the author of several religious books, he is best known for writing the hymn "O Little Town of Bethlehem" (1887). Jewett first heard Brooks preach at Trinity Church in 1869. On 27 November 1870, perhaps inspired by him, she was baptized and confirmed at St. John's Episcopal Church, Portsmouth. Jewett wrote and anonymously published "At the Funeral of Phillips Brooks" (*Atlantic Monthly*, April 1893). In this eloquent eulogy she compares his death to a "great sunset" turning "into dawn." Oliver Wendell Holmes,* Brooks's close friend, especially admired his socially liberal sermons, with their emphasis on Christ's ethical teachings. *Bibliography*: Silverthorne.

BROOKS, TAMSEN. In "The Hiltons' Holiday," she is an aunt of Mrs. John Hilton, who will visit her while her husband takes their daughters, Susan Ellen Hilton and Katy Hilton, to Topham Corners for a little holiday.

BROWN. In "The Coon Dog," he is any of Isaac Brown's sons.

BROWN. In *A Country Doctor*, he provides Nancy Prince with ducks, which she orders cooked for Captain Walter Parish and other special guests.

BROWN. In "Fair Day," this is the name of the owner(s) of the farm property sold by Tobias Bascom when he married Ann (*see* Bascom, Ann) and moved with her and also his mother, Mercy Bascom, to Ann's better property. Mercy's visit to their old house triggers memories.

BROWN. In "The Two Browns," she is the baby daughter of John Benedict Brown and his wife, Lucy Brown.

BROWN, ASA. In "Decoration Day," he is a Civil War veteran who, with Henry Merrill and John Stover, plans the holiday parade. He also intends to decorate "our Joel's grave" with a flag. *See also* Brown, Joel.

BROWN, ISAAC. In "The Coon Dog," he is the father of two or more sons, including John Henry Brown. He and his friend, John York, with their sons, rent 'Liza Topliff's worthless coon dog, Tiger, to go coon hunting. Isaac's good coon dog, Rover, trees the coon.

BROWN, JOE. In "The Life of Nancy," he is a man Addie Porter prefers to Tom Aldis. Tom, who flirted with Addie, is relieved when Nancy Gale, Addie's friend, tells him so.

BROWN, JOEL. In "Decoration Day," he is probably the brother of Asa Brown. Joel was killed during the Civil War.

BROWN, JOHN BENEDICT ("BEN," "SNOOKS"). In "The Two Browns," at twenty-eight, he would rather be an engineer than the fourth attorney in his family line. He is married to Lucy Brown, and they have a baby daughter. Brown begins to lead a double life, that of a so-so but conscientious lawyer (J. Benedict Brown) and that of the adviser and partner (John B. Brown) of Checkley in successfully marketing Checkley's electric potato planter. Three years pass, and Brown and Lucy have a son, also named John Benedict Brown. When Grandison, an inventor whose steam harrow may have inspired Checkley, offers to buy them out, Checkley agrees and Brown resumes his single identity. Checkley calls Brown "Snooks," his school nickname.

BROWN, JOHN BENEDICT ("JOHNNY"). In "The Two Browns," he is the newborn son of John Benedict Brown. Will the child have to be the fifth attorney in the family line?

BROWN, JOHN HENRY. In "The Coon Dog," he is one of Isaac Brown's sons. They go coon hunting with Isaac's friend, John York, and his sons.

BROWN, LUCY. In "The Two Browns," she is John Benedict Brown's trusting wife. The two enjoy summer vacations with her mother in Newport. She does not know of his dual life until he confesses after three years. Jewett characterizes Lucy as unusually callow.

BROWN, MR. In "A Business Man." *See* Craven, John.

BROWN, MRS. In "A Late Supper," she is a cleaning woman Catherine Spring hires when Miss Ashton and Alice West rent rooms from her.

BROWN, MRS. ISAAC. In "The Coon Dog," she is the hunter's wife.

BRUCE. In "Mr. Bruce," he is Philip Bruce's father, a businessman in London.

BRUCE, KITTY. In *Deephaven*, she visits Kate Lancaster and Helen Denis in Deephaven. In "Mr. Bruce," Kitty ("Kate") Bruce is Miss Margaret Tennant's sister, three years older than Margaret. Kitty was named Kate after her father's sister, Kate Hunter. Kitty pretends to be the Tennant family's serving-maid and waits on four dinner guests, including Philip Bruce. She asks her family to call her Katherine, and she puts on an Irish brogue. Her masquerade delays her romance with and marriage to Bruce. They have two daughters. Feminist readers find beautiful Kitty shallow and condescending, even though she is described as "brilliant." *Bibliography*: Roman.

BRUCE, PHILIP. In "Mr. Bruce," he is the handsome, rich son of a London businessman. Philip and three other businessmen are invited to dinner by Tennant, a Boston businessman. Bruce thinks Tennant's daughter Kitty, who pretends to be the family serving-maid, is beautiful but beneath him socially. When he learns her true identity, they get married. By story's end, they have two daughters and have been happily married for nearly thirty years. It may be argued, however, that this "happiest" of marriages is the marriage of a condescending woman and a priggish man. *Bibliography*: Roman.

BRYAN. In "A Landless Farmer," he is any one of Mary Lydia Bryan's lazy young sons.

BRYAN, HENRY. In "A Landless Farmer," he is the deceased husband of Mary Lydia Bryan and was a successful enough businessman.

BRYAN, MARY LYDIA ("MARY LYDDY"). In "A Landless Farmer," she is Henry Bryan's whining widow and the mother of two or more lazy sons, who live with her at Harlow's Mills. Her widowed father is Jerry Jenkins, and her sister is Serena Nudd. Both sisters mistreat their father.

BUCKLAND. In *Betty Leicester*, he is a scientist in London and a friend of Thomas Leicester.

BUNT, ASA. In *A Marsh Island*, he was a hired hand working for Israel Owen until Asa joined relatives in the West. It is hinted that those relatives will filch his savings.

BUNT, DULCIDORA ("DULCY"). In "The Girl with the Cannon Dresses," she is a tomboy, nine, who misses life on the coast, where her father used to fish, and plays at a spring near their farmhome. When she meets Alice Channing, the older girl takes a fancy to her, tutors her a little, sends her reading material, and reveres the memory of the child whose mother made her dresses out of a bolt of calico with a pattern of cannons.

BUNT, JACOB. In "The Girl with the Cannon Dresses," he was Dulcidora Bunt's now-deceased brother.

BUNT, MRS. In "The Girl with the Cannon Dresses," she is Samuel Bunt's wife and Dulcidora Bunt's mother. Mrs. Bunt is happier now that she and her family live on an inland farm. She is critical of Dulcidora and deplores her unfeminine ways.

BUNT, SAMUEL ("SAM"). In "The Girl with the Cannon Dresses," he is Dulcidora Bunt's father. He named her after a schooner he was part owner of. He was happier when he, his wife, and their daughter lived on the coast so he could fish. He misses the sea so much that he brought his boat to their inland farm so he could sit in it occasionally. He wishes Dulcidora were a boy.

BURRILL, CHARLEY. In "A Village Patriot," he is a brisk, neat young shingler from Boston. While working on a job, he boards with Abel Thorndike, a fellow worker. Charley falls in love with Abel's daughter, Phebe Thorndike.

BURT, MISS. In "Mr. Bruce," she is a young woman Philip Bruce meets in Baltimore. He asks her if she knows Kitty Tennant.

BURTON, MARGARET. In "A War Debt," she is Thomas ("Tom") Burton's frail old Bostonian grandmother. She asks him to return the silver cup to the Bellamy family in Virginia. Her son, Thomas Burton, now deceased, pilfered it during the Civil War. Her only uneasiness about her grandson is that he is still unmarried.

BURTON, THOMAS. In "A War Debt," he was Thomas ("Tom") Burton's grandfather, now deceased. He attended Harvard with Colonel Bellamy and visited him in Virginia before the Civil War.

BURTON, THOMAS. In "A War Debt," he was Thomas ("Tom") Burton's father, now deceased. During the Civil War, he pilfered a silver cup from the ravaged estate of Colonel Bellamy and soon thereafter was killed in combat.

BURTON, THOMAS ("TOM"). In "A War Debt," he is the grandson of old Margaret Burton of Boston. She asks him to return the silver cup to the Bellamy family in Virginia. In doing so, he meets and is welcomed by Colonel Bellamy and his frail wife, sees their granddaughter on the train, and is so impressed by her charm that he plans to return to the Bellamys for some Christmas hunting.

"A BUSINESS MAN" (1886). Short story. (Characters: Madame Blanc, William Chellis, Mrs. William Chellis, Jack Craven, John Craven, Mrs. John Craven, Walter.) Some men, clergymen and doctors, for example, choose professions with money as a secondary object. Not so, businessmen. John Craven gets more pleasure totaling his assets than being with his family, and thinks little about society or the next world. One day he grows ill and must slow down; so he transfers control of his vast businesses to his son, Jack Craven, who soon grows overbearing. John Craven and his wife vacation in Europe, where he mainly enjoys checking into commercial connections there. Upon their return, she suddenly dies. He misses her dreadfully, because in recent months they had become more affectionate. Caring nothing for culture, he grows desolate. His sons and daughters, as well as their spouses and children, become ever more busy, materialistic, and indifferent. One day Craven, in an old coat and looking rather poor, walks into a thrifty part of town and idly enters a neat little notions shop. The bright young proprietor, William Chellis, courteously chats with Craven, who sees possibilities in the shop. He learns Chellis plans to marry Miss Brooks (*see* Chellis, Mrs. William), a pretty seamstress, if he can get out of a debt incurred when he stocked his shop. Feeling essentially poorer than this loving couple, Craven, calling himself Mr. Brown, advances Chellis some money, goes into informal partnership with him, works happily in the shop with him, gives Miss Brooks a sizable cash gift for their wedding, but does not attend the ceremony. As time passes, Craven offers several canny suggestions to Chellis, visits less often, grows weaker, is moved by his fretful family to his country house, and dies there. He bequeaths Chellis $5,000 and includes a signed letter thanking him for "kindness and respect to an old man" and warning him not to be all business. Mrs. Chellis expresses surprise at the money gift and is puzzled when Chellis says the gift was more than money. Point of view and details in this excellent parable are poorly handled.

"BY THE MORNING BOAT" (1890). Short story. (Characters: Susy Draper, Elisha, Jim Hooper, Lucy Ann, Lydia, Ma'am Stover, John Sykes.) One summer morning on the coast of Maine, Elisha, fifteen, has a last breakfast with his grandfather, his widowed mother, Lucy Ann, and Lydia, his sister, twelve, before leaving for a job in Boston. Ma'am Stover, a bedridden neighbor lady, gives him a watch. John Sykes wagons him to the steamer. His lonely family is sad at his necessary departure, but Elisha faces the future with grit—if perhaps too much confidence.

C

CAESAR. In *The Tory Lover*, he is Colonel Jonathan Hamilton's "majestic" black servant. Caesar was once a Guinea prince.

CALL, DENNIS. In "Between Mass and Vespers," he is the middle-aged, sturdy teamster who drives Father Ryan into the woods to meet with Dan Nolan. Dennis's wife is ill and tired. Their daughter is Mag Call. Dennis is a typical thrifty, decent, reverent New England Irishman; he speaks Gaelic with John Mulligan after mass.

CALL, MAG. In "Between Mass and Vespers," she is the young daughter of Dennis Call and his wife.

CALL, MRS. DENNIS. In "Between Mass and Vespers," she is Dennis Call's ailing wife.

CALLAHAN, JERRY. In "Elleneen," he is a young man Mary Ann Dunn pretends to regard as a suitor of her sister, Ellen Dunn. Ellen counters by calling him a lout.

CALLAHAN, MIKE. In "The Gray Mills of Farley," he is a mill worker whose house Mary Cassidy says he bought with money inherited from his brother in California.

CALVINN, MISS. In "The Taking of Captain Ball," she is the daughter of Mr. Calvinn, the minister, and is Captain Ball's friend.

CALVINN, MR. In "The Taking of Captain Ball," he is the town minister and Captain Ball's friend.

CALVINN, MRS. In "The Taking of Captain Ball," she is the wife of Mr. Calvinn, the town minister, and is Captain Ball's friend. She and her family are in on the secret that Mrs. Ann French is really Ball's great-niece.

CAMERON, NELLY. In "Mr. Bruce," he is a person Miss Margaret Tennant says is as young as Elly.

CAPLIN. In "The Dunnet Shepherdess," this is the name of the owner of the horse William Blackett uses to draw his wagon when he goes trout fishing and sees Esther Hight. Also, according to a comment of the narrator to gossip-hungry Mrs. Thankful Hight, Caplin is a sea-faring widower about to marry one of the younger Harris women.

CAPLIN. In "The Foreigner," she was a young girl whose poor duet, with Mari' Harris, Mrs. John Tolland objected to, prompting an argument.

CAPLIN, DEACON. In "The Foreigner," he was a church deacon in Dunnet Landing. Mrs. John Tolland objected to the contents of his opening prayer and marched out of the service in tears.

CAPLIN, MRS. In *The Country of the Pointed Firs*, she is a friend of Almira Todd and also attends the Bowden reunion. Mrs. Caplin may be of Irish extraction.

CAPLIN, MRS. In "William's Wedding," she is described as one of several Mrs. Caplins. To gain news of William Blackett's wedding, she visits his sister, Almira Todd, on the pretext of needing a cup of yeast.

CAPLIN, MRS. EDWARD. In *The Country of the Pointed Firs*, she is a friend of Almira Todd and has recently had "her third shock." Almira will inquire about her at the port when the narrator leaves by steamer.

CAPLIN, MRS. ELDER. In "The Queen's Twin," Almira Todd says she is from North Point and loves to visit friends at Dunnet Landing.

CAREW, CAPTAIN. In *Deephaven*, he was a sea captain and ship owner, and the uncle of the church-going Carews.

CAREW, CAPTAIN DICK. In *Deephaven*, he was a former East Indies merchant but lost much of his wealth. He lived in the Carew house with his sisters, Honora Carew and Mrs. Dent. He debated theological points with Parson Lorimer.

CAREW, DANIEL R. In "The Life of Nancy," he is Tom Aldis's friend. The two vacation in East Rodney. Tom happily uses Carew's sprained ankle as an excuse for staying longer than planned, because he is enjoying the company of both sweet Nancy Gale and flirtatious Addie Porter. Carew becomes a member of the New York Stock Exchange.

CAREW, HONORA. In *Deephaven*, she was the sister of Captain Dick Carew and Mrs. Dent. Although she feuded with Rebecca Lorimer, Honora praises Deephaven society in general. She tells Kate Lancaster and Helen Denis about Sally Chauncey's unhappy life.

CARRICK, CAPTAIN JOE. In "A Lost Lover," he is Horatia Dane's "lover." He was from a good Salem family and when orphaned was brought up by his grandmother. He became a sailor, met Horatia in Salem, and was thought to be lost in the South Seas. In reality, he never communicated with Horatia again, married in Australia, and was ruined by drink. Thirty or forty years later, he returned to the United States. Later by chance he begs for food at Horatia's kitchen in Longfield and is fed by her servant Melissa. Horatia, whom he does not recognize but who silently recognizes him, gives him $10 and lets him leave.

CARROLL, ELLEN. In "The Gray Mills of Farley," she is Mike Carroll's wife. The two appeal to Dan, the mill agent, who gives them money after the mills are shut down.

CARROLL, MIKE. In "The Gray Mills of Farley," he is Ellen Carroll's husband. He has a speech impediment. After the mills are shut down, he and Ellen appeal to Dan, the mill agent, who gives them money.

CARROLL, MISS. In "Mr. Bruce," she is the hostess at an evening party in Baltimore that Kitty Tennant attends. She meets Davenport there.

CARROLL, PHIL. In "Elleneen," he is a young man Mary Ann Dunn pretends to regard as a suitor of her sister Ellen, who says she is not interested in him.

CASEY, MOTHER. In "A Little Captive Maid," she is a person who Nora Connelly tells John Balfour would pray for him if he should see her in Glengariff, Ireland, and give her "a trippence."

CASSIDY, MARY. In "The Gray Mills of Farley," she is a mill sweeper. Mary Cassidy is a close friend of Mrs. Kilpatrick, also a sweeper. The two gossip about the French-Canadians. Both feel sorry for Maggie, the little orphan girl, whom Mrs. Kilpatrick soon cares for.

CATESBY. In "A Pinch of Salt," this is the name of one or more of Hannah Dalton's pupils. The Catesby children are called "discreet." Nelly Catesby, one pupil, first broaches the subject of Halloween to Hannah. Nelly's being John Brayton's niece is one reason Hannah thinks so often about John; another is that Hannah has always loved him.

CATHER, WILLA (1873–1947). Author. Born near Winchester, Virginia, she moved at nine with her family to live with her paternal grandfather on his farm in Webster County, Nebraska. Within two years, her father moved the family to nearby Red Cloud. Cather observed immigrant farmers, talked with many cultured ones, and attended plays presented in the local opera house by traveling troupes. After graduating from the University of Nebraska in 1895, Cather was a magazine editor in Pittsburgh, taught English and Latin there, and worked on the staff of *McClure's Magazine* in New York City (1906–1911). She quit her salaried job and finished *Alexander's Bridge* (1912), the first of her thirteen novels. She had already published a collection of poems (1903) and another of short stories (1905). Once established, Cather enjoyed trips to Europe, New Mexico, and Canada. Her best fiction includes *O Pioneers!* (1913), *My Ántonia* (1918), *The Professor's House* (1925), *Death Comes for the Archbishop* (1927), *Shadows on the Rock* (1931), "Old Mrs. Harris" (1932), and "Neighbour Rosicky" (1932); it reflects her love of specific regions—Nebraska, the Southwest, Quebec—and of the people loyal to their roots. Recent critics contend that there is evidence of lesbianism in Cather's life.

Jewett, who had read Cather's 1905 short fiction, met Cather at the home of Annie Adams Fields* (1908), while Cather was in Boston on a *McClure's* assignment. Liking each other at once, they met again that year, in Manchester and South Berwick. Cather soon corresponded with Jewett, who became a role model, mentor, and ideal reader; Jewett successfully advised her to devote all of her energies to the solitary pursuit of her creative writing. Jewett's close relationship with Annie Fields may have helped Cather decide at this time to live permanently with Edith Lewis, her *McClure's* associate. Cather dedicated *O Pioneers!* to Jewett, especially esteemed *The Country of the Pointed Firs*, "The Dulham Ladies," "Martha's Lady," and "A White Heron," and wrote about Jewett with affection and skill. She edited *The Best Short Stories of Sarah Orne Jewett* (2 vols., 1925) and inserted a milestone laudatory preface. In it, she famously predicts that *The Scarlet Letter* by Nathaniel Hawthorne, *Adventures of Huckleberry Finn* by Mark Twain,* and *The Country of the Pointed Firs* are three classics most likely to achieve literary immortality. In *Not Under Forty* (1953), a collection of critical pieces, Cather memorializes her friendship with Annie Fields and Jewett. *Bibliography*: Donovan; Sherman; James Woodress, *Willa Cather: A Literary Life* (Lincoln: University of Nebraska Press, 1987).

CATHERINE. In "Tom's Husband," she is an old servant working faithfully for Tom Wilson and Alice Dunn Wilson. Catherine's niece, Susan, also works for the Wilsons. Catherine's death inconveniences Tom.

CÉLESTINE. In "The Mistress of Sydenham Plantation," she and a girlfriend discuss the fact that on the day before Easter Sunday, for the first time in years, Miss Sydenham has not brought flowers to graves at the cemetery in Beaufort.

CHADBOURNE, JUDGE. In *The Tory Lover*, he is a close friend of Colonel Jonathan Hamilton and Madam Wallingford.

"A CHANGE OF HEART" (1896). Short story. (Characters: Cynthia Bascom, David Bascom, Mrs. Bascom, Isaac Bolton, Sally Martin, Walker.) Sally Martin, a little over thirty and alone in her little farmhouse, visits her neighbor, Mrs. Bascom, one nice April day. They discuss a new house Isaac Bolton is building nearby. Mrs. Bascom gently discusses Sally's love for Isaac, gone awry despite each caring for the other. Sally has heard of Isaac's engagement to marry another woman, but Mrs. Bascom discounts the rumor and says Isaac loves Sally, who was wrong to rebuff him some months ago out of "stubbedness." When Sally says it is undoubtedly too late for her now, Mrs. Bascom says her marriage to her beloved husband was delayed foolishly because of her self-indulgence. Suddenly Cynthia Bascom, the Bascoms' daughter, rushes up to say that Isaac has fallen from his house frame and hurt himself. Cynthia's father, David Bascom, takes Sally to Isaac. He is attended by a reassuring local doctor, who says Isaac broke no bones but will need rest. Sally holds his hand and looks at him "with a sweet and quiet" expression. Their joy and springtime are coming together.

CHANNING. In "The Girl with the Cannon Dresses," he is Alice Channing's father. He is happy to let Alice visit Sophronia Durfee for the summer while he and his wife leave their home in Halifax to vacation elsewhere.

CHANNING, ALICE. In "The Girl with the Cannon Dresses," she is advised by Dr. George, the family physician, to recuperate from a mild illness suffered during the spring by spending the summer with Sophronia Durfee. While there, Alice, seventeen, meets and befriends Dulcidora Bunt, a neglected little tomboy.

CHANNING, MRS. In "The Girl with the Cannon Dresses," she is Alice Channing's mother. She willingly lets her daughter, Alice Channing, spend the summer with Sophronia Durfee.

CHANTREY, GOVERNOR. In *Deephaven*, he is mentioned as having lived in Deephaven. He had important English connections. His mansion burned to the ground. His family is now extinct.

CHARTRES, THE DUCHESS OF. In *The Tory Lover*, she is the wife of the Duke of Chartres. She offered John Paul Jones hospitality near Brest.

CHARTRES, THE DUKE OF. In *The Tory Lover*, he is a French ally of Captain John Paul Jones. They met in Hampton Roads, Virginia, in 1775.

CHASE, JAMES. In *The Tory Lover*, he is an old *Ranger* sailor from Nantucket.

CHAUMONT, LE RAY DE. In *The Tory Lover*, he rents or gives the use of a house in Passy to Benjamin Franklin.

CHAUNCEY. In *Deephaven*, he was Miss Sally Chauncey's father, an aristocrat ruined by the embargo, after which he went insane.

CHAUNCEY. In "A Neighbor's Landmark," he is Joe Banks's close friend. The two men fish together. Chauncey signs the petition to try to save the landmark trees.

CHAUNCEY, MISS SALLY. In *Deephaven*, she is a tall, dignified woman, dressed in old-fashioned garb and living in her crumbling family mansion. Gently insane, she imagines her family to be still intact. She impresses Kate Lancaster and Helen Denis, to both of whom Captain Peter Lorimer later reports Miss Chauncey's death. Old Miss Chauncey is based on Sally Cutts of Kittery, Maine. *Bibliography*: Blanchard.

CHAUNCEY, MRS. WILL. In *A Marsh Island*, she and her husband are guests at the summer home of Mrs. Susan Winchester, Richard Dale's aunt. Dale is too upset to have dinner with them.

CHAUNCEY, WILL. In *A Marsh Island*, he and his wife are Mrs. Susan Winchester's guests.

CHECKLEY ("OLD SHEKELS," "SHEKELS"). In "The Two Browns," he was John Benedict Brown's prep-school classmate, too poor to go on to college. Two years older than Brown, Checkley talks Brown into investing heavily in his electric potato planter. When Grandison, whose steam harrow Checkley may have infringed, threatens to sue but also offers to buy them out generously, Checkley tells Brown to sell. Earlier, Checkley, a fast talker, failed as a patent-medicine salesman.

CHELLIS, MRS. In "A Second Spring," she was a friend of Martha Haydon, who is now deceased. While briefly back in the Atfield neighborhood, Mrs. Chellis reminisces pleasantly about Martha to Maria Durrant.

CHELLIS, MRS. WILLIAM. In "A Business Man," she is the former Miss Brooks, a seamstress who sews a button on John Craven's coat. She marries the notions shopowner.

CHELLIS, WILLIAM. In "A Business Man," he is the bright, ambitious, courteous owner, twenty-two or so, of a notions shop. John Craven, who helps him, sees that Chellis and his girlfriend Miss Brooks, later his wife, are richer because of their love than Craven is with his wealth. Chellis is a rich poor man, whereas Craven is a poor rich man.

CHESTER, DUNCAN. In "The Hare and the Tortoise," he was the father, now deceased, of Mary Chester. When orphaned, Duncan Chester was brought up by his aunts, Anne Duncan and Sophia Duncan.

CHESTER, MARY. In "The Hare and the Tortoise," she is the daughter of the widowed Mrs. Chester, and the great-niece of Anne Duncan and Sophia Duncan. They all live together in Boston. Mary Chester finally prefers the mercurial Richard Dean to the stolid Henry Temple.

CHESTER, MRS. In "The Hare and the Tortoise," she is Duncan Chester's rather passive widow and Mary Chester's mother.

CHICK, ASA. In *Betty Leicester*, he is a handcart man at the Riverport railroad station.

CHICK, MARY ANN. In "The Flight of Betsey Lane," now deceased, she was born the same year Betsey Lane was, according to Betsey.

"A CHRISTMAS GUEST" (1887). Short story. (Characters: General ____, Dr. Gerry, Jarvis, Susan Johnson, Eben Norris, Mrs. Norris, Rebecca, Rebecca.) At her farmhome near Hartland, Mrs. Norris cares for Rebecca, the helpful daughter, now twelve, of her deceased daughter, who was also named Rebecca. The old grandmother's son, Eben Norris, lives there too. On the morning before Christmas, Mrs. Norris feels ill, reluctantly goes to bed, and thinks she has lung fever and may soon die. Eben fetches Dr. Gerry, who leaves medicine for the old woman. Eben hitches their horse and goes through worsening snow to ask his niece, Susan Johnson, a few miles away, to come and help out. Little Rebecca does the chores faithfully, builds up a fire in the stove, checks on her sleeping grandmother, puts a candle in the window for Eben, and feels sad, lonely, and sleepy in the storm-lashed house. Suddenly a tall stranger, first called the Christmas Guest and then General ____, enters from the darkness. He has pressed his weary horse from a tavern in Southfield, ten miles from Hartland, through the dangerous storm, saw Rebecca's light, and seeks shelter before proceeding to the railroad station on his way to Washington during the war. Rebecca is not frightened by the tall, gentle stranger, gives him some good food she has resisted eating herself, and offers him her small bed while she intends to nap beside her grandmother. She sleeps. The General leaves ten dollars and his card in the child's well-worn Bible and departs early in the morning. Eben and Susan enter. He was delayed by a tumble in the snow which dislocated his shoulder, and she was separately hindered by the storm. Old Mrs. Norris is suddenly much improved, the medicine given her having been a helpful sleeping powder. Rebecca tells her excited listeners about the Christmas Guest. After the war, General ——, his wife, and their daughter call on Rebecca and her family.

CHRISTMAS GUEST, THE. In "A Christmas Guest." *See* General ——.

CHURCHILL. In *A Marsh Island*, he is a local deacon and Israel Owen's neighbor. The two have mild little theological disputes.

CLAFLIN, MARY BUCKLIN DAVENPORT (1825–1896). Author, philanthropist, and hostess. Born in Hopkinton, Massachusetts, she became the second wife of William Claflin* in 1845. The couple moved to Newtonville, Massachusetts, built a mansion called "Old Elms" there, and entertained many famous guests. Mary Claflin was a trustee of Wellesley College (1870–1896) and Boston College (1878–1898). In 1876 she founded a society to help young women attend college despite limited financial means. She wrote *Brompton Sketches: Old-time New England Life* (1890), *Real Happenings* (1890), *Personal Recollections of John G. Whittier* (1893), and *Under the Old Elms* (1895). She died in Whitinsville, Massachusetts. In 1877 Jewett was a guest at the Claflins's home. In 1878 she went to Washington, D.C., and paid the Claflins a weekslong visit. Escorted by the Claflins, in one day she met ninety literary and political figures, attended a reception held by Robert Todd Lincoln, helped entertain dinner guests, and met President Rutherford B. Hayes in the White House. Also in 1878 she first met Harriet Beecher Stowe* at the Claflins's home. Later Jewett occasionally visited the Claflins in their Boston townhouse and helped entertain them in the home of Annie Adams Fields.* *Bibliography*: Blanchard; Silverthorne.

CLAFLIN, WILLIAM (1818–1905). Politician. He was born in Milford, Massachusetts, the son of a successful boot and shoe manufacturer. Claflin entered Brown University in 1833 but left without a degree. He learned his father's business, established a wholesale boot and shoe business in St. Louis (1838–1844), saw and loathed slavery in Missouri, and returned to Boston to work with his father. Claflin helped found the Free-Soil Party of Massachusetts (1848), was a state legislator (1849–1853, 1859–1861), lieutenant governor of Massachusetts (1866–1868), and governor (1869–1871). He was the first governor of that state to espouse female suffrage. He signed the charter of Boston University (1871) and was a trustee there and at Wellesley College. He took an interest in Claflin University, Orangeburg, South Carolina, an African-American institution named for his father. Claflin served in the House of Representatives (1877–1881). Three years after the death in 1842 of Nancy Warren Harding, his first wife, Claflin married Mary Bucklin Davenport. *See also* Claflin, Mary Bucklin Davenport.

CLEMENS, SAMUEL LANGHORNE. *See* Twain, Mark.

CLENDENNIN. In "A War Debt," Thomas Burton mentions him as a friend in Washington, D.C., able to give him directions to the Bellamy plantation in Virginia.

CLINTURN. In *Betty Leicester*, he is a famous painter summering at Tideshead. He agrees to give art lessons to Mary Picknell.

CLOVENFOOT, GOVERNOR. In "The Dulham Ladies," he entertained Mrs. Greenaple, the great-grandmother of Harriet Dobin and Lucinda Dobin, in Boston long ago.

CON. In "The Gray Mills of Farley," he is a mill worker and the brother of Ellen Carroll. After the mills close, Dan, the mill agent, tells Ellen to tell Con to come and see him if he needs money.

"A CONFESSION OF A HOUSE-BREAKER" (1884). Sketch. The narrator is a housebreaker; but in her case she quietly breaks out, to stroll before a pretty June dawn into the garden, watch light pour over flowers and trees, walk up the street, hear a sick child cry, and look at a sleeping dog. She returns home, hears the "reluctant" mill bells, goes back to bed, and falls dreamily asleep again.

CONNELLY, BIDDY. In "Bold Words at the Bridge," she is Mary Dunleavy's tiny neighbor. The two argue bitterly but then gently make up, through their common concern over a strange woman's need. Biddy has lived in the mill town five or six years longer than Mary has.

CONNELLY, DAVY. In "A Little Captive Maid," he was the father, now deceased, of Nora Connelly. She reminisces to John Balfour about him. Davy Connelly was from Whiddy Island, fished at Glengariff, and salvaged wine from a vessel sinking off Bantry.

CONNELLY, MRS. DAVY. In "A Little Captive Maid," she was Nora Connelly's deceased mother. Nora reminisces to John Balfour about her mother, who had a fine voice and sang for money at weddings. Nora stole eggs from the trustful woman's hen and sold them.

CONNELLY, NORA. In "A Little Captive Maid," she is an orphan living with a mean aunt near Kenmare, Ireland. She is engaged to John Morris but must go to America to earn money to improve his family farm. Once overseas, she works for John Balfour, and delights and temporarily rejuvenates him because of her loyal work, instinctively quick sympathy, and charming conversation. He wills her $500 and passage money to return to Morris. Nora, with her "delicious Irish voice," is Jewett's most appealing, if too sentimentally drawn, character. Her accent, however, grows tiresome; for example, she says of her mean aunt, " 'Tis herself'll be keenin' after me as if 'twas wakin' me she was.''

CONNOLLY, MRS. In "Miss Esther's Guest," she is a Boston seamstress Mrs. Belton declines to send to Daleham as Miss Esther Porley's Country Week guest.

"THE COON DOG" (1897). Short story. (Characters: Brown, Isaac Brown, John Henry Brown, Mrs. Isaac Brown, Mrs. Price, Rover, Tiger, Abijah Topliff, 'Liza Jane Topliff, York, John York, Mrs. John York.) One late afternoon in September, Isaac Brown and his friend John York are chatting about old Mrs. Price, who attended the circus before making a sympathy visit to her daughter, 'Liza Jane Topliff. 'Liza Jane's husband, Abijah Topliff, has just died "out in Connecticut." Happening by, Mrs. Price tells the two men Abijah left Tiger, a valuable coon dog, and 'Liza Jane will have it soon. A month later, while tramping through their woods, Brown and York encounter a hen-eating coon's track. They persuade 'Liza Jane, now staying with her mother, to rent Tiger for 50¢. Next night, Brown, York, and their sons proceed into the deliciously damp forest with Tiger. Timorous though the dog seems, they let it loose after the coon's scent, build a fire, and wait. After much strange barking, they discern an old coon writhing up a tree. Shot down at last, it is retrieved, not by Tiger but by Rover, Brown's old coon dog, left back home as uselessly fat. Next morning when Mrs. Price calls on Brown, he not only lets her believe the big coon, much talked about by now, was treed by Tiger but also seconds her plan to sell the admirable creature, since 'Liza Jane is no hunter and Mrs. Price does not wish "to harbor him all winter."

COOPER. In *The Tory Lover*, he is a kind old *Ranger* sailor. He knew Roger Wallingford in Berwick. Susan is his sister. Cooper distrusts Dickson.

COPP, MRS. In *A Marsh Island*, she is the wife of Sergeant Copp, in Israel Owen's joke. She complains about her unsatisfactory old cap.

COPP, SERGEANT. In *A Marsh Island*, in Israel Owen's joke, he is the husband of a complaining woman. When she says she lacks a new cap to be buried in, her husband wishes she had died when she had a satisfactory old one.

CORBELL, MARIA. In "Miss Peck's Promotion," she is Eliza Peck's married second cousin. Maria amiably tells Eliza that Eliza could marry the Rev. Mr. Elbury if she knew how to promote her cause. Maria watches with Mrs. Spence over the corpse of Mrs. Elbury.

A COUNTRY DOCTOR (1884). Novel. (Characters: Hattie Barlow, Dr. Bent, Bob, Brindle, Brown, Mrs. Cunningham, Captain Denny, Donnell, Billy Dow,

Drew, Captain Dunn, Dunnell, Eliza Dyer, Jacob Dyer, Martin Dyer, Mrs. Jacob
Dyer, Susan Dyer, Dr. Ferris, Captain Finch, Jim Finch, Miss Eunice Fraley,
Mrs. Fraley, George Gerry, George Gerry, Mrs. George Gerry, Goodsoe, Mrs.
Goodsoe, Graham, Mrs. Graham, 'Miry Gregg, Jim Hall, Dr. Jackson, Jane, Dr.
John Leslie, Parson Leslie, Lester, Major, Margaret, Martha, Marthy, Jerry Mar-
tin, Susan Martin, Friend Meadows, Mrs. Meeker, Miss Betsy Milman, Captain
Walter Parish, Mary Parish, Mrs. Walter Parish, Aunt Parser, Captain Peterbeck,
Phoebe, Adeline Thacher Prince, Captain Jack Prince, Jack Prince, Nan Prince,
Nancy Prince, Priscilla, Sergeant, Sergeant, Captain Slater, Susan, Talcot,
Thacher, Daniel Thacher, John Thacher, Mrs. Daniel Thacher, Marilla Thomas,
Sally Turner, Dr. Wayland, Mrs. Willet, Wills.)

Jacob Dyer and Martin Dyer are twins married to sisters. The pairs live in
adjoining farmhouses near Oldfields. One November night, while their wives
visit nearby Mrs. Thacher, whose son, John, is in town on jury duty, Jacob and
Martin drink cider and smoke before a pleasant fire. Suddenly Martin's wife
bursts in: Mrs. Thacher's daughter, Adeline Thacher Prince, who married badly,
was widowed after two unhappy years, and had an infant, Nan, has returned
home gravely ill. Dr. John Leslie of Oldfields is sent for and soon arrives.
Berating her in-laws with her dying breath, Adeline persuades the doctor to be
Nan's guardian in later years. Adeline's well-to-do sister-in-law, Nancy Prince
of Dunport, asks to care for Nan but is refused. Nan and her aunt remain apart
for years, although the latter sends money for her, which Dr. Leslie carefully
deposits.

John Thacher, who grows fond of Nan, dies, and Mrs. Thacher cares for the
wild little girl. After church one Sunday in June a few years later, old Mrs.
Thacher lets Nan visit Dr. Leslie. The child is thrilled to have dinner, prepared
by the smiling man's officious housekeeper, Marilla Thomas, in his mysterious
home and to wander in his lovely garden. One day on the way to visit a crippled
ex-sailor named Finch, Dr. Leslie chats with meddling Mrs. Meeker and learns
of prankish Nan's loves of the wild creatures of nature. Feeble Mrs. Thacher
calls on Dr. Leslie one summer afternoon and gets him to promise to care for
Nan. That winter the old woman dies and Dr. Leslie takes Nan home, where
she grows "taller," "dearer," and "happier day by day." He tolerates her
dislike of school, encourages her to read, and lets her accompany him on his
calls. When Dr. Ferris, a college classmate, ex-naval surgeon, and great traveler,
visits Dr. Leslie overnight, the two have a long talk, during which Dr. Leslie
says Nan might want to be a doctor. Dr. Ferris recalls Nan's father as his
assistant surgeon at one time.

On a Sunday in November, Dr. Leslie crosses the street to visit Mrs. Graham,
a widow. The two discuss changing times in general, and feisty Nan in particular—her need for better clothes, formal schooling, new adult friends. When
Dr. Leslie says he hopes Nan will be a doctor, Mrs. Graham is upset and recommends marriage for her instead. She invites the girl to tea often, reads helpfully with her, and introduces her to her grandchildren. Dr. Leslie takes the girl

to Boston. She goes away to school, returns to Oldfields, feels uneasy, but suddenly realizes she wants to be a doctor. Dr. Leslie seconds her decision heartily, even as he warns her of difficulties ahead. For a year or more, she studies with him, visits patients with and even without him, is aided by his professional friends, and is respected by the community. She leaves Oldfields to enroll in a medical school for formal training, spending the money sent by Aunt Nancy. Dr. Leslie misses Nan greatly.

One morning in May, Nancy Prince is presiding over the ancestral Prince mansion in Dunport when Miss Eunice Fraley calls for a chat and then Nancy's cousin, Captain Walter Parish, delivers a letter from Nan requesting permission to meet her aunt. Nancy sends her a formal invitation, and Dr. Leslie urges the girl to visit briefly. Nan is nervous on the train in June, goes by carriage to Nancy's home, is greeted with sincere affection, enjoys tea, and is happy to be in her father's boyhood town by the sea. At St. Ann's Episcopal church service next morning, she feels on display; but back at the mansion in the afternoon she wanders in the garden and happily meets two callers—Parish, who soon leaves, and her aunt's admired young lawyer, George Gerry. When Nan casually tells them of her medical plans, Nancy, who has just thought of willing the girl her mansion and now hopes she and George will marry, grows critical. Next morning, Parish takes Nan aboard a damaged vessel he must inspect. He introduces her to his niece, Mary Parish, with whom, along with George and some other young people, Nan goes boating upriver. The group picnic ashore at twilight. Nan and George, who tells her he wants a wider horizon than that of Dunport, go for water to a nearby house, in which they find an injured farmer. Nan sets the man's dislocated shoulder. George is impressed; but Nan, though liking George, arranges for him to pay attention to timid Mary.

After a few pleasant weeks, Mrs. Fraley, Eunice's domineering old mother, invites Nan and her aunt to tea, during which she upbraids the girl for choosing to be a doctor instead of a proper wife and homemaker. Nan holds her own and grows all the more confident and is even displeased when George comes by. He lacks ambition to do much about his dissatisfaction with Dunport but now seeks to show his superiority by persuading Nan to marry him. She grows nervous and decides to return to Oldfields. First, though, they attend a play and next day go boating. Rejecting his proposal, she explains that she loves him as a friend, that he will marry nicely, and that it is God's will for her to minister to the ill and the uninformed. Her "ideals" prove stronger than his "power."

She returns home in late June, and Dr. Leslie is happy to have her practice with him. She earns the respect of his old patients and her new ones. One fine November day, she calls on the two Dyer women near the Thacher farm where Nan's mother returned to die twenty years ago, tends to their medical problems. When she emerges into the open air, Nan thanks God ecstatically for the direction her life is taking.

Jewett liked *A Country Doctor* best among her works. It is considerably autobiographical, both on the externally realistic level and on the personally psychological level. Just as Nan chooses a celibate professional life and admires Dr. Leslie, so Jewett chose to be an unmarried professional writer and revered her physician father, Theodore Herman Jewett* (to whom she dedicated this novel). The story is unified by Nan's being presented with obstacles to be over- come: Marilla Thomas laughs at her ambition to be a doctor, Dr. Ferris initially protests against it, Mrs. Graham suggests marriage instead, and George Gerry tempts her by proposing. The plot has fairy-tale elements, with Nan the Prince(ss), a mother partly evil, a kind surrogate father, a would-be fairy god- mother in rich Aunt Nancy, and a handsome suitor. Nan's choice of a "male" profession spoils the fairy tale but makes *A Country Doctor* a modern, chal- lenging feminist novel. It was translated into French by Thèrése de Solms Blanc* as *Le Roman de la Femme-Médicin* (c. 1893). Critics have compared *A Country Doctor* and two slightly earlier novels featuring female physicians— William Dean Howells's *Dr. Breen's Practice* (1881) and Elizabeth Stuart Phelps's *Dr. Zay* (1882)—with Jewett's novel generally accorded second place after that of Howells. *Bibliography*: Bruno Bettelheim, *The Uses of Enchantment: The Meaning and Importance of Fairy Tales* (New York: Vintage, 1977); Donovan; Ann R. Shapiro, *Unlikely Heroines: Nineteenth-Century American Women Writers and the Woman Question* (Westport, Conn.: Greenwood Press, 1987); Thorp.

THE COUNTRY OF THE POINTED FIRS (1896). Novel. (Characters: Abel, Addicks, Mrs. Addicks, Asa, Mrs. Begg, Sam Begg, Dr. Bennett, Captain Black- ett, Mrs. Blackett, Sarah Jane Blackett, William Blackett, Captain Bowden, Cap- tain Jonathan Bowden, Johnny Bowden, Mrs. Bowden, Mrs. Peter Bowden, Pa'lina Bowden, Santin Bowden, Mrs. Brayton, Nahum Brayton, Phebe Ann Brock, Mrs. Caplin, Mrs. Edward Caplin, Louisa Dailey, Dennett, Mrs. Dennett, Dep'ford, the Reverend Mr. Dimmick, Mrs. Evins, Susan Fosdick, Gaffett, Gil- braith, Harlow, Mari' Harris, Captain Jameson, John, Captain Littlepage, Mary Anna, Miss Augusta Pennell, Monroe Pennell, Talcot, Alva Tilley, Elijah Tilley, Sarah Tilley, Todd, Almira Todd, Edward Todd, Joanna Todd, Mrs. Todd, Mrs. Edward Todd, Nathan Todd, Topham, Captain Tuttle.)

One evening in June the narrator, a writer, returns to Dunnet Landing, engages lodging and meals at the widowed Almira Todd's comfortable little house, and plans to enjoy a working summer vacation. She likes the sibyl-like Mrs. Todd, as well as her conversation, professional herb garden, and spruce beer. The narrator rents the empty schoolhouse nearby and writes there. One day, after observing the "walking funeral" of a townswoman from her schoolhouse win- dow, she is interrupted by Captain Littlepage, one of the mourners and a retired sea captain. He sits on a school bench and tells her how a ship he was com- manding while feverish was lost off Greenland and how he was marooned with Eskimos. While there, he met Gaffett, a Scottish sailor who told of being part of a scientific expedition lost in the region and of sailing north into a foggy place with a town full of mysterious souls caught between this world and the next. Littlepage suddenly quits reminiscing.

One hot sunny day, Mrs. Todd takes the narrator to Green Island, where she was born and where Mrs. Blackett, her widowed mother, and her bachelor brother, William Blackett, live. Mrs. Blackett is quietly, inspiringly hospitable. Shy William walks with the narrator to show her a fine view. Mrs. Todd takes her to where uniquely fine pennyroyal grows and while there shows her some family daguerreotypes. After a chowder meal, William and his mother sing together. The narrator treasures every aspect of this unique visit.

Susan Fosdick becomes Mrs. Todd's guest late in July. The two are old friends, and the narrator enjoys hearing their reminiscences, especially about Joanna Todd, Mrs. Todd's late husband's cousin. When Joanna was jilted, she committed what she regarded as the unpardonable sin of turning wrathful toward God; so in shame she signed over her half of the family farm to her brother, took an old boat, and moved permanently to Shell-heap Island, thirty mostly rocky acres, which their father had owned and built a tiny house on. Joanna had sufficient firewood, fish, berries, potatoes, and hens. Mrs. Todd and the Reverend Mr. Dimmick of Dunnet Landing visited her but could never prevail upon her to return to the mainland. She told Mrs. Todd she felt patient but hopeless. Friends occasionally left gifts and provisions on her shore, respected her privacy, and one pretty September afternoon attended her burial on the island—twenty-two years ago. Captain Bowden takes the narrator to the island, and she finds where Joanna, "plain anchorite," now lies "with eternity well begun."

One beautiful August day, Mrs. Todd, her mother, and the narrator wagon up a country road to a field near a bay and attend the famous Bowden family reunion. As arrivals pour in by land and sea, Santin Bowden, a soldier manqué, directs them in military fashion to well-provisioned tables decorated with leaves and flowers. The "noble feast" is pleasantly formal, with much food, including elaborately baked items. Mrs. Blackett and Mrs. Todd are delighted to see old friends and relatives, some of whom they gossip about harmlessly. On their return to Dunnet Landing, they show the narrator their old family home. One afternoon the narrator calls upon Elijah Tilley, an inconsolably widowered old fisherman, and is pleased to see his tidy home and garden. In late summer Mrs. Todd gives the narrator a prized West Indian basket and is too upset to say goodbye as her esteemed guest takes ship and leaves the lovely coastal town.

The Country of the Pointed Firs, Jewett's finest work, is tighter than a collection of separate stories but looser than a novel. Unity is provided by the evolving friendship of the narrator and Mrs. Todd, their independence and interdependence, the theme of the greatness of "small" rural lives adjusting to a harsh but treasured environment, and by imagery of flowers, sea, and weather. The work was published serially in the *Atlantic Monthly* (1896) and revised, with two final chapters—"Along Shore" and "The Backward View"—added, for book publication. In 1910 "A Dunnet Shepherdess," "The Foreigner," "The Queen's Twin," and "William's Wedding" were also added to continue the story of *The Country of the Pointed Firs*. Jewett wrote a correspondent named Mary E. Mulholland (23 January 1899) that Dunnet's Landing "must be somewhere 'along shore' between the region of Tennants [Tenant's] Harbor and Boothbay [Maine], or . . . eastward in a country that I know less well. It is not any real 'landing' or real 'harbor.' . . ." *The Country of the Pointed Firs*, like several of Jewett's earlier works, shows her indebtedness to Harriet Beecher Stowe's* *Pearl of Orr's Island*, in both setting and themes. (The text used for the plot summary above is that of the first book edition, Boston: Houghton Mifflin, 1896.) *Bibliography*: Joseph Church, *Transcendent Daughters in Jewett's The Country of the Pointed Firs* (Rutherford, N.J.: Fairleigh Dickinson University Press, 1992); Donovan; Patricia Keefe Durso, "Jewett's 'Pointed Firs': An 'Index Finger' to Character Development and Unity of Vision of *The Country of the Pointed Firs*," *Colby Quarterly* 26 (September 1990): 171–81; Cynthia J. Goheen, "Editorial Misinterpretation and the Unmaking of a Perfectly Good Story: The Publication History of *The Country of the Pointed Firs*," *American Literary Realism 1890–1910* 30 (Winter 1998): 28–42; Allison T. Hild, "Narrative Mediation in Sarah Orne Jewett's *The Country of the Pointed Firs*," *Colby Quarterly* 31 (June 1995): 114–22; Michael J. Holstein, "Writing as a Healing Art in Sarah Orne Jewett's *The Country of the Pointed Firs*," *Studies in American Fiction* 16 (1988): 39–49; Philip G. Terrie, "Local Color and a Mythologized Past: The Rituals of Memory in *The Country of the Pointed Firs*," *Colby Quarterly* 23 (March 1987): 16–25.

"THE COURTING OF SISTER WISBY" (1887). (Characters: Phebe Brimblecom, Mrs. Silas Brimblecom, Silas Brimblecom, Mrs. Jerry Foss, Mrs. Goodsoe, Jim Heron, Mrs. Heron, Joshuay, Miss Peck, Widow Peck, Mrs. So-and-So, Ezry Welsh, Eliza Wisby.) One sunny August day the narrator walks to a pasture she knows that seems to be calling her. She encounters Mrs. Goodsoe, who is collecting mulleins for their medicinal value. The two women saunter along, eat peaches the narrator has brought, and rest while Mrs. Goodsoe reminisces, first about Widow Peck and her lovelorn daughter, then about Mrs. Jerry Foss and a fiddler named Jim Heron. When the narrator finds an herb called goldthread, it reminds Mrs. Goodsoe that Eliza Wisby liked that bitter herb. Mrs. Goodsoe recalls that Eliza was courted by Silas Brimblecom, a deacon who briefly abandoned his wife for a "spirit bride"; when his true wife died, he boarded with Eliza during a four-day "Christian Baptist" church meeting. Together they "bawled and talked" at evening services, would soon "give their hearts away" to each other, and decided to have a kind of trial marriage in her nice farmhome starting in November. If both "continued to like," they would wed come spring. But they argued, and "Brimfull" was sent packing, to the amusement of the neighbors. By April Eliza called him back, ostensibly to make him repay winter board by helping with her garden chores. They were soon married "fair an' square." Silas's nice daughter, Phebe Brimblecom, came to live with them, and, in due time, Eliza willed much to the girl. In parting, Mrs. Goodsoe tells the narrator she would like to be buried in the familiar pasture where they have been chatting. "The Courting of Sister Wisby" is unified by Mrs. Goodsoe's humorously folksy lingo and her profound awareness of the beneficence of real religion and the grotesqueness of sham religion. *Bibliography*: Blanchard.

CRADDOCK. In "The First Sunday in June," he is a faithful parishioner of the First Parish church of Dalton.

CRADDOCK, MRS. In "The First Sunday in June," she is a member of the First Parish church of Dalton. Evidently a cold prevented her attendance late in May. But she attends with her husband on the first Sunday in June.

CRANE. In "The Passing of Sister Barsett," he was Mercy Crane's husband and died of sunstroke.

CRANE, FRANK. In *Betty Leicester*, he attends Betty Leicester's tea party. Her father knew his father.

CRANE, MERCY. In "The Passing of Sister Barsett," she is the reclusive widow who welcomes Sarah Ellen Dow for tea, shortcake, and gossip about the inaccurately reported death of Sister Barsett.

CRAPER. In *Deephaven*, he is a sick man from Stone Hill who resolutely takes his five stupid-looking children to the Denby circus.

CRAVEN. In "A Business Man." *See* Walter.

CRAVEN, JACK (JOHN). In "A Business Man," he is the crassly commercial son of John Craven and is representative of the older man's selfish, indifferent, overbearing, materialistic family members in general.

CRAVEN, JOHN. In "A Business Man," he is a man who learns too late that being nothing but a businessman cuts one off from the nonmaterial gifts life offers. His wife dies before they know each other spiritually. His numerous family members grow indifferent. But, calling himself Mr. Brown, he aids William Chellis and his wife, the former Miss Brooks, and hopes they will realize that money is not everything. Craven is a poor rich man, whereas Chellis is a rich poor man.

CRAVEN, MRS. JOHN. In "A Business Man," she is the uncomplaining wife of the businessman who realizes too late that they should have led less materialistic lives. Soon after their fruitless vacation in Europe, she dies.

CRODEN, PARSON. In "An Autumn Holiday," he is a gifted, popular minister whose service is interrupted when Captain Daniel Gunn attends church dressed in his deceased sister Patience Gunn's clothes. Parson Croden is the uncle of Mrs. Ridley, who is the wife of Parson Ridley, his assistant. He is called Dr. Croden. In "A Lost Lover," he was the old parson in Longfield whom Melissa preferred to his replacement.

CROFTON, THE REVEREND MR. In ''Martha's Lady,'' he is the bachelor neighbor of Miss Harriet Pyne. Her cousin Miss Helena Vernon (*see* Dysart, Helena Vernon) sends Martha to him with a gift of cherries. After he is married, he puzzles his wife by blushing when Martha continues to give him cherries. Crofton is a useless churchman as far as improving Harriet is concerned. *Bibliography*: Cary, *Jewett*.

CRONIN. In ''The Guests of Mrs. Timms,'' he was the minister in Baxter when Miss Cynthia Pickett lived there. Miss Pickett tells Mrs. Persis Flagg that Cronin described Nancy Fell as more generous with her limited money than richer parishioners were ''with their much.''

CROSBY. In ''Law Lane,'' he is Abby Crosby's husband and Ruth Crosby's father. He mortgaged the farm to pay legal expenses for a continuation of their feud with their neighbors, Ezra Barnet and Jane Barnet. When it is resolved, Ruth can marry the Barnets' son, young Ezra Barnet.

CROSBY, ABBY. In ''Law Lane,'' she is Crosby's timid wife and Ruth Crosby's mother. Mrs. Harriet Powder calls Abby ''Mis' Much-afraid.''

CROSBY, RUTH. In ''Law Lane,'' she is the submissive daughter of Crosby and Abby Crosby. Ruth is in love with Ezra Barnet, the son of the elder Ezra Barnet and Jane Barnet. Because of the feud over ownership of land between the Barnet and the Crosby farms, the lovers are frustrated until a stratagem by Mrs. Harriet Powder resolves the dispute.

CROSDYCK, MRS. In ''The Green Bowl,'' she is a ''majestic-looking'' old woman. She is one of the people listening to Katie Montague's story.

CROWE, CAPTAIN. In ''All My Sad Captains,'' he is Maria Lunn's tall, clumsy suitor, owns the best house in Longport, and has two domineering sisters. He is rejected gently.

CROWE, DANIEL (''DAN'EL''). In ''Miss Tempy's Watchers,'' he is the well-to-do farmer husband of the woman who watches over Temperance Dent with Sarah Ann Binson.

CROWE, ELIZA. In ''All My Sad Captains,'' she is one of Captain Crowe's domineering sisters.

CROWE, MISS. In ''All My Sad Captains,'' she is one of Captain Crowe's domineering sisters.

CROWE, MRS. DANIEL. In "Miss Tempy's Watchers," she is a rich farmer's wife. Watching with Sarah Ann Binson, a former schoolmate, over the body of Temperance Dent, the night before the funeral, makes "vague and benignant" Mrs. Crowe less niggardly and more compassionate toward Sarah. It is suggested that Miss Tempy planned everything this way.

CUFFEE. In *The Tory Lover*, he is one of Major Tilly Haggens's servants.

CUNNINGHAM, MRS. In *A Country Doctor*, she sends Dr. John Leslie word that Mrs. Thacher is about to pay him a visit.

CURRIER, HENRY. In "From a Mournful Villager," he is mentioned as the mason who built the brick walk for Jewett's paternal grandmother Sarah Orne ("Sally") Jewett.* He proudly signed and dated the walk "H.C., 1818."

CURWEN, SAM. In *The Tory Lover*, he is a Loyalist mentioned by Judge Chadbourne as having defected to England.

CYNTHY. In *Betty Leicester*, she was a friend of Serena, who argued with her. Cynthy died before they ever made up again.

D

DAILEY, LOUISA. In *The Country of the Pointed Firs*, she was Susan Fosdick's sister, now deceased. She lived in Vermont but died in Lynn while visiting her youngest daughter.

DALE, RICHARD ("DICK"). In *A Marsh Island*, he is a rich, dilettantish painter. Orphaned at ten and the ward of Mrs. Susan Winchester, his aunt, he has studied in England, France, and Italy. While painting one summer on Marsh Island, Dick boards with Israel Owen and Martha Owen, his wife. He half falls in love with their daughter, Doris Owen, who, however, finally prefers Dan Lester, a neighbor. Dick too frequently covets what strikes his fancy. After returning to New York City, he successfully exhibits some of his work. Like Jewett, Dick was torn between rural life with its limitations, and urban life with its troubles. *Bibliography*: Roman; Silverthorne.

DALEY, FATHER. In "The Gray Mills of Farley," he is Farley's Irish priest, old-fashioned and hence more eager to minister to the spiritual needs of the mill workers than to collect funds to build a church. He is a close friend of Dan, the mill agent. In "Where's Nora?", Father Daley is mentioned as having given Nora ten shillings when she went to America. Later he helped Tom Flaherty to the hospital when he was ill.

DALLAS, ELDER. In "Decoration Day," he is the Barlow Plains minister. He delivers a patriotic address after the parade and suggests that the veterans should give talks about the war and collect old wartime letters.

DALLETT, CYNTHY. In "Aunt Cynthy Dallett," she is a lonely woman, eighty-four, who lives on a mountainside. When her niece, Abby Pendexter, invites her to live with her, Cynthy counters with the accepted suggestion that Abby come to her. Cynthy promises to will everything to Abby.

DALTON, HANNAH. In "A Pinch of Salt," she is a Winfield school district teacher. Earning thirty dollars a month, she lives with her Aunt Deborah on a farm. Hannah is tired of teaching but has no other options. She fondly remembers John Brayton, a schoolmate from years ago but not seen for ten years. In fulfillment of a Halloween legend about eating only a pinch of salt for supper and then seeing one's lover, John reappears. The two soon get married.

DAMER, 'MANDA. In *Deephaven*, she was a woman who, while dying, was "watched" by Mrs. Dockum and Judith Patton.

DAN. In "The Gray Mills of Farley," he is the mill agent. Orphaned at three, he relied on neighbors in Farley for his upbringing, took classes at Boston's School of Technology, and began mill work at twenty-two. Now forty but looking fifty, he takes orders from the Corporation directors but does all he can to mitigate the suffering of the ill-paid workers. He is Father Daley's close friend. Dan is called "Mr. Agent" by some of the workers.

DANCE, PRISCILLA. In "Miss Tempy's watchers," she is criticized by Mrs. Daniel Crowe for wanting her to waste money on new wallpaper when the old was serviceable if mended.

DANE. In "A Lost Lover," he is mentioned as Nelly Dane's father. He is a civil engineer in the West with Dick Dane, his engineer son. Nelly says she does not miss them much.

DANE, COLONEL. In "A Lost Lover," he was Horatia Dane's father, who, according to Melissa, liked mustard on his beef. He died twenty years earlier.

DANE, DICK. In "A Lost Lover," he is mentioned as Nelly Dane's brother. Dick, whom she says she does not miss much, is a civil engineer in the West, like their father.

DANE, HORATIA ("H'RATIA"). In "A Lost Lover," she is the old patrician spinster owner and occupant, for twenty years now, of the family mansion in Longfield. Early in her life she was deserted by her lover, Captain Joe Carrick. Reported lost at sea, he became an alcoholic wanderer. When decades later he chances to beg for food at her kitchen, he does not recognize her but she silently recognizes him and gives him ten dollars to leave. She secretly wishes he had died, tries to preserve her romantic image of him, and soon dies.

DANE, MRS. In "A Lost Lover," she was Horatia Dane's mother. She informally adopted Melissa and "fetched up" the orphan to be a loyal family servant.

DANE, NELLY. In "A Lost Lover," she is the daughter, twenty, of a civil engineer now in the West. Nelly Dane enjoys a summer visit to Horatia Dane, her deceased mother's cousin, in Longfield. When Nelly says she is engaged to a navy sailor named George Forest, Horatia warns her not to throw away her happiness. Nelly sees Horatia's long-lost lover in her kitchen but never learns his identity.

DAN'EL. In "The King of Folly Island," he is a resident of John's Island. He and his friends speak critically of George Quint.

DANESLEY, LADY MARY. In *Betty Leicester's English Xmas*, she is the owner of Danesley House, invites Thomas Leicester and Betty Leicester for a week at Christmastime, and is gracious to all of her guests, especially Betty. She is Warford's aunt and Mary Duncan's cousin. She combines the qualities of fairy godmother and female authority figure. *Bibliography*: Roman.

DANEWEIGHT, MISS. In "Hallowell's Pretty Sister," she is mentioned as a former girlfriend of Jack Spenser, who has dropped her.

DANFORTH. In "The First Sunday in June," this is the name of a large family attending church on the first Sunday in June.

DANFORTH, MRS. In "An Every-Day Girl," Mary Fleming's mother mentions her as a family friend.

DANFORTH, MRS. In "The King of Folly Island," she is a cousin of George Quint's mother. With a spyglass, Phebe Quint watches the procession of boats going to Wall Island on the occasion of Mr. Danforth's funeral.

DANNY. In *Deephaven*, he is a wharf worker, formerly a sailor, who, after an accident at sea, was nursed back to health by Catholic nuns. He and his friend, Jack Scudder, found a family of cats in a barrel at Manning's warehouse. Danny helps Captain Sands, Kate Lancaster, and Helen Denis with their cunner catch during a shower. Danny is based on George Hatch, whom Jewett knew and fished with at Wells, Maine. *Bibliography*: Silverthorne.

"A DARK CARPET" (1883). Short story. (Characters: Bessie Alison, Sally, Jack Weston, Mary Weston, Mrs. Weston, Nelly Weston, Tom Weston.) When her husband died, Mrs. Weston and their children, Jack Weston, Mary Weston, Nelly Weston, and Tom Weston, found themselves in reduced circumstances in their Boston home. Tom the oldest, was fifteen at the time and went to work in a business office. Now, a few years later, they simply must buy a new carpet for the parlor, although the family is still pinched for money. Jack and Nelly buy a carpet, but when they get it home it is decried as too dark. They soon make it blend in better: Mary fixes up a colorful sofa pillow; Tom uses money saved for Christmas presents to buy a small, tasteful rug; Nelly makes some chair covers out of Mrs. Weston's worn-out silk dresses; and Jack builds a set of wall shelves for the parlor. Jewett points her moral heavily: We can enjoy improving what we too often gripe about.

"A DARK NIGHT" (1895). Short story. (Characters: Betsey, Elizabeth Brent, Captain Fenderson, Rogers, Weymouth.) It is winter in western England. A squire lets his banker persuade him to send gold and notes to Captain Fenderson, a Bristol shipmaster, by Weymouth and Rogers. The squire trusts Weymouth, his friend, but not Rogers, the banker's clerk. On their way on horseback, they take a shortcut suggested by Rogers, who was hurt by a fall. They stop at an ugly inn to rest. The landlady, whom Rogers calls Betsey, gives them brandy, which puts Rogers to sleep, but which Weymouth secretly pours out, fearing it is drugged. While other travelers are entering, Betsey tells Weymouth to rest upstairs in a big bedroom but not disturb an old woman snoring there. Weymouth pretends to be drunk and demands another bottle. He sees two thugs and with them Elizabeth Brent. She and Weymouth met a while ago in Southampton and are in love, but two days ago she strangely spurned his advances. She whispers "the net" to him. He returns upstairs, knocks out the "snorer" (a man), and escapes by throwing a nearby net out the window and sliding down. Elizabeth meets him and helps him run to an honest inn a mile away. She explains: Rogers betrayed Weymouth to the two thugs, who, some time ago, adopted her as an orphan, are thieves whose robberies she has been aiding, and wish to go to America. One of the thugs rides up on Weymouth's horse. Elizabeth tells him Weymouth is in the kitchen of the other inn. When he goes there, Weymouth takes his horse and rides to Bristol. He delivers the gold and notes, gets a receipt from Fenderson, and returns to the squire and the banker. The banker does not believe his condemnation of Rogers, but the squire does and helps him return to the evil inn. Elizabeth and her foster family have gone to America. Weymouth follows across the ocean, becomes a horse trader, and, after almost two years of searching, finds Elizabeth. She explains: She helped the thugs, Betsey, and her husband (the "snorer") get to America. Elizabeth found a job and helped Betsey, first ill and now dead. Her husband was jailed for theft. The thugs disappeared. She did not know Weymouth was to be Rogers's and the thugs' latest victim until she saw and recognized him. She secreted the net upstairs to aid anyone in danger there. Rogers robbed his employer's bank again and went to France. Weymouth and Elizabeth happily marry. "A Dark Night" must rank as Jewett's most ill-managed plot. It was published in four daily, one-page installments in the Philadelphia *Press*.

DARLEY, DR. JOE. In "The First Sunday in June," he has been the minister of the First Parish church of Dalton for twenty years. Attendance has dwindled, and he is stale. On the first Sunday in June, he dusts off an old sermon, figuring it will do. But his wife urges him to put something new into his preaching. When he arrives, he faces an enormous crowd and preaches extemporaneously and inspiringly. The crowd came because Miss Lydia Bent the previous week had urged better attendance.

DARLEY, MRS. In "The First Sunday in June," she is the invalid wife of Dr. Joe Darley, the Dalton minister. She persuades him to preach in a more heartfelt manner and attends church with him on the first Sunday in June.

DARTMOUTH, MRS. In "The Spur of the Moment," she is the well-to-do, bored woman who sends Jenks, her manservant, to Fallon, the cabman, with money and orders to give Miss Peet a ride.

DARWENTWATER, LORD. In *The Tory Lover*, he is mentioned as Charles Radcliffe's brother.

DAVENPORT. In "Mr. Bruce," he is the dejected-looking man Kitty Tennant meets at the party given for Miss Carroll in Baltimore. Kitty finds him so boring that she teases him.

DAVID, FATHER. In "Mère Pochette," he is the priest in Bonaventure summoned to comfort Mère Pochette's dying son-in-law. Father David is later replaced by Father Pierre.

DAVIS. In "An Every-Day Girl," he is a lumber-company clerk in Dolton. He is a lodger in the home of Henry Fleming, Mrs. Fleming, and their daughter, Mary Fleming.

DAVIS, JOHN. In *The Tory Lover*, he is an influential old Bristol merchant and alderman. Since he did profitable business with both Colonel Jonathan Hamilton and Madam Wallingford, he is willing to aid Madam Wallingford and Jonathan's sister, Mary Hamilton, in Roger Wallingford's rescue.

DAVIS, MRS. JOHN. In *The Tory Lover*, she is an old Berwick friend of Madam Wallingford, who knew Mrs. Goodwin, her mother. Davis of Bristol failed to keep his promise to let her visit America every other year. Mother and daughter never saw one another again. Mrs. Davis welcomes Madam Wallingford after a half-century separation.

DAW, ANDREW. In *Deephaven*, he was a son of Peletiah Daw.

DAW, MOSES. In *Deephaven*, he was a son of Peletiah Daw.

DAW, PELETIAH. In *Deephaven*, he was the father of Andrew Daw and Moses Daw and Captain Jacob Lant's foster father. Peletiah had a vision of his nephew, Ben Dighton, at the exact time he was being hanged far away.

DAY. In *Betty Leicester's English Xmas*, she is Betty Leicester's old governess, whom Betty feels she has outgrown.

DEAN. In "A Second Spring," he was the husband of Susan Louisa Dean, Polly Norris's daughter. He died " 'twixt eighty an' ninety year old," Polly tells Maria Durrant.

DEAN, ASA. In "The Quest of Mr. Teaby," he is the head of a family near East Wilby. When his child was sick, Teaby provided salutory medicine.

DEAN, JESSE. In "Decoration Day," he is a crippled Civil War veteran who rides on a wagon during the parade.

DEAN, MARTHA. In "Mary and Martha," she is Mary Dean's older, shorter, more energetic and practical sister. Martha was engaged, but her fiancé died. The two sisters earn their living by sewing and could do better if they had a sewing machine. Their cousin, John Whitefield, with whom they argued, gives them one after they make peace by inviting him to Thanksgiving dinner.

DEAN, MARY. In "Mary and Martha," she is Martha Dean's young sister and is taller, more timid, but nicer. She defers to her sister but is the one to suggest inviting John Whitefield to dinner.

DEAN, MARY ANN. In "Miss Becky's Pilgrimage," she is Susan Beckett's troubled, sick daughter in Brookfield. Learning that Mary Ann Dean has lost several family members and had an alcoholic brother, Becky Parsons visits her to offer comfort. While there, Becky chances to see Beacham the minister.

DEAN, MRS. ASA. In "The Quest of Mr. Teaby," when her child was sick in their home near East Wilby, Teaby was helpful.

DEAN, RICHARD ("DICK"). In "The Hare and the Tortoise," he is the dashing art student who returns to Boston after three years abroad. He defeats the admirable but stolid Henry Temple in the race for Mary Chester's hand.

DEAN, SHEILA. In "The Hare and the Tortoise," she is Richard Dean's deceased sister. Mary Chester knew both of them during their childhood.

DEAN, SUSAN LOUISA. In "A Second Spring," she is Polly Norris's widowed daughter, fifty-one.

DEANE. In *The Tory Lover*, he is one of Benjamin Franklin's colleagues.

DEBBY, MISS. In ''Miss Debby's Neighbors,'' she is a ''tailoress'' who reminisces reflectively, humorously, and with probably unconscious sarcasm about former neighbors, the quarrelsome Ashbys. Her rambling yarn resembles the best similar efforts by Mark Twain.* *Bibliography*: Cary, *Jewett*.

DEBORAH. In ''Lady Ferry,'' she is a servant working for Agnes and Matthew at the Haverford mansion. Deborah rebukes Martha, a younger servant, for gossiping about Lady Ferry.

DEBORAH, AUNT. In ''A Pinch of Salt,'' she is Hannah Dalton's aunt. Aunt Deborah owns half the farm where the two live together.

DECKER. In ''The Flight of Betsey Lane,'' this is the name of friends whom Lavina Dow says Betsey Lane may have gone to visit. The Deckers live on Birch Hill.

DECKER, SIM. In *Deephaven*, he was the sailor who confirmed the accuracy of the vision experienced by Peletiah Daw of Sim Decker's friend Ben Dighton's death.

DECKET. In ''All My Sad Captains,'' he is Captain Shaw's accountant. Shaw boastfully mentions him in conversation with Captain Crowe.

DECKETT, NANCY. In ''The Passing of Sister Barsett,'' she is one of Sister Barsett's selfish, inept sisters. Mrs. Peck is the other. Nancy is or was also married.

"DECORATION DAY" (1892). Short story. (Characters: Barton, Asa Brown, Joel Brown, Elder Dallas, Jesse Dean, Harrison Dexter, Mrs. Harrison Dexter, John Down, Marthy Peck Down, Elwell, Daniel Evins, Henry Merrill, Eben Munson, Stover, John Stover, Tighe, Tighe, John Tighe, Martin Tighe, Joe Wade.) One Saturday evening, a week before Decoration Day, three Civil War veterans—Asa Brown, Henry Merrill, and John Stover—meet at a store in Barlow Plains and discuss placing flags on the graves of dead comrades, including Eben (''Eb'') Munson and John Tighe. They also talk about the war and about some civilians, especially John Down, who remained at home and prospered. The three veterans decide to revive local patriotism by holding a parade. Nine veterans, including three who are crippled, can participate. A week later the parade begins at the church, attracts many spectators, and winds past several farmhouses. Carrying flags and flowers to decorate comrades' graves, the veterans pause at the poorhouse and at paupers' graves, including that of ''Eb,'' who took to drink when Marthy Peck did not wait for him but married Down during the war. Stover and Merrill notice flowers already on Eb's grave. Elder Dallas, the minister, delivers a patriotic address. That same evening Stover and Merrill decide to make the event an annual one, plan to follow Dallas's suggestion to have meeting-house talks about the war, remember the dead, and collect wartime letters "for the benefit o' the young folks." They conclude that Marthy, now widowed, put those flowers on Eb's unmarked grave. Merrill adds that she told him she wants to buy Eb a marker and have it installed. The two men agree that sometimes years pass before events come into proper focus. Under touches of comedy, Jewett hides the moral of "Decoration Day"—that comfortable civilians should not forget the sacrifices of soldiers. She once said that if she were remembered for any of her stories, she hoped it would be for "Decoration Day." Marie Thérèse de Solms Blanc* translated it into "Le Jour de la Décoration" (*Revue des Deux Mondes*, 1 August 1895), and the story also figured for a time in Memorial Day events in Berwick. *Bibliography*: Cary, *Jewett*.

DEDICATIONS. Jewett dedicated ten of the twenty books that she wrote and were published in her lifetime to various friends and relatives. She dedicated *Betty Leicester: A Story for Girls* to Mary Greenwood Lodge, *Betty Leicester's English Xmas: A New Chapter of an Old Story* to Mary Elizabeth Garrett, *Country By-Ways* to Theodore Herman Jewett,* *The Country of the Pointed Firs* to Alice Greenwood Howe, *The Mate of the Daylight, and Friends Ashore* to Annie Adams Fields,* *A Native of Winby and Other Tales* to Caroline Augusta Jewett,* *The Queen's Twin and Other Stories* to Susan Burley Cabot, *The Story of the Normans* to William Perry,* *The Tory Lover* to Theodore Jewett Eastman, *Strangers and Wayfarers* to Sarah Wyman Whitman,* and *A White Heron and Other Stories* to her sister, Mary Rice Jewett.* Cabot, Howe, and Lodge were close personal friends.

DEEMS, LUCY. In "Mrs. Parkins's Christmas Eve," she is Mrs. Deems's little daughter. When the two visit Mrs. Lydia Parkins, they are treated coldly. When Mrs, Parkins reforms, she gives Lucy a basket of the butternuts the girl likes.

DEEMS, MRS. In "Mrs. Parkins's Christmas Eve," she is a sunny little woman who responds with genuine amiability to the chilly welcome accorded her by Mrs. Lydia Parkins. She is Lucy Deems's mother.

DEEPHAVEN (1877). Novel. (Characters: Clorinthy Adams, Andrew, Ann, Anna, Hate-evil Beckett, Judith Beckett, Samantha Barnes Beckett, Bessie, Mrs. Bonny, Chantrey Brandon, Hathaway Brandon, Henry Brandon, Miss Katharine Brandon, Mrs. Chantrey Brandon, Bridget, Kitty Bruce, Captain Carew, Captain Dick Carew, Honora Carew, Governor Chantrey, Chauncey, Sally Chauncey, Craper, 'Manda Damer, Danny, Andrew Daw, Moses Daw, Peletiah Daw, Sim Decker, Denis, Helen Denis, Mrs. Dent, Ben Dighton, Dinnett, Dockum, Leander Dockum, Mrs. Dockum, Tom Dockum, Joshua Dorsey, H—, Hannah, John Hathorn, Mrs. John Hathorn, Ben Horn, Captain Isaac Horn, Exper'ence Hull, Widow Jim, John, Katy, Mrs. Tom Kew, Tom Kew, Lancaster, Jack Lancaster, Jack Lancaster, Kate Lancaster, Mrs. Lancaster, Willy Lancaster, Captain Jacob Lant, Citizen Leigh, Lorimer, Captain Peter Lorimer, Martha Lorimer, Parson Lorimer, Rebecca Lorimer, McAllister, Dolly McAllister, Maggie, Captain Manning, Marilly, Marthy, Mary, Matthew, 'Bijah Mauley, Melinda, Widow Moses, Nora, Parson Padelford, Patey, Jack Patton, Mrs. Oliver Pinkham, Reid, Sands, Captain Sands, Hannah Sands, Jo Sands, Matthew Sands, Mrs. Sands, Mrs. Sands, Mrs. Matthew Sands, Mrs. Matthew Sands, Jack Scudder, Skipper Scudder, Mary Ann Simms, Sabrina Smith, Sophia, Hannah Starbird, Ann'Liza Tanner, Seth Tanner, Margaret Tennant, Mrs. Thorniford, Tobias, Jim Toggerson, Joseph Toggerson, Widow Tully, Captain Wall, Widow Ware, Mary Wendell, Chester White, Lo'isa Winslow.)

Kate Lancaster, a Bostonian whose parents plan to vacation in Europe, invites her visitor and close friend, Helen Denis (the narrator), to spend the summer in the old port town of Deephaven, in a mansion Kate's family has inherited from her great-aunt, Miss Katharine Brandon. Kate and Helen explore the Brandon house, with its ten rooms on two floors, wide hall, garret, fireplaces, and ancient furniture, including an escritoire with packets of old letters. The girls row to the lighthouse, run by Tom Kew and his wife. One woman living near the Brandon mansion is Judith Toggerson Patton, better known as Widow Jim, who was kind to Kate's great-aunt, tells about that fine woman's way of life and generosity, and is the source of much town gossip. The girls amiably observe worshipers at church and take tea with members of the Carew family. Noting the many retired sailors in town and encouraging some to talk, they hear Captain Jacob Lant's account of Peletiah Daw's exact vision of his nephew Ben Dighton's being simultaneously hanged elsewhere at sea; hear Danny tell about being injured at sea, cared for by foreign nuns, and having a pet kitten; and listen as Captain Sands reminisces about a fine Italian sailor who fell and died on deck.

One Saturday Kate, Helen, and Mrs. Kew drive a horse and wagon to Denby, an inland mill town, to see a shabby but well-attended circus—with a band, a singing clown, hand organs, and the "Kentucky giantess." Mrs. Kew recognizes her as an out-of-luck friend named Marilly. The girls attend a dreary lecture on manhood held in the Deephaven church. They go cunner-fishing with old Sands, are almost caught in a shower, and after a walk return to hear his lengthy reminiscences. With Parson Lorimer they go into the woods, find Mrs. Bonny's tiny house in a clearing, and visit the lonely woman. The girls drive with Dockum along a coastal road and pay a forlorn, grateful man named Andrew for watching their horse and wagon. They return some time later with Dockum's son Leander to visit Andrew again. But his wife has died, he took to drink and died, and their children will be scattered. They go to nearby East Parish to visit Sally Chauncey, a genially insane old aristocrat living in a crumbling family mansion. Autumn descends on Deephaven, with its treacherous weather. Helen and Kate philosophize about their summer and their connection with the town—past and future—and will remember it fondly.

Deephaven has thirteen titled chapters. The first, "Kate Lancaster's Plan," and the second, "The Brandon House and the Lighthouse," were first published in the *Atlantic Monthly* in 1873 as "The Shore House." The third, "My Lady Brandon and the Widow Jim," first appeared in *Deephaven*. The fourth, "Deephaven Society," the fifth, "The Captains," the sixth, "Danny," the eighth, "The Circus at Denby," and the thirteenth, "Last Days at Deephaven," were first published in the *Atlantic* (1875) as "Deephaven Cronies." The seventh, "Captain Sands," and the ninth, "Cunner-Fishing," first appeared in *Deephaven*. The tenth, "Mrs. Bonny," the eleventh, "In Shadow," and the twelfth, "Miss Chauncey," were first published in the *Atlantic* (1876) as "Deephaven Excursions." Deephaven, though a fictionally sketched locale, corresponds approximately with York, a coastal town southeast of South Berwick, Maine. Jewett wrote Horace Scudder* (14 September 1876) that "York . . . reminds me of my dear Deephaven though it was 'made up' before I had ever stayed overnight in York. . . ." The character sketches of brave, enduring people in *Deephaven*, as well as its many humorous passages, should not blind readers to the frustration, isolation, and loneliness also portrayed. Jewett bought a horse with her *Deephaven* royalties. *Bibliography*: Blanchard; Joseph Church, "Transgressive Daughters in Sarah Orne Jewett's *Deephaven*," *Essays in Literature* 20 (Fall 1993); 23–50; Judith Fetterley, "Reading *Deephaven* as a Lesbian Text," pp. 164–83, in Susan J. Wolfe and Julia Penelope, eds., *Lesbian Cultural Criticism* (Cambridge, Mass.: Blackwell, 1993); Robert L. Horn, "The Power of Jewett's *Deephaven*," pp. 284–96, in Richard Cary, ed., *Appreciation of Sarah Orne Jewett* (Waterville, Maine: Colby College Press, 1973); Sherman; Silverthorne; Judith Bryant Wittenberg, "*Deephaven*: Sarah Orne Jewett's Exploratory Metafiction," *Studies in American Fiction* 19 (Autumn 1991): 153–63.

"DEEPHAVEN CRONIES" (1875). See *Deephaven*.

"DEEPHAVEN EXCURSIONS" (1876). See *Deephaven*.

DELANE ("DENNY"). In *The Tory Lover*, he was a handsome Dublin actor the teacher Sullivan recalls seeing.

DENIS. In *Deephaven*, he is Helen Denis's father, a navy man.

DENIS, HELEN ("NELLY"). In *Deephaven*, she is the narrator. She and her friend, Kate Lancaster, each twenty-four, spend the summer at Deephaven. They relish associating with townspeople and nearby farmers, and observing the sea, the coast, and the hills—indeed, all of nature. Helen's following the lead of Kate reflects Jewett's behavior in the presence of some of her more forceful friends. In "Good Luck," Nelly and Kate Lancaster are mentioned by Mary

Leslie, the narrator, as friends she visited for a week in a house the two were sharing one summer by the sea. *Bibliography*: Blanchard.

DENIS, NELLY. In "Good Luck." *See* Denis, Helen.

DENNELL, MRS. In *A Marsh Island*, she is a friend of Mrs. Lawton, who is Dan Lester's mother. Mrs. Dennett takes a message from her to Dan.

DENNETT. In "Andrew's Fortune," he is Jonas Dennett's son. When Andrew Phillips visits the property formerly owned by Stephen Dennett and now belonging to Jonas Dennett and his brother, Tim Dennett, Andrew resolves to try to aid Jonas's son.

DENNETT. In *The Country of the Pointed Firs*, this is the name the doughnut-baking farm woman seen along the road to the Bowden reunion tells Almira Todd was her maiden name. She says her first husband's name was Bowden.

DENNETT. In "Miss Becky's Pilgrimage," Rebecca Parsons names her as an aunt she stayed with years ago "over on the Kittery shore."

DENNETT, JONAS. In "Andrew's Fortune," he is the older of the two sons of Lysander Dennett. The other son is Tim Dennett. Andrew Phillips learns that one of the two sons has been a legislator.

DENNETT, LYSANDER. In "Andrew's Fortune," he is Stephen Dennett's cousin. Lysander does not attend Stephen's funeral but quickly appears when he learns that he, not Andrew Phillips, has legally inherited Stephen's property. When Lysander dies, the property goes to his sons, Jonas Dennett and Tim Dennett.

DENNETT, MRS. In *The Country of the Pointed Firs*, she is Almira Todd's neighbor. Almira asks a doctor passing by to ask Mrs. Dennett to close Almira's open door to prevent dust from entering her home.

DENNETT, MRS. In "The Honey Tree," she is the wife of Rev. Mr. Dennett, the Hillborough minister. Mrs. Martin Wells is critical of her housekeeping but is so grateful to the minister that she often provides the Dennetts with excellent baked goods.

DENNETT, MRS. LYSANDER. In "Andrew's Fortune," she is Lysander Dennett's wife and the mother of their sons, Jonas Dennett and Tim Dennett. Mrs. Dennett urges Lysander to agree to inherit the property of his cousin, Stephen Dennett.

DENNETT, MRS. STEPHEN. In "Andrew's Fortune," she was the wife, now deceased, of Stephen Dennett and the aunt of Andrew Phillips.

DENNETT, REV. MR. In "The Honey Tree," he is the Hillborough minister. When Martin Wells and his wife lost their daughter, Dennett's sympathy was something Mrs. Wells remembers gratefully.

DENNETT, STEPHEN. In "Andrew's Fortune," he is a respected, wealthy farmer and town selectman, who dies. His will names as his heir Andrew Phillips, who has lived with him, whom he liked, but whom he never formally adopted. Andrew is the nephew of Dennett's deceased wife. When Dennett's will is missing, his cousin, Lysander Dennett, inherits.

DENNETT, TIM. In "Andrew's Fortune," he is the younger of the two sons of Lysander Dennett. The other son is Jonas Dennett. Andrew Phillips learns that one of the two sons has been a legislator.

DENNIS. In "A War Debt," he is Margaret Burton's courteous servant.

DENNIS, MR. In "An Every-Day Girl," he is the owner of the summer hotel in which Mary Fleming works. She does such a fine job that he will train her in a New York hotel to become the assistant housekeeper under Mrs. Preston, the housekeeper of the summer hotel.

DENNY, CAPTAIN. In *A Country Doctor*, he was an old friend of Nancy Prince's father.

DENT. In "In a Country Practice," this is the last name of two sisters who come to visit Mrs. Ashurst and her daughters, Lizzie and Ashurst and Nelly Ashurst, in Alton, just as the Ashursts receive word that they have inherited $50,000.

DENT. In "Mr. Bruce," he is a person Kitty Tennant dances with during the party given for Alice Thornton, Kitty's friend, in Baltimore.

DENT, KATE. In *A Marsh Island*, she is a dinner guest at the home of Mrs. Susan Winchester, who evidently would like her nephew, Richard Dale, to become interested in Kate.

DENT, MRS. In *Deephaven*, she is a bright, old-fashioned woman, formerly a city resident. She now lives in the Carew house with her siblings, Captain Dick Carew and Honora Carew.

DENT, TEMPERANCE ("TEMPY"). In "Miss Tempy's Watchers," she has just died. At her request, Miss Sarah Ann Binson and Mrs. Daniel Crowe, former schoolmates now estranged, watch over her body in her home the night before her funeral. They discuss Miss Tempy's self-sacrificial generosity, love of nature, and apparent psychic powers. For a last time they view her "wonderful smile." They sample her quince preserves, saved for others. Sarah says Tempy comforted her by explaining that dying is "only a-gettin' sleepier and sleepier; that's all there is." In the course of the night, Sarah and Mrs. Crowe grow friendly and compassionate. Miss Tempy's spirit may be watching over the watchers.

DENTON, CAPTAIN. In "William's Wedding," he is a sea captain who gave Almira Todd two bottles of special State of Maine wine. She opened one on her wedding day and saved the other to celebrate her brother William Blackett's marriage to Esther Hight.

DEP'FORD. In *The Country of the Pointed Firs*, this is mentioned by Mrs. Blackett as the name of a family going to the Bowden reunion.

DESMOND. In "Elleneen," this is the last name of a girl in Ireland whom Elleneen fears Dan Dunn now loves.

DEXTER, HARRISON. In "Decoration Day," he is evidently a deceased Civil War veteran whose grave is to be decorated during the parade.

DEXTER, MRS. HARRISON. In "Decoration Day," she is evidently an old widow who is thrilled when the parade passes her house.

DICKSON. In *The Tory Lover*, he is a *Ranger* junior officer, from Berwick. He cheated the Wallingford family. He spreads lies about Roger Wallingford, stabs him, tries to betray Paul Jones, but is caught. He is described as a yellow-faced Calvinist.

DICKSON, MRS. In *The Tory Lover*, Dickson wants to hoard ill-gotten money to escape in comfort with her to the South or to the West Indies.

DIGHTON, BEN. In *Deephaven*, he was Peletiah Daw's wild nephew. He was an imprisoned privateer who fought with a midshipman and was promptly hanged. Peletiah had a dream of Ben's death.

DILBY. In "Mrs. Parkins's Christmas Eve," this is the last name of the brothers who rent land from Mrs. Lydia Parsons to plant rye "on the halves." They pay her $87.

DILLON, MIKE ("MICKEY"). In "A Landlocked Sailor," he is a former sailor, about forty, hurt in a shipboard accident and tended by Dr. John Hallett. He limps to a farm region near Hallett's home and tells Hallett of his marriage to the pretty daughter of a sturdy woman who owns a hillside farm.

DILLON, MRS. In "Between Mass and Vespers," she is Father Ryan's cook.

DIMDALE, LADY. In *Betty Leicester's English Xmas*, she is Thomas Leicester's friend and is a fellow guest at Lady Mary Danesley's house. Lady Dimdale sings with Frame during the pageant.

DIMMETT, MRS. In "All My Sad Captains," she is Maria Lunn's laundry woman or servant. She has been sick.

DIMMICK. In *The Country of the Pointed Firs*, he is the Dunnet Landing parson described by Susan Fosdick as too "numb in his feelin's" to preach satisfactorily. He and Almira Todd visited Joanna after she marooned herself on Shell-heap Island. Almira says that when a sparrow lit on Joanna's coffin, its song was better than Dimmick's preaching.

DIMMICK, JOHN. In "Told in the Tavern," he is Capt. Asa Fitch's friend and neighbor. Dimmick gossips about Abby Sands in Timothy Hall's Byfleet tavern. He hints that her mother intercepted the last letters Parkins wrote her.

DINNETT. In *Deephaven*, reputed to have been a pirate, he now deep-sea fishes.

DOBIN, HARRIET. In "The Dulham Ladies," she is the older Dulham lady. Her sister, Lucinda Dobin, is younger. Feeling they must uphold traditional values to elevate the townspeople, they only make fools of themselves by wearing outlandish false bangs.

DOBIN, LUCINDA ("LUTIE"). In "The Dulham Ladies," she is the younger Dulham lady. Neither she nor her sister, Harriet Dobin, heed their kind servant Hetty Downs's warning to return the frisettes they bought.

DOBIN, MADAM. In "The Dulham Ladies," she is the deceased widow of Rev. Edward Dobin and was the mother of Harriet Dobin and Lucinda Dobin. She is proud that her grandmother was a Greenaple and took tea with Governor Clovenfoot in Boston. Her daughters revere her as a woman of admirable breeding and hospitality. It is said that the Dobin name, to be pronounced "Do-bin," was originally D'Aubigne. Townspeople ridicule the name by pronouncing it "Dobbin."

DOBIN, REV. EDWARD. In "The Dulham Ladies," he is the deceased father of Harriet Dobin and Lucinda Dobin. He went to Harvard College, was not talented at his post in Dulham's First Parish, was tyrannical at home, wore wigs, and had a stroke twenty or more years before he died.

DOCKUM. In *Deephaven*, he is the Lancaster family handyman at Deephaven.

DOCKUM, LEANDER. In *Deephaven*, he is the oldest son of the handyman Dockum and helps Kate Lancaster and Helen Denis.

DOCKUM, MRS. In *Deephaven*, she cleaned up the Deephaven mansion of Miss Katharine Brandon, Katharine Lancaster's recently deceased aunt.

DOCKUM, TOM ("TOMMY"). In *Deephaven*, he is said to want to see the Denby circus.

DODGE. In "Law Lane," this is the name of the family of Joel Smith's grandmother, according to Mrs. Harriet Powder, his friend.

DOLAN, MOTHER. In "A Little Captive Maid," she is a crippled person who Nora Connelly says could not go to the shore to salvage anything from the vessel sinking off Bantry.

DONAHOE, CORNY. In "Where's Nora?", it is mentioned that his and Dan Donahoe's old aunt, Mary Donahoe, recently died back in Ireland.

DONAHOE, DAN. In "Where's Nora?", it is mentioned that his and Corny Donahoe's Aunt Mary recently died.

DONAHUE. In "A Little Captive Maid," he and his wife are cousins of James Reilly. Donahue recommends Nora Connelly, also the Donahues's cousin, to Reilly to be John Balfour's maid. The Donahues have a son, named Johnny Donahue, and also a daughter.

DONAHUE. In "A Little Captive Maid," she is Nora Connelly's cousin Donahue's bright little girl. Nora suggests bringing the child to see John Balfour, to no avail.

DONAHUE, JOHNNY. In "A Little Captive Maid," he is Nora Connelly's cousin Donahue's son and plays the fife under John Balfour's window.

DONALD. In "A Late Supper," this is the name of a family who are Miss Catherine Spring's neighbors.

DONNELL. In *A Country Doctor*, this is the owner of a farm Dr. John Leslie visits professionally.

DONNELL. In "Mrs. Parkins's Christmas Eve," this is the name of a family whose light Mrs. Lydia Parkins knows she cannot be seeing as she staggers in the snowstorm. The Donnells, she recalls, are not home.

DONNELL. In "A New Parishioner," he is a person whose cabbages Jonas Phipps tells Miss Lydia Dunn he recently helped "get in."

DONNELL, ANN. In "The Becket Girls' Tree," she is the regular teacher of Jess Parsons and John Parsons. They prefer Miss Thomas, who substituted for Ann Donnell at one time.

DONNELL, CAPTAIN. In "A Bit of Shore Life," he is the owner of the horse and wagon the narrator borrows to take Georgie West to visit his aunts, Cynthy West and Hannah West, who live in the country.

DONNELLY. In "Elleneen," this is the name of a neighbor of the Desmond family in Ireland.

DOROTHY. In "The Orchard's Grandmother," she is the older Mary Brenton's faithful servant. The two have been to France, Holland, and Scotland together.

DORSEY, JOSHUA. In *Deephaven*, he is a lawyer who became deaf, lost the woman he loved, and now reads a good deal and fishes regularly.

DOUBLEDAY, MRS. In "The Passing of Sister Barsett," she is a neighbor of Sister Barsett, who regards Mrs. Doubleday as "officious."

DOUGALL, JOHN. In *The Tory Lover*, he is a *Ranger* sailor.

DOUGHERTY. In "A Spring Sunday," the conductor reports a washout of property owned by Dougherty along the new trolley route.

DOUGLAS, MRS. In "The Spur of the Moment," she is a well-to-do woman Fallon gardened for. The indirect result of his being befriended by Mrs. Dartmouth is his being rehired by Mrs. Douglas.

DOW, BILLY. In *A Country Doctor*, he is a person who, according to Mrs. Jacob Dyer, had been drinking before he mistook a horse for a ghost.

DOW, HENRY. In "The Gray Mills of Farley," he is mentioned as a Lancashire man and the cloth-hall overseer at the mills. Although some of his grandchildren are rich and hold important positions away from Farley, he has remained there, doing his regular work and in a position of authority.

DOW, JAMES. In "The Gray Mills of Farley," he is mentioned as a former worker in the cloth-hall in the mills, who is now financially secure.

DOW, LAVINA. In "The Flight of Betsey Lane," she is a resident of the Byfleet Poor-house. Her two closest friends are Peggy Bond and Betsey Lane. In her late eighties, she is rheumatic, fat, and assertive.

DOW, PHOEBE. In "In Dark New England Days," she is Enoch Holt's daughter, who is relieved when her second baby is born with properly formed hands.

DOW, SARAH ELLEN. In "The Passing of Sister Barsett," she is the hardworking helper of Sister Barsett, about whose sisters, Nancy Deckett and Mrs. Peck, Sarah gossips with Mercy Crane. Sarah, older than Mercy and poor, hopes others will later help her as she has helped so many.

DOWN, JOHN. In "Decoration Day," he remained a civilian at Barlow Plains, prospered, and married Marthy Peck. He is now deceased.

DOWN, MARTHY PECK. In "Decoration Day," she was Eben Munson's girlfriend. When he left Barlow Plains to fight during the Civil War, she did not await his return but, rather, married John Down. Her abiding love for Eben, however, is proved by her decorating his grave shortly before the parade and by her planning to erect a marker there.

DOWNER, MRS. In "Sister Peacham's Turn," she is the Reverend Mr. Downer's wife. She is sad because of the recent death of her mother.

DOWNER, THE REVEREND MR. In "Sister Peacham's Turn," he is the minister of the town where Lydia Ann Peacham lives. He was originally from Rhode Island. Lydia invites Mr. Downer and his wife to Thanksgiving dinner, and the two are most grateful. The following Sunday he preaches on "the beauties of hospitality."

DOWNES, JOHNNY. In *The Tory Lover*, he is a *Ranger* sailor.

DOWNING. In "A Visit Next Door," he is the owner of a beach house near Dundalk. Henry Granger considers renting it for a family vacation for two weeks but does not do so.

DOWNS. In "A Financial Failure," he is a bank clerk, under Pendell, and works with Hathaway and Jonas Dyer. Downs and Hathaway, both in their late twenties, constantly belittle Jonas. Downs informs Jonas that Waters is courting Love Hayland.

DOWNS, ANNIE. In "Miss Becky's Pilgrimage," she is Sophia Annis's granddaughter. Annie is a schoolteacher in Brookfield and lives with Julia Downs, her widowed mother. Annie welcomes Becky Parsons at the railroad station.

DOWNS, CAPTAIN PETER. In "The Mate of the Daylight," he is Melinda Downs's father and the close friend of Captain Joseph Ryder and Captain Jabez Ryder. The three are fellow gossipers.

DOWNS, HETTY. In "The Dulham Ladies," she is the faithful, gently critical servant of Harriet Dobin and Lucinda Dobin. She controls the household sanely and warns the sisters—to no avail—not to wear false bangs.

DOWNS, JULIA. In "Miss Becky's Pilgrimage," she is Sophia Annis's widowed daughter Annie Downs's mother. Julia and Annie live together in Brookfield.

DOWNS, MARTHA ("MARTHY"). In "In Dark New England Days," she is the busybody friend of Betsey Knowles and Hannah Knowles, the late Captain Knowles's daughters. She talks with Mrs. Forder about the curse put on Enoch Holt by Hannah following his acquittal of the charge of stealing Captain Knowles's gold coins. Peter Downs, Martha's husband, is domineering, but she survives him by many years. *Bibliography*: Roman.

DOWNS, MELINDA ("MELINDY"). In "The Mate of the Daylight," she is Captain Peter Downs's daughter and helps with his housekeeping.

DOWNS, MRS. 'LISHA. In "A Bit of Shore Life," she is an acquaintance of the narrator. The two observe the auction of the household possessions of the widowed Mrs. Wallis.

DOWNS, PETER. In "In Dark New England Days," he is the chuckling, domineering husband of Martha Downs, who survives him.

DOWNS, SKIPPER 'LISHA. In "A Bit of Shore Life," he is a fisherman who, according to Georgie West, is Captain Abiah Lane's friend.

DRAPER. In "Fame's Little Day," he and Joe Fitch are commission merchants in New York City. Fitch pays Abel Pinkham for a shipment of Vermont maple sugar.

DRAPER, SUSY. In "By the Morning Boat," she is Elisha's girlfriend. Her being away visiting her aunt prevents his saying goodbye to her.

DREW. In *A Country Doctor*, she is Mrs. Meeker's sister. Both women heard a rap on a window shortly before their mother died.

DRUM, MRS. In *Betty Leicester's English Xmas*, she is Lady Mary Danesley's housekeeper.

DRUMMOND. In *Betty Leicester*, he is from London and is traveling in Switzerland.

DRUMMOND, COLONEL. In "Mrs. Parkins's Christmas Eve," he is a rich resident in Holton. Mrs. Deems tells Lucy Deems, her daughter, that only Colonel Drummond is as rich as Mrs. Lydia Parkins is in their town.

DRUMMOND, MISS MARCIA. In *Betty Leicester*, she is a friend Barbara Leicester calls on in Riverport.

DUFF. In *Betty Leicester*, he is mentioned as one of Dr. Prince's patients.

DUFFY. In "The Gray Mills of Farley," this is the name of a family living in a substandard house adjoining the Farley mills. The family is now grievously ill of fever, partly caused by bad plumbing.

DUFFY. In "The Green Bowl," this is the name of a family Mrs. Patton says she thought Katie Montague and Frances Kent were going to visit, just beyond the empty church.

DUFFY, MARY ANN. In "Where's Nora?" she is Nora's mother Mary's sister, Patrick Quin's sister, and Michael Duffy's hard-working wife. The Duffys have a well-married daughter, named Ellen, in nearby Lawrence, Massachusetts.

DUFFY, MICHAEL ("MIKE"). In "Where's Nora?" he is Patrick Quin's lazy brother-in-law. The two are fast friends.

DUKE. In *The Tory Lover*, he is Mary Hamilton's young black horse.

"THE DULHAM LADIES" (1886). Short story. (Characters: Governor Clovenfoot, Rev. Edward Dobin, Madam Dobin, Harriet Dobin, Lucinda Dobin,

Hetty Downs, Harriet Greenaple, Mrs. Greenaple, Hightree, Jones, Paley, Smith, Madam Somebody, Mrs. Woolden.) Harriet Dobin and her younger sister, Lucinda Dobin, are the daughters of Rev. Edward Dobin, the minister of Dulham, now deceased, and his wife, also deceased. The sisters are proud of their family background: Their mother's grandmother, a Greenaple, took tea with Governor Clovenfoot in Boston; their father went to Harvard; and their mother was a woman of "good breeding and exquisite hospitality." The dear ladies, whose relatives are all deceased, are unconsciously aging. They are not treated with due respect in Dulham but are determined to display traditional manners for the public good. Admitting one day that their hair is growing thin, they take the train to nearby Westbury to shop for false bangs. When they see that the establishment where their father bought his hairpieces is out of business, they patronize a French wigmaker, who unloads on them two out-of-fashion chestnut frisettes, which slip down even as they are traveling home. Feeling happy and even girlish, the Dulham ladies ignore their servant Hetty Downs's tactful warning, and doll up and trip off to the local sewing circle. Hetty is certain the two "innocent Christian babes" will be laughed at. "The Dulham Ladies" is one of Jewett's best stories. *Bibliography*: Blanchard; Cary, *Jewett*; Roman.

DU MAURIER, GEORGE (1834–1896). (Full name: George Louis Palmella Busson du Maurier.) Graphic artist and novelist. Paris-born, Du Maurier contributed satirical drawings of high society to *Punch* (from 1860), became a staff member (1864), and illustrated several books. His three novels are *Peter Ibbetson* (1891), *Trilby* (1894), and *The Martian* (1897). Two appealed to Jewett— *Peter Ibbetson*, a fantasy, for its spirited use of the imagination, its supernaturalism, and thoughts in it concerning life after death; *Trilby* for being partly set in the Latin Quarter of Paris, which Jewett visited with the novel in mind. When Jewett and Annie Adams Fields* were in England in 1892, they visited Du Maurier and his family in the coastal village of Whitby. Jewett wrote Sarah Wyman Whitman* (11 September [1892]) to describe the charms of Du Maurier's home, the drawings he showed her and the French songs he sang for her, and the fun she had playing with his terrier. Du Maurier wrote Jewett (2 December 1894) that the idea was "on the brain" for his autobiographical *Martian* (which concerns his studio life on the Continent and his partial blindness). *Bibliography*: Blanchard; Fields, *Letters*; Leonée Ormond, *George Du Maurier* (Pittsburgh: University of Pittsburgh Press, 1969).

DUMPHY. In "The Spur of the Moment," he is a man whose lung fever requires that Fallon temporarily replace him as a cabman driving his old white horse.

DUNCAN. In *Betty Leicester*, he is a man from Scotland about to join his family in Switzerland.

DUNCAN. In "A New Parishioner," he was the dull predecessor of Mr. Peckham, the new minister in Walton.

DUNCAN. In "A Sorrowful Guest," this is the name of the family with whom Helen Ainslie returns from Italy to Boston.

DUNCAN. In "The Spur of the Moment," he was Walton's neighbor. The big coachman knew both Duncan and Walton forty years ago when he cared for their riding horses.

DUNCAN. In "The Spur of the Moment," he was the son of the elder Duncan, who was Walton's close friend. The big coachman served the younger Duncan as coachman for twenty-two years.

DUNCAN, ADA. In *Betty Leicester*, she is Betty Leicester's friend traveling in Switzerland. She and her sister, Bessie Duncan, write Betty.

DUNCAN, BESSIE. In *Betty Leicester*, she is Betty Leicester's friend traveling in Switzerland. She and her sister, Ada Duncan, write Betty.

DUNCAN, DR. In "In a Country Practice," he is a student Dr. Best describes as adequate, as are Dr. Grafton and Dr. Smith, to take up a country practice.

DUNCAN, MARY. In *Betty Leicester*, she is the mother of Ada Duncan and Bessie Duncan. They are traveling in Switzerland. In *Betty Leicester's English Xmas*, she is mentioned as a cousin of Lady Mary Danesley.

DUNCAN, MISS ANNE. In "The Hare and the Tortoise," she is the partly deaf great-aunt of Mary Chester. Anne Duncan, who loves music, is far sweeter than her domineering older sister, Miss Sophia Duncan.

DUNCAN, MISS SOPHIA. In "The Hare and the Tortoise," she is the domineering great-aunt of Mary Chester. Miss Sophia Duncan would like Henry Temple to marry Mary, who finally prefers Richard Dean.

DUNCAN, MRS. In "An Every-Day Girl," she is a guest at the summer hotel where Mary Fleming works. Mary plans to take Aunt Hannah to visit "lovely" Mrs. Duncan.

DUNCAN, MRS. In "Mr. Bruce," she is a friendly woman who offers to provide Mrs. Tennant, her neighbor, with the services of Mary, Mrs. Duncan's maid. Instead, Kitty Tennant performs as the serving-maid.

DUNLEAVY, MARY. In "Bold Words at the Bridge," she is Biddy Connelly's big neighbor. The two argue bitterly but then gently make up, through their common concern over a strange woman's inquiry. Mary has lived in the mill town five or six fewer years than Biddy has. Mary is sad when her goat eats her foxgloves, seeds for which came from Ireland.

DUNN. In "The Honey Tree," he is the Hillborough teacher, disliked by Johnny Hopper and Bill Phillips. Johnny declines to invite Dunn to the Hopper home to sample the honey. One woman says that Dunn is in the hills "botanizing" but that if he expects to find any witch hazel this late he will be disappointed. Jewett, who preferred home schooling to formal classes, delights in holding this teacher up to gentle ridicule.

DUNN. In "Tom's Husband," he is Alice Dunn Wilson's deceased father. He was a manufacturer and saw such "executive ability" in Alice that he wished she were a son.

DUNN, CAPTAIN. In *A Country Doctor*, he was an old friend of Nancy Prince's father.

DUNN, CAPTAIN. In "The Taking of Captain Ball," he is a friend of Captain Asaph Ball, who invites him and Captain Allister to dinner.

DUNN, DAN ("DANNY"). In "Elleneen," he is Elleneen's sister Mary Ann Dunn's brother-in-law and Elleneen's steady boyfriend. She teased him in Ireland before leaving for America and now fears he has gone after a girl whose last name is Desmond. But Dan followed Elleneen to America, and all will be well.

DUNN, ELLEN. In "An Every-Day Girl," she is a friend of Mrs. Fleming, the mother of Mary Fleming. When Mary tells Aunt Hannah her mother is visiting Ellen, Hannah describes Ellen as a conceited seamstress whose sickness will humble her.

DUNN, FATHER. In "A Little Captive Maid," he is the fine priest, born in Glengariff, Ireland, and now Father Miles's successor in John Balfour's town when Nora Connelly works for Balfour. Though knowing it is too late, Father Dunn suggests that he, Balfour, and Nora might go to Ireland to improve Balfour's fatally weakened physical condition.

DUNN, GENERAL. In "Peg's Little Chair," he is Margaret Benning's friend. With his friend, Pomeroy, he tells her General Lafayette will be stopping at her public house.

DUNN, HENRY. In "Elleneen," he is Mary Ann Dunn's older child. Age two, he has an unnamed younger sister.

DUNN, JOHN. In "Elleneen," he is Dan Dunn's older brother, Mary Ann Dunn's husband, and her sister Elleneen's brother-in-law. John works in a gas house.

DUNN, LAWYER. In "A Pinch of Salt," he is the local lawyer who has just arranged the purchase of land by John Brayton.

DUNN, MARGET. In "The Luck of the Bogans," she is Peggy Muldoon's old drinking crony in Bantry.

DUNN, MARY ANN. In "Elleneen," she is Elleneen's sister, John Dunn's wife, and his younger brother Dan Dunn's sister-in-law. Mary Ann arranges for Dan, newly arrived from Ireland, to surprise Elleneen, whom he loves and who loves him.

DUNN, MICKEY. In "Where's Nora?", he delivers Nora's first order of supplies, from McLoughlin's store, to her Birch Plains baking business.

DUNN, MISS LYDIA ("LYDDY"). In "A New Parishioner," she is the proud, independent-minded owner, almost sixty, of a tidy little house in Walton. She hires Jonas Phipps as handyman and gossips with him. She is not deceived for long when smooth Henry Stroud gives her his note for $6,000 out of a sense of guilt that forty years earlier his father, Ben Stroud, cheated Miss Dunn's grandfather, Parson Dunn.

DUNN, MRS. In "A New Parishioner," she was Miss Lydia Dunn's grandmother. Lydia remembers the older woman's calling the period between dinner and breakfast "betwixt hay and grass."

DUNN, NATHAN. In "Aunt Cynthy Dallett," he is a person whose niece Mrs. Hand knows. He arranged his finances carefully, Mrs. Hand recalls, to the extent of separately packaging his own funeral expense money, down to the last 84¢.

DUNN, PARSON. In "A New Parishioner," he is mentioned as Miss Lydia Dunn's grandfather. He was the minister of Walton for forty years.

DUNN, SOLOMON. In "The Stage Tavern," he is a regional genealogist and historian whom General Jack Norton meets at Lizzie Harris's tavern.

DUNNELL. In *A Country Doctor*, he was the owner of the horse Billy Dow thought was a ghost. The Dunnells are said to be "deficient in vitality."

DUNNER. In "The Orchard's Grandmother," this may be the owner of a bay to which Colonel Brenton goes with his family for a ship bound with Puritans for Holland. Instead, the ship takes them to America.

"A DUNNET SHEPHERDESS" (1899). Short story. (Characters: Mrs. Blackett, William Blackett, Bowden, Caplin, Harris, Esther Hight, Thankful Hight, Almira Todd.) In Dunnet Landing one summer morning, Almira Todd smears a pennyroyal lotion and other herbs on her brother William Blackett's face, to protect him from mosquitoes when he goes for a little annual fishing trip. He stops by the schoolhouse where the narrator is writing, and she happily goes with him in his horse-drawn wagon to a trout stream. Speaking little but communicating much, they catch nothing, have lunch, leave some dried fish for a forlorn, grateful farm woman, and press on to the Hight property—unpainted home, potato patch, sheep, and rocky ledge behind. Inside, Thankful Hight, a paralyzed widow, greets the visitors sternly, permits shy William to walk away, and warms up only when the narrator gossips about villagers. When William seems gone too long, the old woman worries that something has happened to her daughter. She is Esther Hight, who gave up teaching, developed a profitable flock of sheep, paid off the mortgage, and now tends both sheep and mother. Esther and William return—shy, uncomprehending "lovers"—and soon say goodbye to each other for another year. The level of this story is raised to that of a pastoral or a mini-epic when Jewett brings in comparisons—Medea anointing Jason (Almira and William), a Millet painting (Esther in a field), a Roman emperor (Mrs. Hight), Chaucerian speech (Mrs. Hight), Atalanta (Esther afoot), and Jeanne d'Arc (Esther as saint). "A Dunnet Shepherdess"—along with "The Foreigner," "The Queen's Twin," and "William's Wedding"—continues the story of *The Country of the Pointed Firs*. *Bibliography*: Donovan; Roman; Sherman.

DUNNING. In "Andrew's Fortune," he is a successful Boston businessman. When he attends the funeral of Stephen Dennett, his friend from boyhood days, he meets Andrew Phillips, likes him, and later helps him get a job in Boston.

DUNNING, KATY. In "A Late Supper," she is a sweet little girl, ten but tiny, and neglected by her aunt. She asks Miss Catherine Spring for a job. After Miss Spring rents some rooms to summer guests, she is able to hire Katy.

DUNNING, MISS ANN. In "A Garden Story," she is a Littletown dressmaker. She takes delight in the flowers of her carefully tended garden. She asks for a needy girl to come from Boston and spend a "country week" with her. When she is sent Peggy McAllister, nine, the little girl quickly becomes so friendly with and useful to Miss Dunning that she arranges to keep her permanently.

DUNSTER. In "The Flight of Betsey Lane," he is a Philadelphia eye specialist. When Betsey Lane seeks to purchase glasses for Peggy Bond, he happens to hear her, says Miss Bond probably has cataracts, and promises to try to help her soon.

DUNSTER, HENRY. In "A Sorrowful Guest," he is Whiston's sneaky cousin who roomed at Harvard with him and John Ainslie. While Whiston and Dunster, along with Ainslie and George Sheffield, were in combat during the Civil War, Dunster was wounded, left for dead, and reported missing in action. He survived, became an alcoholic drifter, and in South America reappeared to Whiston, who had long felt haunted by Dunster.

DUNWATER, LORD. In *Betty Leicester's English Xmas*, he is Lady Mary Danesley's guest. Miss Edith Banfield knows him.

DURFEE. In "The Girl with the Cannon Dresses," he is Sophronia Durfee's farmer husband. They have retired some distance from Halifax.

DURFEE, SOPHRONIA. In "The Girl with the Cannon Dresses," she is a former housekeeper of Alice Channing and her parents in Halifax. While recuperating from a mild illness, Alice spends the summer with Sophronia and during that time meets Dulcidora Bunt, who lives nearby.

DURRANT. In "A Second Spring," he is Maria Durrant's married brother. Before she moves in with Israel Haydon, Maria lives with the Durrants.

DURRANT, JOHNNY. In "A Second Spring," he is the son of Maria Durrant's brother and works for Israel Haydon.

DURRANT, MARIA ("MARI'"). In "A Second Spring," she is the cousin and sister-in-law of Mrs. Durrant, her brother's wife. Maria lives with the Durrants, for whose boarders she cooks, before moving in with Israel Haydon. Maria unselfishly helps others in the region. Gossip almost prevents her from marrying Israel after the death of his first wife, Martha Haydon.

DURRANT, MRS. In "A Second Spring," she is Maria Durrant's cousin and sister-in-law. Maria lives with the two Durrants. Mrs. Durrant is regarded as "worthless" and occasionally makes prolonged visits to a sister in New York state, leaving Maria to cook for her boarders.

DUSTIN, MARY. In "A Village Shop," she sells the contents of her notions shop to Esther Jaffrey and goes west to live with a married sister.

DUTCH, MELINDA. In "In Dark New England Days," she is mentioned as a mourner walking with Enoch Holt in Captain Knowles's funeral procession.

DYER, CAPTAIN ("CAP'N"). In "The Guests of Mrs. Timms," he was Miss Cynthia Pickett's uncle. He willed his home in Woodville to her and her mother.

DYER, ELIZA (" 'LIZA"). In *A Country Doctor*, she is Mrs. Jacob Dyer's sister and the wife of Jacob's twin brother, Martin Dyer. The two women know Mrs. Daniel Thacher and come to love her granddaughter, Nan Prince.

DYER, JACOB ("JAKE"). In *A Country Doctor*, he is Martin Dyer's twin brother and the husband of Martin's wife Eliza's sister.

DYER, JONAS. In "A Financial Failure," he is Jonas Dyer's rich old uncle. Rumor has it the old man gives hugely to tract societies. He gets his nephew a job in the County Savings Bank in Dartford, of which he is a director. When young Jonas, in love with Love Hayland, resigns from the bank, the uncle is irate at first; but when he learns the lad wishes to marry Love, he approves the sensible union and aids the couple financially.

DYER, JONAS. In "A Financial Failure," he is a clerk at the County Savings Bank in Dartford. He works under Pendell, along with Downs and Hathaway. Those two, both in their late twenties, constantly belittle Jonas, who is tall and handsome but only twenty. He falls in love with Love Hayland at first sight, when he sees her while she is with her father, Joel Hayland, doing some banking business. Jonas resigns from the bank and marries Love Hayland.

DYER, MARTIN. In *A Country Doctor*, he is Jacob Dyer's twin brother and the husband of Jacob's wife's sister, Eliza Dyer.

DYER, MRS. In "A Financial Failure," she is the mother, from upcountry, of Jonas Dyer. She attempts to curry favor with Pendell, Jonas's boss at the bank where they both work, by foolishly demeaning her son.

DYER, MRS. JACOB. In *A Country Doctor*, she is Eliza Dyer's sister and the wife of Eliza's husband Martin Dyer's twin brother. Sometimes called Mrs. Jake, she constantly complains of her physical ailments. Both sisters know Mrs. Daniel Thacher and love her granddaughter, Nan Prince.

DYER, SUSAN. In *A Country Doctor*, she is Martin Dyer's granddaughter, about Nan Prince's age. Nan spins stories to her about her rich aunt, Nancy Prince.

DYSART, HELENA VERNON. In "Martha's Lady," she is Harriet Pyne's younger cousin, from Boston. As Helena Vernon, she visits Harriet only briefly but makes a wonderful lifelong impression on Harriet's servant, Martha. Helena marries Jack Dysart, lives in Europe with him, and has sons, deaths in the family, and a daughter who marries. When she returns, tired, bent, and garbed in black, to revisit Harriet forty years later, she notices that Martha has remembered her exquisitely.

DYSART, JACK. In "Martha's Lady," he is a Britisher who marries Helena Vernon in Boston and takes her with him to England and to diplomatic missions to Paris, Madrid, and St. Petersburg. Martha follows their tours of duty by consulting a geography book.

E

EARL. In *The Tory Lover*, he is an inmate in Mill Prison.

EARL, WILLIAM. In *The Tory Lover*, he is a *Ranger* sailor whom Captain John Paul Jones orders to write dispatches for him.

EASTMAN, CAROLINE AUGUSTA JEWETT ("CARRIE") (1855–1897). Jewett's younger sister. During their childhood, Caroline was closer to Mary Rice Jewett,* the oldest sister. But in young adulthood, the three sisters went to the Philadelphia Centennial together in 1876. In 1878 Caroline married Edward Calvin ("Ned") Eastman (1849–1892), the only pharmacist in South Berwick. They had one child, Theodore Jewett ("Stubbs, "Stubby," "Thider") Eastman (1879–1931). When Edward died of peritonitis, Jewett was vacationing with Annie Adams Fields* in Rome, wanted to rush back home, but was persuaded by her sister, Edward's grieving widow, to continue her planned time abroad. Jewett liked Theodore Eastman, her nephew, went boating and hiking with him, discussed books with him, and took him on vacations and to the theater. She minded less when he shot and collected birds than might have been expected, given her portrayal of the ornithologist in "A White Heron." When Caroline died, Jewett became a surrogate parent to him and gloried in his progress through Harvard (A.B., 1901; M.D., 1905). During her 1898 trip with Annie Adams Fields to Europe, Jewett was joined by Mary Jewett and Theodore in France, where they met Marie Thérèse de Solms Blanc.* When Jewett suffered a stroke in Boston early in 1909, Theodore attended her informally. When Theodore, a bachelor, died, he left the Jewett house in South Berwick to the Society for the Preservation of New England Antiquities of Boston, together with $20,000 for its upkeep. *Bibliography*: Blanchard; Cary, *Letters*; Fields, *Letters*; Frost; Silverthorne.

EDERTON. In "Fame's Little Day," he is the *Sun* reporter who embellishes on the report in the *Herald* of the visit to New York City of Abel Pinkham and his wife, Mary Ann Pinkham.

EDGECUMBE, LORD MOUNT. In *The Tory Lover*, he is the commander of the Mill Prison. He is called an earl.

EDWARDS, MARY. In *Betty Leicester*, she is a sick girl Dr. Prince prevents from dying. Her parents were dreadfully worried.

ELBURY. In "Miss Peck's Promotion," she is Rev. Wilbur Elbury's baby daughter. Eliza Peck tenderly cares for her for a year.

ELBURY, MRS. WILBUR. In "Miss Peck's Promotion," she dies giving birth to a baby daughter. Eliza Peck defined her as unselfish.

ELBURY, MRS. WILBUR. In "Miss Peck's Promotion," she is Rev. Elbury's new wife, from a neighboring town. Eliza Peck regards her as weak and only superficially pretty.

ELBURY, REV. WILBUR. In "Miss Peck's Promotion," he is the self-centered minister Eliza Peck generously works for after his first wife dies. His second marriage ends Eliza's timorous hopes of marrying him herself. Elbury is an outrageous example of many "paralyzed men" in Jewett's fiction. *Bibliography*: Roman.

ELDEN. In "A Late Supper," he is the kind old lawyer who advises Miss Catherine Spring to advertise rooms to rent for summer guests.

ELISHA (" 'LISHA"). In "By the Morning Boat," he is a Maine farm lad, fifteen. He must bravely leave his grandfather, his widowed mother, and his little sister at home to take a job in Boston.

ELIZABETH (" 'LIZABETH"). In "An Autumn Holiday," she is the narrator, a country physician's daughter. She enjoys an October walk, muses at a child's grave, and gossips with Polly Marsh and Mrs. Snow about friends both sick, including mentally, and those pretending to be.

ELLEN. In "A Little Traveler," she was the sister, now deceased, of the woman who affectionately welcomes the "little traveler," Ellen's tiny daughter, at the Boston railway station.

ELLEN. In "The Town Poor," she is Rebecca Wright's cousin, married to a man from Parsley.

ELLEN ("ELLENEEN"). In "Elleneen," she is the younger sister of Mary Ann Dunn, who is happily married in America. Before she left Ireland, Ellen teased Dan Dunn, her brother-in-law, and did not tell him she truly loved him. Now working in a cotton mill near Mary Ann's town, she reveals to Mary Ann that she loves only Dan, who is presumably now going after a girl named Desmond back in Ireland; whereupon Mary Ann produces Dan, just arrived and hiding and listening in the next room. All will be well.

ELLEN ("ELLENEEN"). In "Where's Nora?", she is the well-married daughter of Michael Duffy and Mary Ann Duffy. She lives in Lawrence, Massachusetts.

"ELLENEEN" (1901). Short story. (Characters: Jerry Callahan, Phil Carroll, Desmond, Donnelly, Dan Dunn, Henry Dunn, John Dunn, Mary Ann Dunn, Ellen.) One wintry day Mary Ann Dunn, busy ironing and watching her two small children, "innocently" invites a visitor in to her comfortable home. She is Mary Ann's young sister, Ellen ("Elleneen"), who left Ireland last fall and has a steady job in the cotton mills of a nearby town. Mary Ann queries Elleneen about her current boyfriends, but the unhappy girl mainly expresses regret at losing Dan Dunn, Mary Ann's husband John Dunn's younger brother. She says she teased him too much before she left him back in Ireland and can love only him. Mary Ann asks her to check on the dog in an adjoining room. Dan, who just arrived in town and was hidden there by Mary Ann to listen, pops out. The two young people embrace, and Elleneen relishes the familiar smell of turf smoke still in his rough coat.

ELLER, DEACON. In "Miss Manning's Minister," he is a Rinston church official.

ELLER, MRS. In "Miss Manning's Minister," she is the wife of the Rinston church official. When the Reverend Taylor suffers a stroke, she helps arrange for his immediate care.

ELLINOR ("ELLY"). In "Paper Roses," she is the narrator. Ellinor and Kate, her friend, sell items, including paper roses, at a fair to raise funds for a hospital.

ELLIS. In "Mary and Martha," this is the name of a family visited by Martha Dean, who wishes she and her sister lived in town nearer such friends.

ELLIS, AARON. In "The Becket Girls' Tree," he is a neighbor who gives Jess Parsons and John Parsons a lift on his sled toward Eastport, where Jess and John buy Christmas presents for Ann Becket and Lydia Becket.

ELLY. In "Mr. Bruce," she is Aunt Mary's niece, twenty. Elly is the principal narrator. Mary tells her and Ann Langdon her story, told her by Miss Margaret Tennant, about Kitty Tennant and Philip Bruce.

ELTON. In "Marsh Rosemary," he is a Walpole church deacon.

ELTON, MRS. In "Marsh Rosemary," she is the deacon's hypochondriacal wife. She gossips about Nancy Lloyd after Nancy's marriage to Jerry Lane. Under the guise of sympathy, she brings Nancy news, supplied to her by discreet Nathan Low, that Jerry has not drowned but is living with a woman in Shediac. Mrs. Elton does respect Nancy's wish to have the news remain a secret.

ELWELL. In "Decoration Day," he is a Barlow Plains church deacon. His two sons were drowned in a man-of-war during the Civil War.

"AN EMPTY PURSE" (1895). (Full title: "An Empty Purse: A New England Tale for Christmas and Holiday Time.") Short story. (Characters: Ashton, Mrs. Bean, Miss Debby Gaines, Johnson, Mrs. Prender, Nelly Prender, Susy Prender, Rivers, Mrs. Rivers, Mrs. Wallis.) Miss Debby Gaines, a tiny New England seamstress, lost her Christmas money and must give only of herself this season. When Mrs. Rivers complains about the bother of buying presents in a crowded store, Debby says "show[ing] good feelin' " can be better than offering gifts. Three days later, on Christmas, Debby visits Mrs. Prender, a young widow, and babysits a sick daughter for her while she visits her mother with her other daughter; she gives Mrs. Bean, a poorhouse inmate, her own mended, quilted petticoat; she has tea with Mrs. Wallis, who misses her granddaughters; and she does other kind acts. Home again, Debby finds a package of presents from Mrs. Rivers—things she owned and liked—with a note saying she took to heart Debby's comments about the Christmas spirit. This story was privately reprinted as *An Empty Purse: A Christmas Story* in 1905 for sale at Boston's Trinity Chapel Christmas Fair.

ESTES. In "Andrew's Fortune," he is Stephen Dennett's lawyer. Estes drew up Dennett's will, which is missing. Estes is the only lawyer in the area.

ESTES. In "A Landless Farmer," he is Ezra Allen's helper in his wheelwright shop. At one point, Ezra says Estes is sick.

ESTHER, AUNT. In "An Every-Day Girl," she is the aunt of John Abbott, who tells Mary Fleming he is staying with Aunt Esther while briefly in Dolton on some farm business.

"AN EVERY-DAY GIRL" (1892). Short story. (Characters: John Abbott, Mary Arley, Mrs. Danforth, Davis, Mr. Dennis, Mrs. Duncan, Ellen Dunn, Aunt Esther, Farley, Henry Fleming, Mary Fleming, Mrs. Fleming, Aunt Hannah, Haynes, Mrs. Haynes, Nelly Perrin, Mrs. Prescott, Mrs. Preston.) One warm day in May, Mary Fleming, eighteen, returns home from her village school in Dolton in a surly mood. She does not want to become a teacher but wonders what else she can do. Aunt Hannah greets her, here on a visit to Mary's mother, evidently her niece. Hannah's encouraging talk makes the girl feel better. After they have tea, Mary cleans up the untidy yard, which she thinks Henry Fleming, her father, a tired shoe-factory worker, should take care of. John Abbott, Mary's favorite schoolmate, now orphaned and living on a nearby farm, is in town briefly on business. Coming by, he helps her with some pruning and greets her father courteously when he comes plodding home. After a family supper, Mary is delighted when John returns and they take an amiable walk together. At graduation, Mary receives a prize in history but returns home to find her father laid off and sick. Next day she and Mary Arley, a friend working in the shoe factory, decide to get jobs in a nearby summer hotel. The housekeeper there is Mrs. Preston, a cousin of Mary Arley's mother. Soon Mary Fleming, who takes seriously Aunt Hannah's advice to do the best job you can regardless of the job, pleases Mrs. Preston more than happy-go-lucky Mary Arley does. John suddenly appears; he delivers chickens and milk from his farm job to the hotel. One night while Mary Fleming is sleeplessly watching over Mrs. Preston, suddenly ill, she sees the glare of fire over Dolton. The doctor returns and finds Mrs. Preston well again, all because of Mary's ministrations. Given time to go home, Mary finds the fire destroyed much of Dolton but spared her parents' home, which they sell so as to buy a nearby farm with John, whose practical nature they admire. Commended by Mrs. Preston, Mary is given an opportunity to work for a while in a New York hotel with Mr. Dennis, who owns the summer hotel, and then to become her assistant housekeeper at the summer hotel. John wants to marry Mary quickly, but she persuades him to wait until they have both saved a little more money. Jewett takes too little care here in naming her characters. Thus, we have Arley, Farley, Duncan, Dunn, Mary, Mary, Prescott, Preston.

EVINS, DANIEL ("DAN," "DAN'L"). In "Decoration Day," he is Asa Brown's friend. Evins told Brown that he once saw a soldier's patriotic marker in a Confederate cemetery. Brown agrees that the man probably did fight for "his country" too.

EVINS, MRS. In *The Country of the Pointed Firs*, she is a person Almira Todd recalls "favor[ing]" with some catnip and yarrow.

EZRA. In ''The Life of Nancy,'' he is Nancy Gale's farmer uncle. He lives in Milton, a few miles from Boston. When Nancy is visiting his farm, he takes her to Boston, where she chances to encounter Tom Aldis.

EZRA. ''A Native of Winby,'' he is a pupil for whose evident lack of ambition his teacher, Marilla Hender, rebukes him.

FABER. In "Mrs. Parkins's Christmas Eve," he is any of the sons of Mary Faber, the cousin of Mrs. Lydia Parkins, who calls them "prowling boys."

FABER, MARY. In "Mrs. Parkins's Christmas Eve," she is Mrs. Lydia Parkins's cousin. Though not well off, Mary Faber, who lives in Haybury, offers Mrs. Parkins sincere hospitality. After Mrs. Parkins has reformed spiritually, she aids her poor cousin generously.

"THE FAILURE OF DAVID BERRY" (1891). Short story. (Characters: General Barstow, David Berry, Mrs. David Berry, Judge Hutton, Mrs. Lester, Mrs. Lester, Sam Wescott, Mrs. Sam Wescott.) Old David Berry contentedly soles and heels shoes for a shoe manufacturing company, and makes fine footwear too, in a shop beside the house he and his wife have in Lynn. When the town expands away from them, his wife sells the shop to his neighbor, Sam Wescott, who converts it into a shed for his poultry business. David moves his equipment into a poor store he rents downtown. Townspeople prefer inferior ready-made footwear, and his business worsens. A ragged little girl comes to his shop, and he mends her worn sole, gives her an apple, and is happy to welcome her often later. He recalls that a sequence of six parish ministers, whose drives for missionary funds he has regularly supported, have come and gone. One night, when Mrs. Berry is entertaining Wescott and his wife, together with the influential Mrs. Lester and her daughter-in-law, Wescott talks David into borrowing $50 from him and offering a line of ready-mades for sale. Mrs. Berry gets sick, David loses time at work, and the good doctor's moderate fees must be paid.

David falls behind with his shop rent and still owes Wescott $16. Sam gossips to the rent collector and others, and David is shamed in front of curious onlookers as his shop is shuttered and locked. The little girl walks part of the way home with him. Mrs. Berry gets better; but David, trying to repair shoes in his own kitchen, soon dies. Although he finally paid all his debts, he is remembered as a businessman who failed. The little girl attends the funeral. Mrs. Berry auctions her household goods and moves up country. Later Wescott happens to see a biblical verse—"Owe no man anything but to love one another"—pasted on David's old shop wall. Wescott scratches the verse off but is haunted by its message.

"FAIR DAY" (1888). Short story. (Characters: Ann Bascom, Johnny Bascom, 'Liza Bascom, Mercy Bascom, Tobias Bascom, Tobias Bascom, Bassett, Brown, Ruth Bascom Parlet.) One nice October day, Mercy Bascom, tired and depressed but still spry at seventy-seven, is left alone when her son, Tobias Bascom, his wife, Ann, and their children go off to the county fair ten miles away. She wishes they had asked her, although she would have declined. She was left at twenty-eight with three daughters and one son, when her shiftless, alcoholic husband died. She raised her children well, and all are now married. After sewing a patch on her son's coat, she trudges over to her former house, leased to the Browns—now also at the fair—ever since Tobias married Ann and moved to her more substantial place and took his mother along. She regards Ann as cooperative but uppity and lazy. When Mercy enters the Brown house, old sights trigger memories. In the main she regrets only a decades-long argument she had with her husband's sister, Ruth Bascom Parlet, and decides to try to make peace at last. Returning home, she prepares a splendid supper for Tobias and his "folks" and is pleased when he tells her he met Ruth at the fair and she told him she hoped bygones could be bygones. Mercy is agreeable but plans to tell Ruth she "spoke first" about the matter to Tobias. The title "Fair Day" contains a triple pun: while a country fair is held on a fair October day, Mercy turns fair.

FAIRFAX, GEORGE. In *The Tory Lover*, he is a Tory from Virginia, grew tobacco there, and is now living in Bath. Madam Wallingford knew his mother. Mary Hamilton discusses the colonists' grievances with Fairfax, who agrees to help rescue Roger Wallingford.

FAIRFAX, MRS. GEORGE. In *The Tory Lover*, George Fairfax tells Mary Hamilton and John Davis his wife is away from home briefly.

FALES, ASA. In "The News from Petersham," he is a businessman who is happy the rumor of Daniel Johnson's death is false. Fales was aided financially by Johnson and may now help him buy some pine woods.

FALES, JAMES ("THE GRASSHOPPER," "JIM"). In *A Marsh Island*, he is a cocky teenager who works as a hired hand for Israel Owen and bunks in his house. He kids Dan Lester, whistles a lot, carries messages, and gossips.

FALES, MRS. In "The Flight of Betsey Lane," she is a person who Peggy Bond, Lavina Dow, and Betsey Lane agree is not welcome as a part-time resident of the Byfleet Poor-house. Mrs. Fales walks past without entering.

FALES, MRS. In *A Marsh Island*, she is James Fales's mother. She lives a mile or two from Israel Owen's farm.

FALLON. In "The Spur of the Moment," he is the old fellow who temporarily drives Dumphy's horse and carriage. Mrs. Dartmouth befriends Fallon, who drives Miss Peet to a funeral and is befriended by a big coachman. This leads to Fallon's being befriended by Mrs. Douglas, whose gardener he was and becomes so again. Fallon then delivers flowers to Mrs. Dartmouth.

FALLS. In *The Tory Lover*, he is a *Ranger* sailor. He is young and peppy, and plays the fiddle.

"FAME'S LITTLE DAY" (1895). Short story. (Characters: Abel, Draper, Ederton, Joe Fitch, Goffey, Abel Pinkham, Mary Ann Pinkham, Sarah.) A reporter observes Abel Pinkham and his wife, Mary Ann Pinkham, in the Ethan Allen Hotel in New York City, asks the clerk about the pair, and prepares a note about them for the *Tribune*. They are a farm couple from Wetherford, Vermont, in town to have a little pleasure and to be paid for a consignment of maple sugar sent to Joe Fitch, a commission merchant. They feel out of place and homesick until next morning they read in the *Tribune* a flattering story of their visit. Delighted, they begin to feel at home in the big city. When Fitch tells them news of their arrival is also in the *Herald*, they read in it an imaginary interview of Pinkham, one item being the Pinkhams will attend Barnum's circus. Aware of the reporter's fib, they decide to go there anyway, and they have a fine time. Before their departure, the original reporter returns to the Ethan Allen, resists having any more fun, and does not intrude further on the joyful Pinkhams. Though comic, "Fame's Little Day" contains typical Jewett cracks at the inhumanity of the big city in its handling of rustic tourists. *Bibliography*: Cary, *Jewett.*

FANEUIL. In *The Tory Lover*, this is the name of Loyalists who are now refugees in Bristol.

FANNY. In "A Born Farmer," she is Jacob Gaines's old white mare.

FANNY, AUNT. "A Guest at Home," she is the wife of Henry, who is Mrs. Hollis's brother. Fanny and Henry finance the education and fun times in and near New York City of Annie Hollis, Mrs. Hollis's daughter.

FARLEY. In "An Every-Day Girl," he is said by Henry Fleming to be an old worker at the Dolton shoe factory. Farley plans to buy Fleming's house and assume its mortgage.

FARLEY, JOE. In "Miss Peck's Promotion," he has worked for Eliza Peck and will warm her house so Rev. Elbury's baby can stay there comfortably for a brief time.

FARLEY, MISS. In "A Garden Story," she is a teacher Miss Ann Dunning makes dresses for. Miss Farley is about to leave Littletown and go stay with her mother.

FARLEY, MRS. In *A Marsh Island*, she is Mrs. Susan Winchester's talkative friend and visits Israel Owen's farm in her company.

FARLEY, THE REVEREND MR. In "All My Sad Captains," he is the un-married minister who arrives in Longport from a nearby parish. Maria Lunn, who knows him slightly, invites him to be her boarder. This needlessly distresses the three captains courting her.

"FARMER FINCH" (1885). Short story. (Characters: Serena Allen, John Finch, Mary Finch, Polly Finch, Mary Hallett, Jerry Minton, Mrs. Minton, Mrs. Wall.) One bleak December day, Mary Finch serves a gloomy supper to her husband, John Finch, and their daughter, Polly Finch, in their New England farmhome. The bank holding John's deceased father's investment has failed, and Polly, who graduated in June from normal school, has failed to get a teaching job. But Polly perks up, volunteers to help on the farm, says she would rather do so than be a second-rate teacher anyway, milks their two cows, and will be "son and daughter both" to her parents. John admits he is $300 in debt and becomes so sick that Polly goes for the doctor a mile away. Jerry Minton, her next-door neighbor and former boyfriend, offers to accompany her but is rebuffed. The doctor tells Polly her father has a bad heart and must rest; when she tells the doctor she plans to make the farm yield a profit, he offers praise and a loan if need be. John's convalescence is slow; Polly does rough work well and happily; and Jerry, disappointed in a Portsmouth affair, grows friendly—but to no avail. In the winter, Polly reads the *Agriculturist* for farming hints. In April, she starts plowing a big area, which humbles her grateful father. Her summer potatoes are the first to hit the local market. She hires a strong boy to help garden. Her geese, bees, currants, and butter all succeed, although some of her hay is spoiled by wet weather. Girls from her normal school visit, help garden, and ultimately enjoy doing so. By Thanksgiving, the Finch family is out of debt. The doctor praises Polly eloquently for her energetic practicality. The growth in character of Farmer Finch matches her flourishing crops. And if she marries, it will be to a better man than Jerry, rightly spurned.

FEDGE. In *Betty Leicester*, she is the funny-voiced Tideshead choir director.

FELL, NANCY. In ''The Guests of Mrs. Timms,'' she is Miss Cynthia Picket's unmarried friend who still lives in Baxter, where she keeps house for her nephew. Cynthia suggests that she and Persis Flagg call on her; but Mrs. Flagg is reluctant until, rebuffed by Mrs. Timms, the two women do visit her and are hospitably welcomed.

FELLOWS, PAMELA (''PAMELY''). In ''Sister Peacham's Turn,'' she is the widowed Lydia Ann Peacham's older sister, described as ''round and easygoing.'' Pamela, also widowed, lost her husband at sea. When Pamela challenges Lydia Ann to prepare Thanksgiving Dinner for a change, she rises to the occasion, does so admirably, takes too much credit for the idea, but becomes less of a chronic complainer.

FENALD, JOSEPH. In *The Tory Lover*, he is an old Portsmouth sailor on the *Ranger*.

FENDERSON, CAPTAIN. In ''A Dark Night,'' he is a shipmaster to whom Weymouth delivers gold and bank notes in Bristol.

FERRIS. In ''A Neighbor's Landmark,'' he is the timber contractor who wants to buy John Packer's two landmark trees and sell the lumber from them in Boston. Neighbors do not like him, since he buys up farmers' mortgages and then takes their trees at his price. Packer tentatively agrees to sell but changes his mind, to his neighbors' delight. Jewett levels bitter criticism at Ferris and his sort, who viciously strip Mother Nature and leave her to suffer. *Bibliography*: Sherman.

FERRIS, DR. In *A Country Doctor*, he was Dr. John Leslie's college classmate, had an American naval appointment, and supervised Jack Prince when that young man was his assistant surgeon. Dr. Ferris has traveled and wandered widely, and visits Leslie briefly.

FERRY, LADY. In ''Lady Ferry,'' she is the eldritch lady, perhaps more than a century old. Tall, thin, bent, unaging, undrownable, variously garbed, she has a sweet smile and a high voice. Meeting her at the Haverford mansion, Marcia does not fear her, reads about wanderers who never die, and has a dream in which Lady Ferry appears. After years abroad, Marcia returns to the mansion and sees Lady Ferry's grave.

FIELDS, ANNIE ADAMS (1834–1915). Author and hostess. Born in Boston, she was educated at home and in the Boston school for young ladies run by George Barrell Emerson, a cousin of Ralph Waldo Emerson. There she learned to love English literature and committed to Christianity and Christian charitable causes. In 1854 she became the second wife of James T. Fields, the influential Boston publisher, then thirty-seven. (Fields's first wife had been Annie Adams's cousin.) Mrs. Fields established a salon at 148 Charles Street, where her guests over the years included Willa Cather,* Nathaniel Hawthorne, Henry James,* James Russell Lowell,* Harriet Beecher Stowe,* Celia Laighton Thaxter,* and John Greenleaf Whittier.* Annie Fields traveled extensively with her husband, after whose death in 1881 she continued as a hostess and began to welcome Jewett as a frequent guest. Jewett had already been made welcome by Annie and James Fields at their summer home at Manchester, Massachusetts. After Jewett spent the winter of 1881–1882 in Mrs. Fields's Boston home, the two women began to live together about half the time—usually during the winter months. They also took four trips to Europe together. In 1882 they went to Ireland, England, Norway, Belgium, France, Switzerland, and Italy. Jewett met Charles Reade, Alfred, Lord Tennyson,* William Makepeace Thackeray's daughter, and Charles Dickens's family—owing to James Fields's friendship with British authors. Jewett and Mrs. Fields went to England, Italy, and France (1892), meeting Mark Twain* and Marie Thérèse de Solms Blanc.* The two went to England and France (1898), visiting Henry James,* Rudyard Kipling,* and Mrs. Humphry Ward,* among others. Their final trip to Europe took them to Italy, Greece, and Turkey (1900). The two, with Thomas Bailey Aldrich* and his wife, Lilian, accompanied Henry L. Pierce, former Boston mayor, on his yacht on a Caribbean cruise (1896), and Jewett often spent the summer months with Annie Fields in Manchester. Annie Fields was older, petite, wealthy, urban, more classically oriented, and reserved. Jewett, sturdy and vivacious, was more enamored of rural New England and the outdoors. The two complemented and comforted one another well. They read to each other, discussed what they read, shared feelings generated by observations abroad, and wrote each other intimate letters when they were apart. Some commentators refer to such friendships as "Boston marriages." After Jewett's death, Annie Fields edited *Letters of Sarah Orne Jewett* (1911), a work weakened by the deletion—at the urging of their mutual friend, Mark Anthony DeWolfe Howe—of highly personal passages. Annie Fields's writings include *Authors and Friends* (1896), several books of verse, and also biographies of James T. Fields (1881), Whittier (1883), Mrs. Stowe (1897), and Hawthorne (1899). She also coedited Celia Thaxter's letters 1895). Her early involvement in Boston charities is reflected in her book, *How to Help the Poor* (1883). Several recent critics have speculated, on little overt evidence, that the relationship between Jewett and Annie Fields was lesbian in nature. *Bibliography*: Blanchard; Donovan; Lilian Faderman, *Surpassing the Love of Men: Romantic Friendship and Love between Women from the Renaissance to the Present* (New York: William Morrow, 1981); Mark Anthony DeWolfe Howe, *Memories of a Hostess: A Chronicle of Eminent Friendships Drawn Chiefly from the Diaries of Mrs. James T. Fields* (Boston: Atlantic Monthly Press, 1922); Judith A. Roman, *Annie Adams Fields: The Spirit of Charles Street* (Bloomington and Indianapolis: Indiana University Press, 1990).

FILMORE, GEORGE. In "A Visit Next Door," he and his wife live in Dundalk and are the parents of Dick Filmore and Nelly Filmore. George Filmore is indolent and therefore less successful than his neighbor, Henry Granger, a fact that has caused tension between the families. After Mary Granger persuades her mother, Mrs. Henry Granger, to invite the ailing Mrs. Filmore to visit the Granger home for a week, friendship between the families is renewed.

FILMORE, JACK. In "A Visit Next Door," he is the son of George Filmore and his wife and is Nelly Filmore's brother. In later life, Jack and his next-door neighbor, Dick Granger, prosper in business.

FILMORE, MRS. GEORGE. In "A Visit Next Door," she is the indolent George Filmore's wife and the mother of their children, Jack Filmore and Nelly Filmore. Once the ailing, resentful Mrs. Filmore is invited by Mrs. Henry Granger, her more prosperous next-door neighbor, to visit her for a week, the two families get along much better.

FILMORE, NELLY. In "A Visit Next Door," she is the daughter, fifteen, of George Filmore and his wife. She has a fine voice but no piano to practice on. Mary Granger, Nelly's friend next door, persuades her mother, Mrs. Henry Granger, to invite the ailing Mrs. Filmore to visit the Grangers for a week. Soon Nelly is invited to use the Granger piano. In addition, Mrs. Parley, the wife of Mr. Parley, the minister, agrees to give Nelly music lessons.

"A FINANCIAL FAILURE" (1890). (Full title: "A Financial Failure: The Story of a New England Wooing.") Short story. (Characters: Jacob Bean, Downs, Jonas Dyer, Jonas Dyer, Mrs. Dyer, Abel Foster, Hathaway, Hayland, Love Hayland, Mrs. Hayland, Jim Hymore, Pendell, Waters.) Jonas Dyer, twenty and from up country, works with Downs and Hathaway, both in their late twenties. The three all clerk under Pendell, the treasurer of the County Savings Bank in Dartford. Jonas, who got the job through the pull his rich uncle, also named Jonas Dyer, had with Pendell, is demeaned by the other clerks. In truth, Jonas would rather be back on the farm. Shortly after Thanksgiving, Joel Hayland, an Oak Hill farmer eight or nine miles out of town, makes a regular deposit in the bank. While Pendell is tending to the matter, Joel and Love Hayland, Joel's pretty daughter, nineteen, catch each other's eyes—and fancy. In February, Love again accompanies her father to town, asks Jonas to enter a deposit in her bank book, and tells him she is teaching school. In March, while Joel has Pendell handle money from a livestock sale, Love deposits $20 from her salary, which Jonas takes his sweet time recording. When Love asks him whether he has ever been to Oak Hill, her eavesdropping father invites the young man to visit them. Downs alarms Jonas by saying Love is being courted by a middle-aged widower named Waters. The following Sunday, Jonas hires a fine horse and rides through the mud to the Hayland farm. He stays for supper, and he and Love talk a long time in "the best room." Without telling his uncle he hopes to marry Love, Jonas gives his resignation to Pendell, who tells old Jonas that young Jonas, never cut out to do banking, likes Love Hayland. Old Jonas approves the union and gives the happy couple some start-up money. The marriage occurs "in early planting time," and the two agree that it was love at first sight for each.

FINCH, CAPTAIN. In *A Country Doctor*, he is Dr. John Leslie's friend. He gives Leslie a model ship he built. Finch later dies.

FINCH, JIM. In *A Country Doctor*, he is a man whose broken arm Dr. John Leslie set.

FINCH, JOHN. In "Farmer Finch," he is Mary Finch's unenergetic husband and Polly Finch's father. When he falls into debt and grows sick, Polly successfully runs the family farm.

FINCH, MARY. In "Farmer Finch," she is John Finch's old-fashioned wife and Polly Finch's mother.

FINCH, POLLY. In "Farmer Finch," she is the healthy, pretty daughter of John Finch and Mary Finch. She has recently graduated from a normal school. When she fails to obtain a teaching position, she is relieved and works the family farm successfully. She could marry Jerry Minton, a next-door neighbor, but rebuffs him. Polly's real first name is Mary. Polly is an example of an ideal woman to Jewett; she is educated, loves the outdoor life, and is indifferent to marriage. *Bibliography*: Roman.

FINN, PATRICK ("PAT"). In "Between Mass and Vespers," he is a bent little shoemaker. After mass he chats with friends, including Dennis Call, and hence misses a ride home with the Braley family.

FINNERTY, JOHN. In "Between Mass and Vespers," he is the head of a family swindled by Dan Nolan, who was John's pretty daughter Katy Finnerty's boyfriend.

FINNERTY, KATY. In "Between Mass and Vespers," she is the pretty daughter of John Finnerty and Mary Finnerty. Katy works in a mill and gave Dan Nolan, her swindling boyfriend, her savings. So did her parents.

FINNERTY, MARY. In "Between Mass and Vespers," she is John Finnerty's wife and Katy Finnerty's mother.

"THE FIRST SUNDAY IN JUNE" (1897). Short story. (Characters: General Barton, Harriet Barton, Mrs. Barton, Susan Barton, Miss Lydia Bent, Craddock, Mrs. Craddock, Dr. Joe Darley, Mrs. Darley, Danforth, Captain Hanway, Parker, Widow Parker, John Sanford, Mrs. Sanford.) Little old Miss Lydia Bent regularly and happily takes her solitary place in her family pew at the First Parish church in Dalton. Over time she has observed the steady dwindling of church attendance and figures Dr. Joe Darley, the minister of twenty years' standing, must be sad at this development. Miss Lydia, though timid, goes up and down Dalton's streets, toward the end of May, tactfully asking people to attend more faithfully. On the morning of the first Sunday in June, Dr. Darley dusts off an old sermon from a pile dated "1870 to 1880." But his invalid wife, in a moment of inspired frankness, urges him to put something into his "preaching box" for his parishioners to take out. The two walk to the church and are startled, as is Miss Lydia, who has arrived early, as usual, when a crowd enters. Joe puts aside the old sermon, tells his rapt audience that people often avoid church because of the minister; by his extemporaneous sermon he makes many feel he preached that day like an Apostle when "the Christian truth was new to him and all shining with light." Miss Lydia stands and joins the others in singing the last hymn.

FISHER. In "Law Lane," this is the name, according to Mrs. Harriet Powder, of some of her progressive forebears.

FISHER. In "A Pinch of Salt," this is the name of two or more of the little girls who are Hannah Dalton's pupils. They are described as "belles," just as their mother and aunt had been earlier.

FISHER, JIM. In "A Village Patriot," he is one of the six shinglers of the house owned by the Bostonian. Fisher complains that the Fourth of July was too hot a day for him to ride his bicycle.

FITCH, CAPT. ASA. In "Told in the Tavern," he is a retired sailor and "the honored leader" of cronies meeting in Timothy Hall's Byfleet tavern. During a gossip session about Abby Sands, Fitch praises her and also says Parkins, her fiancé, went to Arizona and might have been killed by Indians.

FITCH, JOE. In "Fame's Little Day," he is the New York City commission merchant and Draper's partner. Fitch buys a shipment of maple sugar from Abel Pinkham and tells him the *Herald* has reported Pinkham's arrival in town.

FITCH, MRS. In "Told in the Tavern," when the nine o'clock bell rings, Capt. Asa Fitch says he must go home to his wife.

FITZGIBBON. In "The Gray Mills of Farley," he is the owner of a large Farley boardinghouse. Mrs. Kilpatrick, Michel, and his family live in rooms there.

FLAGG, MRS. PERSIS. In "The Guests of Mrs. Timms," she is a well-to-do Woodville widow. Acting superior, she goes with her timid friend, Miss Cynthia Pickett, to Baxter to call on Mrs. Timms, who is a wealthy widow and who, both "guests" thought, was sincere when earlier she invited them to visit. She rebuffs them with scant hospitality. Reluctant at first to call on Cynthia's friend, Nancy Fell, while still in Baxter, Mrs. Flagg—as well as Cynthia—is welcomed graciously. The unusual name Persis may derive from that of Persis Lapham, wife of the hero of *The Rise of Silas Lapham* by William Dean Howells* (1885).

FLAHERTY, HONORA. In "Bold Words at the Bridge," she is the person the strange woman from Lawrence visited before returning to Ireland to care for her mother. Biddy Connelly had Flaherty cousins.

FLAHERTY, JOHN. In "Where's Nora?", he is Tom Flaherty's father. Patrick Quin knew John in Ireland years ago.

FLAHERTY, TOM. In "Where's Nora?", he is mentioned as recently having a leg amputated and dying.

FLANDERS, EPH. In "The Flight of Betsey Lane," he was Betsey Lane's uncle. While visiting the Centennial in Philadelphia, she fondly remembers his serving popcorn long ago.

FLANDERS, PAPPY. In "In Dark New England Days," he is a friend of Betsey Knowles and Hannah Knowles. He tells them that their father, Captain Knowles, came back from the dead and retrieved his hoard of gold coins and that Hannah was wrong to curse Enoch Holt for the deed.

FLEMING. In "Lady Ferry," he is an officer of her Majesty Queen Anne. Fleming swears to Thomas Highward that Fleming's father saw Mistress Honor Warburton in his youth.

FLEMING, HENRY. In "An Every-Day Girl," he is Mary Fleming's father, in his fifties. He dislikes his work in the shoe factory in Dolton. When he is laid off, he becomes ill, sells his house, and plans to move with his wife to a farm he and Mary's boyfriend, John Abbott, will buy. Curiously, the hero of Stephen Crane's *The Red Badge of Courage*, published three years after Jewett's "An Every-Day Girl," is also named Henry Fleming.

FLEMING, MARY. In "An Every-Day Girl," she is the daughter, eighteen, of Henry Fleming and his wife and is John Abbott's girlfriend. When Mary is advised by Aunt Hannah to worry less about a job than about doing well at whatever work is available, she is happy to quit thinking about becoming a schoolteacher. Her father's loss of his job motivates Mary to work in a summer hotel. She does so well at it that her boss, Mr. Dennis, plans to promote her. Mary modestly defines herself to John as "an every-day girl," which she is not. She and John will soon get married.

FLEMING, MRS. In "An Every-Day Girl," she is Henry Fleming's pleasant wife and Mary Fleming's mother. She is evidently the niece of Aunt Hannah.

FLETCHER. In "Between Mass and Vespers," he is a stable owner or stable worker. He lends Dennis Call the horse and buggy with which he drives Father Ryan into the woods to meet with Dan Nolan.

FLETCHER, ABBY. In "The Flight of Betsey Lane," she is a South Byfleet resident Betsey Lane happens to encounter at the Centennial in Philadelphia.

"THE FLIGHT OF BETSEY LANE" (1893). Short story. (Characters: Mrs. Bland, Peggy Bond, Mary Ann Chick, Decker, Lavina Dow, Dunster, Mrs. Fales, Eph Flanders, Abby Fletcher, George, Lane, Betsey Lane, Katy Strafford, General Thornton, Mrs. Thornton.) One May morning at the Byfleet Poor-house, three old women are in a shed picking over a bushel of cranberry beans. Peggy Bond, seventy-six, has "upsighted" vision; Lavina Dow, in her late eighties, is rheumatic and fat; and Betsey Lane, sixty-nine, has always been eager to travel but lacks money to do so. The three are the intellectual, social leaders of the fifteen or more varied and mostly lonesome poorhouse inmates. After chatting amiably, they are called to dinner. The men come in from corn planting. A visitor is announced. Katy Strafford wishes to see Betsey. Mrs. Strafford is the granddaughter of General Thornton, for whose family Betsey worked long ago; Katy, now living with her children in London, is visiting back home, speaks graciously with Betsey, and gratefully presses $100 on her. Eager to go to Philadelphia and see the Centennial there, Betsey one morning in June dresses in her best, sneaks out early, and makes her way to the railroad tracks near South Byfleet. She agrees to sew on some buttons for one of the amused, courteous workers and in return is given a ride to the Philadelphia-bound train. Another worker gives her the name of his uncle's widow to stay with. While people at the poorhouse wonder where she has disappeared, Betsey has a grand time at the exhibition. She takes in a thousand impressions and buys little presents for her friends back home. When she tries to find some glasses to improve Peggy's eyesight, which she describes in detail, a friendly eye specialist overhears her and promises to come soon to treat the woman, who he says must have cataracts. Nine days after Betsey's flight, Lavina and Peggy, at first annoyed but now worried, go to the Byfield pond, fearing Betsy got depressed and "hove" herself in. But she spryly walks up, tells where she has been, explains her source of funds, says she has $1.35 left, and announces that she has presents and even a specialist's promise to help Peggy in late July or early August. Betsey opines that "What's for the good o' one's for the good of all" and therefore her poorhouse companions will have a full narrative of her adventure. The three close friends walk back home together. Jewett's trip to the Philadelphia Centennial Exhibition of 1876 provided the basis for this story. *Bibliography*: Blanchard; Barbara A. Johns, " 'Mateless and Appealing': Growing into Spinsterhood in Sarah Orne Jewett," in Nagel, pp. 147–65.

FLOYD, NANCY. In "Marsh Rosemary." *See* Lane, Nancy ("Ann") Lloyd.

FOLSOM, MRS. In "The Green Bonnet," rumor has it that she and her sister, Mrs. Pease, both of Walsingham, will be wearing new spring bonnets on Easter Sunday.

FORBES, EDITH EMERSON (1841–1929). She was Ralph Waldo Emerson's second daughter. In 1865 she married William Hathaway Forbes, a valorous cavalry lieutenant colonel during the Civil War. The couple had eight children. Jewett enjoyed visiting the Forbeses on Naushon, an island off the Massachusetts coast owned by Forbes's father, John M. Forbes, the railroad builder, and voyaging along the New England coast on the Forbes family yacht. *Bibliography*: Carlos Baker, *Emerson among the Eccentrics: A Group Portrait* (New York: Viking, 1996).

FORD. In *The Tory Lover*, he is one of Arthur Lee's spies.

FORDER, MRS. In "In Dark New England Days," she is Martha Downs's close friend. They occasionally talk about the late Captain Knowles and his daughters, Betsey Knowles and Hannah Knowles, and about the curse Hannah put on Enoch Holt.

"THE FOREIGNER" (1900). Short story. (Characters: the Reverend Mr. Bascom, Mrs. Beggs, Captain Blackett, Mrs. Blackett, William Blackett, Alick Bowden, Captain Jonathan Bowden, Captain Lorenzo Bowden, Johnny Bowden, Mrs. Jonathan Bowden, Caplin, Deacon Caplin, Mari' Harris, Captain Littlepage, Squire Pease, Elijah Tilley, Almira Todd, Tolland, Captain John Tolland, Eliza Tolland, Ellen Tolland, Mrs. Tolland, Mrs. John Tolland.) One dark late August night during a fierce storm, with lashing winds and roaring seas, Almira

Todd tells the captivated narrator about Captain John Tolland's foreign wife. Thirty or forty years ago, Tolland and three other sea captains, including Mrs. Todd's father, were in Jamaica. They had taken pine lumber there and were loading sugar in Kingston for New England. While they were carousing one night, they heard music from a tavern across the street. Going over, they saw a French woman dancing, playing a guitar, and singing. When some impolite men began teasing her, the four Americans escorted her away and learned she was recently widowed in the French islands, had no immediate family back home, and had recently been robbed. Tolland gave her safe passage to Portland, stepped ashore with her, married her, and returned with her to the Dunnet Landing home he owned with his sister, Eliza Tolland. She and the captain's foreign bride did not get along; so he bought out Eliza, who moved away. The townspeople declined to welcome Mrs. Tolland, whose foreign language and Catholic religion were both strange. One day she was invited to a sociable gathering in the villagers' church vestry but upset the others by suddenly singing and dancing to a rhythmic tune. Only Mrs. Blackett, Mrs. Todd's sympathetic mother, defended the foreigner. Even Mrs. Todd herself, though encouraged by her mother, was slow to offer friendship. When Mrs. Todd's uncle, Captain Lorenzo Bowden, got word that Tolland and his ship had been lost at sea, he and Mrs. Todd broke the news to his widow. The distraught woman went into a decline and within a few months was on her deathbed. Mrs. Blackett sent upriver for a Catholic priest, whose sudden presence moved Mrs. Tolland to ecstasy and who gave her extreme unction. Mrs. Todd and a woman named Mrs. Begg sat watching over the lonely woman. After her death, Mrs. Todd learned that she had been willed Mrs. Tolland's moderate estate. Rumor had it John Tolland might have secreted more money in a sea "chist" in the house; Lorenzo searched for it repeatedly but in vain and one night carelessly left a fire within, which caused the deserted place and its remaining contents—including the woman's guitar—to be destroyed. Coming to the climax of her story, Mrs. Todd tells the narrator that when Mrs. Tolland lay breathing her last, the night was stormy too, just like tonight. The wind even rushed in and made the guitar, hanging on a wall upstairs, start to play. Mrs. Todd was watching and nodding when there appeared in the dark doorway an apparition, shorter than Mrs. Begg, who was napping in another room. Mrs. Tolland recognized it as her mother and, as she lay dying, asked if Mrs. Todd saw it too. Having seen the resemblance between daughter and mother, Mrs. Todd answered, "Yes, dear, I did; you ain't never goin' to feel strange an' lonesome no more." As the storm ends, Mrs. Todd offers the narrator these conclusions: Something of us lives on, we must join two worlds, and we must live in one world only for the other.

Jewett may have been inspired to write "The Foreigner" by knowing her friend, Celia Laighton Thaxter,* after her beloved mother's death held seances to speak with her and, according to her brother, was visited by her when Celia lay dying in 1894. "The Foreigner" is a complex story within a story, each with an outer storm paralleling emotional upheavals. A rumor expressed toward the beginning, that during a storm the devil comes "for his own," is reversed, as the foreigner's mother comes for her child. The narrator fears the story will "haunt my thoughts" but gains beneficent advice. Thus she is akin to the foreigner and is soothed at last by maternal Almira. "The Foreigner," along with "A Dunnet Shepherdess," "The Queen's Twin," and "William's Wedding," continues the story of *The Country of the Pointed Firs*. *Bibliography*: Blanchard; Joseph Church, "Absent Mothers and Anxious Daughters: Facing Ambivalence in Jewett's 'The Foreigner,' " *Essays in Literature* 17 (Spring 1990): 52–68; Marjorie Pryse, "Women 'at Sea': Feminist Realism in Sarah Orne Jewett's 'The Foreigner,' " *American Literary Realism* 15 (1982): 244–52; Sherman; Rosamond Thaxter, *Sandpiper: The Life of Celia Thaxter* (Sanbornville, N.H.: Wake-Brook House, 1962).

FOREST, GEORGE. In "A Lost Lover," he is Nelly Dane's fiancé. He is a navy sailor on a three-year tour of duty to China and Japan.

FORRESTER, JUDGE. In "Peg's Little Chair," he praises Margaret Benning for the fine quality of her public house.

FOSDICK, SUSAN. In *The Country of the Pointed Firs*, she is Almira Todd's old friend. She is a little old woman from Thomaston or near it. All of her eight siblings and many of her children are now dead. In her youth she went to sea with her father, a seaman. She visits Almira, and the two reminisce joyfully.

FOSS. In "The Honey Tree," he is an old sea captain and is now the conversation leader at Joel Simmons's store in Hillborough.

FOSS. In "A Neighbor's Landmark," he is a person on whose "lot" Ferris tells John Packer he will be working next week.

FOSS, JIM. In *Betty Leicester*, he owns a mowing machine being shipped on the Riverport-to-Tideshead packet.

FOSS, JOHNNY. In "Aunt Cynthy Dallett," he is a lad who does chores for Cynthy Dallett. It is likely that the name Ross, used once in the story, is a misprint for Foss, used twice.

FOSS, MRS. In "The Honey Tree," she accompanied her sea-captain husband on some of his voyages. They liked honey aboard ship.

FOSS, MRS. JERRY. In "The Courting of Sister Wisby," she was, according to Mrs. Goodsoe's poignant account, the widowed mother of three children, all of whom died of scarlet fever in a single week. Inconsolable, she turned to marble and only shook her head when spoken to—until Jim Heron came near and played a miraculously soothing tune on his fiddle. Mrs. Foss then sought saving comfort in the arms of Mrs. Goodsoe's compassionate mother.

FOSTER. In *Betty Leicester*, he is the father of Henry Foster and Nelly Foster, was jailed for defrauding friends, injures himself escaping, and dies.

FOSTER. In "Little French Mary," he is a farmer whose hay cart Alexis borrows when he moves out of Dulham to return to Canada.

FOSTER, ABEL. In "A Financial Failure," he is mentioned by Joel Hayland as a friend he recently saw.

FOSTER, ENOCH. In "A Landless Farmer," he is a person who according to Serena Nudd, felt Ezra Allen was "put out" because her husband, Aaron Nudd, defeated Ezra in the election for selectman.

FOSTER, HENRY ("HARRY"). In *Betty Leicester*, he is Betty Leicester's friend, seventeen and interested in naturalistic studies. Thomas Leicester, her father, will help with his education. In *Betty Leicester's English Xmas*, Betty remembers him fondly.

FOSTER, JOHN. In "The Parshley Celebration," he is a storekeeper in Parshley. He brings flags and participates in the Decoration Day parade.

FOSTER, MRS. In *Betty Leicester*, she is the sad wife of Foster, the escaped convict. Barbara Leicester hires her to sew.

FOSTER, MRS. In "The Parshley Celebration," she is John Foster's wife. She walks behind him after they leave church.

FOSTER, NELLY. In *Betty Leicester*, she is Betty Leicester's friend. The two discover Mary's father, mortally injured after escaping from jail.

FOXWELL. In "A Landless Farmer," this is the family name of some children Jerry Jenkins handled trust money for, until Aaron Nudd and Serena Nudd, out of greed, persuaded him to let them do so.

FRALEY, ALBERT. In "The Only Rose," he was Mrs. Bickford's first husband. The two married for love when young. He was handsome, hearty, and friendly, loved his mother, sang well, had a temper, died of fever young, and left their farm encumbered with debts. He is Mrs. Bickford's choice to receive "the only rose" on his grave.

FRALEY, EUNICE. In *A Country Doctor*, she is an unmarried Dunport woman, almost sixty, who lives with her domineering mother and is Nancy Prince's confidante. Eunice loved a young sailor of whom others disapproved and who died of fever in Key West. She offers timid moral support to Nan Prince in the girl's determination to become a doctor.

FRALEY, MRS. In *A Country Doctor*, she is Eunice Fraley's mother and is a conservative, opinionated Dunport society leader. She knew and liked Nan Prince's father and knows Nancy Prince. Mrs. Fraley irately rebukes Nancy's niece, Nan Prince, for wishing to become a doctor.

FRAME. In *Betty Leicester's English Xmas*, he is one of Lady Mary Danesley's guests. He sings with Lady Dimdale at the pageant.

FRANKFORT, JOHN. In "The King of Folly Island," he is a city banker and investor, who vacations briefly on Folly Island in the farmhome of George Quint and his daughter, Phebe Quint. Frankfort soon realizes he has been just as selfish and grasping as George, misses the chance to befriend sick Phebe, and learns almost too late from her self-sacrificial life to be more generous. It has been noted that his name suggests he is walled in by currency. *Bibliography*: Roman.

FRANKFORT, PHOEBE. In "The King of Folly Island," this is the name of John Frankfort's deceased mother, whose book of William Wordsworth's short poems he treasures.

FRANKLIN, BENJAMIN (1706–1790). American diplomat, inventor, and statesman. In *The Tory Lover*, Captain John Paul Jones and Roger Wallingford, whose mother Franklin knew, confer with Franklin in Passy. He is sorry he cannot secure *L'Indien* for Jones to command. Franklin is described as a canny listener.

FRENCH, ANN. (Full name: Ann Ball French.) In "The Taking of Captain Ball," she is Captain Asaph Ball's grand-niece. When his sister, Ann Ball (for whom Ann Ball French was named) dies, the younger Ann, married to a man named French who soon died, obtains the position of Ball's housekeeper, as Mrs. French from Massachusetts. Making herself needed and ultimately liked by Ball, she remains.

FRENCH, ELDER. In "The Passing of Sister Barsett," he is a churchman whose manner of preaching Mercy Crane and Sarah Ellen Dow criticize.

FRENCH, LIZZIE. In *Betty Leicester*, she is a Sin Book Club member.

FRENCH MARY. In "Little French Mary," she is the daughter, about six, of Alexis and Marie. Work brings Alexis to Dulham, where French Mary's timid courtesy charms a group of old men. They miss her when she returns to Canada with her parents.

"FROM A MOURNFUL VILLAGER" (1881). Essay. (Character: Henry Currier.) Jewett laments the "extinction of front yards." Old English customs are dying out as Western ways sweep New England. Village life was once more pleasant. Women were more confined at home and therefore controlled their front-yard gardens as "pleasure grounds" where they planted "slips and cuttings" brought from England. The absence of fences makes yard activities too visible now, and we miss their former reserve and sanctity: "[W]e Americans had better build more fences than take any away from our lives." Jewett likes dandelions, French pinks, lavender, lilacs, and poplars, but dislikes lemon verbena. Railroad travel brings visitors from afar, but neighbors therefore visit less often. She remembers being a favored guest of old ladies, including her proud, solemn (paternal step-) grandmother [Mary Ricc Jewett*], from whose tea-rose bush she thoughtlessly plucked a tender bud. When five, Jewett was terrified by news of the old woman's death but enjoyed participating in the ensuing "grand public" funeral. Jewett here voices her clear preference for past over present. *Bibliography*: Cary, *Jewett*; Sherman; Silverthorne.

FRY, ELDER. In "The Quest of Mr. Teaby," he is a churchman, thrice married and widowered, to whom Sister Hannah Jane Pinkham says she is "kind o' half promised." However, his voice has given out because of shouting. His ambition to enter the butter business is offputting for her; so she now inclines toward Teaby.

FULHAM, MRS. EBEN. In "Aunt Cynthy Dallett," she was a woman living near Staples's Corner to whom Mrs. Hand paid a surprise visit one summer. Delighted, Mrs. Fulham prepared a pleasant tea. She died that fall.

G

GAFFETT. In *The Country of the Pointed Firs*, he is a Scottish sailor marooned with Moravians close to the North Pole while on a voyage of discovery. This, according to Captain Littlepage, who later bunked with Gaffett and heard and believed his account of seeing a foggy town of ghostly people evidently waiting between this world and the next.

GAINES, ADELINE ("ADDIE"). In "A Born Farmer," she is Jacob Gaines's wife and the mother of Jacob Gaines and Mary Ellen Gaines. Adeline thinks she dislikes life on the farm but only until she moves with her family to Boston when her brother persuades Jacob to invest in his lumber business. Once in the big city, she grows depressed and sick and is happy to return home.

GAINES, JACOB. In "A Born Farmer," he is Adeline Gaines's husband, forty-nine, and the father of Jacob ("Jakey") Gaines and Mary Ellen Gaines. They work on their farm in Pine Hill, near Upton Corners. When Jacob inherits $50,000 from Nat, his cousin, he is persuaded to invest in the lumber business of Adeline's brother in Boston. The Gaines family moves there; all but Jakey, however, are soon discontent and happily return home. A potato distributor in the Boston market sizes up Jacob as "a born farmer."

GAINES, JACOB ("JAKEY"). In "A Born Farmer," he is the son, eighteen, of Jacob Gaines and Adeline Gaines. When the family moves to Boston, only Jakey likes the city. He will flourish there in his uncle's lumber business, in which his father invested.

GAINES, MARY ELLEN. In "A Born Farmer," she is the young daughter of Jacob Gaines and Adeline Gaines. She moves with her family from their farm to Boston but is soon discontent. Once back home, she begins to like John Ray, a neighbor lad.

GAINES, MISS DEBBY. In "An Empty Purse," she is a New England seamstress, who, having lost her Christmas money, visits various persons to bestow the gift of personal kindness and good feeling.

GALE. In "The Life of Nancy," he is Nancy Gale's rugged father. He and his family live on their farm in East Rodney, Maine. He tells Tom Aldis she is crippled by rheumatism.

GALE, ASA. In "The Life of Nancy," he is Nancy Gale's brother. While in Boston, she buys him a biography of Napoleon.

GALE, MRS. In "The Life of Nancy," she is Nancy's mother. Tom Aldis vacationed briefly one summer at their home in East Rodney.

GALE, NANCY. In "The Life of Nancy," she is a member of the Gale family of East Rodney, Maine. She met Tom Aldis at a dance while he was vacationing there from Boston. It is thought that her Spanish grandmother must have provided her with dancing genes, so light are the girl's movements. Nancy meets Tom again by chance in Boston, while accompanying Ezra, her uncle, when he delivers farm produce to the Boston market. Tom escorts Nancy around Boston, takes her to Papanti's dancing school to watch some lessons there, and introduces her to his aunt, Mrs. Annesley. Severe rheumatism ends Nancy's career as a teacher and renders her sedentary, after which in her parents' home she coaches dancing etiquette, tutors bright students, and helps slow ones. Seventeen or so years later when Tom revisits East Rodney and calls on Nancy, she inspires him by her selfless courage.

GALE, SAM. In "The Life of Nancy," he is Nancy Gale's brother. While in Boston, she buys him a book about birds.

GALES. In "The Two Browns," he is a witty lawyer who often lunches with John Benedict Brown. Fortuitously, Gales is away during Brown's assumption of his second identity, that of John B. Brown.

"A GARDEN STORY" (1886). Short story. (Characters: Miss Ann Dunning, Miss Farley, Sister Helen, Peggy McAllister, Mike O'Brien, Mrs. West.) Each August, Miss Ann Dunning, a Littletown dressmaker, protects her garden of lilies, marigolds, mist plants, poppies, petunias, sweet peas, and zinnias against frost soon to come. She lets her gardener, Mike O'Brien, cultivate beans and potatoes but not flowers. She generously provides blooms for church, weddings, and funerals. One June she asks to accept a little girl from Boston for a "country week." Mrs. West sends Peggy McAllister, a sweet little orphan, nine, who has been staying at a hospital on Blank Street. Sister Helen is sorry to see her go. Miss Dunning and Peggy take to each other at once. Peggy persuades her not to thin her seedlings but to nurture them and send the blooms to the hospital. Miss Dunning soon arranges to keep the delighted Peggy on a permanent basis.

GARDNER. In *The Tory Lover*, he is Captain John Paul Jones's steersman when they are in port at Quiberon.

GARROW. In "Jenny Garrow's Lovers," he is Jenny Garrow's father. He is a farmer and has no other children.

GARROW, JENNY ("JEN"). In "Jenny Garrow's Lovers," she is the beautiful, innocent, and naive heroine. Her delayed preference for Richard Tyler instead of William Tyler, his brother, causes William to go to sea for five years. This results in Richard's conviction on charges of murdering William. Jenny dies of fever before the truth is revealed.

GENERAL ____. In "A Christmas Guest," he is the "Christmas Guest" who suddenly enters the home of the sick Mrs. Norris and Rebecca, her little granddaughter, during a snowstorm on Christmas Eve. He is an old soldier on his way to Washington during "the war." While Mrs. Norris sleeps, Rebecca gives the stranger food and the use of her little bed. Leaving $10 and his card with a message of gratitude, General ____ departs at dawn. After the war he, his wife, and their daughter visit Rebecca and Mrs. Norris. A quotation from Matthew 25:35, about a stranger being welcomed, and suggestions of "no room at the inn" make both Rebecca and General ____ biblical-story Christian figures, albeit enigmatically cast here.

GEORGE. In "The Flight of Betsy Lane," he is the sea captain son of an acquaintance of Lavina Dow, who recalls that George's mother sailed with him to Callao. The mother would have voyaged longer but for being kicked by a cow.

GEORGE, DR. In "The Girl with the Cannon Dresses," he is the physician who tells Alice Channing's parents she ought to recuperate from a mild illness by spending the summer with Sophronia Durfee and her husband.

GEORGIE. In *Betty Leicester*, he is a Riverport boy whose mother briefly fears that he and Ida, his sister, are lost.

GERRY, DR. In "A Christmas Guest," he is the local physician who calls on Mrs. Norris and leaves a sleeping powder for her.

GERRY, GEORGE. In *A Country Doctor*, he was George Gerry's father, of whom, according to Walter Parish, Nancy Prince was fond.

GERRY, GEORGE. In *A Country Doctor*, he is a Dunport lawyer, aided in his education and profession by Nancy Prince. He is discontent in Dunport but lacks ambition to move elsewhere. George, twenty-six, likes Mary Parish, until Nan Prince visits Nancy, her aunt. He falls in love with Nan, proposes to her, but is rejected, because Nan, though loving him, intends to be a doctor and remain single. George will probably wed Mary. George Gerry is typical of several supercilious young men in Jewett's fiction who, though possessed of little talent and strength of character, think they should dominate women. George Gerry is meant to be regarded as a stick figure, whose passion Jewett cannot convey to the reader and whose very name delimits him. *Bibliography*: Cary, *Jewett*; Renza; Roman.

GERRY, MRS. GEORGE. In *A Country Doctor*, she is young George Gerry's feeble, dull, widowed mother. She tells Nancy Prince that Hattie Barlow is going to get married.

GERRY, SUSANNAH. In "Jenny Garrow's Lovers," she is a friend from Tarrow who tells Margery Blake that William Tyler has disappeared.

GIFFORD, MARY LIZZIE. In "The Only Rose," she is the fiancée of John Parsons, the nephew of Mrs. Bickford, who likes her and will help the two when they marry.

GILBRAITH. In *The Country of the Pointed Firs*, he is an old man who attends the Bowen reunion with his sister. Almira Todd notes their disappointment at not being seated "among folks they can parley with."

GILMAN, NICHOLAS. Jewett's great-great-grandfather; he was a colonel during the American Revolution, and also a New Hampshire politician, a continental loan officer, and a receiver general. He had three sons: John Taylor Gilman, governor of New Hampshire; Nicholas Gilman, delegate to the second constitutional convention, member of the staff of George Washington,* and congressman; and Nathaniel Gilman, New Hampshire politician, father-in-law of William Perry,* and grandfather of Caroline Frances Perry Jewett* (Sarah's mother). Hence, Jewett had numerous Gilman relatives and visited them in Exeter and elsewhere. In *The Tory Lover*, Jewett introduces Nicholas Gilman as an Exeter man Sam Adams asked for money to support the troops; Gilman is Major John Langdon's friend. *Bibliography*: Blanchard; Richard Cary, "Jewett's

Cousins Charles and Charlie," *Colby Library Quarterly* 5 (September 1959): 48–58; Cary, "Jewett and the Gilman Women," *Colby Library Quarterly* 5 (March 1960): 94–103.

"THE GIRL WITH THE CANNON DRESSES" (1870). Short story. (Characters: Dulcidora Bunt, Jacob Bunt, Mrs. Bunt, Samuel Bunt, Channing, Alice Channing, Mrs. Channing, Durfee, Sophronia Durfee, Dr. George, Joe, Mrs. Thomson.) Alice Channing, seventeen, is the narrator. She is ill in March and better in May; but she is delighted when Dr. George, the family physician, persuades her parents to let her leave their home in Halifax for a summer with Sophronia Durfee, their former housekeeper, now retired with her husband on their farm. Sophronia escorts Alice by "cars and stages" for three or four days to the Durfee place two miles from the Corners. One day while Alice is reading and napping by a spring a mile or two away, Dulcidora ("Dulcy") Bunt suddenly appears. Dulcy, a little tomboy, nine, says she lives with her mother and her father, Samuel Bunt, a retired sailor, on a farm near the Durfees. She is wearing one of several dresses her mother made of material from a bolt of calico with a pattern of cannons on wheels and "Union" spelled out in big letters. During the summer, Dulcy and Alice become fast friends. They hike and picnic together, and Dulcy's mother is delighted when Alice tutors Dulcy a little. Two years later, Dulcy is attending classes at a country academy, and Alice, who occasionally sends her some reading material, treasures memories of that summer and also a tintype of Dulcy in a cannon dress. Horace Scudder,* as editor of the *Riverside Magazine*, accepted "The Girl with the Cannon Dresses." Earning $36, it was the first story signed "Sarah Jewett." Jewett later wrote Scudder (13 July 1873) that " 'Cannon Dresses' . . . is the dearest and best thing I have ever written." *Bibliography*: Fields, *Letters*.

GODDARD, MRS. In "The Green Bowl," she is one of the people listening to the story told by Katie Montague. It may be in this pleasant woman's home that the storytelling takes place.

GOFFEY. In "Fame's Little Day," he is the reporter for the New York *Herald* who embellishes on the *Tribune* report concerning Abel Pinkham and his wife, Mary Ann Pinkham, by saying the Pinkhams are going to Barnum's circus. Though aware of the fib, the Pinkhams do go and enjoy themselves.

"GOING TO SHREWSBURY" (1889). Short story. (Characters: Barnes, Isabella, Isaiah Peet, Josh Peet, Mrs. Peet, Mrs. Wayland, Mrs. Winn.) The narrator sees Mrs. Peet, widowed and childless, on the train. She has been cheated out of her farm by her nephew, Isaiah Peet, and is going with a little bundle of possessions to Shrewsbury to live with Isabella, who is the daughter of Mrs. Peet's sister, Mrs. Wayland, and who is comfortably married. The independent old woman, seventy-six, hopes to be useful there. To the sympathetic narrator, she explains her circumstances: Her husband, never "forehanded," paid off debts to everyone but Isaiah, who then seized the property, including "[t]he rain-blackened little house." Mrs. Peet refuses to be "demeaned" by staying on with him. In the spring, the narrator learns that Mrs. Peet enjoyed winter concerts and lectures in Shrewsbury and that her four nieces, the daughters of her sister, Mrs. Winn, in Shrewsbury, had thoughts of buying back Mrs. Peet's farm and staying there with her. But Mrs. Peet preferred life in Shrewsbury and has just died. Jewett's two main points here, made elsewhere as well, are that men can easily victimize women and that a country woman cannot enjoy city life for very long. *Bibliography*: Cary, *Jewett*; Roman.

GOOD'IN, DEACON JACK. In "In Dark New England Days," he is a man Hannah Knowles's father, Captain Knowles, prevented her from marrying. Martha Downs later says Knowles was right to do so.

"GOOD LUCK" (1879). (Full title: "Good Luck: A Girl's Story.") Short story. (Characters: Alice, Mrs. Anderson, Ashurst, Birney, Annie Birney, Mrs. Birney, Nelly Denis, Kinlock, Kate Lancaster, Mary Leslie, Mrs. Leslie, Parkhurst Leslie, Tom Leslie, Nancy, Mrs. Phillips.) The family of Polly Leslie, the narrator, has had financial reverses in Boston. So her mother, Mrs. Leslie, rents their house and will spend the summer in the country place inherited from Kinlock, her late husband's granduncle, which is four miles outside Hilton, New Hampshire. In June, Polly and Tom Leslie, her younger brother, go there to clean up the old square house, which they call Windywalls, and which, according to rumor, has a secret chamber with money left in it by old Kinlock. Tom and Polly start to tidy the place and soon welcome their mother and Parkhurst ("Park") Leslie, their older brother. One day, while Mrs. Leslie, Park, and Mr. Ashurst, the local clergyman, are in the village, Tom and Polly prepare for Aunt Alice's arrival by cleaning the fireplace in a spare bedroom. They discover a hidden den between the back of the fireplace and the loose wall of a closet in another room. They must delay further exploration because of the return of Park and their mother, both of whom next morning they send on errands back to the village. In the secret room, Tom and Polly find a desk, books and papers, out-of-date bank notes, old letters, and a few hundred dollars in old coins. When Mrs. Leslie and Park return, they show them the den. But Mrs. Leslie offers even better news: By letter she has just learned that Mrs. Anderson, her mother's old friend in Baltimore, has died and willed Mrs. Leslie a large sum of money. "Good Luck" is one of Jewett's poorest stories. The relationship of the Leslies to their country neighbors the Birneys is undeveloped. Nancy, the Leslies's servant, and Ashurst, a visiting minister, are merely hinted at. Parkhurst remains shadowy. And Jewett digresses to inveigh against Annie's impractical seminary instruction.

GOODSOE. In *A Country Doctor*, he was a sailor who knew Captain Jack Prince, the grandfather of Nan Prince. Goodsoe is now keeper of a vessel damaged and docked at Dunport and chats with Captain Walter Parish.

GOODSOE. In "A Native of Winby," this is the name of a Winby family whose features Joseph K. Laneway recognizes in one of Marilla Hender's pupils.

GOODSOE, MRS. In "Andrew's Fortune," she is one of Stephen Dennett's neighbors. She is "a dismal, grasping soul," disliked by some of the other women.

GOODSOE, MRS. In *A Country Doctor*, she is the plain wife of the keeper of the damaged vessel.

GOODSOE, MRS. In "The Courting of Sister Wisby," she is the narrator's friend. When the two meet in a pasture, Mrs. Goodsoe tells several stories concerning old neighbors. The two best are about Mrs. Jerry Foss and about Eliza Wisby and Silas Brimblecom. Mrs. Goodsoe has inherited "the second sight" from her maternal Scotch-Irish forebears. She prefers the old ways and deplores changes occasioned by the railroad and the telegraph. An environmental regionalist, she is a gifted herbalist even while modestly saying her mother was a more expert one. Mrs. Goodsoe prefigures Almira Todd of *The Country of the Pointed Firs*. *Bibliography*: Blanchard.

GOODWIN, GENERAL. In *The Tory Lover*, the maids at Colonel Jonathan Hamilton's house can look out and see General Goodwin's beautiful elm trees.

GOODWIN, HETTY. In *The Tory Lover*, she is the mother of Madam Wallingford's cousin, Mrs. John Davis. Her maiden name was Plaisted. She was kidnapped and taken to Canada by Indians, who killed one of her many children before her very eyes.

GORSMANTOWN, LORD. In *The Tory Lover*, he was a well-dressed aristocrat whom the teacher Sullivan remembers seeing in Dublin.

GRAFTON, DR. In "In a Country Practice," he is a student Dr. Best describes as adequate, as are Dr. Duncan and Dr. Smith, to take up a country practice.

GRAHAM. In *A Country Doctor*, he was the husband of Dr. John Leslie's now-widowed friend and said Leslie "thought twice for everybody else's once."

GRAHAM, MRS. In *A Country Doctor*, she is Dr. John Leslie's widowed, lame neighbor across the street. He often visits her in her nice house. She tries to influence Nan Prince toward conventional feminine domesticity but succeeds only in improving her taste in reading. *Bibliography*: Sherman.

GRANDISON. In "The Two Browns," he is John Benedict Brown's neighbor, knew and respected Brown's lawyer father and lawyer grandfather, and admires Brown's seeming ambition as a lawyer. Grandison is a successful old inventor, whose steam-harrow patent Checkley has probably infringed in devising his own electric potato planter, which Checkley and Brown are profitably marketing. They accept Grandison's offer to buy them out. Grandison never knows that John Benedict Brown is also John B. Brown.

GRANGER, DICK. In "A Visit Next Door," he is the son of Henry Granger and Mrs. Granger and is Mary Granger's brother. In later life, Dick and his next-door neighbor, Jack Filmore, prosper in business.

GRANGER, HENRY. In "A Visit Next Door," he and his wife, who live in Dundalk, are the parents of Dick Granger and Mary Granger. Henry is a successful businessman in Dundalk. He and his neighbor, the indolent George Filmore, are estranged but will become more friendly again after Mrs. Granger invites the ailing Mrs. Filmore to vacation at the Grangers's home for a week.

GRANGER, MARY. In "A Visit Next Door," she is the daughter, fifteen, of Henry Granger and his wife. She practices on her own piano but has little musical talent. Nelly Filmore, her neighbor and friend, also fifteen, sings beautifully but lacks a piano and will benefit from practice. Mary Granger persuades her mother, Mrs. Henry Granger, to invite Nelly's mother, the ailing Mrs. George Filmore, to visit in their home for a week. This reinvigorates the two families' weakened friendship.

GRANGER, MRS. In "A Visit Next Door," she is Henry Granger's wife and the mother of Dick Granger and Mary Granger. The relative success of the Granger family, in comparison to that of their neighbor George Filmore and his family, causes unfriendliness until Mrs. Granger persuades Mrs. Filmore to visit her for a week.

GRANT. In *The Tory Lover*, he is a rather stupid *Ranger* sailor.

GRANT, ELLEN. In *Betty Leicester*, she and her sister, Mary Grant, are the Tideshead minister's daughters. They are Sin Book Club members.

GRANT, JOHN. In "A Village Shop," he is a wealthy farmer and a village selectman, widowed a dozen years. He persuades Esther Jaffrey to provide room and board for his young daughter, Nelly Grant, to improve the girl in general ways. He heads the delegation offering Esther's brother, Leonard Jaffrey, the position of town librarian.

GRANT, MARY. In *Betty Leicester*, she and her sister, Ellen Grant, are the Tideshead minister's daughters and are Sin Book Club members.

GRANT, MR. In *Betty Leicester*, he is the Tideshead minister. He is delighted when Betty Leicester and Mary Beck ask him to explain a parable.

GRANT, MRS. In *Betty Leicester*, she is the Tideshead minister's wife. She worries about providing tea for too many children at one time.

GRANT, NELLY. In "A Village Shop," she is the teen-aged daughter of John Grant, a well-to-do widower. Soon after she begins rooming and boarding with Esther Jaffrey, she falls in love with her brother, Leonard Jaffrey, who tutors her in Latin and philosophy. Ill suited though the two are, they will get married, probably in part because her father excessively admires the tradition of the old Jaffrey family.

GRANT, THANKFUL. In *The Tory Lover*, she is mentioned by Elizabeth Wyat as a weeping maid.

GRAY. In *The Tory Lover*, he is mentioned by Judge Chadbourne as a Loyalist who defected to London's high society.

"THE GRAY MAN" (1886). Short story. (Characters: none named). Legend has it that a certain decaying farmhouse is haunted. One day a gray-looking stranger strides through the town and lights the place that evening, soon buys provisions in town, is friendly, and offers valuable advice concerning crops, household chores, and rearing children. But he is soon regarded with suspicion—he never smiles. He grows unwelcome. One winter evening he is ordered to leave a wedding, and by summer he is an outcast. He grows his own food and for companionship has only tamed birds and a few books. A stray hunter once saw an empty chair glide toward him as he silently read by his fire. When "the war of the rebellion" begins, a wounded lad sees the gray man on a tall horse. He is death, teaching and serving us and waiting to be our friend. The gray man's spoiling a wedding recalls Nathaniel Hawthorne's "The Minister's Black Veil," and so does Jewett's parable style here. *Bibliography*: Cary, *Jewett*.

"THE GRAY MILLS OF FARLEY" (1898). Short story. (Characters: Ahern, Mike Callahan, Ellen Carroll, Mike Carroll, Mary Cassidy, Con, Father Daley, Dan, Henry Dow, James Dow, Duffy, Fitzgibbon, Mrs. Kilpatrick, Maggie, Michel, Mary Moynahan, Mrs. Mullin, Sullivan.) The mills of Farley, a grim-

looking village by the river, and the crowded houses of the mill workers are
congested together. In late autumn the Corporation, against the advice of Dan,
the unselfish agent of the mills, declares a 9 percent dividend for the stock-
holders. This causes the mill's stock to rise, prompting a sell-off and the closing
of the mills until orders accumulate. The English, Irish, and "Canadian-French"
workers begin to suffer. Mrs. Kilpatrick, a mill sweeper, takes Maggie, a little
orphan, to her room at the Fitzgibbon house. A rich director gives the child a
50-cent piece. A few French-Canadians agitate, but then many leave town. Jewett says it is the same old story of capital versus labor. Mrs. Kilpatrick phrases
it thus: " 'Tis a worrld where some has and more wants." When the bitter
winter ends, Dan, whose salary continues, gives the survivors seed potatoes from
his garden for spring planting and even money from his personal savings to
help the neediest workers and their families. Some people get temporary farm
work and jobs repairing the mills. In August, though still "sadly idle," several
workers spend some money patronizing a traveling show "for a little cheerful-
ness." The Duffy family is near death because of fever caused by bad plumbing,
inadequately repaired. One warm September day, Dan and Father Daley, the
compassionate local priest, are discussing money, charity, and old- and new-
fashioned religion, when word comes that the mills will reopen. Two weeks
later, all is ready and the mill bell signals the welcome start-up. In Jewett's
gallery of males, Dan and Father Daley are unusually decent. The happy ending
to this otherwise naturalistic story, with its harsh criticism of industrial, capi-
talistic "progress," is too saccharine—unless Jewett's intention is to suggest
that the workers have been infantilized, dependent on the big-daddy Corporation
and living in what Jewett calls toy-like houses. *Bibliography*: Cary, *Jewett*; Morgan
and Renza; Roman.

GREEN, DR. EZRA. In *The Tory Lover*, he is the *Ranger* surgeon and purser.
From Dover, he socializes with Dickson and accompanies Captain John Paul
Jones on the Whitehaven raid.

GREENAPLE. In "The Dulham Ladies," this is the name of relatives Madam
Dobin's grandmother boasts of having visited.

GREENAPLE, HARRIET. In "The Dulham Ladies," this is a deceased cousin
who, Madam Dobin boasts, would have provided Harriet Dobin and Lucinda
Dobin both "enjoyment" and "social education."

"THE GREEN BONNET" (1901). (Full title: "The Green Bonnet: A Story
of Easter Day.") Short story. (Characters: Bent, Mrs. Folsom, McFarland, Esther
McFarland, Ethel McFarland, Eunice McFarland, Martha McFarland, Mrs.
McFarland, Sarah McFarland, Mrs. Martin, Mrs. Pease, Aunt Sarah, John Tanner, Mrs. Tanner, Mr. West.) Well-to-do Aunt Sarah has given Sarah McFarland,
her beautiful niece, eighteen, an atrocious green velvet bonnet with ostrich feath-

ers. Young Sarah lives with her parents and four younger sisters on a farm near
the Walsingham township, north of Boston, where the aunt lives. For the Easter
Sunday church service, on April 8, Sarah is invited to read a special poem,
while her pleasant friend, John Tanner, a successful young blacksmith, twenty-
four or -five, is invited to sing. Because her father cannot afford to buy her a
new hat, she must wear the green velvet bonnet, which remains embarrassingly
ugly even though she trims and modifies it. Shortly before the big day, Esther
McFarland, Sarah's mischievous sister, seven, takes the green bonnet, wears it
in the rainy woods, and hangs it in a tree. On Easter morning it cannot be found,
and Sarah must don a hood Martha McFarland, another sister, offers, and go
hatless to church. She is delighted when all girls walking to the platform are
told to remove their hats. The performance is faultless. Sarah and Esther find
the bonnet, now ruined, and Sarah pleases Esther by saying John told her nobody
cared a thing about the girls' Easter bonnets.

"THE GREEN BOWL" (1901). Short story. (Characters: Bob, Mrs. Crosdyck,
Duffy, Mrs. Goddard, Frances Kent, Aunt Mally, Katie Montague, Mrs. Patton.)
Katie Montague and Frances Kent are telling Mrs. Crosdyck, Mrs. Goddard,
and some other auditors about their recent bold travel. Such trips are instigated
by Katie. Katie does most of the talking, while Frances timidly interrupts at
times, only to be often silenced. One autumn day, they drove by horse and
buggy into the country, took a byroad, got lost, and were caught in a "drowning
rain." They found a shed, put Bob, their horse, in it, and took shelter in an
empty church nearby. They used pages from an old hymn book to start a pine-
wood fire in the stove. Next morning while Frances was still asleep, Katie
answered a knock on the door by Mrs. Patton. She was the church cleaning
woman and said she saw the young women light lamps in the church the night
before. She cordially invited them to her house for a marvelous breakfast, partly
already prepared for them. Katie's storytelling manner suddenly changes. She
says she instantly sensed Mrs. Patton would be "a real friend." Amid queries
from some of the listeners, Katie continues. Mrs. Patton's pie was a "creation."
When Katie and Frances noticed a green bowl with three yellow apples, Mrs.
Patton explained that a "wild" sailor brought two such bowls from China and
gave them to his brother, who was the orphaned Mrs. Patton's great-aunt's
husband. The great-aunt kept the bowls fifty years, gave them to Mrs. Patton
before her death, and has been dead forty years. Mrs. Patton told Katie the
bowls "have some sort of charm," details of which she could reveal to only
one person—Katie, not Frances, who has remained in peevish ignorance. Mrs.
Patton proceeded to tell her visitors' fortunes: One had been in danger; the other,
in shadows; Katie's uncle having died, Katie would have more money, would
prefer love to money; both young women would visit a house by a river with
many people there. Katie enigmatically continues. Mrs. Patton said the wild
sailor wanted to make money telling fortunes but was killed in an accident. The
possessor of the second bowl, long her "companion," died two days before

Katie and Frances appeared on the scene. To work, companions must own the bowls. Mrs. Patton took Katie into a small bedroom, closed the door, told her the secret, gave her one of the bowls, and made Katie her "companion." Frances sees Katie step away from their listeners. Staring into her glittering bowl, Katie whispers to Frances: She sees two people among those present here; they are saying farewell, and one will die. A male guest rouses from a nap and asks where "you . . . young ladies" will vacation next. Katie says they will visit Mrs. Patton's "dear little house" and tell her what "happened about the green bowl." Though pressed, she refuses "to tell anything more" to her listeners.

"The Green Bowl" is a puzzling tour de force. Mrs. Patton is one of Jewett's potent seeresses. What Katie knows remains largely unshared. The residence in which Katie and Frances tell their story is uncertain. It is probably Mrs. Goddard's home, because Jewett writes that Katie at one point takes "some of Mrs. Goddard's treasured bits of lightwood" from "the great china jar" by the hearth to feed "the bright coals." *Bibliography*: Elizabeth Ammons, "Jewett's Witches," in Nagel, pp. 165–84.

GREGG, 'MIRY. In *A Country Doctor*, she is Mrs. Meeker's sister-in-law's cousin and grows poppies.

GRIMSHAW, MRS. In *Betty Leicester*, she is a neighbor Barbara Leicester and Mary Leicester can occasionally call on for help.

GROSVENOR. In *The Tory Lover*, he is a *Ranger* sailor Captain John Paul Jones worked hard at the wheel.

GROVER. In "The Hiltons' Holiday," this is the name of some boys who visit the teacher at the Becker home when Susan Ellen Hilton and Katy Hilton are there. Mary Speed and Sarah Speed are also there.

"THE GROWTOWN 'BUGLE' " (1888). Short story. (Characters: Deacon Burrow, Jim Bush, Abby Cook, Sam'el Cook, Miss Prudence Fellows, Lizzie Peck, Mrs. Peck, Mrs. Streeter, Simeon Streeter, Simeon Streeter, Junior.) While ironing one damp morning in Simmsby, not far from Boston, Miss Prudence Fellows happens to read a notice in a newspaper. Sheets from the Growtown *Bugle* had been wrapped around some asparagus Prudence bought from Abby Cook, whose son Sam'el must have sent the paper to her from Growtown, Kansas. The item invites people to invest in town lots being offered by Simeon Streeter, Growtown's treasurer. Dissatisfied with her regional investments, Prudence subscribes to the *Bugle*, reads about and writes Streeter, is encouraged by his response, and decides to invest $500 secretly, out of her income from mill stock and woodlands inherited from her father, instead of letting Deacon Burrow put her spare money into spool-factory stock he has recommended. Growtown enjoys a land boom when a railroad line is built nearby. Prudence's $500 grows to $2,000, which she reinvests in more Growtown lots. Meanwhile, she is becoming conceited and even more furtive, and sends Simeon Streeter, Junior, money for a bicycle which the *Bugle* reports he would like to own. When Prudence learns that Mrs. Peck, her widowed neighbor, is ailing, she criticizes the woman for complaining; when Lizzie Beck, the widow's pale, skinny child, runs an errand for Prudence, she restrains herself from tipping her 5¢, because she would expect such a gift every time. Still, Prudence idly thinks she might befriend Lizzie later, maybe even send her to school. One rainy day a neighbor rushes by to tell Prudence that Mrs. Peck is "at death's door" and that Lizzie has just died, half starved, of lung fever. Prudence faints, comes to, and feels "never . . . so poor in her life. . . ."

"A GUEST AT HOME" (1882). Short story. (Characters: Aunt Fanny, Aunt Harriet, Uncle Henry, Hollis, Annie Hollis, Jack Hollis, Lonny Hollis, Mrs. Hollis.) Annie Hollis has been financed by her Uncle Henry, the brother of Mrs. Hollis, her mother. Annie has spent three years studying at a city boarding school, traveling on vacations, and living with Henry and Aunt Fanny, his wife, in New York City. Now Annie returns home in June to help her aging parents and her young brothers, Jack Hollis and Lonny Hollis, at their farmhome near Brookfield. Instead of complaining, she delights, as she puts it, in giving rather than continuing to take. In her spare time, she aids Aunt Harriet, half-paralyzed and a burden on Mrs. Hollis, in renewing her old sewing skills. Annie, who took art lessons in the city, paints some watercolors depicting nearby rural scenes and sells them. Jewett adds the explicit moral: "[A] girl who makes the best of things in one place, will do it in every place." Still, there are indications that rural life is oppressive. Annie's father wanted to go to college but could not. Annie has money to hire a neighbor girl to help her worn-out mother with the housework. And both of Annie's parents are said to "feel like horses in a treadmill."

"THE GUESTS OF MRS. TIMMS" (1894). Short story. (Characters: Barlow, Bascoms, Ezra Beckett, Mrs. Ezra Beckett, Susan Beckett, Cronin, Captain Dyer, Nancy Fell, Persis Flagg, John Marsh, Miss Cynthia Pickett, Captain Timms, Mrs. Timms.) One June afternoon Miss Cynthia Pickett calls on Mrs. Persis Flagg, who is condescending. Former residents of Longport, both now live in Woodville. The two met again at a county conference in Danby. Cynthia, though timid, ventures to hope they can go together to Baxter and visit Mrs. Timms, who is Captain Timms's widow, formerly of Longport, where Mrs. Flagg knew Mrs. Timms. She spoke amiably to both Mrs. Flagg and Cynthia at Danby. Next morning the two women, who call themselves Orthodox (Congregational) church members, take the stage driven by John Marsh and share seats with a strange woman who calls herself a Freewill (Baptist) church member. She gets off at Beckett's Corner and calls on Mrs. Ezra Beckett, whom she says she met at a state conference. Although Mrs. Beckett seems not to recognize the stranger, they begin to talk and Marsh therefore drives on toward Baxter.

Mrs. Flagg and Cynthia consider calling on Nancy Fell, a former member of their church back home who now lives with her nephew. Mrs. Flagg is reluctantly agreeable until she glimpses the Timms mansion, and the two guests hasten to its front door. Mrs. Timms, expressing surprise, lets them into her dark "best room," but the conversation is strained. She offers her guests wine and cake, but only as they are about to leave. Mrs. Flagg walks "stiffly away," and Cynthia's "usual smile . . . burnt itself out into gray ashes." As she retrieves her companion's heavy leather handbag, she suspects it was packed in the hope of an invitation to stay overnight. The two have ample time to call on Nancy, who, "poor [but] good-hearted," greets them with a gush of friendship and serves them dandelion greens, pork, biscuits, and potatoes. On the way back, the two travelers stop to talk with Mrs. Beckett, who asks Marsh to bring a trunk containing the strange woman's summer things, left at the Woodville station, because her guest, now ostentatiously rocking by a window, will be staying a while. As Marsh drives on, Mrs. Flagg expresses a desire to call on Mrs. Beckett soon. Different welcomes unify the story: Cynthia is not put at her ease at Mrs. Flagg's; Mrs. Timms is frigidly formal; Nancy is warm and generous; and Mrs. Beckett proves to be hospitable. Jewett characterizes Mrs. Flagg and Miss Cynthia Pickett with unusually deft touches. At first Mrs. Flagg seems only lofty, but gradually the depths of her hypocrisy become clear. Cynthia is mumblingly timid but ridicules Mrs. Beckett and demonstrates her resentment of Mrs. Flagg. Jewett makes her moral too obvious when Cynthia quotes the Bible: "Better is a dinner of herbs where love is." Equally obvious is the fact that none of these churchgoing females is very nice. While Jewett was in Athens in 1900, she was pleased to learn that a dramatized version of "The Guests of Mrs. Timms" was presented by a club in South Berwick. *Bibliography*: Blanchard; Cary, *Jewett*; Cary, *Letters*; Roman.

GUINEY, LOUISE IMOGEN (1861–1920). Author. She was born in Boston, the only child of Robert Patrick Guiney, an Irish Catholic from Tipperary, Ireland, who became a lawyer in Maine and a general (at twenty-eight) in the Civil War, during which he was grievously wounded. He became an editor and an assistant district attorney and died in 1877 (at forty-two). Louise Guiney graduated from Elmhurst Academy, Providence, Rhode Island, and the following year began publishing extensively. Need for income to support herself and her mother prompted her to become postmistress at Auburndale, Massachusetts (1894–1897), and cataloguer at the Boston Public Library (1899–1900). She was hounded from the former position by a boycott organized by anti-Irish, anti-Catholic, and anti-female bigots. She had been recommended for the library job by Jewett, whom Guiney met through their mutual friend Annie Adams Fields* and who admired her poetry and essays. Guiney traveled with her mother in England, Ireland, and France (1889–1891) and returned to England to do research into Catholic literary history (1901–1909). After her mother's death in 1910, Guiney, enfeebled by two breakdowns and quite deaf, moved in England.

Her best publications include *A Roadside Harp* (1893), *Patrins: A Collection of Essays* (1897), *Robert Emmet* (1904), *Blessed Edmund Campion* (1908), and an anthology of Catholic poets (*Recusant Poets* [1938]). *Bibliography*: Henry G. Fairbanks, *Louise Imogen Guiney* (New York: Twayne, 1973); Judith A. Roman, *Annie Adams Fields: The Spirit of Charles Street* (Bloomington and Indianapolis: Indiana University Press, 1990).

GUNN, CAPTAIN DANIEL ("DAN'EL"). In "An Autumn Holiday," he is an old bachelor and former militiaman. Gunn suffered a sunstroke and after the death of his sister, Patience Gunn, grew mentally unstable and took to wearing her clothes occasionally. So garbed, he once went to church and also crashed a female missionary society meeting. Polly Marsh gossips about him. In several stories, Jewett has characters dressing or acting like members of the opposite sex. But Daniel Gunn is unique in her fiction for being a male dressing like a female and thinking he is one. *Bibliography*: Roman.

GUNN, JACOB. In "An Autumn Holiday," he was Daniel Gunn's nephew. Jacob, Polly Marsh, and her cousin, Statiry, attended the church service disrupted by Daniel Gunn's appearance. Polly declined Jacob's proposal of marriage, according to her sister, Mrs. Snow.

GUNN, PATIENCE. In "An Autumn Holiday," she was Daniel Gunn's unmarried sister. After her death, he took to wearing her clothes.

H

H——. In *Deephaven*, he owns the Boston store where Mary Wendell works.

HACKETT. In *The Tory Lover*, he is the shipmaster who built the *Ranger*.

HAGGENS, MAJOR TILLY. In *The Tory Lover*, he is a fiery old revolutionary. He is a friend of Colonel Jonathan Hamilton and Mary Hamilton. He helps drive the mob from the home of Madam Wallingford, despite her Tory leanings. He is of Huguenot extraction, and his family name was Huyghens.

HAGGENS, NANCY. In *The Tory Lover*, she is Major Tilly Haggens's hospitable old sister.

HAINES. In "The Spur of the Moment," a coachman at the funeral of Walton says Haines long ago paid a high price for the horse, once strong but now old, that Fallon has hitched to the carriage he uses to drive Miss Peet to the funeral.

HAITON, JOHN. In "Jenny Garrow's Lovers," he is the farmer in whose home his daughter, Phebe Haiton (*see* Winnis, Phebe), is married.

HAITON, PHEBE. In "Jenny Garrow's Lovers." *See* Winnis, Phebe.

HALL, JIM. In *A Country Doctor*, he was a man Martin Dyer said Adeline Prince should or might have preferred to marry.

HALL, LIEUTENANT. In *The Tory Lover*, he is one of Captain John Paul Jones's *Ranger* officers; he helps with the Whitehaven raid.

HALL, TIMOTHY. In "Told in the Tavern," he is the Byfleet tavern owner. Rather quiet during the gossip session about Abby Sands, Hall is described as sometimes jocose.

HALLETT, ADDIE. In "A Spring Sunday," she was the frail little daughter, now deceased, of Alonzo Hallett and Mary Ann Hallett. They reminisce tearfully about the child during their picnic at Miller Falls.

HALLETT, ALONZO ("LONZO"). In "A Spring Sunday," he is Mary Ann Hallett's successful businessman husband. Married sixty-two years, they reminisce during a Sunday picnic back in Miller Falls, their original hometown.

HALLETT, DR. JOHN. In "A Landlocked Sailor," he is an assistant surgeon in the navy, home on leave after three years at sea. While fishing, he encounters Mike Dillon, whom he tended more than two years earlier after a shipboard accident. Mike tells him about his marriage.

HALLETT, JAKE. In *Betty Leicester*, he is mentioned by Plunkett as his wife's cousin, just returned to Riverport.

HALLETT, JOSEPH. In "A Spring Sunday," he is the grown-up son of Alonzo Hallett and Mary Ann Hallett, married, with a family, and well respected.

HALLETT, MARY. In "Farmer Finch," she is a Portsmouth girl with whom Jerry Minton became friendly. This helps spoil his chances to marry Polly Finch, his next-door neighbor; Mary later married a Boston commission-firm partner.

HALLETT, MARY ANN. In "A Spring Sunday," she is Alonzo Hallett's wife. Married sixty-two years, the two enjoy a trolley ride ten miles to Miller Falls and a Sunday picnic there. They lived with their children—including Addie Hallett, Joseph Hallett, and Oliver Hallett—in Miller Falls before moving to the city.

HALLETT, OLIVER. In "A Spring Sunday," he is the son of Alonzo Hallett and Mary Ann Hallett. Like his brother, he is a respected family man.

HALLOWELL. In "Hallowell's Pretty Sister," he is the widowed father of Alice Hallowell, Dick Hallowell, and Tom Hallowell. He is not at his mansion some distance from Boston when Dick Hallowell brings Jack Spenser and Phil there for a visit.

HALLOWELL, ALICE. In "Hallowell's Pretty Sister," she is the beautiful sister of Dick Hallowell and Tom Hallowell. Tom impersonates Alice during her absence from home. When Alice, delayed by a snowstorm, finally arrives, she meets Jack Spenser. Later Alice and Jack get married.

HALLOWELL, DICK. In "Hallowell's Pretty Sister," he is the brother of Alice Hallowell and young Tom Hallowell, and the close friend of Jack Spenser and Phil. The three are juniors at Harvard together. To tease Jack, who fancies himself quiet a ladies' man, Dick arranges to have Tom impersonate their lovely sister when Jack and Phil visit the Hallowell mansion.

HALLOWELL, TOM. In "Hallowell's Pretty Sister," he is the brother, fifteen, of Dick Hallowell, who is a junior at Harvard. When Dick brings his college friends Jack Spenser and Phil home for a holiday visit, Tom agrees to impersonate Alice Hallowell, his and Dick's lovely sister. The ruse works until the real Alice tardily arrives. Jack quickly prefers the real Alice.

"HALLOWELL'S PRETTY SISTER" (1880). Short story. (Characters: Miss Daneweight, Hallowell, Alice Hallowell, Dick Hallowell, Tom Hallowell, John, Phil, Jack Spenser.) Dick Hallowell, Jack Spenser, and Phil, who is the narrator, are close friends at Harvard, where they are members of the junior class. Earlier, Jack was more amiable. This year he has become too enamored of fancy clothes and is somewhat snobbish. When Jack, well aware of his charms, sees a photograph of Alice Hallowell, Dick's beautiful sister, he begins to socialize more with his former pals and eagerly accepts the invitation, as does Phil, to visit Hallowell's country mansion some distance from Boston. He expects to meet and make a conquest of Alice. The three young students arrive over the snowy Washington's birthday holiday. Dick explains that his widowed father is away, as is Tom, Dick's brother, fifteen. John, the butler, helps the guests. Dick brings his sister downstairs and introduces her. She is a fresh-faced, blond beauty, intriguingly demure; but she has a cold and a husky voice and sits part of the time behind a screen to protect her eyes from the firelight. Still, Jack domineers her, not least when he plays the piano and reads poetry to her. Dick hints to Phil, who feels neglected and even jealous, that a joke is in the offing. After Sunday church services, the real Alice arrives. She was prevented by a storm from being at home when Dick, Jack, and Phil arrived. Tom, present all along and impersonating his sister brilliantly, joins in the laugh. And so does Jack. He and Phil happily visit Dick's home later. In fact, Dick and the real Alice get married in the fall. Tom is suggested as chief bridesmaid. Still later, Jack graduates from law school. The stuffiness of these Harvard lads may be indicated by Phil's considerable overuse of the word "capital" in his description of events.

HAMILTON, COLONEL JONATHAN ("JACK"). In *The Tory Lover*, he is Mary Hamilton's brother, a self-made Berwick shipping merchant, now rich, thirty-five, and a Revolutionary army officer.

HAMILTON, MARY. In *The Tory Lover*, she is Colonel Jonathan Hamilton's beautiful young sister. They live in Berwick. Roger Wallingford loves her, as does Captain John Paul Jones briefly. She accompanies Roger's mother, Madam Wallingford, to Bristol, persuades John Davis and others to work for Roger's release from prison, through Jones's efforts is reunited with Roger near Bristol, and will marry him when they arrive back home. Mary is a beautiful and intelligent young woman and an accomplished equestrienne; but in her brother's house she is mainly decorative, and with Roger she is mostly vapid and trembly. *Bibliography*: Roman.

HAMMET. In *The Tory Lover*, he is a sailor wounded when he and Roger Wallingford escape from prison. Roger helps him get to the inn near Bristol.

HANCOCK, JOHN (1737–1793). American statesman and revolutionary. In *The Tory Lover*, he mentioned as Judge Chadbourne's friend.

HAND, MRS. In "Aunt Cynthy Dallett," she is an old woman who visits aging Abby Pendexter, tells her about visiting Mrs. Eben Fulham, and with Abby calls on Abby's aunt, Cynthy Dallett. The result is that Abby promises to move in with Cynthy.

HANNAH. In *Deephaven*, she is mentioned as Mrs. Tom Kew's sister.

HANNAH. In "Martha's Lady," she is Harriet Pyne's cook when Helena Vernon Dysart visits her cousin, Harriet, late in the cousins' lives.

HANNAH. In "Miss Sydney's Flowers," she has been Miss Sydney's maid, now "venerable," for fifty years.

HANNAH. In "Mr. Bruce," she is one of Mrs. Tennant's servants but is away when the dinner party must be served.

HANNAH. In "Paper Roses," she is probably the daughter of the old invalid who makes paper flowers. The old woman says Hannah brought her paper of too light a pink color.

HANNAH, AUNT. In "An Every-Day Girl," she is evidently the aunt of Mrs. Fleming, the mother of Mary Fleming. Aunt Hannah, who wears a Shaker bonnet, is a welcome guest wherever she goes. When she visits the Flemings, she advises Mary to be the best worker she can be in whatever job is available.

Aunt Hannah is an almost magical creature, appearing opportunely and advising where she can do the most good.

HANNAN, JERRY. In "Between Mass and Vespers," he is the father of a newborn who had fits. Father Ryan was called to christen it fast.

HANSCOM. In *The Tory Lover*, he is a *Ranger* sailor from Berwick. He is Cooper's chum and is described as practical.

HANWAY, CAPTAIN. In "The First Sunday in June," he is an old friend of Miss Lydia Bent's father. When Hanway hobbles into church, Miss Lydia is pleased, even though he tells her he has not attended church for five years and is too deaf to hear any sermon.

"THE HARE AND THE TORTOISE" (1883). Short story. (Characters: Angelo, Becket, Duncan Chester, Mary Chester, Mrs. Chester, Richard Dean, Sheila Dean, Miss Anne Duncan, Miss Sophia Duncan, Hovey, Polly, Henry Temple, Mrs. Temple, Winterford.) Pretty Mary Chester trips daintily along Beacon Street in Boston on a nice April day, briefly sees and is noted appreciatively by a well-dressed young man, and enters the curious household of which she is a peppy part. Mrs. Chester, her sad mother, lives with her deceased husband's two aunts, the domineering Miss Sophia Duncan, and the sweet, rather deaf younger Miss Anne Duncan. The wealthy, widowed Mrs. Temple and Henry Temple, her stolid son, are guests at dinner. Then three people—Mary, Henry, whom she admires but enjoys teasing and whom family members expect her to marry, and deaf Anne Duncan—attend a concert at the Music Hall. When Henry says Richard ("Dick") Dean has just returned from studying art for three years abroad, Mary realizes it was Dick who saw her on the street, and they renew their friendship. Mary remembers she knew him and his now-deceased sister when they were all children. Visiting her several times, Dick charms Mary's mother and great-aunts, and Mary contrasts his kind attention to Anne with Henry's, which seems clumsy and patronizing. Mary and Dick discuss his travels, sketches, and society life. When Sophia ridicules his habit of describing things as "lovely" and says she prefers Henry, Mary responds by saying Dick is like champagne and paté, unlike Henry's sherry and soup. The month of May is rainy, but June is pleasant. Dick goes out with Mary often, which alarms Henry. Feeling more loved than loving, Mary is uncertain whether to prefer Henry and the well-known routine of Boston life, or Dick, who, rumor has it, may soon be off sketching in Europe. Dick invites Henry to go riding, but he says he has a 3 P.M. appointment with Mary. Dick goes to his club, naps a little too long, checks the time, and rushes off to Mary's house, popping in just ahead of the sedately trudging Henry. The hare, not the tortoise, gains the victory this time.

HARLOW. In *The Country of the Pointed Firs*, he is mentioned by Mrs. Caplin as long-winded at a county conference. Since she calls him "Fayther," he may be a priest.

HARLOW. In "A Landless Farmer," he is the owner of a shop where Serena Nudd bought blankets for her father, Jerry Jenkins. Ezra Allen, who knows Harlow, saw her make the purchase with Jerry's money.

HARRIET, AUNT. In "A Guest at Home," she is the half-paralyzed, complaining relative living in the home of Annie Hollis's parents. When Annie returns, she sweetens the old woman's life, partly by encouraging her to exercise her ability at needlework again.

HARRIS. In "The Dunnet Shepherdess," she is "one of the younger Harrises" whom Caplin, a seafaring widower, is engaged to marry. The narrator tells gossip-hungry Thankful Hight about this development.

HARRIS, JOHN. In "The Stage Tavern," he is Major Tom Harris's courteous son and Lizzie Harris's brother. Lizzie runs the tavern and uses part of the profits to send John to college.

HARRIS, JOHNNY. In "The Night before Thanksgiving," he is a soldier's orphaned son. When Johnny was injured, Mary Ann Robb fed, housed, and otherwise aided him. Promising to return, he went west but returns just in the nick of time to save Mrs. Robb from being sent to the poorhouse by the townspeople.

HARRIS, LIZZIE. In "The Stage Tavern," she is Major Tom Harris's pretty daughter and John Harris's sister. She graduated from Radcliffe two years earlier. Her mother died, and Lizzie Harris must run the Stage Tavern at Westford to support her blind father and pay for John's college expenses. General Jack Norton meets Lizzie, is immediately attracted to her despite the difference in their ages, and will undoubtedly marry her.

HARRIS, MAJOR TOM. In "The Stage Tavern," he is the son of Squire Harris, the former owner, now deceased, of the Stage Tavern. Tom Harris is an ex-soldier, blinded by a wound incurred during the Civil War. His delicate wife has recently died, and his daughter, Lizzie Harris, runs the tavern. Tom is delighted when his old friend, General Jack Norton, visits him.

HARRIS, MARI'. *See* Harris, Maria.

HARRIS, MARIA ("MARI' "). In *The Country of the Pointed Firs*, Mari' is identified as Captain Littlepage's housekeeper. Almira Todd and Mrs. Caplin contend that her arguing, being "sordid" and homely, and having a "Chinee" look cause Littlepage to be "disconsolate." In "The Foreigner," Mari' was a woman whose poor duet with a young Caplin girl Mrs. John Tolland objected to, thus causing an argument. In "William's Wedding," Maria visits Almira to gain news of her brother William Blackett's wedding. Maria, called Almira's "arch enemy," uses the ineffective excuse that she wants to borrow a weekly paper to give to Littlepage.

HARRIS, SQUIRE. In "The Stage Tavern," he was a great politician in the Westford region. Now deceased, he owned the Stage Tavern, was Major Tom Harris's father, and the grandfather of Lizzie Harris and John Harris. General Jack Norton, while a college student, stayed at the tavern with his friend, Tom, and met Squire Harris.

HART. In "The Quest of Mr. Teaby," he is the husband of Ann Maria Hart, the niece of Teaby. He says Hart is stingy.

HART, ANN MARIA. In "The Quest of Mr. Teaby," she is the niece of Teaby, who is an itinerant peddler and who occasionally stays with her.

HARTLEY, DAVID. In *The Tory Lover*, he is a British parliamentarian who tries to help Benjamin Franklin aid Americans in British prisons.

HATHAWAY. In "A Financial Failure," he is a bank clerk, under Pendell, and works with Downs and Jonas Dyer. Downs and Hathaway, both in their late twenties, constantly belittle Jonas.

HATHAWAY, FRED ("THE PRETTY SAXON"). In "A Sorrowful Guest," he was a handsome soldier whose death John Ainslie recalls when he and George Sheffield are reminiscing about Civil War horrors.

HATHORN, JOHN. In *Deephaven*, he is mentioned as Captain Sands's cousin's deceased husband.

HATHORN, MRS. JOHN. In *Deephaven*, she is Captain Sands's cousin. She sensed her husband's death as it was occurring thirty miles away.

HAVERFORD, COLONEL. In "Lady Ferry," he was the Englishman who built the mansion by the ferry 150 years ago. He lived well and was mysterious. When he and his son died, the place was used as a tavern for many years.

HAVERFORD, MISTRESS. In "Lady Ferry," she was a woman Martha talks about. She says it was said that Mistress Haverford was hanged as a witch and that Lady Ferry wears her clothes.

HAWKES, WIDOW MARTHA. In "An Only Son," she is the housekeeper for Captain Abel Stone; he often swears at her volcanically but harmlessly. This occasions Jewett's aside that some profanity is not injurious.

HAYDEN, JOSH. In "A Landless Farmer," he is a lawyer—"what there is of him"—says Asa Parsons, who, Asa adds, arranged with Aaron Nudd to have Jerry Jenkins deed his farm to Aaron and his wife, Serena Nudd, Jerry's greedy daughter.

HAYDON, ISRAEL ("ISR'EL"). In "A Second Spring," he is a prosperous, dignified farmer, sixty-seven, near Atfield. He is disconsolate and helpless when his wife, Martha Haydon, dies after their happy marriage of forty years. His married son, William Haydon, invites him to pay a long visit, but Israel declines. Later, at William's suggestion, he lets Maria Durrant become his housekeeper. A year later the two marry.

HAYDON, MARILLA. In "A Second Spring," she is Israel Haydon's daughter-in-law. Her mother-in-law caused a brief period of trouble by not regarding Marilla as good enough for her son, William Haydon.

HAYDON, MARTHA ("MARTHY"). In "A Second Spring," she was Israel Haydon's wife, recently deceased. They were happily married for forty years.

HAYDON, WILLIAM. In "A Second Spring," he is the son of Israel Haydon and Martha Haydon, who is now deceased. William has a successful "milk farm" nearby. According to Mrs. Stevens, Israel's sister-in-law, Martha "made a kind of girl of him." William invites Israel to come live for a while with him and his wife, Marilla Haydon. After Israel declines, William suggests that Marilla's cousin should become Israel's housekeeper. This leads to Israel's marrying Marilla.

HAYLAND, JOEL. In "A Financial Failure," he is a farmer living in Oak Hill. He regularly has his old friend, Pendell, the treasurer of the County Savings Bank in Dartford, eight or nine miles from his home, handle his deposits. When Jonas Dyer inquires about Joel Hayland, Pendell recommends him as a "comfortable" farmer and an "honest . . . man." Hayland encourages Jonas to court Love Hayland, Joel's daughter.

HAYLAND, LOVE. In "A Financial Failure," she is the pretty, nineteen-year-old daughter of Joel Hayland of Oak Hill and his wife, Mrs. Hayland. Love falls in love with Jonas Dyer at first sight. She tells him she is "keeping school." Although she is allegedly pursued by Waters, a middle-aged widower, she and Jonas get married.

HAYLAND, MRS. In "A Financial Failure," she is Joel Hayland's kind little wife and Love Hayland's mother. When she wishes to contribute to the repair of the meeting-house, her husband happily agrees to do so.

HAYNES. In "An Every-Day Girl," he is a farmer John Abbott works for. They raise poultry.

HAYNES, MRS. In "Andrew's Fortune," she is a neighbor of Stephen Dennett, whom she admires. Described as good-hearted but tactless, Mrs. Haynes proves to be helpful following Dennett's death.

HAYNES, MRS. In "An Every-Day Girl," she is mentioned as the wife of the farmer John Abbott works for. Mrs. Haynes knows Aunt Hannah.

HELEN, SISTER. In "A Garden Story," she works in the hospital on Blank Street in Boston. She loves Peggy McAllister, is sorry to see the little orphan go to Miss Ann Dunning's house in Littletown, but soon learns she is happy there.

HENDER, ABBY HARRAN. In "A Native of Winby," she is a worn but sturdy farm widow near Winby. John Hender, one of her three sons, was killed at Fredericksburg. John's daughter, Marilla Hender, lives with Abby. Her other two sons are away buying cattle in Canada when Joseph K. Laneway—a year younger than she, and her sweetheart "Joe" during their teen years in school— calls on her, fifty-eight years or so later, for an evening of reminiscing. She is an example of a fine, generous, intelligent person remaining in the rural environment of her childhood, unlike Laneway, a millionaire, senator, and general.

HENDER, JOHN. In "A Native of Winby," he was one of Abby Harran Hender's three sons. He was killed at Fredericksburg, and his wife is also dead. Their schoolteacher daughter, Marilla Hender, lives with his widowed mother, Abby Harran Hender.

HENDER, MARILLA. In "A Native of Winby," she is the teacher at the Winby roadside school and lives with her widowed grandmother, Abby Harran Hender. Marilla is thrilled when Joseph K. Laneway visits her school and lectures her pupils on worthy ambitions and hard work. She feels left out when he pays attention only to Abby during his visit to their home and densely wonders why Abby cries after saying good-bye to "Joe."

HENDERSON. In "Peg's Little Chair," he is Margaret Benning's father and Margaret ("Peg") Benning's grandfather. Henderson was a sea captain who traveled to the East Indies, England, and Holland. When his daughter's husband was lost at sea off Henderson's ship, Henderson helped provision her public house.

HENDERSON, HANNAH. In "Peg's Little Chair," she is Margaret Benning's mother and Margaret ("Peg") Benning's grandmother. Hannah helps her daughter run her public house.

HENRI, FATHER. In "Mère Pochette," he is the "saintly" priest who replaces Father Pierre in Bonaventure. Father Henri shows Mère Pochette the letter he has received that reveals that her deceased son-in-law's family has willed her granddaughter, Manon, a substantial sum of money.

HENRY. In "The Becket Girls' Tree," he is Mrs. Parsons's brother. When he writes that his wife, Sarah Ann, is gravely ill, Mrs. Parsons leaves at once for Gloucester, where Henry and Sarah Ann live.

HENRY. In "A War Debt," he is a friendly old guest Margaret Bellamy welcomes to her home in Boston.

HENRY, UNCLE. "A Guest at Home," he is Aunt Fanny's husband and Mrs. Hollis's brother. Henry and Fanny finance the education and fun-time in and near New York City of Annie Hollis, Mrs. Hollis's daughter.

HEPSY. In "Martha's Lady," she is Miss Harriet Pyne's kitchen servant; she teaches Martha the ropes because, as she says, she was awkward herself at first.

HERBERT, CHARLES. In *The Tory Lover*, he is an American in the Mill Prison. Age twenty, he is called the scribe.

HERON, JIM. In "The Courting of Sister Wisby," in Mrs. Goodsoe's gripping story, he was the first Irishman seen in her region of New England. He married a Peck girl (*see* Peck, Widow). He had "the second sight" and played the fiddle magically—to accompany dances and also in a way to evoke a kind mother's gentle voice. When widowed Mrs. Jerry Foss's three children all died of scarlet fever in one week, she turned stony and would soon have died but for Heron's coming by and playing a Celtic song that called her shattered being back to comfort and sanity.

HERON, MRS. JIM. In "The Courting of Sister Wisby," Mrs. Goodsoe says that Mrs. Heron complained that Jim's music made her nervous.

HERTEL. In *The Tory Lover*, he is mentioned as a victor, alongside French and Indian fighters, against Berwick settlers long ago.

HICKS, MRS. In "All My Sad Captains," she is Maria Lunn's dying cousin. Mrs. Lunn visits her and later inherits her property.

HIGHT. In *The Tory Lover*, this is the family name of a guest at Colonel Jonathan Hamilton's party.

HIGHT, ESTHER. In "The Dunnet Shepherdess," she is the aging daughter of paralyzed Thankful Hight, whom she is caring for. Esther was a teacher but returned to the family farm after her father's death, paid off the mortgage, tends sheep, and sees her "lover" William Blackett only once a year. The narrator says Esther's smile is "of noble patience, of uncomprehended sacrifice." In "William's Wedding," Esther, shy though in her sixties, is freed by her mother's death to marry William after their forty-year courtship. She brings to the ceremony a motherless little white lamb.

HIGHT, THANKFUL. In "The Dunnet Shepherdess," she is Esther Hight's paralyzed mother, over eighty. William Blackett takes the narrator to meet and talk with her while he goes off with Esther Hight, the old woman's sheep-tending daughter. In "William's Wedding," Thankful Hight's death frees Esther to wed her William.

HIGHTREE. In "The Dulham Ladies," this is the name of relatives Madam Dobin's mother boasted that her grandmother visited.

HIGHWARD, THOMAS. In "Lady Ferry," he is described as an early eighteenth-century author of a book on his travels in the American colonies. In his book he discusses Mistress Honor Warburton, doomed never to die.

HILL. In *The Tory Lover*, this is the name of a guest at Colonel Jonathan Hamilton's party.

HILL. In *The Tory Lover*, he is a *Ranger* midshipman who takes part in the Whitehaven attack.

HILL, MARTHA. In *The Tory Lover*, she is a guest at Colonel Jonathan Hamilton's party and behaves coquettishly before Judge Chadbourne.

HILTON. In "A Late Supper," he is the son of Mrs. Hilton, one of Miss Catherine Spring's neighbors. He delivers the good-news letter from Alice West to Miss Spring.

HILTON, CATHARINE WINN. In "The Hiltons' Holiday," she is fondly recalled as John Hilton's deceased mother. She attended school with Masterson, who became a judge and remembers her well. She was a schoolteacher.

HILTON, JOHN. In "The Hiltons' Holiday," he is a farmer living in the hills seventeen miles from Topham Corners, "a creature of the shady woods and brown earth, instead of the noisy town." He and his wife have had three children, John (evidently deceased), Susan Ellen Hilton, and Katy Hilton. John Hilton works especially hard one long spring day so he can take his daughters to town the following day for a memorable holiday.

HILTON, JOHN. In "The Hiltons' Holiday," he was the son of John Hilton and his wife and is evidently deceased. The couple discuss losing him.

HILTON, KATY. In "The Hiltons' Holiday," she is the younger daughter of John Hilton and his wife. She is almost nine and is shy and reserved. She is a good pupil at school and may become a teacher. She helps her father with farm work. Not likely to marry, she is the character in the story Jewett most closely identifies with. *Bibliography*: Roman.

HILTON, MRS. In "A Late Supper," she is Miss Catherine Spring's neighbor. She gives Miss Spring cream for the tea she offers her guests, Joseph Spring, Martha Spring, and Miss Stanby.

HILTON, MRS. JOHN. In "The Hiltons' Holiday," she is the patient, somewhat domineering wife of John Hilton, who takes their two daughters, Susan Ellen Hilton and Katy Hilton, to Topham Corners for a little holiday. She tells her husband not to buy her any "kickshaws" in town.

HILTON, SUSAN ELLEN. In "The Hiltons' Holiday," she is the older daughter of John Hilton and his wife. She feels grown up and is less well behaved than her sister Katy. Susan helps her mother with housework and is likely to marry.

"THE HILTONS' HOLIDAY" (1893). Short story. (Characters: Barstow, Mrs. Becker, Tamsen Brooks, Grover, Catharine Winn Hilton, John Hilton, John Hilton, Mrs. John Hilton, Katy Hilton, Susan Ellen Hilton, Adeline Marlow, Judge Masterson, Ira Speed, Mary Speed, Sarah Speed.) John Hilton has been up since shortly after four in the morning planting potatoes and is now resting at eight at night. He and his wife discuss their daughters, Susan Ellen Hilton and Katy Hilton, who are about to return from visiting their teacher. Hilton plans to take the girls to Topham Corners in the morning for a holiday. Mrs. Hilton decides to stay home. In the morning, father and daughters take their wagon seventeen miles to the village. Hilton is proud to stop at the home of Judge Masterson, who attended school with Hilton's mother and speaks to the Hiltons with impressive courtesy. Hilton talks with a friend so old he longs to die. Hilton has his photograph taken with the girls and buys himself a new straw hat, a fancy pepperbox for his wife, and candy for the girls. When they return to their farm, Mrs. Hilton senses a new maturity in the girls. Hilton confesses that he forgot to buy a needed hoe and some turnip seeds. Darkness falls on "[t]he great day." Jewett's country characters here feel, though Jewett does not, that they are inferior to town folks. John may be too boyish in his desire to make this trip, while his wife, in a role reversal, may be too much in command—and uncomfortably so—at their farmhome. The name Topham may derive from that of Topsham, Maine. Only a few months before her death, Jewett read "The Hiltons' Holiday" to 150 female students at Simmons College in Boston and remained afterwards to converse with the girls from Maine. *Bibliography*: Roman.

HITTY, AUNT. In "Andrew's Fortune," she is a relative Mrs. Jonas Beedle recalls. She says Hitty was a half-sister of her "grand'ther," grew simple-minded, babbled, died at ninety-three, and had a big funeral.

HODGDON. In *The Tory Lover*, she is named as a widow whose son, Humprey Hodgdon, was killed by the British.

HODGDON, HUMPHREY. In *The Tory Lover*, he was a soldier the British killed.

HODGDON, PHEBE. In *The Tory Lover*, she is a servant in Colonel Jonathan Hamilton's house. She was said at one point to be accompanying Mary Hamilton to Bristol but is unmentioned later. *See also* Phoebe.

HOLLIS. In "A Guest at Home," he is Annie Hollis's old father. He and his wife also have two sons, Jack Hollis and Lonny Hollis. Hollis appreciates his daughter's essential goodness.

HOLLIS, ANNIE. In "A Guest at Home," she is the daughter of Hollis and his wife and is the sister of Jack Hollis and Lonny Hollis, both younger than she. With funds provided by Uncle Henry, her mother's brother, and his wife, Aunt Fanny, Annie has gone to school, traveled, and enjoyed herself for three years in and near New York City. Now she returns home to help her needy family and does so with great good nature. She encourages Aunt Harriet, her mother's aunt, to resume her skillful needlework; Annie also paints nearby rural scenes in watercolors and sells her landscapes.

HOLLIS, FRED. In "The Lost Turkey," he is a friend of John Jones, who tells his mother, Sarah Jones, that the Hollis family is having lots of guests for Thanksgiving dinner.

HOLLIS, JACK. In "A Guest at Home," he is Annie Hollis's brother, twelve. He is shy when she returns home, but only at first.

HOLLIS, LONNY. In "A Guest at Home," he is Annie Hollis's brother, fourteen. He is briefly shy when she returns home.

HOLLIS, MRS. In "A Guest at Home," she is Hollis's good-natured wife and the mother of their children, Annie Hollis, Jack Hollis, and Lonny Hollis. Mrs. Hollis, who is kind to Aunt Harriet, an invalid living in their home, gratefully welcomes Annie's return from New York City.

HOLMES, OLIVER WENDELL (1809–1894). Physician, educator, and author. He was born in Cambridge, Massachusetts, graduated from Harvard (1829), and attended its law school (1829–1830), the Tremont Medical School in Boston (1830–1833), and a medical school in Paris (1833–1835). Once Harvard granted him a medical degree (1836), he taught at Dartmouth (1838–1840), practiced in Boston (1840–1847), and taught and was an administrator at Harvard (1847– 1882). In 1840 he married Amelia Lee; they had three children, including the eminent jurist Oliver Wendell Holmes, Jr. The elder Holmes combined a busy social and academic life with voluminous writing—medical treatises, poetry, humorous items, books of essays, "medicated" novels, biographies, and a travel book. In 1857 he helped establish the *Atlantic Monthly*, for which he provided the title and in which he published upwards of 120 items. His many friends included Ralph Waldo Emerson, James T. Fields and Annie Adams Fields,* Nathaniel Hawthorne, Julia Ward Howe,* Henry Wadsworth Longfellow, James Russell Lowell,* Celia Laighton Thaxter,* and John Greenleaf Whittier.* Holmes was a conservative humanist, a gentle critic of Calvinist and Unitarian rigidities, and a pioneering physician.

Jewett associated with Holmes because of their mutual friendship with the Fieldses and also undoubtedly felt a special bond with him because both he and her father, Theodore Herman Jewett,* were physicians. She and Holmes both appreciated the sermons of Phillips Brooks.* She was a guest at the breakfast reception given in Boston by the *Atlantic Monthly* (3 December 1879) for Holmes on his seventieth birthday and attended by Thomas Bailey Aldrich,* the Fieldses, Julia Ward Howe, William Dean Howells,* Harriet Beecher Stowe,* Charles Dudley Warner,* Whittier, and others. Holmes attended the reading (1887) in Boston, which was designed to raise funds for a Longfellow memorial and which Jewett helped organize. Holmes concluded an 1892 letter to Annie Fields "with affectionate regards and all sweet messages to Miss Jewett." *Bibliography*: Blanchard; Annie Fields, "Oliver Wendell Holmes: Personal Recollections and Unpublished Letters," *Century* 49 (February 1895): 505–15; M. A. DeWolfe Howe, *Holmes of the Breakfast-Table* (New York: Oxford University Press, 1939); Howe, *The Atlantic Monthly and Its Makers* (Boston: Atlantic Monthly Press, 1919); Ellery Sedgwick, *The Atlantic Monthly, 1857–1909: Yankee Humanism at High Tide* (Amherst: University of Massachusetts Press, 1994); Silverthorne.

HOLT. In "In Dark New England Days," he is the young man whose right hand is shot off on the frontier. He returns home to get married. The loss of his hand fulfills part of Hannah Knowles's curse put on Enoch Holt, one of young Holt's forebears. His mother also loses the use of her right wrist and hand.

HOLT, ENOCH. In "In Dark New England Days," he is accused by Betsey Knowles and Hannah Knowles of stealing their father Captain Knowles's hoard of gold coins. Acquitted in court, he swears his innocence by his right hand, whereupon Hannah curses his right hand and those of his descendants. Later Enoch loses his right arm in a house-building accident. Another member of his family loses his right hand, and yet another the use of her right wrist and hand.

HOLT, MRS. In "In Dark New England Days," she is the mother of a young man whose right hand is shot off on the frontier. She is thrown from a wagon and suffers a mangled right wrist. Thus, she and her son fulfill part of the curse put on right hands of Holt family members by Hannah Knowles.

HOLT, MRS. In "In Dark New England Days," she is the bride of the man whose right hand was shot off on the frontier.

"THE HONEY TREE" (1901). Short story. (Characters: Mrs. Dennett, Rev. Mr. Dennett, Dunn, Foss, Mrs. Foss, Ann Sarah Hopper, Asy Hopper, Johnny Hopper, Jenkins, Bill Phillips, Mrs. Prime, Joel Simmons, John Timms, Martin Wells, Mrs. Wells.) One Friday night in October Joel Simmons's store in Hillborough is alive with talk. Johnny Hopper has found a honey tree, with an estimated fifty pounds of honey, on the Hopper property. Several men discuss the value of the find, how some would like to buy a little of it, and whether Johnny and his friends will dirty it by pawing it and eating some themselves. Next day a bunch of men go up the hill, smoke the angry bees away, cut the hollow tree down, wedge its trunk, and take out the treasure. Ann Sarah Hopper, Johnny's mother, and Mrs. Prime, her spry old mother, arrive with bowls and carry the honey home. Neighbors help. Later a hungry bear scoops up what has dripped onto the ground. When the crowd returns to the Hopper house, they find seven or eight friends waiting to partake of samples, partly on cake and bread provided by generous Mrs. Wells. Rev. Mr. Dennett impresses Johnny by trading a four-bladed knife for a taste of honey. Dunn, the disliked teacher, was off in the woods seeking witch hazel and missed the little feast. When the visitors have left, not much honey remains. But Johnny's father has saved some for his rueful son, and Mrs. Prime philosophizes: It is always necessary "to have somethin' pleasant to draw folks round ye." This Faulknerian tale is livened by folksy New England dialogue.

HOOPER, JABEZ. In "Aunt Cynthy Dallett," he is Cynthy Dallett's friend. He brought flour to her, and she wishes she had asked him to ask Abby Pendexter to visit her on New Year's Day.

HOOPER, JIM. In "By the Morning Boat," he is a friend of Elisha, who decides to free his caged woodchuck and not, after all, give it to Jim. The woodchuck's sudden liberty parallels that of Elisha, now on his way to a job in Boston.

HOPPER, ANN SARAH. In "The Honey Tree," she is Mrs. Prime's daughter, Asa Hopper's wife, and Johnny Hopper's mother. She participates in the gathering and sampling of the honey Johnny located.

HOPPER, ASA. In "Miss Debby's Neighbors," he is the owner of the farm the Ashby family once owned next to Miss Debby's old family farm.

HOPPER, ASA (ASY). In "The Honey Tree," he is Ann Sarah Hopper's husband and Johnny Hopper's father. He helps gather the honey.

HOPPER, JOHNNY. In "The Honey Tree," he is the feisty child who found the honey tree. His pal is Bill Phillips. They dislike Dunn, their teacher. Johnny is willing to give some honey to Foss, an old sea captain, and his wife and also to Joel Simmons, a pleasant storekeeper; but "plague take the rest of 'em!" He wanted to sell the honey and buy skates and "a man's gun" with the proceeds. Johnny's father cheers him up, and, in gratitude for sharing some of the honey, Rev. Mr. Dennett gives Johnny a fine pocketknife.

HORACE. In "The Queen's Twin," he was Abby Martin's brother and the master of the vessel on which she and her husband Albert sailed to England in the 1840s. While there, Abby saw Queen Victoria.

HORN, BEN. In *Deephaven*, he is a man Kate Lancaster and Helen Denis dig clams with.

HORN, CAPTAIN ISAAC. In *Deephaven*, he is a representative old sea captain. A Bristol cloth merchant once tried unsuccessfully to cheat him.

HOVEY. In "The Hare and the Tortoise," this may be the owner of a store where Mary Chester shops.

HOWE, JULIA WARD (1819–1910). Woman of letters and reformer. Julia Ward was born in New York City, was privately educated, and in 1843 married Samuel Gridley Howe (1801–1876), the humanitarian. After traveling abroad for a year, the Howes established their residence in Boston and began an association with abolitionists and advocates of other liberal causes. Of their six children, three—Florence Marion Howe Hall, Laura Elizabeth Howe Richards, and Maud Howe Elliott—became writers. Mrs. Howe's vast literary production includes poetry, drama, travel writing, biographies, and works on social issues, notably feminism and prison reform. A gifted linguist and lecturer, she knew most of the established figures of her era, including the publisher James T. Fields and his wife, Annie Adams Fields.* Jewett was acquainted with Mrs. Howe through her friendship with Annie Fields. In 1879 Mrs. Howe invited Jewett to read from her works at the Saturday Morning Club, which she had established as an informal school for young women. The two often met later. In Boston both attended the *Atlantic Monthly* reception honoring Oliver Wendell Holmes* (3 December 1879) and an authors' reading to raise funds for a memorial to Henry Wadsworth Longfellow (1887); Jewett also heard Mrs. Howe lecture at the Berwick Women's Club (7 December 1901) and provided hospitality in her home for Mrs. Howe and Laura, her daughter. *Bibliography*: Blanchard; Silverthorne.

HOWELLS, WILLIAM DEAN (1837–1920). Author and editor. He was born in Martin's Ferry, Ohio, was a typesetter and reporter, studied literature and languages on his own, wrote the campaign biography of Abraham Lincoln, and was rewarded by being made consul to Venice (1861–1865). In Paris in 1862 he married Elinor Mead, cousin of Rutherford B. Hayes, the future president, whose campaign biography Howells also wrote. When he returned to the United States, he became an influential editor, with the *Nation* in New York City (1865–1866), as James T. Fields's assistant with the *Atlantic Monthly* (1866–1871), and as *Atlantic* editor (1871–1881). He and his family then moved to New York. Earlier, he had helped the cause of literary realism; later, he turned toward socialism, anti-imperialism, and progressivism. He and his wife, who had three children, traveled frequently in the 1890s. He wrote more than a hundred books, which include novels, travel sketches, literary criticism, biography, and autobiography. His greatest novels include *A Modern Instance* (1882), *The Rise of Silas Lapham* (1885), and *A Hazard of New Fortunes* (1890). Notable are his *Criticism and Fiction* (1891) and *Literature and Life* (1902). Howells concerned himself with frontier democracy, snobbery, feminism, miscegenation, ruthless industrialism, crime, spiritualism, and social reform. Although he championed literary realism, he seems timid by more relaxed modern standards. Revealingly, he once wrote his friend, John Hay (18 March 1882), that there would never be "palpitating divans in my stories." Among his many other friends, the closest were Henry James* and Mark Twain.* Younger writers he encouraged include Stephen Crane, Henry Blake Fuller, Hamlin Garland, and Frank Norris. The Howellses's daughter Winifred, suffering from anorexia, hypochondria, and vertigo, was misdiagnosed as neurasthenic by S. Weir Mitchell, the Philadelphia physician-novelist and a friend of Jewett's; Winifred died in 1889.

In "Looking Back on Girlhood," Jewett mentions that after publishing stories in *Young Folks* and *The Riverside*, she had a "sketch" accepted by "Mr. Howells for the *Atlantic*" when she "was between nineteen and twenty." That sketch was "Mr. Bruce" (1869). Howells and Fields had rejected at least two earlier Jewett submissions, and after "Mr. Bruce" they declined two more. She grew so depressed that she asked whether she should continue trying, and was encouraged by Howells to do so by all means but with fiction rather than poetry.

Next, she sent him "The Shore," which he deftly told her how to improve, and before long he became a treasured mentor. The two met soon thereafter, and Jewett was often a guest of the Howellses in Cambridge and Belmont, Massachusetts, and at their summer home at Kittery Point, Maine. Howell had a hand in shaping her "Deephaven" pieces, which he suggested could be made into a novel, and in otherwise pointing out as her greatest assets her compassion for rural folks and their often cramped lives, her knack for catching the timbre of their revealing speech, and her ability to write with restrained realism. Since Howells liked supernatural yarns, it is odd that he rejected Jewett's "Lady Ferry." In his *Literary Friends and Acquaintance* (1900), Howells praises Jewett's "exquisitely realistic art." *Bibliography*: Blanchard; Kenneth S. Lynn, *William Dean Howells: An American Life* (New York: Harcourt Brace Jovanovich, 1971).

HOWTH, LORD. In *The Tory Lover*, he is a fancy aristocrat the teacher Sullivan remembers seeing in Dublin.

HULL, EXPER'ENCE. In *Deephaven*, she and her sister, Mrs. Ware, attend church together in Deephaven.

HULL, MIRANDA ("MIRANDY"). In "The Taking of Captain Ball," she is a dressmaker who works for and gossips with Mrs. Captain Topliff.

HUNTER, KATE. In "Mr. Bruce," she is the sister of Tennant, the father of Kitty Tennant and Margaret Tennant. Kate Hunter welcomes Kitty for a visit to her Baltimore home, where Kitty momentously encounters Philip Bruce again.

HUNTER, ROBERT ("BOB"). In "Mr. Bruce," he is the husband of Kate Hunter, who is the sister of Tennant, the father of Kitty Tennant and Margaret Tennant. Hunter is a businessman in Baltimore. While he is away on business in Savannah, Kitty visits Kate, her aunt. When Hunter returns, he invites Philip Bruce to dinner. The two men had met in London earlier.

HUTCHINGS, SOLOMON. In *The Tory Lover*, he is a *Ranger* sailor. He breaks his leg.

HUTCHINSON, GOVERNOR THOMAS (1711–1780). American colonial administrator. In *The Tory Lover*, Roger Wallingford remembers seeing his mother, Madam Wallingford, at the governor's birthday party at the Province House.

HUTTON, JUDGE. In "The Failure of David Berry," he is a person whose best boots David Berry makes for a while.

HYMORE, JIM. In ''A Financial Failure,'' he is known to Joel Hayland as a careless investor. Hayland mentions the fact to Pendell, the treasurer of the County Savings Bank in Dartford, and adds that he prefers moderate but certain interest.

IDA. In *Betty Leicester*, she is a Riverport girl whose mother briefly fears that she and Georgie, her brother, are lost.

"IN A COUNTRY PRACTICE" (1894). Short story. (Characters: Dr. Ashurst, Dr. John Ashurst, Lizzie Ashurst, Mrs. Ashurst, Mrs. Ashurst, Nelly Ashurst, Dr. Best, Dent, Dr. Duncan, Dr. Grafton, Sarah, Dr. Smith). Dr. John Ashurst graduates first in his class in medical school, whereupon his finest teacher, Dr. Best, invites him to join him in his lucrative practice in New York. But the young physician prefers to return to Alton, where his father practiced country medicine before him. Years later Dr. Ashurst, married now and with two daughters, takes a train one wintry day, after a distant call, for a twenty-mile trip home to Alton. In the cold car he meets a very sick man just back from business in Cuba, diagnoses him accurately, writes a prescription for him, and even loans him for needed warmth a Scotch plaid blanket sent him by Dr. Best. He gives the man his name and address, and the stranger returns the blanket in due time but without an accompanying note. More time passes, and Dr. Ashurst suffers a fatal attack of pneumonia. The failure of a bank in which he invested heavily has left his wife, their daughter, Lizzie Ashurst, now a schoolteacher, and Nelly Ashurst, their younger daughter, almost destitute—especially since he often treated not only many charity patients but also several forgetful ones. The day before Thanksgiving a letter arrives explaining that a businessman, recently dying in Cuba, has willed Dr. Ashurst and his heirs $50,000 in remembrance of his kind and invaluable help. The Ashurst women use part of the money to continue Dr. Ashurst's habit of generosity to those in need. Since Jewett's father, Theodore Herman Jewett,* was also a country doctor and the head of a loving family including daughters, "In a Country Practice" has several autobiographical touches.

"IN DARK NEW ENGLAND DAYS" (1890). Short story. (Characters: Phoebe Dow, Martha Downs, Peter Downs, Melinda Dutch, Pappy Flanders, Mrs. Forder, Deacon Jake Good'in, Holt, Enoch Holt, Mrs. Holt, Mrs. Holt, Betsey Knowles, Captain Knowles, Hannah Knowles.) Captain Knowles, a former slave trader, has just died in May at his farm near Riverport. Martha Downs helps his daughters, Betsey Knowles and Hannah Knowles, each over sixty, at their house afterwards and feels insulted when they rush her out in the dark evening to her home nearby. Her husband, Peter Downs, meets her and laughs when she admits she got little news. That night Betsey and Hannah open their stingy father's sea chest and find, under miscellaneous clothes and papers, a hoard of gold and silver coins, and some bank bills. They do not see the eye of a man peering at them through a shutter knothole. Leaving everything in the kitchen, they go upstairs to bed. In the morning the treasure is gone. They formally accuse Enoch Holt, who once argued with their father over a timber sale, did attend his funeral, but then supposedly left by horseback for Boston. At his trial in August, the verdict is "not proven." When Hannah curses him, he swears his innocence by his right hand. So she curses his right hand—"yours and all your folks' that follow you." Enoch sails on a vessel out of Salem he is part owner of and returns with a profit from the pepper trade. To support themselves, the Knowles sisters work at their wheel and loom, resemble two Furies, waste away, and are subject to gossip: Did old Knowles return from the dead and take his coins? Is a shadowy spirit living with the pair in their house? When Enoch's married daughter, Phoebe Dow, has a second baby, she is relieved to note his properly formed hands. Next April, Mrs. Forder visits Martha, and over tea the two ponder the efficacy of curses. One June evening years later, Martha, now a widow, and Mrs. Forder reminisce after attending the wedding of a young Holt. He returned from the frontier with his right hand shot off. When his mother was thrown from a wagon, her right wrist was mangled. While Enoch was building his new house, the frame fell and crushed his right arm, which had to be amputated. Under a glorious New England sunset, Martha and Mrs. Forder suddenly see bent old Enoch crossing a meadow and resembling "a malicious black insect" and with his empty sleeve fluttering. *Bibliography*: Elizabeth Ammons, "Jewett's Witches," in Nagel, 165–84; Joseph Church, "Fathers, Daughters, Slaves: The Haunted Scene of Writing in Jewett's 'In Dark New England Days,' " *American Transcendental Quarterly* 5 (September 1991): 205–24; Roman.

ISABELLA. In "Going to Shrewsbury," she is one of Mrs. Wayland's daughters and is a niece of Mrs. Peet, who is going to stay with Isabella. Isabella is married to the carriage shop overseer, has four daughters, and dislikes housework. Mrs. Peet expects to be useful.

J

JACK. In "Miss Sydney's Flowers," he is Bessie Thorne's uncle. He tells her about a job available in a museum. She tells Miss Sydney, who recommends Becky Marley for it.

JACK. In *The Tory Lover*, he is mentioned as a typical "poor" sailor under the rigorous command of Captain John Paul Jones.

JACKSON. In "Hallowell's Pretty Sister," he is a person whose house is inferior to Dick Hallowell's, according to the snobbish Jack Spencer.

JACKSON. In "Told in the Tavern," he is a drover who enters the Byfleet tavern and describes the weather up north.

JACKSON. In "Tom's Husband," he is the "chief aid" whose advice Mary Dunn Wilson relies on when she runs the Wilson factory.

JACKSON, DR. In *A Country Doctor*, he is a man mentioned by Dr. John Leslie as an unusually ignorant diagnostician in Oldfields.

JACKSON, JERRY. In "An Only Son," he is the Dalton town tax collector. He dutifully hands selectmen John Kendall, Deacon John Price, and Captain Abel Stone the $735 he collected. Deacon Price's agreeing to deposit the cash the next day occasions all the trouble.

JACOBS, JOHN. In "Miss Debby's Neighbors," he is a neighbor of old John Ashby and his family. For a dollar, Jacobs uses his oxen to help John Ashby and his son, also named John Ashby, haul the farmhouse of Joseph Ashby, young John's brother, down the road.

JAFFREY. In "A Village Shop," he was the early-dying clergyman father of Esther Jaffrey and Leonard Jaffrey.

JAFFREY, ESTHER. In "A Village Shop," she is the long-suffering manager of a notions shop in the old Jaffrey mansion. Her work totally supports the indolent lifestyle of her younger brother, Leonard Jaffrey. She fears for the future if he marries Nelly Grant; but Nelly's father, a wealthy widower, so admires the once-aristocratic Jaffrey family that all will be well. When Leonard suggests that Esther close her shop, she vehemently declines.

JAFFREY, JUDGE. In "A Village Shop," he was a respected jurist and was the great-grandfather of Esther Jaffrey and Leonard Jaffrey.

JAFFREY, LEONARD. In "A Village Shop," he is a pompous, indolent bookworm. He quits Harvard, returns home, and lets his older sister, Esther Jaffrey, support him. When John Grant gets her to take in his teen-aged daughter, young Nelly Grant, as a roomer and boarder, Leonard tutors her in Latin and philosophy. Although he is now middle-aged, the two fall in love and will marry, and comfortably, because Grant appoints him town librarian at $1,000 a year. Simpering Leonard's relationship with dumb Nelly has been called a parody of sentimental romantic fiction. *Bibliography*: Roman.

JAFFREY, MADAM. In "A Village Shop," she is the widowed mother of Esther Jaffrey and Leonard Jaffrey. She sacrifices to send useless Leonard to Harvard, soon dies, and leaves her children in precarious financial circumstances.

JAFFREY, MARLBOROUGH. In "A Village Shop," he was a distinguished forebear of Esther Jaffrey and Leonard Jaffrey. Marlborough studied at Oxford, migrated to America, and became a successful colonial merchant.

JAMES, HENRY (1843–1916). Novelist, short-story writer, and critic. Born in New York City, he received his early education in England and on the Continent, began publishing in the 1860s, established residence in London in 1876, and wrote with prodigious fecundity. His production includes *The American* (1877), *The Europeans* (1878), *The Portrait of a Lady* (1881), *Hawthorne* (1879), "The Art of Fiction" (1884), *A Little Tour in France* (1884), *The Bostonians* (1886), *The Aspern Papers* (1888), "The Turn of the Screw" (1898), *The Wings of the*

Dove (1901), *The Ambassadors* (1902), *The Golden Bowl* (1903), and *The American Scene* (1907), as well as collections of short fiction, volumes of criticism and autobiography, and plays.

Early in her reading of James, Jewett disliked the characters and their amorality in *The American* but admired its author's clever style. Later she extolled much of his short fiction. Jewett met James at his home south of London in 1898 when she and Annie Adams Fields* were vacationing in England. Fields records his praise of Jewett's work for being true, exact, elegant, and "not . . . overdone." In a letter to Jewett (5 October 1901) he criticized *The Tory Lover* as "misguided" and "cheap," and advised her to return to the time and place of *The Country of the Pointed Firs*. During his 1904–1905 tour of the United States, James visited William Dean Howells,* their mutual friend, then at Kittery Point, Maine, and with him called on Jewett shortly before James returned to England in June. James's *Bostonians* features an intimate relationship between two female characters similar to that of Jewett and Annie Fields, and of James's sister Alice James and the Bostonian Katharine Peabody Loring as well. James's short story, "Flickerbridge," was partly inspired by Jewett's "A Lost Lover." *Bibliography*: Blanchard; Robert L. Gale, *A Henry James Encyclopedia* (Westport, Conn.: Greenwood, 1989); Nagel.

JAMESON, CAPTAIN. In *The Country of the Pointed Firs*, he was a sea captain who, according to Captain Littlepage, knew a great deal about Solomon's temple and made a model of it.

JANE. In *A Country Doctor*, she is Marilla Thomas's assistant servant in Dr. John Leslie's home when Nan Prince returns after attending finishing school.

JANES. In "The Town Poor," he is mentioned by Miss Ann Bray as the considerate little son of Abel Janes and Mrs. Abel Janes.

JANES, ABEL. In "The Town Poor," he is the owner of the house where the Hampton selectmen have placed Miss Ann Bray and her sister, Mandana Bray, for $5 a month. Janes provides the sisters with a miserable upstairs room.

JANES, MRS. ABEL. In "The Town Poor," she opens her chilly house to Mrs. William Trimble and Miss Rebecca Wright when they seek to visit Miss Ann Bray and her sister, Mandana Bray.

JARVIS. In "A Christmas Guest," he is any one of the Jarvis boys. He helps Susan Johnson get to the nearby farmhome of Mrs. Norris, reportedly ill, so Susan can offer help.

JENKINS. In "The Honey Tree," he hears about the honey tree while at Joel Simmons's store. Jenkins tells the men gathered there about his mother's "aunt

by marr'ge'' who was ''deadly p'soned'' and ''was throwed into complete fits''
when she ate a lot of honey once.

JENKINS. In ''A Landless Farmer,'' he is or was Jerry Jenkins's brother who
went to California seeking gold.

JENKINS. In *The Tory Lover*, he is Major Tilly Haggens's Portsmouth business
acquaintance. Jenkins sells fine apples.

JENKINS, JERRY. In ''A Landless Farmer,'' he is a sick old widower. His
daughter, Serena Nudd, and her husband, Aaron Nudd, persuade him to deed
them his farm. Jerry's other daughter, Mary Lydia Bryan, gets the house he
owns but has let her live in. Jerry's long-absent son, Parker Jenkins, returns
from Colorado, rescues Jerry, and brings him back to health. Jerry's nephew,
Ezra Allen, is sympathetic.

JENKINS, MRS. JERRY. In ''A Landless Farmer,'' she was Jerry's deceased
wife, whom he remembers as more helpful and affectionate than their daughters.

JENKINS, PARKER. In ''A Landless Farmer,'' he is Jerry's son. Unsuited for
farming and a heavy drinker, he went to Colorado, was long out of touch with
his family, but returns with $25,000, rescues his father from the clutches of his
vicious sister, Serena Nudd, and brings him back to health. Parker plans to grow
cranberries in a nearby swamp. Jewett, profeminist wherever possible, says Parker's goodness is inherited from his mother. *Bibliography*: Roman.

JENKINS, SILAS. In ''The Taking of Captain Ball,'' he was the sea cook for
Captain Asaph Ball, who hires him briefly after the death of Ann Ball, the
captain's sister. Jenkins is too incompetent to remain on staff.

JENKS. In *A Marsh Island*, he is a hired hand for Israel Owen now that work
has slackened off during the dull summer season at the Sussex shipyard, where
he is normally employed.

JENKS. In ''The Spur of the Moment,'' he is Mrs. Dartmouth's servant. She
sends him to Fallon, the cabman, with money to use to offer Miss Peet a ride.

JENKS. In ''The Two Browns,'' he is a member of the law firm of Jenks and
Rowley. Thinking they are getting old, Grandison decides to retain John Benedict Brown instead. His doing so enables Brown to avoid detection.

"JENNY GARROW'S LOVERS" (1868). Short story. (Characters: Margery
Blake, Mrs. Blake, Tim Blake, Garrow, Jenny Garrow, Susannah Gerry, John
Haiton, Lady Tarrow, Sir John Tarrow, Mrs. Tyler, Richard Tyler, William

Tyler, Phebe Winnis, Stephen Winnis.) The scene is near Haverwell, England, in the year 180–. Margery Blake, the narrator, is Jenny Garrow's close friend. Jenny cannot decide between Richard ("Dick") Tyler and his brother, William ("Will") Tyler. Dick is tall and dark; Will, fair and graceful. To tease and test Dick, Jenny lets Will escort her to the harvest-moon country wedding of a girl they all know. Dick sees Jenny and Will together and disappears. At the dance afterwards, Will asks Jenny to marry him. Deciding she prefers Dick, she declines. When Will, who turns angry, cannot be located later, evidence against Dick results in his conviction for murdering Will. In the spring, Jenny and Margery visit Dick, serving a life sentence in Haverwell prison. In September, Jenny dies of fever. Much later, Will reappears and explains that after the dance he immediately left the region, went to sea for five years, and has just returned home. Dick is released, but neither brother ever marries. Margery offers the narration some forty years later. "Jenny Garrow's Lovers," Jewett's first story, was published under the pseudonym A. C. Eliot on 18 January 1868 in *The Flag of Our Union*, a Boston weekly.

JEWETT, CAROLINE AUGUSTA (1855–1897). Jewett's younger sister. *See also* Eastman, Caroline Augusta Jewett.

JEWETT, CAROLINE FRANCES PERRY (1820–1891). Jewett's mother (often called Mar). Her father was William Perry;* her mother, Abigail Gilman Perry.* Frances Jewett, as she was usually called, enjoyed cooking, sewing, gardening, boating, church and town activities, and visits to relatives in Brunswick and Portsmouth, Maine, and Exeter, New Hampshire. She had gracious manners, relished village gossip, read sentimental fiction, and was gentle and ceremonious. She suffered from a long illness, which caused her to be a semi-invalid for her last decade; it remained mysterious and was finally fatal. Jewett was one of the family "watchers" at the end. Although tender mother-daughter relationships are often presented in her fiction, she and her mother were evidently truly close only toward the end of her mother's life. Jewett wrote Thomas Bailey Aldrich* (letter unlocated) that she truly knew her mother only after her death. *Bibliography*: Blanchard; Frost; Matthiessen; Sherman.

JEWETT, DEARBORN (?–?) Jewett's great-grandfather. As a child he served in the Revolutionary army, wintering at Valley Forge when only twelve. He married Mary Furber (?–1837), an ensign's daughter. Their son, Theodore Furber Jewett,* was Jewett's grandfather. Later in their lives, Dearborn and Mary Jewett lived on a farm near South Berwick. *Bibliography*: Blanchard.

JEWETT, MARY RICE (?–1854). Jewett's paternal step-grandmother. In "From a Mournful Villager," Jewett describes her visits to this proud, solemn woman, that woman's preference for Jewett's better-mannered older sister, Mary

Rice Jewett,* and her death and grand funeral. *Bibliography*: Blanchard; Frost; Silverthorne.

JEWETT, MARY RICE ("O.P.," "OLD PEG") (1847–1930). Jewett's older sister. She was closer emotionally to Caroline Augusta Jewett Eastman,* the youngest of the three Jewett sisters, and mothered Caroline for a time. Mary was confirmed in the Episcopal faith in 1871 with Sarah. Mary, a fine pupil at school, was interested in gardening, history, library work, and funerals. Sarah and Mary devotedly cared for their mother, Caroline Frances Perry Jewett,* during her final illness. In 1898 Mary visited France with her nephew, Theodore Jewett Eastman,* and rendezvoused with Sarah there. In 1904, not long after Sarah was injured in the carriage accident, Mary took her to Johns Hopkins Medical Center, in Baltimore, for treatment that proved ineffective; soon thereafter, Mary was also thrown from a carriage but was not seriously injured. Through Sarah, Mary became a close friend of Willa Cather.* *Bibliography*: Blanchard; Frost; Sherman; Silverthorne.

JEWETT, SARAH ORNE ("SALLY") (1794–1819). Jewett's paternal grandmother. The daughter of a Portsmouth sea captain, she was married at nineteen to Theodore Furber Jewett* and gave birth to three sons, including Jewett's father, Theodore Herman Jewett.* In "River Driftwood," Jewett suggests that the older Sarah had a brief love affair with a French sailor named Ribère, briefly a prisoner in or near Portsmouth during the French and Indian Wars. *Bibliography*: Blanchard; Silverthorne.

JEWETT, THEODORA SARAH ORNE. This was Sarah Orne Jewett's full name.

JEWETT, THEODORE FURBER (1787–1860). Jewett's paternal grandfather. As a boy he ran away to the sea and became a whaler and then a captain, trading between Portsmouth and the West Indies. Captured in 1813 during the War of 1812, he was briefly held on the Dartmoor prison ship at Bristol, England. His first wife was Sarah Orne ("Sally") Jewett* the elder, who was the mother of Jewett's father, Theodore Herman Jewett,* and who died in 1819. T. F. Jewett's second wife was Olive Walker, also a Portsmouth sea captain's daughter; he moved with her to South Berwick. In Berwick he was a timber dealer, a bank director, and a town leader. He and his brothers established a shipyard on nearby Salmon Falls River. He and his second wife had two sons. After her death at thirty-two his third wife was Mary Rice Jewett,* who died in 1854 after twenty-five years of marriage. He then married Eliza Sleeper, his brother Nathan Jewett's widow. In "Looking Back on Girlhood," Jewett summarizes her paternal grandfather's career as youthful sailor, sea captain, shipbuilder, and timber dealer. She says that around 1825 he bought the Berwick family house, built about 1750, and moved his family there from Portsmouth. He is also mentioned in "River Driftwood." *Bibliography*: Blanchard; Frost; Silverthorne.

JEWETT, THEODORE HERMAN (1815–1878). Jewett's father. He attended Berwick Academy and then Bowdoin College, graduating in 1834. He taught briefly, attended lectures on medicine at Dartmouth College and in Boston, and worked in Boston military and charity hospitals. He studied at Jefferson Medical College in Philadelphia, obtained a medical degree there in 1839, and practiced with William Perry* in Exeter, New Hampshire. In 1842 Theodore Jewett married Perry's daughter, Caroline Frances Perry (*see* Jewett, Caroline Frances Perry). Soon after their first daughter, Mary Rice Jewett,* was born in 1847, they moved to South Berwick. Theodore Jewett established a permanent practice there and nearby. He occasionally taught, lectured, and consulted away from home—at Bowdoin Medical School, at the Medical College of Maine, and at Maine General Hospital in Portland (during some of the Civil War years). Sarah Orne Jewett adored her companionable father, sought and respected his advice, and was devastated at his death. In "Looking Back on Girlhood," she praises her father for encouraging her to read, observe nearby people and things lovingly, and write honestly. He was impatient, she says, only with insincerity and affectation. She accompanied him "like an undemanding little dog" when he visited the sick. He recognized, even before she was aware, that she would become a writer. She sought to characterize him, though inadequately, in *The Country Doctor*. *Bibliography*: Blanchard; Cary, *Letters*; Frost; Sherman; Silverthorne.

JIM. In "Jim's Little Woman," he is the sailor-husband of Martha, his "little woman." Of mixed New England and Spanish blood and orphaned as a teenager, he ships on the *Dawn of Day*, meets Martha in Maine, and within days marries her there. They sail to the house he inherited from his mother in St. Augustine, Florida. A sometimes-abusive alcoholic, he returns to the sea for a final profitable time, is reported dead, but reappears as a successful hand on a yacht—and all is well.

JIM. In "Jim's Little Woman," he is the son of Jim and Martha. She cares for him devotedly. Young Jim later has a little sister.

JIM, WIDOW. In *Deephaven*, this is the nickname of Judith Toggerson Patton, married thirteen years to Jack Patton. She is a bright little neighbor Kate Lancaster and Helen Denis enjoy talking with. Kate's aunt, Katharine Brandon, remembered Widow Jim handsomely in her will. Widow Jim sews, makes rugs and carpets, and helps with funeral arrangements. She warns the girls about the dangers of marriage.

JIMMY. In *Betty Leicester*, he is the old black horse belonging to Barbara Leicester and Mary Leicester.

"JIM'S LITTLE WOMAN" (1890). Short story. (Characters: Joe Black, Jim, Jim, Lizzie, Martha, Jim Peet). Jim is cared for by his mother, of New England extraction and deserted by her husband of Spanish blood, in the St. Augustine, Florida home of her retired Yankee sea-captain father. When Jim's grandfather and mother die, the teen-ager goes off to sea with an alcoholic captain of the schooner *Dawn of Day*. In June they put into Boothbay Harbor, Maine, for fresh water. Broad-shouldered, tall, handsome Jim meets Martha, a red-haired, orphaned lobster-factory worker described as "small and queer." They fall in love instantly and get married at Mount Desert. Once the captain sells his cargo of pine and conch shells and loads on dried fish and flour, they sail back to St. Augustine. Martha brightens Jim's "coquina house." They have a baby son, named Jim, and then a daughter. Jim is often abusive and roisters with his captain and crew so irreponsibly that Martha is glad when he sails away again. She supports herself and her infants by becoming a laundress, a seamstress, and a scrubwoman. Jim returns home, rationalizing that hard work in tropical Caribbean weather has forced him to drink. In truth, his Northern and Spanish blood jangle within him. Chagrined, Jim promises to settle down with her after one last profitable voyage. She dreams of his safe return but grows fearful as months pass, until the *Dawn of Day* returns with the message that Jim has died in Jamaica. Martha's life becomes a daze, until Jim returns home again and in the fine uniform of a yacht hand. He explains that he gave a quarter to a fellow in Kingston to write her he had a splendid new job and would soon return. A different crew member, thought to be Jim, had died. Soon Jim, his little woman, and their children, happily reunited, set sail for a visit to Maine. The best feature of "Jim's Little Woman" is Jewett's word pictures of St. Augustine, which she and Annie Adams Fields* visited at least twice in the 1880s.

JOE. In "The Girl with the Cannon Dresses," he is the independent, grinning dog owned by Sophronia Durfee. Joe accompanies Alice Channing when she goes to the spring where she chances to meet Dulcidora Bunt.

JOE, PEACH-TREE. In "Peach-tree Joe." *See* Peach-tree Joe.

JOHN. In *The Country of the Pointed Firs*, he was Susan Fosdick's brother, a year younger than she. He is now deceased.

JOHN. In *Deephaven*, he is mentioned at the Denby circus as a farmer whose brother-in-law is to be consulted regarding a pig's weight.

JOHN. In "Hallowell's Pretty Sister," he is the butler at the Hallowell home. Dick Hallowell brings guests there. John is in on the ruse to have Dick's brother, Tom Hallowell, impersonate their sister, Alice Hallowell.

JOHN. In "A Late Supper," he is the husband of Mary, who is Miss Catherine Spring's niece. They live in Lowell. Since his sister is going to help them with their children during the summer, they do not need Miss Spring's help.

JOHN. In "Miss Sydney's Flowers," he is Miss Sydney's stableman, coachman, and greenhouse keeper.

JOHN. In "Mr. Bruce," he is the coachman of Tennant and his family.

JOHN. In "The Parshley Celebration," he was a soldier from Parshley who died during the Civil War. The marchers stop at the home of John's parents and praise their son.

JOHN. In "Peach-tree Joe," he is "an old soldier and the master-of-horse" for the narrator's family. John reminisces about Peach-tree Joe, killed beside him in Virginia during the Civil War in the summer of 1861.

JOHN. In "The White Rose Road," he is the narrator's carriage driver. Called "the master of horse," he says a bunch of talkative country children are discussing "[o]ld times." The children are perhaps descendants of regicides who fled England and settled in New England after the death of Charles I. In "A Winter Drive," John, called "the Captain of Horse," is Jewett's driver and tells her the clam man is "well off" and "lives at the Gunket." John is based on John Tucker, who was the Jewett family's faithful hostler and handyman for thirty years, until his death in 1902. *Bibliography*: Silverthorne.

JOHNSON. In "An Empty Purse," he is Mrs. Wallis's "elderly man-servant." He shows Miss Debby Gaines in for a visit.

JOHNSON. In *A Marsh Island*, he was Susan Winchester's coachman, discharged after fourteen years of service.

JOHNSON. In "The News from Petersham," he is the son of Jesse Johnson, who is the son of Daniel Johnson. This Johnson tells Mrs. Peak his grandfather is ill but has not taken to his bed.

JOHNSON, DANIEL ("DAN'EL"). In "The News from Petersham," he is the wealthy, generous old Petersham resident whose death is greatly exaggerated, first by Mrs. Peak and then by several others.

JOHNSON, JESSE. In "The News from Petersham," he is Daniel Johnson's son and William Johnson's brother. Jesse's wife is Lydia Johnson.

JOHNSON, LYDIA. In "The News from Petersham," she is Jesse Johnson's wife and Daniel Johnson's daughter-in-law. She starts the rumor of Daniel's death by exaggerating the severity of his cold.

JOHNSON, MRS. WILLIAM. In "The News from Petersham," she is Daniel Johnson's daughter-in-law. It is said she would like to move west with her husband, perhaps to join her sister there, if Daniel dies.

JOHNSON, SUSAN. In "A Christmas Guest," she is Eben Norris's niece and Rebecca's cousin. Eben Norris goes through the snowstorm to ask for Susan Johnson to come help Mrs. Norris, his mother, who has become ill.

JOHNSON, WILLIAM. In "The News from Petersham," he is Daniel Johnson's son and Jesse Johnson's brother.

JONAS. In "Miss Debby's Neighbors," he is Miss Debby's brother. His death obliges her to move into the village. She recalls his minor activities.

JONAS. In "The New Methuselah," he is a servant in Dr. Asa Potterby's household.

JONATHAN. In *Betty Leicester*, he is the loyal old servant of Barbara Leicester and Mary Leicester. He is based on John Tucker, the long-time servant of Jewett's parents in South Berwick.

JONES. In "The Dulham Ladies," he is evidently a Dulham minister who took the place of the Reverend Edward Dobin when he died.

JONES. In "Stolen Pleasures," he is the man whose barge the factory friends of John Webber plan to hire to take them to the beach.

JONES, CAPTAIN JOHN PAUL (1747–1792). American Revolutionary War naval officer. In *The Tory Lover*, Captain John Paul Jones, called Paul Jones (and John Paul Jones only once), falls in love with Mary Hamilton in Berwick, sails his *Ranger* to France, confers with Benjamin Franklin in Passy, is promised but then denied command of *L'Indien*, and raids Whitehaven. Disguised as a Spanish sailor in Bristol, he foils the traitorous plot of Dickson, his yellow-faced officer, and helps Roger Wallingford meet Mary at an inn. Jones is mentioned in "River Driftwood."

JONES, GRANDMA. In "The Lost Turkey," she is Grandpa Jones's wife, Sarah Jones's mother-in-law, and John Jones's grandmother. She happily hugs little John when the family feud ends.

JONES, GRANDPA. (Real name: Henry Jones.) In "The Lost Turkey," he is John Jones's stubborn grandfather. He never approved of his deceased son's marriage to Sarah Jones. Harsh words kept the two apart until by chance the turkey Grandpa Jones bought for himself rattled to the back of his wagon and John Jones, his estranged little grandson, thinks it is a present and takes it. This act breaks the ice, and Grandpa Jones, his wife, his daughter-in-law, and his grandson are reconciled.

JONES, JOHN ("JOHNNY"). In "The Lost Turkey," he is Sarah Jones's little son and the grandson of Grandma Jones and Grandpa Jones. His thinking his grandfather's turkey is meant as a gift results in the happy ending of an unfortunate family feud.

JONES, SARAH. In "The Lost Turkey," she is little John Jones's widowed mother. Her father-in-law, Grandpa Jones, never approved of her. Her harsh words in response caused a longlasting family feud, which ends when John thinks Grandpa Jones's turkey is a gift.

JOSEPH. In "Andrew's Fortune," he is mentioned by Mrs. Haynes as having brought news of Stephen Dennett's sudden illness. Joseph may be Ann's husband.

JOSEPHINE. In "Mère Pochette," she is Father Pierre's housekeeper. He selfishly discourages her ambition to become a Catholic sister because he wants to retain her as his excellent cook.

JOSHUAY ("JOSH"). In "The Courting of Sister Wisby," Mrs. Goodsoe mentions him as her oldest brother. He kidded Silas Brimblecom when Eliza Wisby ejected him from the trial marriage he had been enjoying in her home.

JOSIAH. In "Mary and Martha," he is Maria Whitefield's brother. Josiah gave Maria a sewing machine and is reportedly doing well in New York.

K

KALEHAN, JIM. In "The Luck of the Bogans," he is a Bantry shoemaker who bids goodbye to Mike Bogan, his wife, Biddy Flaherty Bogan, and their infant son, Dan Bogan, when they leave for America.

KATE. In "Paper Roses," she and her friend Ellinor sell items at a hospital fair. One item is a bunch of paper roses, purchased though seemingly unattractive. Kate later meets the bedridden old shut-in who made them and delights her by reporting that the sale brought money for the hospital.

KATHERINE. In "Mr. Bruce." *See* Bruce, Kitty.

KATY. In *Deephaven*, she is Captain Sands's daughter-in-law. He says she sensed that her daughter, fifteen miles away, was crying.

KATY. In "The White Rose Road," this may be the name of the thin little girl who tends a sage-bordered rural garden. She may also be called Becky.

KEAY. In *The Tory Lover*, this is the name of a Berwick family active in the French and Indian War.

KEITH, JOHN. In "Mr. Bruce," he is a man discussed by Bowler and Philip Bruce as having married his mother's nursery maid. Bowler praises the girl's charming manner. Philip's uppityness about it all betrays his class consciousness.

KENDALL, JOHN. In "An Only Son," he is a grist miller and also a Dalton selectman, along with Deacon John Price and Captain Abel Stone.

KENT, FRANCES. In "The Green Bowl," she is the young companion of Katie Montague, who domineers Frances. The two spend the night in the empty church and are given breakfast the next morning by Mrs. Patton. When Mrs. Patton tells Katie the secret of the green bowl, Katie will not share the secret with Frances.

KERSAINTE. In *The Tory Lover*, he is a French commodore who was with the Duke of Chartres at Hampton Roads, Virginia, in 1775. Captain John Paul Jones met them both there at that time.

KEW, MRS. TOM. In *Deephaven*, Vermont born, she helps her husband tend the Deephaven lighthouse. Kate Lancaster and Helen Denis find her amiable and pleasantly gossipy. They go to the Denby circus together.

KEW, TOM. In *Deephaven*, he is a former whaler, who is now the Deephaven lighthouse keeper. He tells sea yarns and ghost stories.

KILGORE, HATE-EVIL. In *The Tory Lover*, she was Nancy Haggens's neighbor and has a name popular in Round-head times.

KILLAHAN, MOTHER. In "A Little Captive Maid," she is mentioned by Nora Connelly as a feeble but devout member of her American church.

KILLOREN, DINNY. In "A Little Captive Maid," he is the owner of a sidecar in Kenmare, Ireland. He brings Nora Connelly home to her lover, John Morris.

KILPATRICK, MRS. In "The Gray Mills of Farley," she is a mill sweeper. Mrs. Kilpatrick is a close friend of Mary Cassidy. Mrs. Kilpatrick rents a room from Fitzgibbon; gossips about Michel, a French-Canadian; and befriends Maggie, the little orphan.

KIMBALL. In "Andrew's Fortune," he is mentioned as the owner of a tract of wood Mrs. Towner had a lot on.

"THE KING OF FOLLY ISLAND" (1886). (Characters: Dan'el, Mrs. Danforth, John Frankfort, Phebe Frankfort, George Quint, Mrs. George Quint, Phebe Quint, Jabez Pennell, Mrs. Jabez Pennell, Wash'n'ton.) John Frankfort, a bachelor of forty-two or -three, is taking a September vacation from his ruthlessly successful banking and investment business in the city. He sails to John's Island, off the coast of Maine, with Jabez Pennell, its old merchant-postmaster. From there Frankfort decides to stay briefly on Folly Island, purchased twenty-six years ago by George Quint, who, when he lost the appointment as postmaster of John's Island, vowed never to set foot on any land but his own. George agrees to sail Frankfort out to his island retreat. Called "King George" by former friends, he took his wife and daughter, Phebe, to his island. His wife died there of loneliness; Phebe, once beautiful, patiently languishes there, coughing a great deal. George fishes and raises hogs, chickens, and sheep, while Phebe does what chores she can, which includes raising potatoes. She welcomes Frankfort, to whom she is wistfully attracted. He pities her stoic loneliness and senses she is near death. Within a few days Frankfort and George come to realize they are similar: Successful fishing and successful investing are equally chancy and can make people equally callous. When George takes Frankfort, his vacation ended, back to John's Island, he wonders whether Frankfort would like to marry and care for Phebe and accept his considerable savings in "hard cash" in the process. Frankfort, although he has thought of offering sick Phebe medical help, declines. A little later he sends the Quints some useful Christmas gifts, for which King George writes his thanks and adds that Phebe is weakening. She soon sends Frankfort a touchingly ugly toy meeting-house she crafted of cardboard and seashells, and with it a letter saying that she has led a useless life, whereas he must be "a sight of use" to the world, and also that her father would love to see him again. Her praise stings Frankfort, who realizes he has been too grasping and determines, in gratitude to Phebe, to aid others—beginning with his "bright young" office boy. Aspects of this story owe something to the father of Celia Laighton Thaxter,* who was called "The King of the Island Empire" because of his control over the Isles of Shoals. *Bibliography*: Donovan.

KINLOCK. In "Good Luck," he was the granduncle of Mary Leslie's father. The Leslie family inherits moody old Uncle Kinlock's house near Hilton, New Hampshire.

KIPLING, RUDYARD (1865–1936). British author, born in Bombay. He was a journalist in India, and wrote short stories, novels, and books for children and about animals. The following are among his early book publications: *The Phantom 'Rickshaw* (1888), *Soldiers Three* (1888), *Plain Tales from the Hills* (1888), *The Light That Failed* (1890), *Mine Own People* (1891, with an introduction by Henry James,* his friend and admirer), *Barrack-Room Ballads and Other Verse* (1892), *The Jungle Book* (1894), *Captains Courageous* (1897), and *Kim* (1901). From 1887 to 1889 Kipling traveled widely, in India, China, Japan, and the United States. He married Caroline Balestier, an American, in 1892, and lived with her in Brattleboro, Vermont, her home town, until they returned to England in 1896. Jewett admired Kipling's short stories and met the Kiplings two or three times during their New England stay. In a letter (January 1897) he offered this prescient praise of *The Country of the Pointed Firs*: "I don't believe even *you* know how good that book is." He also esteemed "The Only Rose." During their 1898 visit to England, Jewett and Annie Adams Fields* called on the Kiplings at their home in Rotterdean. Charles Eliot Norton, whose daughter Sara Norton* was one of Jewett's closest friends, wrote a biography of Kipling (1899). *Bibliography*: Blanchard; Stuart Murray, *Rudyard Kipling in Vermont: Birthplace of the Jungle Books* (Bennington, Vt.: Images from the Past, 1997).

KIPP, MISS TEMPERANCE ("TEMP'RANCE," "TEMPY"). In *A Marsh Island*, she is Martha Owen's wise, garrulous, observant servant. She supports Dan Lester in his anemic courtship of Doris Owen.

KNOWLES. In "A New Parishioner," he is mentioned as the owner of nearby mills.

KNOWLES, BETSEY. In "In Dark New England Days," she is the older daughter, over sixty, of Captain Knowles. At his death, she and her sister, Hannah Knowles, open his sea chest and find a hoard of gold coins. It is immediately stolen from them, presumably by Enoch Holt. When he swears his innocence on his right hand, Hannah curses his hand and those of his descendants. Betsey and Hannah seem accursed themselves in later life.

KNOWLES, CAPTAIN ("CAP'N"). In "In Dark New England Days," he was a slave-trading, devilish sea captain. At his death, his daughters, Betsey Knowles and Hannah Knowles, whom he dominated dreadfully, find his hoard of gold coins. They are stolen from them, presumably by Enoch Holt, with whom Captain Knowles had an argument over money. Rumor has it that Captain Knowles returned for his coins and hovered shadow-like in his daughters' home thereafter.

KNOWLES, HANNAH. In "In Dark New England Days," she is the younger daughter, over sixty, of Captain Knowles. At his death, she and her sister, Betsey Knowles, find his gold coins, but they are stolen from them. When Enoch Holt, the presumed thief, is acquitted in court, Hannah, though always more timid than Betsey, boldly curses his right hand and those of his descendants. The curse comes true, but in the process both sisters turn witch-like.

L

"LADY FERRY" (1879). Short story. (Characters: Agnes, Deborah, Lady Ferry, Fleming, Colonel Haverford, Mistress Haverford, Thomas Highward, Jack McAllister, John McAllister, Marcia, Matthew, Mistress Honor Warburton.) When the parents of little Marcia, now the grown-up narrator, go abroad, they leave her with a cousin named Matthew and his wife, Agnes, in the big old Haverford mansion by a ferry near a river. Marcia hears her parents remark that they hope she will not be frightened by a certain crazy old lady, now also living there. Agnes and Matthew treat Marcia graciously. Agnes is like a surrogate mother. Before bedtime the first night, Marcia is allowed to wander in the garden. Feeling lonely, she calls out for her faraway mother, then turns and sees Lady Ferry—tall, thin, bent, in a white dress that has a chilly rustle. Marcia lets the lady hold her hand, and they walk and talk about dead queens. A servant's gossip about the lady adds to the mystery, and Marcia also reads about wanderers doomed never to die. Agnes, who is a little ill, lets Marcia visit the lady in her rooms. The lady explains that she has her chairs all placed properly for her own funeral, for the morrow (but often postponed). With her sweet smile, pleasantly high voice, and trail of faint fragrance, she assuages Marcia's fears by showing her antique jewelry and Chinese carvings—thus delighting the girl. The two kiss. They discuss historical figures, some of whom the lady seems to have known. One day John McAllister, Matthew's middle-aged friend, calls at the house; the lady, mistaking John McAllister for his grandfather, calls him Jack McAllister, lost more than seventy years ago at sea. In the garret, Marcia finds a curiously shaped book and reads in it about a woman named Mistress Honor Warburton in Boston, saddled with the curse of unending life. Marcia has a dream about a stately old dance in the empty parlor below Lady Ferry's rooms; Marcia has a vivid sense of harpsichord music, candlelight, velvet, brocade, cloaks, ruffs, and low-voiced guests departing by boats. In the fall, Marcia says farewell to Lady Ferry. Marcia lives abroad for years; during this time her mother, Matthew, and Agnes all die. In Amsterdam before she and her father return to America, Marcia happens upon the book about Miss Warburton and reads further. Home again, she visits the old mansion, empty and now regarded as haunted. Marcia smiles, because in the family burial ground she sees "my Lady Ferry's grave"; so the ancient woman is surely dead.

The old Haverford mansion is based on the house in Portsmouth, by the Piscataqua River, inherited by Jewett's old friend, Anne Rice, from her sea-captain father. Jewett called her "Aunt Anne" and also knew her daughter, Marcia, whose name she took for the narrator of "Lady Ferry." *Bibliography*: Elizabeth Ammons, "Jewett's Witches," in Nagel, pp. 165–84; Blanchard; Silverthorne.

LAFAYETTE, GENERAL (1757–1834). (Full name: Marie Joseph Paul Yves Roch Gilbert de Motier, Marquis de Lafayette.) French officer, statesman, and hero of the American Revolution. In "Peg's Little Chair," when General Lafayette arrives at the public house of Margaret Benning, the mother of Margaret ("Peg") Benning, the child places her little chair for him to step down on to descend from his carriage. Lafayette kisses Peg and gives her a silver coin.

LANCASTER. In *Deephaven*, he is Kate Lancaster's father. He and his wife live in Boston and are summering in Europe. They have inherited Katharine Brandon's Deephaven house.

LANCASTER, JACK. In *Deephaven*, he was Kate Lancaster's beloved uncle. He took her to a circus when she was seven. He died in Canton, not long out of college and still in his twenties.

LANCASTER, JACK. In *Deephaven*, he is one of Kate Lancaster's young brothers, new at school. He visits Kate at Deephaven once.

LANCASTER, KATE. In *Deephaven*, she is Helen Denis's friend. Kate, twenty-four, and Helen spend the summer in Deephaven, in the big mansion the Lancasters have inherited from Kate's aunt, Katharine Brandon. The two girls enjoy reading, hiking, fishing, and gossiping with local residents. In "Good Luck," Mary Leslie mentions having visited Kate Lancaster and Nelly Denis in Deephaven. (*See* Denis, Helen.) Some readers regard Kate as a little too class conscious. She is probably based on Kate Birckhead, Jewett's close friend. *Bibliography*: Josephine Donovan, "The Unpublished Love Poetry of Sarah Orne Jewett," in Nagel, pp. 107–17; Sherman.

LANCASTER, MRS. In *Deephaven*, she is Kate Lancaster's mother. She and her husband live in Boston and are vacationing in Europe.

LANCASTER, WILLY. In *Deephaven*, he is one of Kate Lancaster's young brothers, now at school. He visits her at Deephaven once.

"A LANDLESS FARMER" (1883). Short story. (Characters: Allen, Ezra Allen, Susan Allen, Dr. Banks, Bryan, Henry Bryan, Mary Lydia Bryan, Estes, Enoch Foster, Foxwell, Harlow, Josh Hayden, Jenkins, Jerry Jenkins, Mrs. Jerry Jenkins, Parker Jenkins, Nudd, Aaron Nudd, Serena Nudd, Parsons, Asa Parsons, Mrs. Asa Parsons, Jack Townsend, Washington Tufts, Henry Wallis.) One nice spring Sunday in New England, Asa Parsons and Henry Wallis, both of whom are farmers, meet Ezra Allen, a farmer-wheelwright, at a bridge by a swamp. Ezra tells them he sat up the night before with Jerry Jenkins, his sick uncle. Jerry's daughter, Serena Nudd, talked him into deeding his homestead to her and her husband, Aaron Nudd; deeding his improvident, widowed daughter, Mary Lydia Bryan, the house he owns that she is living in with her lazy sons; and cutting out his own absent son, Parker Jenkins, a drinker and a poor farmer, but a good fellow. Two days later, Ezra encounters Serena at his house and argues with her while she rationalizes. In June, Jerry feels a bit stronger and is about to be delivered to Mary Lydia for the summer when he discovers that Serena has sold his treasured "chist o' drawers" for money to buy a sewing machine. He grows too feeble to object for long. Jerry no sooner arrives at Mary Lydia's rundown house in Harlow's Mills than she whines about her "neurology." They chat pleasantly enough for a week, after which homesick Jerry is pleased when Ezra wagons by on business, takes him along, and listens as he complains about his selfish daughters. Simultaneously, handsome Parker returns from the Colorado mining fields with $25,000, learns from Susan how his father was treated, goes to Serena and rebukes her for cheating him and Mary Lydia, then brings his father home. The upshot is that Jerry's health improves, Parker considers growing cranberries in the swamp, Aaron takes Serena to Harlow's Mills and gets a good job in a shoe factory, and Asa's pretty daughter has her eye on Parker, which pleases her parents. Jewett avers that many New England farmhouses hide tales of Juliets, Ophelias, Shylocks, and Lears. Ironically Serena, the evil sister, prospers financially after her move with Aaron to the mill town and is accepted socially by members of the church there, although she practices few Christian doctrines relating to the well-being of others, whereas Parker will care lovingly for their father although he "ain't one to talk religious." *Bibliography*: Blanchard.

"A LANDLOCKED SAILOR" (1899). Short story. (Characters: Mike Dillon, Dr. John Hallett, Parlow.) Dr. John Hallett, an assistant surgeon in the navy, is just back from Valparaiso and then Brooklyn after three years at sea. He is relaxing at his family's inland home. One early June morning, he walks through familiar surroundings to a trout-fishing spot he knows. He feels spiritually refreshed. Suddenly Mike Dillon emerges from the woods. Mike, about forty, was a sailor whose bones, badly broken in a shipboard accident, Hallett helped treat more than two years earlier. While the two men rest and smoke in the noonday sun, Mike, who says he is married now, tells his story. After being discharged, he made his way painfully on imperfectly mended legs to this region and was able to help a farm woman because he had been on a farm during his youth. He favorably impressed the woman, who was close to sixty but still good-looking, by scaring crows away from her corn planting. She saw, he says, "me heart was honest and me luck very bad." Dr. Hallett is glad for the man's "[g]ood harborage" but is surprised to learn it was the old woman's pretty niece that Mike wed. Mike does not mind that one of his legs is now shorter than the other, because the farm he and his wife expect to inherit is on a hillside anyway. In this story, Jewett combines beautiful description of the natural setting, a charming Irish monologue, and an O. Henry ending.

"THE LANDSCAPE CHAMBER" (1887). (Characters: none named.) The narrator, a native of New England, seeks a little summer adventure on horseback to improve her weakened health. When her horse develops shoe trouble three or four days later, she leads it a few miles along a road to an old mansion, once elegant but now dilapidated, and looks there for help and rest. She is given food, lodging, and reluctant hospitality by the haggard old owner—alternately gentle in expertly tending her horse and sourly offputting and miserly—and by his wretched daughter as well. The pallid woman explains that she is obliged to care for her father by a promise made to her deceased mother. The pair seem as doomed to decay as their house, in one room of which the daughter lets the narrator sleep. Called "the landscape chamber," the room has a quaint, century-old painting of the mansion in its former glory, erect and vivid, with brilliantly caparisoned occupants and guests. To the prying queries of the narrator, the old man says both mansion and inhabitants are cursed by the inescapably damning greed of an avaricious ancestor. The narrator offers to provide companionship for the daughter, at least for a time, and to debate free will and the restorative beneficence of nature with the father. But to no avail. Rooted, neither will budge. So, her mount well again, the narrator reluctantly rides away. This Hawthorn-esque, Poesque tale is one of Jewett's most brilliant, with many extraordinary touches. The old man had a mare that broke its neck trying to escape; he saved one of her ears as a souvenir. His china and silverware are lush, but the accompanying food is juiceless. Healthy mother nature beckons the narrator when a sparrow chirps on a windowsill near the stagnant chamber with the painting. The old man "clutch[es]" the money the narrator gives him. Best, she urges his imprisoned daughter to be modern and escape a tyrannical male. *Bibliography*: Blanchard; Cary, *Jewett*; Roman; Thorp.

LANE. In "The Flight of Betsey Lane," he is Betsey Lane's brother. She remembers that he brought her a bundle-handkerchief from the East Indies fifty years earlier.

LANE, BELL. In "Mrs. Parkins's Christmas Eve," she is one of the daughters of Mr. Lane, the new minister in Holton, and his wife. Their other children are John Lane and Mary Lane.

LANE, BETSEY. In "The Flight of Betsy Lane," she is a Byfleet Poor-house resident. Her two closest friends are Peggy Bond and Lavina Dow. Betsey, of seafaring stock and spry at sixty-nine, worked loyally for General Thornton, whose granddaughter, Katy Strafford, gives her $100 in gratitude. Sneaking off in defiance of likely criticism by the town selectmen, Betsey spends the money at the Philadelphia Centennial. For nine days she delights in wondrous sights, buys presents for friends back at the poorhouse, and tries to purchase glasses to improve Peggy's vision. Betsey returns home loaded with subjects to regale her friends with. She is typical of many Jewett characters who combine independence of spirit and love of community.

LANE, CAPTAIN ABIAH. In "A Bit of Shore Life," he attends Mrs. Wallis's auction. While there, the skinny old fellow talks with Skipper 'Lisha Downs about fish.

LANE, JERRY. In "Marsh Rosemary," he is a handsome, shiftless young sailor who lures middle-aged Nancy Lloyd into marriage, then contributes little or no work to managing her home near the Walpole marsh, and goes off to sea. Not drowned as reported, he marries a young woman in Shediac and has a child with her. Nancy goes to Shediac to expose him, but sees their domestic contentment by peeping through their window, and spares him the disaster of being charged with bigamy.

LANE, JOHN. In "Mrs. Parkins's Christmas Eve," he is the crippled son of Mr. Lane, the new minister in Holton, and his wife. Their other children are Bell Lane and Mary Lane. Mrs. Lydia Parkins pays for surgery in New York, which successfully repairs the boy's leg.

LANE, MARY. In "Mrs. Parkins's Christmas Eve," she is one of the daughters of Mr. Lane, the new minister in Holton, and his wife. Their other children are Bell Lane and Mary Lane.

LANE, MR. In "Mrs. Parkins's Christmas Eve," he is the new minister in Holton. He and his wife have three children—Bell Lane, John Lane, and Mary Lane. When Mr. Lane and his family welcome Mrs. Lydia Parkins, who almost dies in a snowstorm near the parsonage, she is spiritually reformed and pays for the successful operation in New York on John's crippled leg.

LANE, MRS. In "Mrs. Parkins's Christmas Eve," she is the gracious wife of Mr. Lane, the Holton minister. They have three children—Bell Lane, John Lane, and Mary Lane. Although Mrs. Lydia Parkins used to scowl at Mrs. Lane during church services, Mrs. Lane is sincerely hospitable to the woman when Mr. Lane brings her from the snowstorm into their home.

LANE, MRS. JERRY. In ''Marsh Rosemary,'' she is the second wife of the bigamist, Jerry Lane. They live in Shediac and have a baby.

LANE, NANCY ("ANN") LLOYD. In ''Marsh Rosemary,'' she is the lonely, resolute, middle-aged seamstress whom Jerry Lane, a shiftless sailor, lures into marriage. Knowing she is ''the better man of the two,'' she works harder than he at making a go of their marriage. He runs off to sea and marries a younger woman in Shediac. Deciding not to expose him as a bigamist, the abandoned wife is a combination of foolish romantic and admirably forgiving woman.

LANEWAY, JOSEPH ("JOE") K. In ''A Native of Winby,'' he is an illustrious Winby native. When he was about thirteen, he went west to the state of Kansota, became a millionaire and a senator, and was a general in the Civil War. After fifty-eight or so years, he returns to Winby, visits Marilla Hender's roadside school, and calls on her widowed grandmother, Abby Harran Hender, his childhood sweetheart a year older than he. They reminisce one evening, and he leaves the next morning. He is called General Laneway, the Honorable Joseph K. Laneway, and the Senator.

LANGDON, ANNE. In ''Mr. Bruce,'' she is a long-time friend, fifty, of Elly's Aunt Mary and Miss Margaret Tennant. She has heard Margaret's story about Kitty Tennant, who became Kitty Bruce, and Philip Bruce but enjoys hearing Margaret tell it again, to Mary.

LANGDON, MAJOR JOHN. In *The Tory Lover*, he is a Portsmouth friend to whom Roger Wallingford reluctantly pledges allegiance to the revolutionary cause. Benjamin Franklin mentions remembering Langdon. He is First Lieutenant Simpson's brother-in-law.

LANT, CAPTAIN JACOB. In *Deephaven*, he was an orphan, became a sea captain, quit the ocean reluctantly, and started farming two miles inland.

"A LATE SUPPER" (1878). Short story. (Characters: Miss Ashton, Mrs. Brown, Donald, Katy Dunning, Elden, Hilton, Mrs. Hilton, John, Mary, Rand, Miss Catherine Spring, Joseph Spring, Martha Spring, Miss Stanby, Alice West.) Old Miss Catherine Spring of Brookton, short of money because a railroad company failed to pay her a dividend, advertises in Boston for summer guests but gets no reply. She considers writing Mary, her niece in Lowell, offering to care for her children there. Little Katy Dunning comes to the door and asks to be her maid, which Katy's aunt has suggested. Declining regretfully, Miss Spring gives the hungry ten-year-old all of her milk and little cakes to eat. Miss

Spring's nephew, Joseph Spring, his wife, Martha Spring, and their friend, Miss Stanby, pay a surprise visit from a nearby town and are invited to stay for supper. Joseph saddens Miss Spring by reporting that Mary's husband John's sister is going to help with their children. Though flustered, Miss Spring starts some baking to replace the missing cakes and then scurries off to a neighbor to borrow cream for tea. When a train blocks her return, she boards it to cross to the other side, only to be carried away as the train starts north. She makes friends with Miss Ashton and her niece Alice West, who are aboard the train and heading for a vacation in the mountains. Miss Ashton likes the looks of Brookton and says she wishes she had answered a certain advertisement for rooms there. Miss Spring says the advertisement was hers. Alice West gives Miss Spring money for her round-trip ticket to the next town, and soon she is home again—to the relief of her worried guests. Once the substantial, if late, supper, is completed, the guests leave. Next day Miss Spring feels a dreadful letdown—until she receives a letter from Alice West saying she and her aunt dislike their vacation accommodations and wish to rent two rooms from her, at $20 a week, until October. So all is well; and Miss Spring, who can now hire Katy, is happy. Jewett ends this seriocomic story with much didacticism and even quotes the bromide about old age from Robert Browning's "Rabbi Ben Ezra." *Bibliography*: June Howard, "Unraveling Regions, Unsettling Periods: Sarah Orne Jewett and American Literary History," *American Literature* 68 (June 1996): 365–84.

"LAW LANE" (1887). Short story. (Characters: Miss Lyddy Bangs, Ezra Barnet, Ezra Barnet, Grandsir Barnet, Jane Barnet, Crosby, Abby Crosby, Ruth Crosby, Dodge, Fisher, Asa Packer, Powder, Mrs. Harriet Powder, Joel Smith, Mrs. Smith, Mrs. Topliff.) After completing her ironing one Tuesday morning in July, old Mrs. Harriet Powder meets Miss Lyddy Bangs, ostensibly to gather blueberries but really to gossip. They discuss the ongoing court case of the Barnet family and the Crosby family, who are adjacent neighbors feuding over the precise ownership of a lane of land—called Law Lane—between them. Mrs. Powder favors the Crosbys, who would combine disputed strips into a public lane. Her neighbor boy, Joel Smith, has just told her the Barnets won their appeal in court. Mrs. Powder reveals to Miss Bangs that Ezra Barnet and Ruth Crosby, children of the rivals, are secretly in love. Suddenly Joel, stung by hornets, falls out of the hemlock tree under which the two women have been talking. They fear Joel heard their talk and will tell his mother, and gossipers will spread news of the lovers. Mrs. Powder promises Joel a reward if he keeps his mouth shut, but to no avail. That evening, as Ezra is telling his gloating mother that Ruth's father had to sell a horse to pay legal costs, Ezra's father returns from town and demands to know whether news that Ezra has "took a shine" to Ruth is true. Ezra admits his love, rebukes everyone for the "heathen" land dispute, and is ordered to leave home forever. On Christmas Eve, as Ezra, a railroad employee now, heads toward home, Joel, who is out trapping rabbits, tells him Ezra's mother has just been badly injured in a fall. Meanwhile, Mrs.

Powder, summoned to nurse Mrs. Barnet until the doctor comes, keeps her husband out of the room and persuades her she is near death (which she is not) and gets her to wish the lawsuits were ended, peace declared between the rival families, and Ruth would marry her son. Mrs. Powder sends for the Crosbys, greets Ezra as he tramps in and warns him to hide and wait for her signal. Ruth and her parents enter. Once Mrs. Powder gets Mrs. Crosby to send the lovers her blessing, she summons Ezra. His father, shunted to the kitchen in a daze earlier, makes peace with his son. Mrs. Barnet gets her son and future daughter-in-law to hold hands and soon falls asleep. The doctor comes and praises the mending woman's able nurse.

Two notable features of this seriocomic yarn of a rustic Romeo and his Juliet are the skillful point-of-view shifts and the fine-lined etching of season-varied New England scenery. *Bibliography*: Thorp.

LAWTON. In "The Becket Girls' Tree," this may be the name of the neighbor on whose property, or near it, John Parsons chops down the Christmas tree.

LAWTON, MRS. In *A Marsh Island*, she was Simeon Lawton's wife, by her second marriage, and is Dan Lester's lonely mother.

LAWTON, SIMEON. In *A Marsh Island*, he was the second husband, now deceased, of Dan Lester's mother. He was careless with the money he came into by marrying her. Dan never like Lawton and was happy when he died.

LEE, ARTHUR. In *The Tory Lover*, he is a weak American commissioner of the Marine Committee of the colonies in France. He hates Captain John Paul Jones, who scorns him in return. Lee is a traitor and employs Ford, Thornton, and others as spies.

LEICESTER, BARBARA ("BAB," "BARB'RA"). In *Betty Leicester*, she is Thomas Leicester's aunt and Betty Leicester's grandaunt. Her younger sister is ill-tempered Mary Leicester. Barbara is sweet, kind, and sensible. In *Betty Leicester's English Xmas*, Betty remembers both old women fondly.

LEICESTER, BETTY ("BETSEY," "SISTER BETTY"). (Real name: Elizabeth Leicester.) In *Betty Leicester*, she is Thomas Leicester's only child, fifteen. He leaves her with his Tideshead aunts, Barbara Leicester and Mary Leicester, for the summer. She renews and makes friendships, has fun, but is glad when her father returns. In *Betty Leicester's English Xmas*, Betty and her father accept Lady Mary Danesley's invitation to spend a week during Christmas season at Danesley House. They go; and Betty has a nice time, meets Miss Edith Banfield and Warford (among others), and finds in lovely Lady Danesley a surrogate mother.

LEICESTER, MADAM. In *Betty Leicester*, she is the well-remembered matri-archal Tideshead figure, the mother of Barbara Leicester and Mary Leicester.

LEICESTER, MARY. In *Betty Leicester*, she is Thomas Leicester's aunt and Betty Leicester's grandaunt. Her older sister, Barbara Leicester, is peppier than Mary, who is frequently scolding and grumpy. In *Betty Leicester's English Xmas*, Betty remembers both old women fondly.

LEICESTER, THOMAS. In *Betty Leicester*, he is Betty Leicester's father, thirty-nine. He is a naturalist and has lived much of his widowerhood in Europe with Betty. He leaves her in Tideshead to go to Alaska, returns, and promises they will soon make their home in Tideshead. He is patterned closely after Jewett's father, Theodore Herman Jewett.* In *Betty Leicester's English Xmas*, Leicester is happy to interrupt his work at the British Museum on American Indians so he and Betty can spend a week during the Christmas season at Lady Mary Danesley's estate north of London. *Bibliography*: Roman.

LEIGH, CITIZEN. In *Deephaven*, he is a sea captain and, according to Captain Sands, was once a captive of Algerine pirates.

LEJAY. In *The Tory Lover*, he was a professor in the French school the teacher Sullivan and the future Duke of Boufflers attended.

LESLIE, DR. JOHN. In *A Country Doctor*, he is a brilliant physician who wants to practice only in Oldfields. His wife and daughter have died. He becomes Nan Prince's guardian and encourages her ambition to become a country doctor herself. For twenty years she regards him as a father figure and admires him tremendously, as do all of his fellow villagers and patients both in town and in the countryside beyond. Dr. Leslie is partly based on Jewett's father, Dr. Theodore Herman Jewett.* The name Leslie may derive from that of Dr. Horace Granville Leslie, a book-loving physician from Amesbury, Massachusetts, whom Jewett knew. *Bibliography*: Silverthorne.

LESLIE, MARY ("POLLY"). In "Good Luck," she, the narrator, is the wid-owed Mrs. Leslie's daughter and the sister of Parkhurst Leslie and Tom Leslie. During their stay one summer in a house the Leslies have inherited near Hilton, New Hampshire, she and Tom discover a secret closet containing some old papers and some gold coins.

LESLIE, MRS. In "Good Luck," she is the mother of Mary Leslie, Parkhurst Leslie, and Tom Leslie. She rents her Boston residence and stays one summer in a house inherited from her deceased husband's granduncle, a man named Kinlock. Then she inherits a large sum of money from Mrs. Anderson of Baltimore, who knew Mrs. Leslie's mother.

LESLIE, PARKHURST ("PARK"). In "Good Luck," he is Mary Leslie's older brother, stays briefly in the family summer home, and will soon study medicine in Paris.

LESLIE, PARSON. In *A Country Doctor*, he was Dr. John Leslie's grandfather.

LESLIE, TOM. In "Good Luck," he is Mary Leslie's younger brother and is about to go to college in Cambridge. While staying in the family summer home, he discovers a secret closet in which he and Mary find old papers and gold coins.

LESTER. In *A Country Doctor*, this was evidently the maiden name of Nancy Prince's mother. *See also* Prince, Nancy.

LESTER. In *A Marsh Island*, he was Dan Lester's father, now deceased. He was a skillful boat maker. He fought in the Civil War alongside young Israel Owen, and saw him wounded and die.

LESTER, DAN ("DANNY"). In *A Marsh Island*, he is Mrs. Lawton's son. After his father's death, she married Simeon Lawton. Dan works as a blacksmith at the Sussex shipyard, lives near Israel Owen, and timidly courts Doris Owen, his daughter. Doris vacillates between wanting Dan and wanting Richard Dale, the painter temporarily in their neighborhood. Dan becomes indifferent to land he owns that is suddenly worth thousands and, lovelorn, decides to go to sea. Doris pursues him, and they become betrothed.

LESTER, MRS. In "The Failure of David Berry," she is a person from nearby West Farms whose visit, accompanied by her daughter-in-law, to Mrs. David Berry causes that social-climbing woman to encourage David to expand his shoe business, with disastrous results.

LESTER, MRS. In "The Failure of David Berry," she is the older Mrs. Lester's daughter-in-law.

LETTY. In *Betty Leicester*, she is a servant, as is the more important Serena, of Barbara Leicester and Mary Leicester. In *Betty Leicester's English Xmas*, Betty remembers both servants fondly.

LEWIS, DAN ("DAN'L"). In "The Mate of the Daylight," he is Susan Ryder's boyfriend. Seemingly unambitious, he appears willing to bide his time and profit from her expected inheritance. Suddenly he becomes master of his uncle's *Daylight*, when her captain is lost at sea and her first mate falls ill. Dan returns home and marries Susan. He is predictably parasitic most of the time and appears to be transformed only by a deus ex machina. *Bibliography*: Roman.

LEWIS, MRS. In "The Mate of the Daylight," she is Dan Lewis's poor mother, who lives nearby.

"THE LIFE OF NANCY" (1895). Short story. (Characters: Aldis, Mrs. Tom Aldis, Tom Aldis, Tom Aldis, Mrs. Annesley, Joe Brown, Daniel R. Carew, Ezra, Gale, Asa Gale, Mrs. Gale, Nancy Gale, Sam Gale, Lorenzo Papanti, Jacob Parker, Addie Porter, Abby Snow.) Nancy Gale, a native of East Rodney, Maine, is visiting Ezra, her uncle, in Milton, four and a half miles from Boston. When the two come by wagon to deliver farm produce at the market, she and Tom Aldis see each other on the street. Tom, a Harvard graduate, twenty-two, is the son of a real-estate investor. Tom and his "chum," Daniel R. Carew, vacationed the previous summer at East Rodney, where Tom met Nancy at a dance. He was pleased by her innocent freshness, and remains so. Ezra lets Nancy and Tom spend a delightful afternoon together in Boston. He points out the sights, takes her to observe a lesson at a dancing school run by Papanti, and introduces her to Mrs. Annesley, his pleasant, aristocratic old aunt. During the next two years, he sends reading material to Nancy, including a book about dancers, but they drift apart. He marries in Boston and has children. Fifteen or so years pass. Tom visits East Rodney, where his father bought a point of land and some nearby islands, to consider land development in the beautiful region. While looking in at a local dance held to raise money for a school bell, Tom encounters Nancy's rugged father, who tells him that Nancy became a teacher, was crippled by rheumatism, and is virtually bedridden. She coaches children in dancing moves and in manners and also tutors slow school children. Tom visits her and is both thrilled and saddened by her courageous philosophy of life. She tells him she has always remembered his aunt's comment to her: ". . . to be happy and useful . . . the only way is to be self-forgetful." She says she is sorry she cannot get out to cheer up some old neighbors she knows. A year later Tom is at East Rodney again, this time with his wife and children. On his property there, he has built a fine summer home. He and others carry Nancy to it. She delights in the fine view. He tells her of his decision not to commercialize the region. He says he often wishes . . . but then he pauses. She says she has thought of him every day since their brief time together in Boston.

LIGHTFOOT. In *The Tory Lover*, this is one of the horses owned by John Davis.

"A LITTLE CAPTIVE MAID" (1891). Short story. (Characters: John Balfour, Barton, Mother Casey, Davy Connelly, Mrs. Davy Connelly, Nora Connelly, Mother Dolan, Donahue, Donahue, Johnny Donahue, Mrs. Donahue, Father Dunn, Mother Killahan, Dinny Killoren, Father Miles, John Morris, Mrs. Morris, Mrs. Nash, James Reilly, Johanna Spillane, Dan Sullivan.) In early winter in Kenmare, Ireland, Nora Connelly bids a temporary farewell to John ("Johnny") Morris, a dirt-poor young farmer. Although they love each other, she must leave her wicked aunt, who dislikes Johnny, and go to a relative named Donahue in America, earn and save about a hundred pounds, and return to her lover and marriage. She arrives at a thriving American town and is soon recommended to James Reilly, also a cousin of the Donahues and a servant, as is the widowed Mrs. Nash, of wealthy, feeble John Balfour, a retired sea captain and then a businessman. Nora is hired as a "little maid," and her youthful freshness, touching sympathy, and sparkling talk rejuvenate Balfour to a degree. This relieves Reilly and Mrs. Nash of some of their work. Nora suggests that Balfour try the salt-sea air of Glengariff, Ireland, for his health. She tells him how she and her parents visited Baltimore, beyond Glengariff and near Bantry, how she stole eggs to sell from under her trusting mother's "spickled" hen, and how she, her father, and his friends once salvaged oranges and wine from a wrecked ship off Bantry. She tells about Johnny back home and their plans. Nora praises Father Dunn, her priest; so Balfour gets her to help him walk to the rectory. Nora tells Father Dunn that Balfour would like to visit Glengariff. Though sensing Balfour's grievous feebleness, Father Dunn describes the beneficent Irish sea town, which he knows well, and wonders idly whether the three of them could go there in the summer. He then helps his visitors back to fatigued Balfour's fine old house. The old man weakens, dies in the autumn, and leaves his house to a nephew and generous gifts to his servants, including $500 and passage money home to Nora, whom he praises tenderly in his will. One evening in the Irish twilight not long after, Johnny sees Nora, three years gone from him now, coming to him in a friend's cart. The faithful pair marry, use her money to turn his little farm into a prosperous one, and flaunt their good fortune in her mean aunt's face. Nora often prays for the repose of good Balfour's soul in her village church. This story reverses the myth of the American Dream foreigners have. *Bibliography*: Morgan and Renza.

LITTLEFIELD, PHEBE. In "Miss Becky's Pilgrimage," she is Mahaly Parker's sister, in whose home, during a tea party, Becky Parsons meets Beacham, the widowed Brookfield minister.

"LITTLE FRENCH MARY" (1895). Short story. (Characters: Alexis, Foster, French Mary, Marie, Ezra Spooner, Henry Staples, Captain Weathers.) Alexis, a French-Canadian, moves to the neighboring American town of Dulham with his wife, Marie, ill from poor drainage and factory work in a nearby town, and their little daughter, French Mary, about six. Alexis quickly does admired handiwork. French Mary's gentle, courteous ways delight the old men loitering in the local store. They give her candy and other presents. When the family moves back to Canada, the old men miss the child dreadfully.

LITTLEPAGE, CAPTAIN. In *The Country of the Pointed Firs*, he is a retired sea captain, over eighty but dapper and often articulate. The narrator is fascinated when Captain Littlepage reminisces about being shipwrecked near the

North Pole, bunking with Gaffett, and relating how Gaffett told him he saw a foggy town of ghostly creatures seemingly caught between this world and the next. In "The Foreigner," Littlepage is a sea captain whose house, according to Almira Todd, has a big garret, unlike Captain John Tolland's house. In "William's Wedding," Littlepage is mentioned by the narrator as someone she would like to visit. Littlepage's obsessive recital of his eldritch tale may owe something to *The Rime of the Ancient Mariner* by Samuel Taylor Coleridge. *Bibliography*: Blanchard.

"A LITTLE TRAVELER" (1880). Short story. (Characters: Ellen, Martha, Nelly.) While traveling on the train, the narrator sees Nelly, an unattended little girl who says her mother has just died. The conductor explains that Nelly's father, a freight conductor, was killed almost two years ago, his widow died of pneumonia last week, and Nelly is to be met in Boston by an aunt. Fellow passengers take a loving interest in the well-mannered child, and the narrator is relieved to see her aunt greet her affectionately at the station. This slight tale is livened by pungent sketches of the other passengers—shy newlyweds, two loud old women, a priest, some businessmen, and a woman with birds.

LIZZIE. In "Jim's Little Woman," she is Martha's friend in Maine. Martha wants her to visit in St. Augustine, but their reunion will occur only after Jim and Martha sail north, which they finally plan to do.

LONGBROTHER, THE REVEREND DANIEL. In "The Town Poor," he was the friend of Deacon Bray, who is now deceased. The two are said to have been conservative in their theology.

LONGFELLOW, ALICE (1850–1928). Daughter of Henry Wadsworth Longfellow (1807–1882). In 1835, the poet's first wife, Mary Storer Potter Longfellow, died. In 1843 he married Frances Elizabeth Appleton, and they had six children before she burned to death in 1861. In his famous poem, "The Children's Hour," Longfellow describes his "Grave Alice and laughing Allegra/ And Edith with golden hair." Jewett greatly admired Longfellow and his immensely popular poetry, probably first met him through Annie Adams Fields* in the 1870s, and soon became Alice's close friend. In 1877, Jewett helped establish a memorial fund for Henry Wadsworth Longfellow in Boston. Alice Longfellow made herself highly visible in the Cambridge area as an activist in the establishment of Radcliffe College, which opened in 1879 and of which she was a trustee. In 1888 and 1889, and perhaps again later, Alice invited Jewett to vacation with her on Mouse Island in Boothbay Harbor, Maine, where Jewett found that the mineral springs helped her arthritis. Jewett could not keep pace with the unusually athletic Alice at sailing and rowing, and more calmly delighted in the woods, water, and people of the island. *Bibliography*: Blanchard.

"LOOKING BACK ON GIRLHOOD" (1892). Essay. (Characters: William Dean Howells, Theodore Furber Jewett, Theodore Herman Jewett, Nathan Lord.) Jewett is grateful to those who taught her to observe and be interested. She loves her New England region, with its hills, forests, evidence of Indians and the English, rivers, sea nearby, and fisheries. Berwick was settled in 1627. Her grandfather (Theodore Furber Jewett*) was a Portsmouth sea captain and then a Berwick businessman. Barter between lumbermen and farmers was then more common than money transactions. Jewett hated to see huge, "unreplaceable" oaks and pines cut and hauled away. Her elders spoke of a way of life already waning, with stories of three wars: Louisburg (during the French and Indian War), the Revolution, and "the last war"—that of 1812. Berwick citizens were highly patriotic. Jewett names Sullivans, Colonel Hamilton, and the Chadbourne and Lord families. Her father (Theodore Herman Jewett*) encouraged her to read, took her with him when he called on the sick along the coast in York and Wells, and offered this advice: "Don't try to write *about* people and things, tell them just as they are!" His only dislikes were insincerity and affectation. One should "make the most of whatever is in one's reach," as she has done with "country characters and rural landscapes . . . which I had been taught to love with all my heart." After a few early publishing successes, she had a piece ("Mr. Bruce") accepted by "Mr. [William Dean] Howells[*] for the *Atlantic*" when she was nineteen.

LOOMIS, 'LIZA. In *Betty Leicester*, she is a Riverport resident whose singing voice Seth Pond recognizes.

LORD. In *The Tory Lover*, this is the last name of several girls who are said to be entertaining Mary Hamilton at cards when in reality Mary is going with Caesar to aid Madam Wallingford after her son Roger Wallingford was falsely called a traitor.

LORD, BILLY. In *The Tory Lover*, he is reported as a colonial soldier now missing.

LORD, CATO. In *The Tory Lover*, he is one of the black servants in the home of John Lord and his family. Cato Lord is a friend of Caesar.

LORD, HUMPHRY. In *The Tory Lover*, he is a boy sailor who sails off with Captain John Paul Jones on the *Ranger* as his mother weeps.

LORD, ICHABOD. In *The Tory Lover*, he is an American sailor in the Mill Prison.

LORD, JOHN. In *The Tory Lover*, he is a merchant from Somersworth. John Lord is too ill to join the Revolutionary army. He works with Colonel Jonathan Hamilton and helps Mary Hamilton board a ship bound for Bristol.

LORD, NATHAN. In "Looking Back on Girlhood," he was a prisoner of the British during the Revolution. He challenged an insulting captor, defeated him in a fair fight, and was praised and rewarded for his courage by his opponent— the Duke of Clarence, later King of England. In *The Tory Lover*, Nathan Lord is mentioned as a commander of Berwick soldiers during the Revolution. A General Lord is mentioned in "River Driftwood."

LORIMER. In *Deephaven*, he is the father of Parson Lorimer, the present Deephaven minister. Captain Sands knew the older man.

LORIMER, CAPTAIN PETER. In *Deephaven*, he was a sea captain who brought fine silk to his sister, Martha Lorimer.

LORIMER, MARTHA. In *Deephaven*, she was Katharine Brandon's unmarried neighbor. She was the aunt of Parson Lorimer of Deephaven and his siblings, Captain Peter Lorimer and Rebecca Lorimer. Mrs. Bonny offers to send Martha some bitters.

LORIMER, PARSON. In *Deephaven*, he is the Deephaven minister and is the brother of Captain Peter Lorimer and Rebecca Lorimer. The minister conducted Katharine Brandon's funeral. He debates theological points with Dick Carew. Mrs. Bonny reveres him.

LORIMER, REBECCA. In *Deephaven*, she is Parson Lorimer's sister. Widow Jim says Rebecca was Martha Lorimer's niece.

"A LOST LOVER" (1878). Short story. (Characters: Andrew, Joe Carrick, Croden, Dane, Colonel Dane, Dick Dane, Horatia Dane, Mrs. Dane, Nelly Dane, George Forest, Melissa.) Young Nelly Dane writes to ask Horatia Dane, her deceased mother's cousin, if she may pay a summer visit to the old patrician woman in her mansion in Longfield, some eighty miles from Boston. Nelly heard that Horatia was to marry a sailor but he was lost at sea. Through Melissa, Horatia's old servant, Nelly learns details. The man, Joe Carrick, sailed out of Salem, where the couple had met, and was reported lost in the South Seas. Over tea, Nelly tells Horatia she loves a navy man named George Forest, now on a three-year voyage to China and Japan. Horatia warns the girl to be careful and that night remembers her own lover even more fondly. Next morning, while Nelly is mending a dress, she hears a beggar at the kitchen door ask Melissa for food. Melissa feeds him and asks Horatia to watch him while she tends to some chickens. He explains that he was a sailor from Salem, was married in Australia, was ruined by drink, and returned to the United States thirty or forty years ago. He soon leaves with $10 from Horatia, who then faints. Neither Nelly nor Melissa ever knows the truth: The man was Horatia's long-lost lover. Preferring her fantasy of him as an ever-youthful lad, she wishes he had died and soon ages noticeably. Finding "A Lost Lover" charming, Henry James used it as the basis for his story, "Flickerbridge." *Bibliography*: Leon Edel and Lyall H. Powers, eds., *The Complete Notebooks of Henry James* (New York: Oxford University Press, 1987); Thorp.

"THE LOST TURKEY" (1902). Short story. (Characters: Asa, Barton, Fred Hollis, Grandma Jones, Grandpa Jones, John Jones, Sarah Jones.) Sarah Jones, the widowed mother of young John ("Johnny") Jones, feuded with her father-in-law both before and after her husband's death. She lives with Johnny in the country not far from Grandma Jones and Grandpa Jones. Johnny is sad when Sarah says they lack money to buy a turkey for tomorrow's Thanksgiving dinner. In the village is a store run by Barton, who is also the postmaster. The local doctor sees Grandpa Jones there and urges him to make peace with poor Sarah. But he remains huffy and puts his gigantic Vermont turkey, just purchased, into his wagon. As he heads out, Barton gives him a bundle of mail to take to Sarah, and also a paper the doctor wants Johnny to have. Grandpa Jones goes along the bumpy road, and the turkey slides into the back of the wagon. Stopping reluctantly, he calls Johnny to come get something from the postmaster. Johnny takes the turkey; and Grandpa Jones, "perfectly unconscious of such an involuntary benefaction," rattles on home in the darkness. When his wife wonders where their turkey is, they conclude it fell off the back of the wagon and got lost in the snow. At daybreak next morning, Johnny plods over to his grandparents' house for the first time ever—to convey Sarah's "best respects," thank them for the turkey, and invite the old pair to dinner. Grandpa Jones wonders where their turkey came from, and Johnny says from his wagon. While Grandma Jones gives Johnny a hot breakfast, Grandpa hitches up the colt to his sleigh to take his grandson home. When Sarah sees the two approaching amiably, she feels glad she took the second step after Grandpa Jones took the first step. Soon their family Thanksgiving dinner is a success.

LOW, CAPTAIN. In "Marsh Rosemary," he is Nathan Low's brother. Jerry Lane ships out with Nathan Low.

LOW, NATHAN. In "Marsh Rosemary," he is the skipper aboard whose schooner, the *Susan Barnes*, Jerry Lane ships. They ply the waters between Shediac and Newfoundland. The schooner sinks, but neither is aboard, because Nathan sold his interest, and Jerry happened to stay in Newfoundland to visit. Nathan discreetly tells Mrs. Elton of Jerry's bigamy.

LOWELL, JAMES RUSSELL (1819–1891). Man of letters, educator, and diplomat. Born in Cambridge, Massachusetts, he attended Harvard (1834–1838) and its law school (1840), and soon began to publish essays of literary criticism and poetry, including *A Fable for Critics* (1848) and *The Biglow Papers*, first series (1848). He taught languages and literature at Harvard (1856–1872 [succeeding Henry Wadsworth Longfellow] and 1874–1877), was the first editor of the *Atlantic Monthly* (1857–1861), and coedited the *North American Review* (1863–1872, at first with Charles Eliot Norton [1863–1868]). Lowell was the American minister to Spain (1877–1880) and Great Britain (1880–1885). In 1882 he acted as godfather to Virginia Stephen (later Virginia Woolf), whose father, Sir Leslie Stephen, he knew in England. In 1844 Lowell married the frail poetess Maria White; they had four children, three of whom died before she died in 1853. In 1857 he married Frances Dunlap; mentally unstable, she died in 1885, in London. Returning to Cambridge, Lowell lectured but continued to travel widely. He was clever, sparkling, and perhaps too versatile for his own good. He knew most of the establishment figures of his era. Jewett probably first met Lowell in 1886 at the home of James T. Fields and Annie Adams Fields;* the latter found him egotistical. Jewett read and admired his works, was a frequent guest at his Cambridge home, grew fond of him, was happily introduced by him to the poetry of John Donne, and was the target of his gentle mimicry of her Maine accent. In 1887 she persuaded Lowell to participate in the authors' reading to raise funds for the Henry Wadsworth Longfellow Memorial in Boston. While fatally ill in 1891, Lowell wrote a puff for a London edition of selected Jewett stories praising their pathos, humor, and exquisite style. Jewett was also a close friend of Mabel Lowell Burnett, Lowell's one surviving child. After his death, Jewett wrote Annie Fields (Wednesday, 1891) that she felt like a member of Lowell's family. One of Jewett's closest friends, Sara Norton,* was the daughter of Charles Eliot Norton, who wrote a biography of Lowell (1893) and edited many of his letters (1893) and much of his writing (1904). *Bibliography*: Blanchard; Matthiessen; Silverthorne.

"THE LUCK OF THE BOGANS" (1889). Short story. (Characters: Tom Auley, Biddy Flaherty Bogan, Dan Bogan, Jerry Bogan, Mary Ellen Bogan, Mike Bogan, Marget Dunn, Jim Kalehan, Father Miles, Peggy Muldoon, Patrick O'Brien, Biddy O'Hern, Corny Sullivan, Tom Whinn.) Mike Bogan, persuaded by his wife, Biddy Bogan, leaves Bantry, Ireland, in the spring with their infant son, Dan Bogan, to try their luck in "Ameriky." Many friends, including a one-eyed beggar named Peggy Muldoon, bid them farewell. In the American town where some of Biddy's relatives house them briefly, Mike works in a carriage-shop forge, and he and his wife have three daughters. Dan goes to school, learns arithmetic but also foul words, and is abusive to his sisters. Buying a saloon, Mike prospers as a decent, moderate purveyor of liquor. The growing family lives upstairs. Father Miles, a priest from Bantry, Ireland, admires him and the aging Biddy as well; but he also warns Mike about the dangers of drink. It is an unwritten family rule that Dan, growing handsome but also conceited and conniving, should stay out of the saloon. But one October evening, Dan stumbles into the place drunk and with rowdy companions, to Mike's embarrassment and that of his convivial but temperate customers. One sailor suggests that, if Mike sent Dan off to sea "wid a good captain," it would improve him. Desperately saddened, Mike closes the saloon early and gets Dan up to bed. One winter night, while Mike, sick and worried, groans in his sleep and Biddy prays, some men carry Dan home to them, stabbed to death in a fight. When Mike hears, he rushes downstairs and destroys his supply of drink, is comforted when Father Miles arrives, but soon lies dying upstairs and dreaming of Bantry "with our luck smilin' us in the face." The pathos and humor of this story blind many readers to defects in the Bogans. Biddy wants to leave Ireland, where they are comfortably situated; but then she blames Mike, though but briefly, for their difficulties. Their motives are greed and making their son, favored over their daughters, into a gentleman. Ironically, liquor causes Mike's material rise and Dan's fatal fall. Jewett delivers a lecture on the need to sympathize with Irish immigrants, homesick in a new, strange, and often materialistic world. "The Luck of the Bogans" is the first of eight Irish stories by Jewett. Although Jewett listened to the Irish accent carefully, it is overdone here (and elsewhere as well). For example, one Irishman says "Anybody that meddles wid wather 'ill have no luck while they live, faix they 'ont thin." Also, Jewett regularly has her Irish characters pronounce "talk" as "tark." *Bibliography*: Morgan and Renza; Roman; Thorp.

LUCY ANN. In "By the Morning Boat," she is a widow living on a poor farm in Maine with her crippled father, her son, Elisha, fifteen, and her daughter, Lydia, twelve. Lucy Ann is sad when Elisha must leave to take a job in Boston.

LUNN, CAPTAIN PETER. In "All My Sad Captains," he was the shipmaster husband of Maria Lunn, his second wife, who is now widowed for four years.

LUNN, MARIA. In "All My Sad Captains," she is a reasonably attractive woman, widowed in Longport by Captain Peter Lunn's death four years earlier. She lives on Barbados Street and is now seeking a new husband. Three ex-shipmasters, Captain Crowe, Captain Asa Shaw, and Captain John Witherspoon, court her. She lets the Reverend Mr. Farley become her boarder to precipitate proposals and then accepts Witherspoon.

LYDIA ("LYDDY"). In "By the Morning Boat," she is Elisha's sister, twelve. They play together briefly before he leaves for a job in Boston. She is sad at his departure, especially when she sees how mature his prospects are making him.

LYMAN. In *The Tory Lover*, this is the family name of guests from York at Mary Hamilton's wedding.

M

MACALISTER, MR. In *Betty Leicester's English Xmas*, he is young Warford's old schoolmaster. He participates in the Christmas pageant Betty Leicester organizes.

MACDUFF, JEAN. In *The Tory Lover*, Captain John Paul Jones mentions her as his old aunt who would be proud of him.

MCALLISTER. In *Deephaven*, he was Dolly McAllister's father and was in Deephaven once long ago on business.

MCALLISTER, DOLLY. In *Deephaven*, she was, according to old papers, Katharine Brandon's dear friend, who died in 1809, at age eighteen.

MCALLISTER, JACK. In "Lady Ferry," he is a person Lady Ferry remembers as a sea captain. When she sees his grandson, John McAllister, she mistakes John for Jack, who was lost at sea more than seventy years earlier.

MCALLISTER, JOHN. In "Lady Ferry," he is Matthew's friend. When he visits, Lady Ferry mistakes him for his grandfather, Jack McAllister.

MCALLISTER, PEGGY. In "A Garden Story," she is a sweet little orphan, nine, sent from Boston for a "country week" with Miss Ann Dunning in Littletown. The two like each other so well that they make the stay permanent. When Peggy persuades Miss Dunning not to thin her seedlings but to nurture them instead, it is easily seen that Jewett is presenting Peggy as a saved seedling herself.

MCFARLAND. In "The Green Bonnet," he is a hard-working milk farmer. He and his wife have five daughters: Sarah McFarland, eighteen; Ethel McFarland, fourteen; Martha McFarland, twelve; Esther McFarland, seven; and Eunice McFarland, five.

MCFARLAND, ESTHER ("ESSIE"). In "The Green Bonnet," she is the fourth daughter, seven, of McFarland and his wife. Called "dreadful," she wears a dress and the green bonnet belonging to her sister, Sarah McFarland, in the rain. Sarah happily forgives her.

MCFARLAND, ETHEL. In "The Green Bonnet," she is the second daughter, fourteen, of McFarland and his wife. She is called "a good scholar" but will replace her sister, Sarah McFarland, as a worker on the family farm in due time.

MCFARLAND, EUNICE. In "The Green Bonnet," she is the fifth and last daughter, five, of McFarland and his wife. Her sister, Esther McFarland, occasionally leads Eunice, called "mild and timid," into mischief.

MCFARLAND, MARTHA. In "The Green Bonnet," she is the third daughter, twelve, of McFarland and his wife. She loans a hood to her sister, Sarah McFarland, to replace the missing green bonnet for Easter Sunday church service.

MCFARLAND, MRS. In "The Green Bonnet," she is the wife of McFarland, a milk farmer living just outside Walsingham with her and their five daughters. She is described as a "hard-worked, delicate woman."

MCFARLAND, SARAH. In "The Green Bonnet," she is the oldest daughter, eighteen, of McFarland and his wife. She hates the green bonnet given to her by her Aunt Sarah of Boston, but feels she must wear it. She is relieved when it is temporarily lost. She wears a hood and no hat, sings at the Easter Sunday church service in Walsingham, and pleases her friend, John Tanner, a young village blacksmith. Sarah expects to go to Boston and become a milliner.

MCINTIRE. In *The Tory Lover*, he is the source of a Scottish joke told by Captain John Paul Jones.

MCLOUGHLIN. In "Where's Nora?", he is the Birch Plains storekeeper from whom Nora first orders supplies for her baking business.

MAGGIE. In *Deephaven*, she is a Lancaster family servant in Boston, as is Ann. Both are from Deephaven and accompany Kate Lancaster and Helen Denis there.

MAGGIE. In "The Gray Mills of Farley," she is a little orphan child in Farley. Mrs. Kilpatrick informally adopts her.

MAJOR. In *A Country Doctor*, he is Dr. John Leslie's horse.

MAJOR. In *A Marsh Island*, he is Israel Owen's old horse.

MAJOR. In "Mrs. Parkins's Christmas Eve," he is Mrs. Lydia Parkins's horse. She almost gets Major killed in the snowstorm overtaking them between Haybury and Holton. Mr. Lane, the Holton minister, saves both Mrs. Parkins and Major.

MALLY, AUNT. In "The Green Bowl," she was the great-aunt who gave the two green bowls to Mrs. Patton, who explains that Mally "was the doctor's wife's mother over to Jopham Corners." When the doctor moved with his family to Meriden, Mally remained in her Jopham Corners home.

MANDER, JOHN. In "The Night before Thanksgiving," he is Mary Ann Robb's neighbor and wants to seize her acreage. He loaned the old widow money, repaid himself by dishonestly cutting wood from her lot, scolds her for helping others, and even plans to plow over her family graveyard. Though briefly sketched, he is one of the most odious male characters in all of Jewett's writings. *Bibliography*: Roman.

MANNING, CAPTAIN. In *Deephaven*, he is a retired, bachelor sea captain. Danny works at his warehouse. Widow Jim says Captain Manning used to play whist with Katharine Brandon.

MANNING, MISS NARCISSA. In "Miss Manning's Minister," she is fifty, regularly attends the First Congregational church in Rinston, Connecticut, and admires the Reverend Edward Taylor's sermons. When the minister suffers a stroke, she volunteers to care for him in her home. The two slowly fall in love. When cured, he takes a position some distance from Rinston but soon returns, and the two get married. Miss Manning is "a Narcissa . . . in actions, who saw the beauty of her deeds reflected in his [Taylor's] gratified sense of comfort." She is anti-Calvinist to the extent of preferring Sunday afternoon sermons following "a good, warm dinner."

MANON. In "Mère Pochette," she is the pretty granddaughter of Mère Pochette, who raises her, objects when she falls in love with Charles Pictou, but finally accepts him and even blesses their marriage.

MARCIA. In "Lady Ferry," she is the little girl (and narrator) whose parents leave her for the summer with Matthew and Agnes. Matthew is the parents' cousin, and Agnes is his wife. The two live in an old house near the ferry by the river. Marcia meets, is apprehensive of, likes and kisses, and is gently befriended by Lady Ferry. Years later Marcia returns to the house and sees the old woman's grave. Marcia's name derives from that of Marcia, the daughter of Anne Rice. As a child, Jewett visited the Rice family mansion in Portsmouth on the Piscataqua River. *Bibliography*: Blanchard; Silverthorne.

MARGARET. In *A Country Doctor*, she was Mrs. Graham's aunt. Dr. John Leslie remembers Margaret's funeral.

MARIE. In *Betty Leicester*, she is an Interlaken hotel maid mentioned by Bessie Duncan in a letter to Betty Leicester.

MARIE. In "Little French Mary," she is Alexis's wife and French Mary's mother. Marie does household chores in Dulham. When the family moves back to Canada, some old men in town miss sweet little French Mary.

MARILLY. In *Deephaven*, she is the "Kentucky giantess" at the Denby circus. Mrs. Tom Kew knew her earlier and speaks kindly to her. The 400-pound woman's troubles began when she married an incompetent, alcoholic man.

MARION, AUNT. In "A Sorrowful Guest," she is an aunt of John Ainslie and his sister, Helen Ainslie. She briefly welcomes Helen home to Boston after her return from Florence. John and Helen do not like Aunt Marion.

MARLEY, BECKY. In "Miss Sydney's Flowers," she is Polly Sharpe's widowed old sister. They live together in a cramped apartment. At a street stand, Becky, who is rheumatic, painfully sells the molasses candy Polly makes. When Becky moves her stand near Miss Sydney's greenhouse to improve sales, Miss Sydney sees and befriends her.

MARLOW, ADELINE ("AD'LINE"). In "The Hiltons' Holiday," she is a cousin of Mrs. John Hilton, who asks her husband to call on her in Topham Corners to get some news. Ad'line is not mentioned again.

MARR, JOHN. In *The Tory Lover* (1901), he is reported as a colonial soldier now missing. Jewett may have taken this name from that of the retired sailor in Herman Melville's *John Marr and Other Sailors* (1888).

MARSH. In *Betty Leicester*, he is a Tideshead teacher Betty Leicester says is coming to see her father, Thomas Leicester.

MARSH, DR. In "A Born Farmer," he is a physician in Upton Corners for whom Jacob Gaines and his son Jacob ("Jakey") Gaines prepare a cord of chestnut oak.

A MARSH ISLAND (1885). Novel. (Characters: Allen, Asher, Bangs, Bennet, Mrs. Bennet, Bradish, Asa Bunt, Mrs. Will Chauncey, Will Chauncey, Churchill, Mrs. Copp, Sergeant Copp, Richard Dale, Mrs. Dennell, Kate Dent, James Fales, Mrs. Fales, Mrs. Farley, Jenks, Johnson, Miss Temperance Kipp, Mrs. Lawton, Simeon Lawton, Lester, Dan Lester, Major, Maxwell, Mrs. Nash, Parson Nash, Nelly, Doris Owen, Israel Owen, Israel Owen, Martha Owen, Bill Simms, Mrs. Simms, Mrs. Susan Winchester.)

Richard ("Dick") Dale is a dilettantish artist with a New York City studio. He has strayed from the hospitality of his rich aunt and former guardian, Mrs. Susan Winchester, at her summer home and is sketching on Marsh Island, in Sussex County, one August day. When his promised ride back does not materialize, he walks to the farmhouse of Israel Owen, his wife, Martha Owen, and their attractive daughter, Doris Owen. They agree to let him stay there temporarily. He enjoys supper with them and their hired hands, now cutting salt marsh hay, but is oddly nonplussed when Dan Lester, a neighbor working as a shipyard blacksmith in nearby Sussex, takes Doris to a choir meeting in the village. Israel tells Dick that his son was killed in the Civil War and wistfully adds that Dick resembles him. Dan is prevented from proposing to Doris by another girl's presence on the ride home from the village. In the morning, Dick walks out to consider various views for future paintings, trips and badly injures an already lame ankle, and is helped to the house by Doris. A nearby doctor bandages Dick's foot and says he remembers seeing Dick at Mrs. Winchester's place. Israel and his men go east by his hay boat, cut more hay, and are joined by Dan. James ("Jim") Fales, one of Israel's hired hands—the two others are Allen and Jenks—hints to Dan that Doris may prefer Dick. Getting Israel's approval, Dan on their return boldly asks Doris to walk a little with him, only to be rebuffed.

By September Dick has made a studio out of the Owen's unused spinning room. He is ambitious to take a portfolio back to his New York studio and show his colleagues his superior ability. Doris admires his work. Martha, testy at first about a boarder, likes this one more and more, and asks him to escort Doris, by horse-drawn wagon, to Sussex to see a sick relative. Doris visits the relative, then takes Dick to Dan's smithy. Still hurt, Dan speaks curtly to her, and she sadly goes back home with Dick. Miss Temperance ("Tempy") Kipp, back from a few days off, returns to work for Martha and breaks confidence by telling her Dan, whom Tempy hopes Doris will marry, has family land in the West now worth $6,000. Martha silences her, goes to inspect absent Dick's studio

room, and is impressed by his work. Dan, alternately glad and angry he rebuffed
Doris, goes home Saturday evening. When his lonely mother tells him the land
in the West has become valuable, he says he does not care and will marry Doris
or nobody. Next morning he meets Israel and Martha on their way to church
and wonders suspiciously why Doris is absent. While strolling idly through the
woods and then toward the water, Doris suddenly happens upon Dick, who
borrowed her boat, rowed to a far shore, and is napping. Their talk skirts inti-
macy, while neither expresses a commitment. Doris says she likes her homeland,
while Dick feels repulsed by the idea of rustic winters. They return by water to
the house as her parents are coming home. That evening they welcome some
neighborhood visitors. While everyone is talking amiably, Dan comes in, gets
Doris outside in the moonlight, and proposes. Asked to be patient, he abruptly
leaves. Dick ponders taking Doris away from her prosaic region.

In October Dick's aunt, Mrs. Winchester, suddenly arrives with a friend in a
victoria driven by a new coachman; they are now lost. The Owens provide brief
hospitality, and his aunt persuades Dick to guide them home. He reluctantly
agrees. Now feeling out of place in Mrs. Winchester's lavish mansion, he does
not join her other dinner guests and becomes defensive when she urges him not
to return to the Owens's farm and certainly not to marry Doris. Next day that
uneasy girl goes with her father to the coast. While he dickers to sell a load of
hay to the owner of a magnificent estate near Westmarket, she looks at the
mysterious sea and the familiar land, and thinks they symbolize her choices—
or rather what others might choose for her.

That night Dick, back with the Owens again, sends Jim Fales to the village
with a letter telling his artist friends, who want to sketch and hunt with him in
this region, to stay away. He feels out of place here but wonders what his place
may be. Jim returns with news: Dan is shipping out of Westport to the Banks
on a short-handed new schooner. Dick senses that Martha and Tempy regard
him as an interference. That night Doris quits weighing her options, goes before
dawn toward Westport, and encounters Dan in the street there. They return,
pledged to wed. Dick returns to New York and resumes his career. On a crisp
winter day, Doris looks at the ice, thinks of Dick fondly, and reads about Dick's
successful exhibition of a Sussex landscape in a New York paper he sent Israel.
Doris and Dan are happy in their Marsh Island home.

Jewett was encouraged by John Greenleaf Whittier* to follow her second
novel, *A Country Doctor*, with a third, which became *A Marsh Island*. Its plot,
however, is only that of a long short story. Rowley and Essex, Massachusetts,
become Sussex; Choate and Hog islands, the main marsh island. Jewett describes
her idyllic scene with a watercolorist's skill, while her depiction of the shipyard
provides the sharp contrast of a charcoal sketch. To some the style is marred
by overuse of curious double negatives, such as "not displeased," "not infre-
quently," and "not seldom." Thematically, country wins over city here. Doris
and Dan are based on patients treated by Jewett's father, Theodore Herman
Jewett.* Their pallid love affair Jewett stumbled into and developed with reluc-

tance. Current feminist critics seize on Jewett's few hints that Doris would be better off not marrying at all. *Bibliography*: Blanchard; Cary, *Jewett*; Randall R. Mawer, "Setting as Symbol in Jewett's *A Marsh Island*," *Colby Library Quarterly* 12 (June 1976): 83–90; Roman.

MARSH, JOHN. In "The Guests of Mrs. Timms," he is the stage driver in Woodville. He transports Mrs. Persis Flagg and Miss Cynthia Pickett to Baxter to call on Mrs. Timms. His remarks to Mrs. Ezra Beckett at Beckett's Corner make it clear that he guesses Mrs. Timms has treated the two women inhospitably.

MARSH, MISS POLLY. In "An Autumn Holiday," in her late sixties, she is Mrs. Snow's sister. Elizabeth, the narrator, and her father call her Aunt Polly. She is a nurse. Fifty years earlier, she treated Captain Daniel Gunn and is now the source of anecdotes about his mental derangement. She declined the proposal of Gunn's nephew, Jacob Gunn.

"MARSH ROSEMARY" (1886). Short story. (Characters: Amandy, Deacon Elton, Mrs. Elton, Jerry Lane, Mrs. Jerry Lane, Nancy Lloyd Lane, Low, Nathan Low.) Nancy Lloyd is a middle-aged, unmarried tailor, with a neat little home near a marsh by Walpole. Jerry Lane, a shiftless young sailor, who has been eyeing Nancy, wanders along the marsh one hot August afternoon and blandishes her into inviting him in for supper. They kiss. Though half-fearing she is making a mistake, she soon marries him, decently outfaces town gossipers, including Deacon Elton's wife, and wins everyone's respect—and sympathy. Jerry does little work in the house, barn, or garden, drinks habitually with his cronies, and to them once even calls Nancy his "Grandma." She alternates between criticism and forgiveness. One June he goes off to sea on trips between Shediac and Newfoundland, nicely outfitted by her needle and promising to return with money in September. But in the spring his ship, the *Susan Barnes*, goes down; Nancy, donning the black of widowhood, feels relief but also begins to build up a romantic image of him. Two years later she is secretly informed, one afternoon in September, by the supposedly sympathetic Mrs. Elton that Jerry, having stopped off a while in Newfoundland, is alive and living with a woman in Shediac. Nancy goes there to savage him and after some difficulty finds his house; but, peeping through his window, she observes her contented husband, his "trig" young second wife, and their happy baby. Feeling "alternate woe and comfort," Nancy returns home, unwilling to break another woman's heart, aware that "her best earthly hope" has failed, and confronting lonely old age as bravely as a prim, gray marsh rosemary. Jewett wrote Annie Adams Fields* ("Home, Saturday afternoon") that "dear, dull old Wells is a first-rate place to find stories in. Do you remember how we drove up that long straight road across the marshes last summer? It was along there the Marsh Rosemary grew." *Bibliography*: Fields, *Letters*.

MARTHA. In *A Country Doctor*, she is Mrs. Graham's servant.

MARTHA. In "Lady Ferry," she is a young servant at the house in which Matthew and Agnes live. She gossips to Marcia about Lady Ferry.

MARTHA. In "A Little Traveler," she is the niece in Stockbridge whom the woman on the train with birds is going to visit.

MARTHA. In "Martha's Lady," she is the handmaiden of prim, dense Miss Harriet Pyne of Ashford. From "up country" and working to support her mother and little brothers, Martha is tall and at first ungainly; but Miss Helena Vernon (*see* Dysart, Helena Vernon), Harriet's lively, considerate cousin, teaches Martha refining little touches during a short visit. Martha treasures her memory of Helena, her ideal of a lady and a friend to please in absentia. Forty years later, Helena revisits her cousin, sees Martha again, and for the first time realizes the indelible impression she has made on her.

MARTHA. In "The News from Petersham," she is Mrs. Peak's niece. Martha lives in Petersham and is amused when her aunt revisits her to attend the funeral of Daniel Johnson, who, rumor falsely has it, has died.

MARTHA ("MARTY"). In "Jim's Little Woman," she is Jim's tiny, red-haired wife. They meet in Maine, where she is a lobster-factory worker. Quickly marrying, they live in his house in St. Augustine, Florida, and have a son named Jim and then a daughter. Martha does menial work because Jim is unreliable. Although he is sometimes abusive and is reported dead in Jamaica, she dreams of his return, which finally occurs—to her delight.

"MARTHA'S LADY" (1897). Short story. (Characters: the Reverend Mr. Crofton, Helena Vernon Dysart, Jack Dysart, Hannah, Hepsy, Martha, Miss Harriet Pyne, Judge Pyne.) In early summer, Miss Harriet Pyne, thirty-five, welcomes into the conservative Pyne home in Ashford her younger cousin, Miss Helena Vernon (*see* Dysart, Helena Vernon), visiting from Boston. Harriet is prim and unimaginative; Helena, peppy and considerate. Whereas Harriet worries that Martha, her new "hand maiden" from "up country," may prove embarrassing to guests, including her bachelor neighbor, the Reverend Mr. Crofton, Helena sweetly encourages the ungainly girl. She even helps her climb a cherry tree for fruit, shows her how to arrange an attractive dish of cherries with leaves, and sends her off with the gift to Crofton. Martha hears Helena praise her to Harriet and from that moment on worships the gracious lady forever. Crofton sends Helena a book of his sermons. As she prepares to depart for an August vacation with her family, Helena speaks tenderly to Martha and asks her never to forget her; the timid servant promises to think of her every day. Forty years pass. Martha gradually became a thoughtful, dignified servant, happy to be "pleasing the ideal, that is to say, the perfect friend." Helena married Jack Dysart, a brilliant British diplomat, and wanted Harriet to bring Martha to the ceremony and thus let her see Boston. But Harriet thought it "unnecessary"; so Helena before going abroad sent Martha a silver-cased mirror, a tiny pair of scissors, and a lace-edged handkerchief as keepsakes. Harriet aged but never essentially changed. One Sunday afternoon in June, while Martha is fondling her precious keepsakes, Harriet announces the imminent arrival of "the Honorable Mrs. Dysart" and asks if Martha remembers her. Together the two greet the guest; while the cousins embrace, Martha, ever self-effacing, sobs at sight of her ideal—now old, bent, and in black, but with the same smile and youthful eyes. That night Martha prepares the guest room in old ways familiar to "Miss Helena," who now sees the lasting effect she has had on Martha. They kiss one another good night. Although Martha has lived a more emotionally satisfying life than Harriet, recent scholarship has made perhaps too much of the close relationship of Martha and Helena Vernon Dysart. After all, Martha never fully realized her emotional potential. *Bibliography*: Donovan; Glenda Hobbs, "Pure and Passionate: Female Friendship in Sarah Orne Jewett's 'Martha's Lady,' " *Studies in Short Fiction* 17 (1980): 21–29.

MARTHY. In *A Country Doctor*, she is the wife of a farmer whose dislocated shoulder Nan Prince sets. The couple live upriver.

MARTHY. In *Deephaven*, she is the half-sister of Andrew, who briefly tends Kate Lancaster's horse. When Andrew dies of sorrow and drink, Marthy feels she has to "fetch up" his two smallest children. Marthy's husband is considerably more gentle.

MARTIN. In "A Second Spring," he is Abby Martin's husband and Israel Haydon's brother-in-law.

MARTIN, ABBY. In "The Queen's Twin," she is a widow who lives alone in a farmhouse on a hill. Almira Todd and the narrator visit her and hear her tell about her connection with Queen Victoria. Both Abby Martin and Queen Victoria were born on the same day; Abby's husband was named Albert, as was Queen Victoria's; and there are other similarities. Abby saw the queen in London once, in the 1840s. Jewett handles the dementia of the "Queen's twin" with touching delicacy.

MARTIN, ABBY. In "A Second Spring," she is Israel Haydon's sister. When Israel's wife, Martha Haydon, dies, Abby helps Israel for a brief time. She theorizes to Mrs. Stevens, Israel's similarly helpful sister-in-law, that "Men is boys . . . [and] always want motherin'."

MARTIN, ALBERT. In "The Queen's Twin," he was Abby Martin's husband. A good accountant, he went as supercargo with Abby aboard her brother Horace's vessel to England. Albert evidently was not a good provider and was sick a long time before he died.

MARTIN, ALBERT EDWARD. In "The Queen's Twin," he is one of Abby Martin's children. Abby's husband gave the baby the name Albert after his own name and the name Edward after his brother's name. Later Abby learned that Queen Victoria had a son identically named.

MARTIN, ALFRED. In "The Queen's Twin," he is one of Abby Martin's children. She so named him because Queen Victoria had a son with that name.

MARTIN, ALICE. In "The Queen's Twin," he was one of Abby Martin's children, now deceased. Abby named her Alice because Queen Victoria had a daughter with that name.

MARTIN, JERRY. In *A Country Doctor*, he is a handyman. Captain Walter Parish tells Nancy Prince that Jerry will come to work for her tomorrow.

MARTIN, MISS. In "An Autumn Holiday," she is a person named in gossip by Miss Polly Marsh and Mrs. Snow, and is known by the father of Elizabeth, the narrator.

MARTIN, MRS. In "The Green Bonnet," she lives near Mr. West's parsonage and is in charge of aspects of the Easter Sunday service there.

MARTIN, NATHAN. In "Andrew's Fortune," he is Stephen Dennett's neighbor. He feels superior to his friends because he once worked in a shipyard.

MARTIN, SALLY. In "A Change of Heart," she is a farm woman, a little over thirty and living alone. She loves but has rebuffed Isaac Bolton after hearing he was once engaged to someone else. Mrs. Bascom, her kind neighbor, gently tells Sally that she is too stubborn and Isaac loves only her. Sally admits she has inherited "setness" from her grandfather, Walker. When Isaac is injured in a fall, Sally rushes to him, and all will be well.

MARTIN, SUSAN. In *A Country Doctor*, she is an Oldfields seamstress whose silk bonnets, made for Miss Betsy Milman and Sally Turner, Mrs. Graham praises.

MARTIN, VICTORIA. In "The Queen's Twin," she is one of Abby Martin's children. She says, "I called her Victoria after my mate."

MARY. In *Deephaven*, she is Helen Denis's aunt and lives in Lenox. She briefly visits Helen and Kate Lancaster in Deephaven.

MARY. In "A Late Supper," she is Miss Catherine Spring's niece. Miss Spring would like to go live with Mary and her husband, John, in Lowell and care for their children. But John's sister is going to provide the help instead, to Miss Spring's immense disappointment.

MARY. In "Little French Mary." *See* French Mary.

MARY. In "Mr. Bruce," she is the maid of Mrs. Duncan, who is the neighbor of Tennant and his family. Kitty Tennant squelches the idea of borrowing Mary, since Kitty wants to play maid herself.

MARY. In "Where's Nora?", she is mentioned as the old aunt of Corny Donahoe and Dan Donahoe. She recently died in Ireland.

MARY. In "Where's Nora?", she is the sister of Mary Ann Duffy and Patrick Quin and is Nora's mother. Nora comes to America and returns to visit her mother two years later, with her baby boy and with her uncle, Patrick Quin.

"MARY AND MARTHA" (1885). Short story. (Characters: Martha Dean, Mary Dean, Ellis, Josiah, Torby, John Whitefield, Maria Whitefield.) Martha and Mary Dean are sisters. Martha is older, shorter, practical, and impatient. She had a fiancé, but he died. Mary is taller, gentler, and timid. Having lost most of their money in a railroad failure, they live in their small house outside the village and sew for income. Martha is also an occasional housesitter, while Mary is sometimes called to tend the sick. They wish they had a sewing machine, to enable them to handle more work. One November day they talk about their cousin, John Whitefield, whom their family helped, whose father evidently cheated the sisters' father, and who has ignored their poverty now. Sulky Martha reluctantly follows Mary's meek suggestion and sends old John a cool letter inviting him for Thanksgiving dinner. He accepts; and while Martha prepares a dinner of chicken and cranberries, he talks sadly to Mary not only about their family dispute but also about his deceased wife, Maria Whitefield. Suddenly he promises to give the "girls" Maria's sewing machine, which was a gift from her brother Josiah. Next day, after John leaves, Martha praises Mary for wanting to invite John, and Mary praises Martha for the well-prepared dinner.

MARY ANNA. In *The Country of the Pointed Firs*, she is a poet at the Bowden reunion. Her last name may be Bowden.

MARY, AUNT. In "Mr. Bruce," she is Elly's aunt, fifty, and relishes hearing Miss Margaret Tennant recount stories about Kitty Tennant, who became Kitty Bruce, and about Philip Bruce. Mary and Anne Langdon are old friends.

MASTERS. In "The New Methuselah," he is a pompous physical scientist. Dr. Asa Potterby supports Masters while he theorizes impractically and without attempting to run practical tests. He discusses an electrical marine railway. Jewett, however, does give him some startling prescience: Masters borrows Potterby's typewriter to tinker with it, having "conceived an idea that the machine should be made to count its own words."

MASTERSON. In "The Orchard's Grandmother," this is the last name of the child to whom Mary ("Polly") Brenton entrusts her little apple tree when Polly must return from Massachusetts to England with her family.

MASTERSON, JUDGE. In "The Hiltons' Holiday," he is a prominent Topham Corners lawyer and judge. John Hilton, who served on a jury in his court once, respects him greatly. When Hilton takes his daughters, Susan Ellen Hilton and Katy Hilton, into the village, he sees the judge at his fine home. The judge talks to the little girls with delightful courtesy; says Katy's face "recalls" that of her grandmother, Catharine Winn Hilton, whom he remembers tenderly; and invites the Hiltons to visit him later that day. They are touched by his manners but do not stop there again.

"THE MATE OF THE DAYLIGHT" (1882). Short story. (Characters: Captain Peter Downs, Melinda Downs, Dan Lewis, Mrs. Lewis, Captain Jabez Ryder, Captain Joseph Ryder, Melinda Ryder, Mrs. Jabez Ryder, Susan Ryder, Sand, Captain Joseph Sewall, Mrs. Stark, Tarbell.) One summer morning Captain Joseph Ryder, his deaf cousin, Captain Jabez Ryder, and Captain Peter Downs, three retired sea captains, discuss the foolishness of Dan Lewis, known for his carelessness, in going out to fish in a fog at night. Susan Ryder, who is Dan's girlfriend and Joseph's granddaughter, is annoyed by their gossip and argues with Joseph, who is well off and, who with his single daughter, Melinda (Susan's aunt), has cared for Susan since her childhood. That evening Jabez and his wife walk over to Joseph's house to calm him down. Jabez relieves Susan by reporting that Dan lost some trawls but returned to port safely. Joseph criticizes her for demeaning him in front of others and, further, for continuing to admire worthless Dan. Next morning Dan announces that his uncle in New York wants him to ship out at once as second mate on the *Daylight*, which the uncle owns, to Liverpool to load freight for the East Indies. Joseph reluctantly but sailor-like wishes him "a good v'y'ge." Thus encouraged, Dan asks him for Susan's hand in marriage. Joseph, first off, demands some assurance of financial stability but then promises to aid the couple. Melinda, whose fiancé, Captain Joseph Sewalk, was lost at sea, goes to the family burial ground and laments at a slate slab with his name on it. Dan returns in September, healthy and with money. The captain of the *Daylight* was swept overboard during a storm, the first mate fell ill, and Dan is now the ship's master. When he takes the *Daylight* to sea again, Susan, now his wife, accompanies him. It is hard, if not impossible, to follow Jewett's handling of the names Downs and Melinda here. Why would Melinda think it only "likely" that her father will leave her some of his money? Also, Dan's promotion to master and hence to Ryder family acceptability is a weak deus ex machina.

MATHES. In "Andrew's Fortune," he is Susan Mathes's father.

MATHES, MRS. In "Andrew's Fortune," she is Susan Mathes's mother.

MATHES, SUSAN. In "Andrew's Fortune," she is Andrew Phillips's girl-friend. Pretty but materialistic, she will not marry him once he decides not to contest Lysander Dennett's inheritance of Andrew's uncle Stephen Dennett's estate. Her parents contend they do not want her to go to Boston with Andrew. She regrets marrying locally when she learns that Andrew has prospered.

MATTHEW. In "Lady Ferry," he is the cousin of Marcia's parents, who leave her with Matthew and his wife, Agnes, in their house by the ferry near the river. Matthew treats Marcia considerately, lets her plant a small garden, and condones her association with Lady Ferry.

MATTHEW. In "The Orchard's Grandmother," he is named by Mrs. Brenton as a cousin fighting "with the Roundhead army" against the forces of King Charles I.

MATTHEW. In *The Tory Lover*, he is John Davis's old groom. Matthew accompanies Davis and Mary Hamilton from Bristol to Plymouth.

MATTHEW, UNCLE. In *Deephaven*, he was Captain Sands's hot-tempered uncle and was in the West Indies trade. He ordered Sands's father, Matthew, named after him, to put cherries in a barrel of rum. By mistake, the lad put them in a barrel of gin instead, ruined the gin, and ran away from home in fear.

MAULEY, 'BIJAH. In *Deephaven*, he is a trawl owner with Joe Sands. Mauley allowed circus posters to be placed on his barn.

MAX, GEORGE. In *Betty Leicester*, he is Betty Leicester's tennis-playing friend. He will later go to sea.

MAX, MRS. In *Betty Leicester*, she is a woman Betty Leicester naughtily regards as an ugly old gossip.

MAXWELL. In *A Marsh Island*, this is the name of a family the members of which, according to Mrs. Bennet, attend funerals most sociably.

MEADOWS, FRIEND. In *A Country Doctor*, she is Dr. John Leslie's Quaker friend.

MEEKER, MRS. In *A Country Doctor*, she is an unpleasant, meddling neighbor of Mrs. Daniel Thacher and her family. She lives on a desert-like farm but does grow nice flowers.

MELINDA. In *Deephaven*, she may be Tobias's wife.

MELISSA. In "A Lost Lover," she is Horatia Dane's loyal if crotchety old servant. Horatia's mother, Mrs. Dane, found her in a Deerfield orphanage and "fetched [her] up," as Melissa puts it. She provides Nelly Dane with details concerning Captain Joe Carrick, Horatia's lost lover. Melissa serves him a hearty breakfast when he returns as a beggar, but she never learns his identity. Melissa is better adjusted to reality than dreamy Horatia. *Bibliography*: Roman.

"MÈRE POCHETTE" (1888). Short story. (Characters: Marie Binet, Father David, Father Henri, Josephine, Manon, Julie Partout, Charles Pictou, Father Pierre, Philippe, Jeanne Pochette, Joseph Pochette, Mère Pochette, Justin Pochette, Rispé.) Joseph Pochette of Quebec moves to the river town of Bonaventure, buys lands there, and soon dies, survived by his wife, Manon, called Mère Pochette, and a daughter named Jeanne. Mère Pochette opens the village shop in her house and raises Jeanne in a tyrannical, tight-fisted fashion. She makes a profit by selling some of her land to the incoming railroad. Jeanne marries an engineer from the States, goes with him to the West, has a daughter, also named Manon, and dies. The sick husband returns to Bonaventure with the child and soon dies. When Father David, the kind old priest, dies, he is replaced by Father Pierre, who is conceited and selfish. The town grows. Mère Pochette works and saves, hoping to provide a dowry for a fine marriage for little Manon. But she becomes a handful for the crotchety woman. Manon, who likes church but also the great outdoors, combines her mother's beauty and her father's persuasiveness. She attracts handsome young Charles Pictou, with whom, despite Mère Pochette's fierce objections, she falls in love. Given some money by Josephine, Father Pierre's housekeeper, Charles goes to the States for work, promises to write Manon faithfully, and plans to return for her. But Father Pierre, to whom Charles addresses his letters, shares them with Mère Pochette, who then burns them. Manon prays faithfully for his return, languishes because of his silence, and is not comforted when Mère Pochette offers to take her to Quebec to combine sightseeing and husband-seeking for her. Instead, she grows desperately ill. Mère Pochette repents; but after Father Pierre leaves and goes overseas, she does not know what to do. She would willingly accept Charles now and even finance his marriage to Manon. One happy day, Father Henri, the new priest, calls her to him and shows her a letter. It reveals that Manon's father's family has sought the girl to give her an inheritance. Mère Pochette offers Manon a profound apology and is embraced. The same day Charles returns, still handsome and now financially successful. Manon grows well again, and the lovers wed and go to the States. Mère Pochette is happy in her garden. "Mère Pochette" is not typical of Jewett and is mainly notable for its depiction of several dreadful French-Canadian women. Oddly, it is marked by innumerable run-on sentences, which contribute to its resembling a stiff literal translation from a foreign language. Also, why does Jewett name so many of her fourteen characters so strangely? She has a Joseph, a Josephine, a Justin and a Julie, two Manons, and eight characters whose names begin with "P," including a Poulette to go with three Pochettes. *Bibliography*: Thorp.

MERRILL, HENRY. In "Decoration Day," he is a Civil War veteran and, with Asa Brown and John Stover, plans the holiday parade. Merrill tells Stover that Marthy Peck Down plans to erect a marker on Eben Munson's grave.

MEYNELL, ALICE (1847–1922). British poet and essayist. Born Alice Thompson in Barnes, England, she began to write poetry at seven, and gained quick fame with *Preludes* (1875), the first of nine volumes of poetry containing lines John Ruskin praised excessively. She was confirmed in the Anglican faith in 1864 and converted to Roman Catholicism four years later. She married the journalist-biographer Wilfred Meynell, also a Catholic, in 1877; they had eight children. She helped him edit the Catholic *Weekly Register* (1881–1898). When Alfred, Lord Tennyson* died in 1892, Alice Meynell's fame was so great she was nominated to be his successor as poet laureate. (Alfred Austin was so named, in 1896.) Meynell also published several books of essays, the first being *The Rhythm of Life* (1893); later came a biography of Ruskin (1900) and much else. Contemporary critics praise her delicate craftsmanship but find her subject matter too reticent for modern taste. During a visit to the United States (September 1901–April 1902), Meynell called on Annie Adams Fields* in March and met Jewett, whose works Meynell had long admired and who, in turn, valued the austerity and compression of Meynell's poetry. Jewett and Meynell became friends at once and corresponded during Jewett's final years. In such poor health in 1904 that she was ordered not to read, Jewett wrote Meynell (14 December 1904) she was grateful when a nurse smuggled a copy of Meynell's poetry into her room anyway. Fields asked Meynell to provide an introduction to her edition of Jewett's letters in 1911. Meynell tactfully declined on the grounds that any preface by Fields would be more than sufficient. *Bibliography*: June Badini, *The Slender Tree: A Life of Alice Meynell* (Padstow, Cornwall: Tabb House, 1981); Blanchard; Matthiessen.

MICHEL. In "The Gray Mills of Farley," he is a mill worker in Farley. He is the head of a French-Canadian family of nine, including a daughter whose Christian talk Mrs. Kilpatrick approves of.

MIDDLETON. In "The Mistress of Sydenham Plantation," he is mentioned by Sibyl, an ex-slave, as the man Mistress Sydenham bought her from. Sibyl adds that, as infants, she and Middleton nursed at the same breast.

MILES, FATHER. In "The Luck of the Bogans," he is the Irish priest, born in Bantry, who befriends Mike Bogan and his wife, Biddy Flaherty Bogan. Though addicted to coffee and drinking liquor in moderation, he lectures Mike on the evils of alcohol. He says that Mike's and Biddy's daughter, Mary Ellen Bogan, should go to school. He tries to comfort Mike when his son, Dan Bogan, is killed and administers extreme unction when Mike lies dying of terrible grief. In "A Little Captive Maid," Father Miles is remembered by Father Dunn as his predecessor. John Balfour knew and respected Father Miles.

MILMAN, MISS BETSY. In *A Country Doctor*, she is a person Susan Martin makes silk bonnets for. Sally Turner also wears Susan Martin's bonnets. Dr. John Leslie says Betsy and Sally mend his clothes. The two may be sisters.

MILTON. In "A War Debt," he is the emancipated black servant of Colonel Bellamy and his wife in Virginia.

MINTON, JERRY. In "Farmer Finch," he is Polly Finch's next-door neighbor. The two came close to marriage, but he preferred Mary Hallett of Portsmouth, who then married someone else. When Jerry tries to resume his friendship with Polly, she rebuffs him.

MINTON, MRS. In "Farmer Finch," she is Jerry Minton's and Polly Finch's neighbor, and is described as "croaking" and "unpleasant." When Mrs. Minton boasts that her son, Jerry, is interested in Mary Hallett, Polly happily tells her that Mary has married another man.

"MISS BECKY'S PILGRIMAGE" (1881). Short story. (Characters: Daniel Annis, Sophia Annis, Beacham, Susan Beckett, Mary Ann Dean, Dennett, Annie Downs, Julia Downs, Phebe Littlefield, Parker, Joshua Parker, Mahaly Parker, Becky Parsons, the Rev. Mr. Joseph Parsons, Prescott, Prescott, Adaline Emery Prescott, Cynthy Rush, Sands.) Rebecca ("Becky") Parsons, and her brother, Joseph Parsons, lived together for forty years. He was a Congregationalist minister who left their native town of Brookfield, Maine, to preach in New York state, then Devonport, in western New York state; she was his contented housekeeper and was always proud of him. The two were planning to visit Brookfield in September, but he suddenly died. The following spring, Becky writes her old cousin, Sophia Annis, in Brookfield, about making a visit, takes a train to Boston, after which, on the train for Brookfield, she chances to meet Mahaly Parker, an old friend, twice widowed, also going to Brookfield. They reminisce all the way to Brookfield, the sight of which makes Becky not only happy but also apprehensive of change. Mahaly, though offering to let Becky stay with her and her sister, Phebe Littlefield, if need be, abruptly leaves her at the railway station alone—until Sophia's granddaughter, Annie Downs, a Brookfield schoolteacher, meets her and takes her to the home she shares with her widowed mother, Julia Downs. They make Becky feel wonderfully welcome. To make amends for forgetting Becky at the station, Malahy and her sister invite her to a tea party, where she meets Beacham, the widowed Brookfield Congregationalist minister. Becky enjoys his sermons, although she feels her brother's were a bit better. When Becky, always generous and now suddenly popular, informally nurses Mary Ann Dean, a sick woman, she happens to meet Beacham, who is there to pray for Mary. One warm June afternoon in the Annis garden, shaded by grape vines, Beacham proposes gallantly to Becky, who tearfully accepts. They go for their wedding trip to Devonport, where Becky, looking not a day over fifty-five, gives away some belongings with characteristic generosity and returns to Brookfield with the rest of her things. She feels that the events of her life have "happened just right," with "other people's affairs" connecting wonderfully. Beacham would have pronounced everything providential. For even "the dullest life," Jewett concludes, "much machinery is put in motion."

"MISS DEBBY'S NEIGHBORS" (1884). Short story. (Characters: Ashby, John Ashby, John Ashby, Joseph Ashby, Marilla Ashby, Mrs. Ashby, Mrs. John Ashby, Susan Ellen Ashby, Miss Debby, Asa Hopper, John Jacobs, Jonas, Cyrus Parker, Tommy Simms.) Miss Debby, an old tailor, has moved from her family farm into the village. She likes to reminisce, to her auditors' delight, about John Ashby and his quarrelsome family. Combining reflection and humor, she reveals that John Ashby joined with his son, also named John Ashby, in "twitt[ing]" his other son, Joseph Ashby. Joseph's wife, Susan Ellen Ashby, had money but was dumb; neither John liked her. Old Mrs. Ashby, the brothers' grandmother, worn out by the squabbling, died, and soon so did her daughter, Marilla Ashby, Debby's friend. Joseph was a good carpenter and built a house for himself and Susan Ellen on the Ashby farm. One day both Johns got John Jacobs, a neighbor with oxen, to help them drag the house a half a mile away. When they saw it, Joseph made a fist but then laughed while Susan Ellen cried. Joseph obtained a machine-shop job in town, and he and his wife had a son. Young John married a vixen named Miss Pecker, who persuaded him to work in a mill. Meanwhile, Joseph wanted to return to the family farm. To frustrate him, John and his wife tried to haul the family house to town, but it got stuck on the railroad tracks. Old John died. Susan Ellen's son became a sailor and was lost—either at sea or by fever. When young John died, Susan Ellen, with an estate of several thousand dollars, was snapped up by "a roving preacher," and the pair sold out and went "up country" to his old region. Debby's rambling yarn is unified by her steady preference for the old ways rather than the new. She concludes that railroads and store-bought clothes have contributed to smoothing away people's proper distinctions. "Miss Debby's Neighbors" has tall-tale features, with asides concerning a six-quart pail to spoon a gift of preserves into, a convenient liquor jug, and a house stalled on railroad tracks. *Bibliography*: Cary, *Jewett*; Roman.

"MISS ESTHER'S GUEST" (1893). Short story. (Characters: Barnard, Barstow, Mrs. Belton, Mrs. Connolly, Esther Porley, Mr. Rill, Deacon Sparks, Mrs. Sparks, Wayton, Mr. Wayton, Mrs. Wayton.) Miss Esther Porley, a seamstress in Daleham, is sixty-four, single, and lonely since her mother's death. One summer morning, Miss Esther agrees to let Mrs. Wayton, the minister's wife, tell Mrs. Belton, chairman of the Country Week in Boston, to send her a person to room and board with her for a short vacation. Mr. Rill, an Englishman and a retired seal engraver, old and bent but clean, is chosen and reports by train to Daleham. Miss Esther, though surprised her guest is male, greets him, and they soon become friendly. Mr. Rill spruces up her old-fashioned house and grounds, and stays a month. Miss Esther shyly tells Mrs. Wayton that she and Mr. Rill may advance "judicious[ly]" in the fall; after all, he left his caged bullfinch with her. Sex hardly looms in the pair's future. Miss Esther sees Mr. Rill as a replacement for her father or her brother and oddly refers to him as her "old lady" in talking to Mrs. Wayton. Moreover, Mr. Rill sees Miss Esther as a replacement for his deceased sister. *Bibliography*: Roman.

"MISS MANNING'S MINISTER" (1883). Short story. (Characters: Susan Allen, Deacon Eller, Mrs. Eller, Miss Narcissa Manning, Jonas Peters, Mr. Raynor, the Reverend Edward Taylor.) Miss Narcissa Manning, fifty, takes pleasure in the text from the Apocrypha read at the morning service by the Reverend Edward Taylor the last Sunday in May. Taylor, in his late forties, has just replaced Mr. Raynor, the recently deceased old minister, at the First Congregational church in Rinston, Connecticut. Taylor spent years as an only partly successful missionary in India and is glad to be back in the United States, though single and with no near relatives. One day he misses the afternoon service and is found to have suffered a paralytic stroke in the garden of his rectory, leaving him unable to walk or speak beyond a mumble. He is replaced by another minister, and the church leaders voice uncertainty about Taylor's care, until Miss Manning, normally shy, steps up, rebukes them for stinginess—there was even talk of sending him to the almshouse—and promises to welcome him into her home, where she will care for him. Arrangements are made, and before long Miss Manning finds a new meaning to her life. She cooks for and reads to Taylor, is assisted by Jonas Peters, her "factotum," and rejoices to see improvement in her patient. When he stammeringly wonders if he must always be dependent on her kindness, she replies she is the one who owes him. All the same, he hopes for freedom. One day a distinguished physician is called to Rinston and happens to learn about Taylor. The two were classmates. The physician takes Taylor for treatment "by electricity" to a small hospital in New York. Miss Manning, though lonely again, is happy to hear of Taylor's marvelous improvement. He calls on her again, walking with a cane and speaking slowly, before taking a position in a missionary society. One day the following spring, he returns to her, says he cannot be happy without her, and the two get married. The nearby robins and lilacs rejoice. The gentle moral is that "each had been both giver and receiver."

"MISS PECK'S PROMOTION" (1887). Short story. (Characters: Maria Corbell, Elbury, Mrs. Wilbur Elbury, Mrs. Wilbur Elbury, the Rev. Mr. Wilbur Elbury, Joe Farley, Colonel Tom Peck, Eliza Peck, Tom Peck, Harriet White Peck Pigley, Noah Pigley, Mrs. Spence, Ezra Weston.) When the father of Eliza Peck, who is single and forty, died, he left her the family's Vermont farm and her brother, Tom Peck (*see* Peck, Colonel Tom), the money part of the estate. Tom married Harriet White (*see* Pigley, Harriet White Peck), had three children, including a son also named Tom ("Tommy") Peck, went off to the war, was promoted to colonel, and was killed. Eliza, who adores her nephew, Tommy, but dislikes selfish Harriet, is alone as winter approaches. Harriet has married Noah Pigley. One night Eliza is called to the parsonage of the Rev. Mr. Wilbur Elbury, whose wife has just died giving birth to a baby girl. Eliza, whose brother always said she deserved a promotion for generosity, takes charge of the "ease-loving" minister's home so nicely that town gossip says she and Elbury, three years her junior, can wed if she knows how to promote her cause. A year passes. One day Elbury returns from a neighboring city, where he has been a guest preacher, with a prissy new Mrs. Elbury. Eliza, who has rented her farm, goes home, half relieved, to the old familiar place, open to long vistas; she is especially happy that Tommy will now live with her. She can pass on to him much of the learning she incidentally got while reading in Elbury's well-stocked library.

"MISS SYDNEY'S FLOWERS" (1874). Short story. (Characters: Hannah, Jack, John, Becky Marley, Polly Sharpe, Miss Sydney, Bessie Thorne, Mrs. Thorne, Mrs. Welch.) Old Miss Sydney, wealthy, aloof, and self-centered, dislikes the idea that a new street is being built right next to her greenhouse of beautiful flowers. She is further distressed that the authorities are naming the street Grant Place rather than Sydney Street, after her important family. But soon numerous pedestrians—some busy, others tired—while using the new street pause to have a look at her beautiful blooms. The sight of her geraniums even reminds one young man of his mother, and he mends his sinful ways. Lame Polly Sharpe makes molasses candy which Becky Marley, her rheumatic widowed sister, sells on a windy street corner nearby. Becky moves her stand to Grant Place to capitalize on the increased foot traffic there. When Miss Sydney ventures to look at her flowers from the outside, she sees a girl with a baby and impulsively buys them some candy. When Miss Sydney talks to Becky and learns that she and her sister are short of money, she gives them a substantial sum. When Bessie Thorne, the daughter of a woman who used to know Miss Sydney well, decides to call on the lonely woman, she is welcomed graciously and is given flowers for the children's hospital, which Miss Sydney decides to visit. When Bessie learns of a job in a museum nearby and tells Miss Sydney, she recommends Becky for the position. The following Sunday, while Miss Sydney's radiant smile at Bessie puzzles the congregation, the minister preaches about flowers springing up behind a good woman's footsteps. Though marred by preachy passages about friendship, self-examination, and reform, "Miss Sydney's Flowers" has genuine power to strengthen its old-fashioned pathos. *Bibliography*: Cary, *Jewett*; Donovan.

"MISS TEMPY'S WATCHERS" (1888). Short story. (Characters: Sarah Ann Binson, Daniel Crowe, Mrs. Daniel Crowe, Priscilla Dance, Temperance Dent, Mrs. Owen, Dr. Prince, Lizzie Trevor.) Temperance ("Tempy") Dent lies dead one April evening in her little house in a New Hampshire farming village. Two of her oldest friends, Mrs. Daniel Crowe and Sarah Ann Binson, former schoolmates, sit in Tempy's cozy kitchen as her asked-for watchers through the night before her funeral. Well-to-do Mrs. Crowe is knitting a stocking for her husband while Sarah Ann, single and overworked because she feels obliged to support a widowed sister-in-law and her six whining children, is sewing indifferently. Mrs. Crowe and Sarah Ann never got along well, but both admire Tempy's self-sacrificial virtues. While a brook murmurs outside and the wind makes the house tremble, they remember how Tempy gave Lizzie Trevor, a tired, financially strapped local teacher, money for a vacation to "Niagary Falls," which Tempy herself wanted to see but never did. Tempy supported herself mostly by caring for others when they were sick. Her spirit prompts Mrs. Crowe to admit to former selfishness and prompts Sarah "to defer to others," including Mrs. Crowe, more sympathetically. Tempy's spirit even helps the two brush aside a minor church dispute that once caused them anguish. They check on Tempy's body and admire her still-present "wonderful smile." They sample Tempy's quince preserve, kept for the ill. They doze off, and Tempy watches the watchers as dawn breaks on a fair day. *Bibliography*: Nina Auerbach, *Communities of Women: An Idea in Fiction* (Cambridge: Harvard University Press, 1978); Edward Garnett, *Friday Nights: Literary Criticisms and Appreciations*, First Series (New York: Alfred A. Knopf, 1922).

"THE MISTRESS OF SYDENHAM PLANTATION" (1888). Short story. (Characters: Barnwell, Célestine, Middleton, Peter, Rhett, Sibyl, Mistress Sydenham.) Twenty years after her husband and sons were killed in the Civil War, and with her mind ruined and her property destroyed, old Mistress Sydenham orders her one remaining faithful servant, ex-slave Peter, to take her from her home in Beaufort (probably in Tidewater Maryland) by boat to her plantation on St. Helena's Island. Once there, she imagines her mansion and her field workers are all as they once were. In reality, the house is ruined and the land has been distributed to the emancipated blacks, one of whom, old Sibyl, is as demented as her former mistress. The following day is Easter, and Peter escorts the frail lady to church.

MONTAGUE, KATIE. In "The Green Bowl," she is the independent-minded young woman who goes by horse and buggy with Frances Kent, her compliant companion, for a little vacation. They get lost in the woods, are given breakfast by Mrs. Patton, and see her green bowl. Mrs. Patton gives a companion bowl to Katie, tells her it has a charm, confides its secret to her, and makes Katie her companion. Evidently, Katie thus gains the ability to foresee the future.

MOODY. In *The Tory Lover*, he is a Berwick minister who praises the teacher Sullivan and his distinguished ancestors.

MOOLLY. In "A White Heron," she is the cow, called Mistress Moolly, belonging to Mrs. Tilley and affectionately tended by her granddaughter, Sylvia.

MORRIS, BETSEY. In "Andrew's Fortune," she is Stephen Dennett's faithful housekeeper. She is hospitable to numerous neighbors when he is dying and later at his funeral. Lysander Dennett inherits Stephen's estate, honors Stephen's request, and gives Betsey $500. She goes to live with her sister. Andrew Dennett later learns of Betsey's death.

MORRIS, JOHN ("JOHNNY"). In "A Little Captive Maid," he is Nora Connelly's faithful lover. They separate for three years, while Nora works in America to earn enough money to improve his family farm so they can get married. She succeeds, returns, and they do so.

MORRIS, MRS. In "A Little Captive Maid," she is John Morris's mother. Nora Connelly sends her some money from America, but it is mostly used to maintain, rather than improve, the farm.

MORRIS, ROBERT (1734–1806). American banker and supporter of the Revolution. In *The Tory Lover*, Robert Morris is mentioned by Benjamin Franklin, who says Morris sent him a letter.

MOSES, WIDOW. In *Deephaven*, she is a Deephaven resident critical of anyone misguided enough to leave the city with its "many privileges."

MOULTON, CAPTAIN. In *The Tory Lover*, he is mentioned as commanding a company of American soldiers.

MOYNAHAN, MARY. In "The Gray Mills of Farley," she is the housekeeper for Dan, the mill agent.

"MR. BRUCE" (1869). Short story. (Characters: Ann, Bowler, Bruce, Kitty Bruce, Philip Bruce, Miss Burt, Nelly Cameron, Miss Carroll, Davenport, Dent, Mrs. Duncan, Elly, Hannah, Kate Hunter, Robert Hunter, John, John Keith, Anne Langdon, Mary, Aunt Mary, Peggy, Madame Riché, Tennant, Miss Margaret Tennant, Mrs. Tennant, Thornton, Miss Alice Thornton, Mrs. Walkintwo, Harriet Wolfe.) Aunt Mary tells her niece, Elly, twenty, about meeting Miss Margaret Tennant during a vacation in the mountains and visiting her in her Boston home the following winter. Mary's friend, Anne Langdon, was there. Margaret and Anne were old friends and knew Margaret's story of Philip Bruce. Margaret repeats it for Mary's benefit; and all three spinsters, each about fifty, find it pleasant.

Here is the story. When eighteen, out of boarding school and in Madame Riché's finishing school, Margaret's sister Kitty, three years older than she, becomes the center of a family ruse. During the Easter season, their father sends a note home saying he is bringing four businessmen to dinner—two from South America, one from New Orleans, and Bruce from London. Mrs. Tennant worries because three of their white servants are away and their black cook cannot serve at table. Kitty volunteers to don an apron and be the serving-maid. She puts on a brogue, and all goes nicely. She and Bruce eye each other, but he soon leaves. Kitty graduates in July and is a November debutante. She is invited to the Baltimore home of Kate Hunter, who is the sister of Kitty's father, while her husband, Robert Hunter, is on business in Savannah. During a dance party in Baltimore at the home of Miss Alice Thornton, a fellow Riché graduate, Kitty meets an Englishman, who is a friend, named Bruce, of Alice's father. He and Kitty Tennant agree they must have met somewhere before. Kitty cannot remember; but when he seems to do so, he turns into "a perfect icicle"—as Kitty says in one of her letters to Margaret. The two occasionally meet again—at a dinner, at a dance, at a whist party. Once, when the two discuss girls rising socially above their "position," he grows puzzlingly distant. When Hunter returns to Baltimore, he and his wife invite Bruce to dinner, Hunter having met him on business in London and having found messages from Bruce at his office. The truth comes out: Kitty is Kate's niece from Boston and the daughter—not servant—of a businessman whom Bruce met there. Although he was a dinner guest at the man's home, he forgot his host's name but did remember his pretty servant with the brogue. Bruce apologizes for his rudeness, they talk and walk together, and soon get married. He becomes his father's American partner, settles in Boston, and has now been Kitty's husband for almost thirty years. They have two daughters.

The farcical plot of "Mr. Bruce" was based on an anecdote Jewett heard from her step-grandmother, Eliza Sleeper Jewett (*see* Jewett, Theodore Furber), on 5 August 1869. Within four days, Jewett finished and made a fair copy of the story. It was accepted by William Dean Howells* and became her first story to appear in the *Atlantic Monthly*, under the pseudonym of A[lice]. C. Eliot. It is Jewett's most needlessly convoluted piece of fiction, with Elly telling about Aunt Mary's telling Elly and their friend, Anne Langdon, about Margaret Tennant's telling about her sister Kitty Bruce, whose letters Margaret quotes extensively. For profeminist readers, decent and independent Margaret and her rapt female auditors, Elly and Anne, are more significant than shallow Kitty and uppity Mr. Bruce could ever be. *Bibliography*: Cary, *Jewett*; Frost; Roman.

"MRS. PARKINS'S CHRISTMAS EVE" (1890). Short story. (Characters: Lucy Deems, Mrs. Deems, Dilby, Donnell, Colonel Drummond, Faber, Mary Faber, Bell Lane, John Lane, Mary Lane, Mr. Lane, Mrs. Lane, Major, Parkins, Parkins, Lydia Parkins, Nathan Parkins.) On December 21, widowed Lydia Parkins is sitting alone in her farmhouse near Holton. She is as cheerless as the cold, bleak day outside. Her two sons are grown and employed elsewhere. When Mrs. Deems and her little daughter, Lucy Deems, come calling, Mrs. Parkins offers them scant welcome. When Mrs. Deems praises Mr. Lane, the new minister, Mrs. Parkins speaks coldly about him and his family. Next day Mrs. Parkins does some ironing. On Wednesday she feels neuralgic. On Thursday she goes by her horse and wagon to Haybury, eight miles away. After depositing in the bank $87 paid to her by the Dilby brothers for use of some of her land, she visits her widowed cousin, Mary Faber, who is having a difficult time raising her two sons. Mrs. Parkins resists the temptation to give the woman some money as a Christmas present. She might expect more such presents later. Though invited to stay overnight, since it is Christmas Eve, she hitches up her horse, starts to drive back to Holton, but is caught in a sudden snowstorm. Releasing her horse, she staggers through drifts. In danger of freezing to death, she is rescued by Mr. Lane, who saw the horse approaching the shelter of the parsonage. Mr. Lane, his gracious wife, their crippled son, John Lane, and their two daughters, Bell Lane and Mary Lane, join to warm Mrs. Parkins with tea, blankets, a dressing gown, a heartfelt hymn, and a biblical reading about the birth of Christ and "no room that night at the inn." Mrs. Parsons no longer feels scared, lonely, cold, or even selfish. Never again will her heart be like a cold inn. Touched to her soul, she gives Mary Faber hospitality and supplies, little Lucy Deems a peck of coveted butternuts, and Mr. Lane money for an operation on John's leg. When Bell and Mary find Mrs. Parkins's old bonnet, lost in a snowdrift now melted, they put it on the parsonage scarecrow at corn-planting time.

MULDOON, PEGGY ("PEG"). In "The Luck of the Bogans," she is a one-eyed old Bantry beggar, whose drinking cronies include Marget Dunn and Biddy O'Hern. When Mike Bogan is leaving for America, he gives her five shillings and later sends her a pound for Christmas. She curses him for not sending more later.

MULLET, MRS. In *The Tory Lover*, she is George Fairfax's housekeeper in Bath. She serves Mary Hamilton "a dish of tea."

MULLIGAN, JOHN. In "Between Mass and Vespers," he is a person older men speak with in Gaelic after mass.

MULLIN, MRS. In "The Gray Mills of Farley," she is a person Maggie says is "always . . . scolding" about collections Father Daley takes up. Mrs. Kilpatrick is critical of Mrs. Mullin for doing so.

MUNSON, EBEN ("EB"). In "Decoration Day," he was a Civil War veteran. When he returned to Barlow Plains and found his girlfriend, Marthy Peck (*see* Down, Marthy Peck), married to John Down, "Eb" took to drink and died a pauper. Marthy, now widowed, plans to erect a marker on his grave.

MURDON, MISS. In *Betty Leicester*, she is mentioned by Thomas Leicester as a former servant or teacher of Betty Leicester.

MURPHY, PETER. In "Where's Nora?", he is reported as recently dying back in Ireland, as did his brother in Ballycannon the same week.

N

NANCY. In "Good Luck," she is the old servant of the family of Mrs. Leslie and her children, Mary Leslie, Parkhurst Leslie, and Tom Leslie. She accompanies Mrs. Leslie to their summer home near Hilton, New Hampshire.

NANCY. In *The Tory Lover*, she is an old Whitehaven resident. Captain John Paul Jones once "wintered" with her and borrows a light from her to start fires during the Whitehaven raid.

NANCY, AUNT. In "The Passing of Sister Barsett," she is mentioned lugubriously by Sarah Ellen Dow as an aunt who died suddenly.

NASH, MRS. In "A Little Captive Maid," she is one of John Balfour's servants. Mrs. Nash, now widowed, was born in Northern Ireland. Her first husband was an American. She welcomes Nora Connelly, is good to her, inherits money at Balfour's death, and will marry James Reilly, another of Balfour's servants, and go with him to her farm.

NASH, MRS. In *A Marsh Island*, she is the former Sussex minister's widowed wife. She was annoyed when young Israel Owen, as a child, dressed and preened himself like her for a joke.

NASH, MRS. In "A Second Spring," this is a generous person whose family, according to gossipy Polly Norris, has "all . . . passed away."

NASH, PARSON. In *A Marsh Island*, he was the Sussex minister, now deceased, who laughed when young Israel Owen mimicked his wife. Mrs. Nash, however, was not amused.

NAT. In "A Born Farmer," he was Jacob Gaines's cousin and his playmate during their childhood. Nat went to Minnesota, made a fortune, died, and left Jacob $50,000. This bequest enables Jacob and his family to move from their farm to Boston. But Jacob, his wife, Adeline Gaines, and their daughter, Mary Ellen Gaines, dislike city life. Only Jacob's son, Jacob ("Jakey") Gaines, remains in Boston.

"A NATIVE OF WINBY" (1891). Short story. (Characters: Ezra, Goodsoe, Abby Harran Hender, John Hender, Marilla Hender, Joseph K. Laneway, Johnny Spencer, Winn.) While teaching her class at a roadside school near Winby one hot May afternoon, Marilla Hender repeats the story of Joseph J. Laneway. He was an industrious lad who studied years ago in this same schoolhouse, went west, and gained fame in the state of Kansota as a millionaire, senator, and army general. Laneway enters, listens to Marilla, identifies himself, and rather pompously tells the children he determined as a lad to be rich and enter politics, and later was proud to fight for his country. He adjures his audience to "[w]ish for the best things, and work hard to win them." He recruits a boy to drive his horse back to the Four Corners so he can stay in the area a while, learns from Marilla that her widowed grandmother, Abby Harran Hender, often speaks of attending classes here with Laneway and would love to see him. Laneway walks past familiar spots, notes that his family farmhouse is obliterated but finds a rosebush his mother planted, feels let down, and decides to knock on the Hender house door that evening. Marilla has been telling Abby about Laneway. She recognizes him as "Joe" and welcomes him into her cheerful kitchen, where they reminisce amiably. Abby, who says she has followed and admired Joe's career, married and had three sons, one of whom, Marilla's father, John Hender, was killed at Fredericksburg, and his wife also died; the other two sons are now away buying cattle in Canada. Laneway reminds her that his wife and only son are dead. Abby, with Marilla's help, prepares a country supper for their guest— rye drop-cakes, tea, salt fish, cheese, baked beans, and bread and honeycomb. Marilla studies while Abby and Joe talk—she about the varied fortunes of mutual friends, and he about politics, which, he notes, she understands astutely. When Marilla retires, the two old people get some tangy cider from the cellar and look at Abby's small library in her "best room." It includes his biography, with letters saved in it that he wrote to her. Feeling he neglected her, he promises to send her some books. Next morning the two friends kiss "gravely" and say good-bye. Marilla drives Laneway to Winby and returns with news: Crowds awaited the great man, who, the selectmen say, met earlier with them and has promised a new town hall with names of Winby soldiers displayed. Marilla wonders why her grandmother has been crying. "A Native of Winby" is one of Jewett's several return-of-the-native stories. Originally intending to have Lane-way go west to Iowa, she agreed with Horace Scudder,* editor of the *Atlantic Monthly*, that she should make the state fictitious. She wrote Scudder (28 February [1891]) that she thought of either Wi-owa or Kansota as a substitute.

NEAL, HANNAH. In *The Tory Lover*, she is a demure servant in Colonel Jonathan Hamilton's home.

"A NEIGHBOR'S LANDMARK" (1894). (Full title: "A Neighbor's Land-mark: A Winter Story with a Christmas Ending.") Short story. (Characters: Joe Banks, Fox'l Berry, Chauncey, Ferris, Foss, Bill Otis, John Packer, Lizzie Packer, Mary Hannah Packer.) One cold December day, surly John Packer half-promises Ferris, a conniving timber contractor, to accept $80 and let him cut down his two immemorially old landmark pine trees, one of which, five feet in diameter at the base, is of great value. Packer's wife, Mary Hannah Packer, and their daughter, Lizzie Packer, sadly watch the deal being struck from the window of the Packer farmhouse, less than a mile from the sea. Lizzie seems especially distressed. Meanwhile two fisherman—Joe Banks, who loves Lizzie, and Chaun-cey—are making their cold way to shore, with a poor catch, by taking "a steady sight" on the two pines. The two discuss not only the danger of fishing on into January but also the landmark trees and a petition being signed to present to Packer, whom they know to be hot-tempered. Chauncey signed the petition, and Joe reluctantly says he will too. December 23 turning sunny, Packer goes to his boat by Joe's fish house, is surprised at the young man's unfriendly refusal to fish with him, and rows far out alone. Suddenly he sees Ferris and his French woodsmen bearing down on the landmark trees, decides he will not sell, and rows furiously toward shore. Will he be in time to stop them? On Christmas Eve the neighbors, including happy Joe, surprise Packer with a party at the Packer house and praise him for standing up to Ferris in time to save the trees. Packer offers his best cider to one and all, the petition goes unmentioned, and the two trees look down toward the Packers' glowing windows. The best element in this story, the suspenseful aspects of which are clumsily handled, is the sug-gestion that the two "archaic" trees think, talk to each other, and are "mates." Jewett's earlier "A Winter Drive" prefigures several aspects of "A Neighbor's Landmark."

NELLY. In "A Little Traveler," she is the orphaned child traveling by train to begin life with her aunt in Boston. The narrator happily sees the aunt welcome the child with genuine affection.

NELLY. In *A Marsh Island*, she is evidently Mrs. Susan Winchester's daughter, married and with children.

NEVINS. In "Law Lane," he is a village coffin maker. Thinking she is dying, Jane Barnet tells Mrs. Harriet Powder not to allow Jane's husband to permit Nevins to make her coffin of hemlock.

NEWBURGH, LORD. In *The Tory Lover*, he is Charles Radcliffe's son and hence the nephew of Lord Darwentwater, who is Radcliffe's brother. Newburgh is an old friend of the teacher Sullivan, who sends him a mysterious letter that results in Newburgh's trying to get Roger Wallingford released from the Mill Prison. Mary Hamilton meets Newburgh and persuades him to be more sympathetic toward the American colonists' complaints and rights.

"THE NEW METHUSELAH" (1890). Short story. (Characters: Nancy Bland, Jonas, Masters, Dr. Asa Potterby, Madam Potterby, Madam Powers, Thomas, Mrs. Ann Yard.) Dr. Asa Potterby has considerable inherited wealth, is catered to by a practical housekeeper named Mrs. Ann Yard, theorizes endlessly about experimenting to prolong individual life beyond the traditional span, and finances the airy notions of a physical scientist named Masters. Over her objections, Dr. Potterby even sends Mrs. Yard over to Masters and his housekeeper, Nancy Bland, carrying baskets of food which they accept ungratefully. Dr. Potterby listens sympathetically when Masters proposes a transoceanic electric railway. To test his own theory, Dr. Potterby adopts Thomas, a tiny orphan, and, with Mrs. Yard's assistance, starts to raise him scientifically as to diet, fresh air, and bedroom temperature. The child might grow up and live to be at least 150. But when he is nineteen months of age, he toddles into the garden, eats a hard green apple, and dies. This underdeveloped Hawthornean parable presents three failures: a scientist born too late, a scientist born too early, and a common-sense woman who should not have let a child (Thomas) in her care ingest poisonous fruit. If Thomas had survived, he might have become "the new Methuselah."

"A NEW PARISHIONER" (1883). Short story. (Characters: Ashby, Bangs, Beckett, Donnell, Duncan, Miss Lydia Dunn, Mrs. Dunn, Parson Dunn, Knowles, Otis, Parson Peckham, Phipps, Jonas Phipps, Mrs. Phipps, Silas, Asa Singer, Mary Ann Singer, Ben Stroud, Henry Stroud, Mrs. Ben Stroud, Mrs. Henry Stroud, West, Mrs. West, Whitehouse.) In September, Miss Lydia Dunn, the deceased Walton minister's old granddaughter, is cleaning her house when her handyman, Jonas Phipps, comes by. He says Henry Stroud has returned to the area after forty years. Lydia recalls that Henry's father, Ben Stroud, cheated her grandfather, old Parson Dunn. Parson Peckham, the present minister, who wants a new vestry, toadies up to Stroud, who seems wealthy, says he is old and sick, and boards with Mrs. West, who with her husband now occupies the old Stroud farm. Stroud makes gifts to the church and needy people, calls on Lydia, but cannot allay her distrust. She becomes the target of adverse town gossip. When he visits her again in December, he tells her that he did not know his father was a cheat, praises her tidy little home, and gives her an I.O.U. for

$6,000 redeemable in a year—probably from his estate, he adds lugubriously. She says she does not want his gift but holds the note and is distressed to learn that he has told her neighbors about it. Still, she serves him some tasty ginger-bread in her kitchen one day and briefly imagines marrying, caring for, and traveling with him. After a Wednesday evening church service, two officials take Stroud, wanted for fraud, over to snowy Walpole, to catch the train to New York. He dies in Walpole, leaving a trail of debts, including one to a quarry owner for a new vestry foundation. When Phipps, a spokesman for the chagrined townspeople, commends Lydia for being the only one not taken in by the smooth-speaking Stroud, he asks her who could have paid for Stroud's Walpole funeral, which makes her look "a little conscious." She waxes critical of her neighbors for first cozying up to Stroud and then berating him after his death. Jewett makes symbolic use of a lilac stick—the "twisted mockery of a human being"—which Lydia props up so that it "look[s] into the kitchen wistfully"; she is relieved when, after Stroud's exposure, it blows away. *Bibliography*: Cary, *Jewett*.

"THE NEWS FROM PETERSHAM" (1894). Short story. (Characters: Asa Fales, Johnson, Daniel Johnson, Jesse Johnson, Lydia Johnson, Mrs. William Johnson, William Johnson, Martha, Mrs. Peak, Mrs. Rogers, Mrs. Smith, Mrs. West.) Mrs. Peak is visiting her niece, Martha, in Petersham, her old hometown, which is accessible by train from the town where she now lives alone. She learns from Lydia Johnson that Daniel Johnson, her well-to-do father-in-law, was too ill to attend church on Thanksgiving Day. Home again, Mrs. Peak tells Asa Fales, Mrs. West, and Mrs. Rogers that the generous old man will be missed, and they begin to wonder about the disposition of his estate. At church on Sunday, the story grows, and that evening Mrs. West tells Mrs. Peak that Mrs. Smith said that Johnson is dead. Mrs. Peak dutifully returns next morning to Petersham to attend his funeral but first reports to Martha, who amid chuckles tells her Johnson had a bad cold but is fine again. Mrs. Peak returns home, reveals the truth to her neighbors, but adds that she will always welcome "what news there is a-goin'." Jewett's use of the name Petersham, which is a town in Massachusetts, is clever, since petersham is a cheap, knotted cloth.

"THE NIGHT BEFORE THANKSGIVING" (1895). Short story. (Charac-ters: Ezra Blake, Johnny Harris, John Mander, Mary Ann Robb.) Townspeople have decided to take Mary Ann Robb, a sick old widow, to the poorhouse before winter so no individuals will have to provide for her. She remembers gladly helping many unfortunate persons in the past, including Ezra Blake, a poor, deaf lad, and Johnny Harris, the orphaned, injured son of a soldier and now in the West. She owes money to John Mander, a grasping farmer who has cheated her, wants her acreage, and even scolded her for her foolish generosity in the past. As Mary Ann Robb huddles before her fire the night before Thanksgiving, Johnny returns as he promised he would, bringing food, fuel, and cheer, and assurances that she will be comfortable as long as she lives.

NOLAN, DAN ("DANNY"). In "Between Mass and Vespers," he is the ne'er-do-well who was an altar boy with Father Ryan. Dan went briefly to a seminary, left for the West to work on the railroads, and swindled John Finnerty and his daughter, Katy Finnerty, Dan's girlfriend, out of money he supposedly would invest in a gold mine. When Dan returns home, Father Ryan befriends him.

NOLAN, TOM. In "Between Mass and Vespers," he is mentioned as Dan Nolan's father.

NORA. In *Deephaven*, she is a servant who is to take care of the Lancasters' Boston home while members of the family are away.

NORA. In "A Spring Sunday," she is the servant of Mary Ann Hallett and Alonzo Hallett. Mary Ann is glad she gave Nora the day off to attend the christening of her sister's baby. The Halletts stage a picnic out of town.

NORA. In "Where's Nora?" *See* O'Callahan, Nora.

NORRIS, EBEN. In "A Christmas Guest," he is old Mrs. Norris's son, deceased Rebecca's brother, and the uncle of little Rebecca and Susan Johnson. When his mother becomes ill, Eben goes through a snowstorm to seek help. By the time he returns, his mother is much better.

NORRIS, MRS. In "A Christmas Guest," she is the mother of Eben Norris and the deceased Rebecca, and little Rebecca's grandmother. When Mrs. Norris gets sick, Dr. Gerry leaves a sleeping powder for her to take; her son goes for help; and Rebecca, a resourceful child, is left in charge. By morning Mrs. Norris is better.

NORRIS, POLLY. In "A Second Spring," she is the widowed Susan Louisa Dean's improvident, gossipy mother. Polly upsets Maria Durrant when she says gossip has it that Maria is setting her cap for Israel.

NORTHUMBERLAND, THE HONORABLE MISS. In *Betty Leicester's English Xmas*, she is one of Lady Mary Danesley's guests.

NORTON, GENERAL JACK. In "The Stage Tavern," he is an ex-soldier who was wounded during the Civil War, remained in the army, fought in the West against Indians, retired, and made a fortune in Arizona mining. He returns to the East to visit his old army friend, Major Tom Harris, who, now widowered, lives in the Stage Tavern near Westford, Maine. While there, General Norton meets Tom's charming young daughter, Lizzie Harris, who is running the tavern.

They fall in love and, despite the difference in their ages, will undoubtedly get married.

NORTON, SARA ("SALLY") (1864–1922). Eldest daughter of Charles Eliot Norton (1827–1908), who was a nephew of rich Boston merchants (for whom he traveled around the world), eminent scholar, editor of the *North American Review* (with James Russell Lowell*), cofounder of the *Nation*, and translator. He married Susan Ridley Sedgwick in 1862; they had six children. During one of their trips abroad, his wife died in Germany, in 1872. A year later, Norton began his career as professor of art history at Harvard (to 1898). He knew many important writers of his era, including Thomas Carlyle, Charles Dickens, Ralph Waldo Emerson (whose Liberalism he disliked), William Dean Howells,* Henry James,* Rudyard Kipling* (whose biography he wrote), Henry Wadsworth Longfellow, James Russell Lowell (whose letters he edited and whose biography he wrote), Francis Parkman, and John Ruskin (with whom he corresponded voluminously). One of Jewett's closest friends was Sara Norton, whom she met in the early 1870s and saw again when the Norton family began to live in Cambridge. One of the most revealing letters Jewett ever wrote (3 September [1897]) is addressed to Sally. In it she says, "This is my birthday and I am always nine years old . . ." It continues thus: "There is something transfiguring in the best of friendship. One remembers the story of the transfiguration in the New Testament, and sees over and over in life what the great shining hours can do, and how one goes down from the mountain where they are, into the fret of everyday life again, but strong in remembrance." These comments conflate Jewett's endearing youthfulness, practical Christianity, and worship of friendship. Unfortunately, like many unmarried New England women, Sara Norton, an accomplished cellist and a very bright person, sacrificed her life to her brilliant father; she accompanied him various places, helped him in countless ways, and after his death assembled his letters and provided biographical details thereon. *Bibliography*: Sara Norton and M. A. DeWolfe Howe, *Letters of Charles Eliot Norton with Biographical Comment*, 2 vols. (Boston and New York: Houghton Mifflin, 1913).

NUDD. In "A Landless Farmer," he is the unpleasant son of Aaron Nudd and Serena Nudd.

NUDD, AARON. In "A Landless Farmer," he is Serena Nudd's husband and conspires with her to get her father, Jerry Jenkins, to deed them his farm. Aaron incurs the enmity of Jerry's nephew, Ezra Allen, whom Aaron further annoys by defeating him in the election for selectman. Ultimately Aaron leaves the region, obtains a good job in a shoe factory at Harlow's Mills, and takes Serena with him.

NUDD, SERENA ("SERENY"). In "A Landless Farmer," she is Aaron Nudd's wife, Jerry Jenkins's daughter, and the sister of Parker Jenkins and Mary

Lydia Bryan. She gets her sick father to deed his farm to her and Aaron, to deed a house to Mary Lydia, and to cut out Parker. But Parker returns from Colorado and sets everything right. Serena then moves with Aaron to Harlow's Mills. Serena Nudd is one of Jewett's most despicable characters. She sells her father's beloved ''centennial'' desk, gobbles up doughnuts entrusted to her to give her father, and prospers after her move to the mill town.

O

O'BRIEN, MIKE. In "A Garden Story," he is a gardener who works for Miss Ann Dunning in Littletown. She trusts him with her beans and potatoes but not her flowers. O'Brien worked for a lord back in his native land.

O'BRIEN, PATRICK. In "The Luck of the Bogans," he is the subject of an anecdote Mike Bogan heard on board the ship to America. "Pathrick" said he would not stop at Silver Street but would go on to Gold Street, where more valuable money would be available to pick up.

O'CALLAHAN. In "Where's Nora?", he is the infant son of Nora O'Callahan and Johnny O'Callahan. When Nora visits her mother in Ireland, she takes her baby along.

O'CALLAHAN, JOHNNY. In "Where's Nora?", he is a handsome young man from Kerry, Ireland, now working as a railroad brakeman in America. His mother has been dead for two years. Johnny is the one who suggests that Nora might bake buns to sell to passengers at Birch Plains. He and Nora marry and have a son.

O'CALLAHAN, NORA. In "Where's Nora?", she migrates from Dunkenny, Ireland, to a mill town in "Ameriky," reports to her uncle, Patrick Quin, and her aunt, Mary Ann Duffy, there, and tells them of deaths back home. Nora establishes a bakery and lunch-counter business at a railroad station at Birch Plains. She marries Johnny O'Callahan, and they have a son. After an absence of two years, Nora, with Uncle Patrick, visits Mary, her old mother, and takes her son along.

"AN OCTOBER RIDE" (1881). Essay. (Character: Sheila.) Jewett rides her mare, Sheila, one cloudy October day into a hidden part of a forest, where she finds the sunken cellar of an old farm. The place becomes Jewett's "kingdom." She ponders the relationship of "untamed nature," which takes over such a place, and formerly "cultivated" areas. Life cycles occur, but God overarches all—old and new—and nature prevails. Jewett was told by a friend that an old woman, famous for spinning and weaving, had once lived alone at the farm-house. Jewett tries to imagine the woman's life and even her funeral. As Jewett rides on, rain falls. She puts Sheila into a shed, enters a deserted, falling-down parsonage, inspects its rooms, finds "1802" written on a door, and imagines the old minister's life there: He read, pondered, enjoyed an occasional "mug of flip," and helpfully advised varied visitors. Jewett finds a chair, builds a fire of corn husks and old boards, and sits before it. When the shower ends, she rides home, fancying that ghosts are watching her depart. Hers might be the last fire there. Conclusions? "I am only a part of one great existence which is called nature," and "[o]nly God . . . can plan and order it all." In February 1880 Henry Mills Alden, editor of *Harper's Magazine*, rejected "An October Ride," which Jewett thought contained some of her best writing to its date and which she first published in her *Country By-Ways*. *Bibliography*: Cary, *Jewett*; Renza.

O'DONNELL, JOHNNY. In "Between Mass and Vespers," he is Mary O'Donnell's sick son.

O'DONNELL, MARY. In "Between Mass and Vespers," she is Dennis Call's widowed niece. She cares for her sick son, Johnny O'Donnell. She is delighted when Dennis invites her for dinner after mass.

O'FLAHERTY, MRS. In "Between Mass and Vespers," she is the owner of a donkey that neither goes nor stands, in a story Father Ryan knows.

O'HERN, BIDDY. In "The Luck of the Bogans," she is Peggy Muldoon's drinking crony in Bantry.

"THE ONLY ROSE" (1894). Short story. (Characters: Bickford, Mrs. Bick-ford, Albert Fraley, Mary Lizzie Gifford, Eliza Parsons, John Parsons, Tommy Parsons, Miss Abby Pendexter, Wallis.) One early summer morning, Miss Abby Pendexter drops in on her neighbor, Mrs. Bickford, whose house is at the edge of Fairfield. She is preparing three potted flower plants to decorate the graves of her three late husbands and wonders who should get the only rose. While talking with Miss Pendexter, Mrs. Bickford reveals her husbands' personal traits.

The third one, Bickford, left her well off but was dull. Her second husband, Wallis, was an entertaining talker, had an inventive mind, but was impractical. Albert Fraley came first; a handsome "boy," he sang sweetly and "had a hasty temper" but also "a good word for everybody." Before Albert died of fever, "we was dreadful happy," says Mrs. Bickford. She invites Abby to have some tea; but the girl, revealing that she herself once loved a lad unrequitedly, remembers her hostess dislikes unexpected guests and therefore departs. Next morning, Mrs. Bickford is escorted by John Parsons, her good-looking, friendly nephew, to the cemetery. Still unable to choose which grave should get the only rose and feeling a little giddy in the sunlight, she asks John to carry the three pots to the three graves. Having done so, he returns to his aunt wearing the rose in his buttonhole and planning to give it to his fiancée, Mary Lizzie Gifford. Mrs. Bickford, who likes Lizzie, does not mind in the least and promises to help the two when they marry. She tells John that he resembles her first husband and adds that "[t]he flower he first give me was a rose."

"AN ONLY SON" (1883). Short story. (Characters: Austin, Jacob Austin, Asa Ball, Widow Martha Hawkes, Jerry Jackson, John Kendall, Otis, Deacon John Price, Mrs. John Price, Mrs. John Price, Warren Price, John Stacy, Mrs. Starbird, Captain Abel Stone, Eliza Storrow.) Three Dalton selectmen—John Kendall, Deacon John Price, and Captain Abel Stone—are discussing town business one hot July morning when Jerry Jackson, the tax collector, enters and leaves them $735. Deacon Price, twice widowered, agrees to hold the cash and deposit it the following day in their town account in the South Dalton bank. He puts the money in his wallet, takes it with him when he goes home for noon dinner, and hides it carefully under his pillow. Eliza Storrow, his niece and housekeeper, and his cousin, Mrs. Starbird, who comes by, are about to go to a golden wedding celebration in nearby Somerset and will be away two nights. Price is unhappy with Warren, his only son, who is inept as a farmer and keeps foolishly tinkering with an invention instead of helping around the place. The two women leave. Price mends a fence neglected by Warren, returns to discover his wallet missing, and suspiciously recalls seeing his son hastily scurrying away toward the railroad station. After a restless night, Price goes to Stone, a retired sea captain, who is well off financially and is now farming indifferently, and asks for $800 against the future sale of a parcel of land to some neighbors. Stone readily agrees, and Price officially deposits the money. Next day, Eliza returns home, puts ordinary clothes on again, and hands Price the missing wallet, which she carelessly put in her calico work dress while making his bed. Price laconically agrees he was a bit worried, but she thinks he should have guessed she put it somewhere safe. Warren returns from Lowell, where he conferred with a mechanic who staked him to money for a patent on what proves to be his successful machine, in exchange for a share of expected large profits. Price claps his son on the shoulder, and the two agree to spruce up the farm together. Price explains everything to Stone, who plans to use the returned cash to buy an interest in a new ship being built by the Otis family. A thunderstorm ends a literal drought and symbolizes the end of the Prices's spiritual drought as well.

"THE ORCHARD'S GRANDMOTHER" (1871). Short story. (Characters: Brenton, Colonel Brenton, Mary Brenton, Mary Brenton, Mrs. Brenton, Dorothy, Dunner, Masterson, Matthew, Tom.) One September day in England during the time of Oliver Cromwell's rebellion against King Charles I, Mary Brenton gives her granddaughter, Mary ("Polly") Brenton, a beautiful apple to eat and encourages the child to plant its seeds. Polly does so, and one of them soon starts to grow. One wintry night, Cromwell's men are pursuing Polly's father, Colonel Brenton, who is loyal to the king. He takes his wife and Polly, who hugs a flower pot with her apple sapling in it, to a ship he thinks will take them to Holland. Instead, it is bound for America. After a long voyage, they are placed with fellow royalists in a prison garrison at York, in Massachusetts. Polly plants her little tree there. The displaced royalists endure many hardships, including a raid by hostile Indians. The following September, the Brentons return home to England. Two hundred years later a farmer offers the narrator a special apple and tells her it came from a tree grafted by his father from a certain old tree, shaky but still standing, and said to have been carried in a pot by one of the first settlers from England. The narrator calls the tree the present orchard's grandmother.

OTIS. In "Andrew's Fortune," he has sold "them sticks o' rock-maple" to some shipbuilders, according to neighborhood gossip.

OTIS. In "A New Parishioner," he is a boy Miss Lydia Dunn tells Jonas Phipps she thought would be helping him prepare kindling wood for her.

OTIS. In "An Only Son," he is a Dalton shipbuilder whose three-masted schooner Captain Abel Stone invests in, once Deacon John Price returns the $800 he borrowed from Stone.

OTIS, BILL. In "A Neighbor's Landmark," he is a person in whose shoe shop Joe Banks tells Chauncey he may soon be working. Joe adds that Bill Otis may go west to visit his uncle's folks, since he recently lobstered profitably.

OWEN, DORIS. In *A Marsh Island*, she is the tall, slender, beautiful daughter of Israel Owen and Martha Owen. Doris does little farm work, sews on occasion, but can handle horses and wagons well. She went to school with Dan Lester, who loves her. She seems to prefer Richard Dale, the painter who wanders into the Owens's region and boards one summer with them. When Dan, feeling cut out, decides to go to sea, she goes after him at Westmarket. He decides to stay home, and they are betrothed. Current feminist critics contend that Doris need not have chosen either deficient man but that, given then-current options for women, she felt obliged to accept one or the other. *Bibliography*: Roman.

OWEN, ISRAEL. In *A Marsh Island*, he was the son of Israel Owen and Martha Owen. He was a first lieutenant during the Civil War and was killed in action. Dan Lester was his close friend.

OWEN, ISRAEL ("ISR'EL"). In *A Marsh Island*, he is a prosperous, kind farmer, well over sixty. He is Martha Owen's husband and Doris Owen's father. His son, Israel Owen, was killed during the Civil War. When Richard Dale boards with the Owens, Israel sees a resemblance in him to his dead boy. Miss Temperance Kipp refers to Israel as "the 'Square." He is happy when Doris and Dan Lester decide to get married.

OWEN, MARTHA ("MARTHY"). In *A Marsh Island*, she is the wife, almost sixty, of Israel Owen and is Doris Owen's mother. Discontented with her place in life because of thwarted social ambitions, Martha vacillates between hoping Doris will marry Richard Dale, the sophisticated painter who boards with the Owens, and favoring Dan Lester, a neighbor who suddenly comes into wealth. Jewett is of two minds concerning Martha Owen and treats her ambivalently. *Bibliography*: Donovan.

OWEN, MRS. In "Miss Tempy's Watchers," she is mentioned by Sarah Ann Binson as Temperance ("Tempy") Dent's friend. Mrs. Owen visited Tempy shortly before Tempy's death.

P

PACKER, ASA. In "Law Lane," he is the storeowner Joel Smith says Mrs. Harriet Powder "git[s] some opodildack" from for injured Jane Barnet.

PACKER, JOHN. In "A Neighbor's Landmark," he is a farmer and fisherman, and is Mary Hannah Packer's husband and Lizzie Packer's father. Beneath his irascible exterior, Packer wants to be friendly. Ferris seeks to buy Packer's two landmark pines, cut them down, and sell the lumber. Packer half-agrees to sell them for $80, changes his mind at the last minute, and saves them—to the delight of his neighbors, all of whom regard the trees as lovable, valuable guides to their safety.

PACKER, LIZZIE. In "A Neighbor's Landmark," she is the timorous daughter of John Packer and Mary Hannah Packer. She and Joe Banks are in love.

PACKER, MARY HANNAH. In "A Neighbor's Landmark," she is hot-tempered John Packer's sweet, long-suffering little wife and Lizzie Packer's mother.

PADELFORD, PARSON. In *Deephaven*, he is a preacher whose sermons on foreordination Mrs. Bonny likes because she cannot understand them. She prefers Padelford to Reid.

PAGET, VIOLET (1856–1935). Woman of letters, whose pen name was Vernon Lee. She was born near Boulogne, France, of British parents. A precocious writer, Paget lived in her villa outside Florence, Italy, beginning in 1871. Her forty or so books include long and short fiction, drama, and essays in various intellectual fields, most notably Italian culture. She had a formidable intellect, was friendly with innumerable important people of her era—including Bernard Berenson, Marie Thérèse de Solms Blanc,* Anatole France, Henry James,* Ouida, Walter Pater, John Singer Sergent, and H. G. Wells—and evidently had lesbian tendencies. From the 1880s on, Jewett admired Paget's writings. During her trip to Europe with Annie Adams Fields* in 1898, Jewett met Paget at her Florentine villa. Jewett wrote Paget at least three letters (17 March 1907, July 1907, 3 January 1908) about the latter's work and also their close mutual friend, Madame Blanc; these letters are sentimental, even gushy, possibly to impress Paget. At this time Jewett, though in poor health, tried without success to obtain an American publisher for a book of Paget's essays and also a producer for *Ariadne in Mantua: A Romance in Five Acts* (1903), Paget's closet drama. *Bibliography*: Cary, *Letters*; Peter Gunn, *Vernon Lee, Violet Paget, 1856–1935* (London: Oxford University Press, 1964).

PAGOT. In *Betty Leicester's English Xmas*, she is Betty Leicester's faithful maid. She is happy to accompany Betty and her father, Thomas Leicester, when they go to Lady Mary Danesley's house for Christmas, because Pagot knows other servants there.

PALEY. In "The Dulham Ladies," he was a Westbury store proprietor who sold wigs to the Reverend Edward Dobin. Paley's wife died a year or two earlier. When Harriet Dobin and Lucinda Dobin go to Westbury to buy false bangs, and to offer belated sympathy to Paley, they find his shop boarded up.

PAPANTI, LORENZO. In "The Life of Nancy," he was the real-life founder of a famous Boston dancing school. When Tom Aldis takes Nancy Gale there, she delights in watching some lessons. Later she incorporates this knowledge in dancing classes she conducts back in East Rodney, Maine, which is her hometown. *Bibliography*: Lucius Beebe, *Boston and the Boston Legend* (Boston: Appleton-Century, 1935).

"PAPER ROSES" (1879). Short story. (Characters: Mrs. Ashurst, Ellinor, Hannah, Kate, Phebe.) Ellinor and her friend, Kate, sell items made by country people at a fair to raise money for the hospital. Just when they fear that they cannot sell an "ungainly and forlorn" bunch of paper flowers put on their table, a sweet old lady comes up, says the nosegay reminds her of similar ones she made as a youth, and buys it. Later Kate writes Ellinor that while accompanying a friend to visit some shut-ins, she saw identical paper flowers in the room of a bright old woman bedridden for years because of a fall. She told Kate that she had made some for the hospital fair last spring. Kate delighted her by reporting that one of her nosegays brought a considerable sum.

PARISH, CAPTAIN WALTER. In *A Country Doctor*, he is Nancy Prince's old cousin, friend, and business agent and is Mary Prince's uncle. He becomes friendly with Nan Prince and advises her to marry George Gerry.

PARISH, MARY. In *A Country Doctor*, she is Captain Walter Parish's young, sweet niece. She likes George Gerry, is worried when he prefers Nan Prince, but is likely to marry him later.

PARISH, MRS. WALTER. In *A Country Doctor*, she, though Walter's wife, attends a different church in Dunport than his.

PARKER. In "The First Sunday in June," this is the last name of any little daughter of Widow Parker. The daughters attend the First Parish church of Dalton.

PARKER. In "Miss Becky's Pilgrimage," he is mentioned by Mahaly Parker as her father-in-law. She courteously refers to him as "Father Parker." He was crippled by frostbite.

PARKER, CYRUS. In "Miss Debby's Neighbors," he is old John Ashby's neighbor. While haying at Parker's farm, the two get drunk on some New England rum.

PARKER, JACOB. In "The Life of Nancy," he is the owner of a new barn in East Rodney, Maine. Tom Aldis danced there with Nancy Gale and Addie Porter.

PARKER, JOSHUA. In "Miss Becky's Pilgrimage," he was Mahaly Parker's second husband. A Gloucester man, he sailed out of Salem, then Boston, and was lost at sea fourteen years ago.

PARKER, MAHALY. (Real first name: Mahala.) In "Miss Becky's Pilgrimage," she was Mahaly Robinson, Becky Parson's friend from forty years ago in Brookfield. The two meet again on the train from Boston. Mahaly was married for three years to a man named Sands, who died. She was then married for fourteen years in Salem and then Boston to Joshua Parker, who died. Mahaly tells Becky she had six children in all. Mahaly invites Becky to stay with her and her sister, Phebe Littlefield, in Brookfield; to make up for forgetting Becky at the railway station, she is happy to have Phebe invite Becky to a tea party. While there, Becky meets Beacham, the sisters' minister, whom Becky later marries.

PARKER, WIDOW. In "The First Sunday in June," she does not attend the First Parish church of Dalton but sends her little daughters. Miss Lydia Bent rationalizes that Widow Parker works hard all week.

PARKINS. In "Mrs. Parkins's Christmas Eve," he is Mrs. Lydia Parkins's son who has a good job in a shoe factory. He does not figure in the story.

PARKINS. In "Mrs. Parkins's Christmas Eve," he is Mrs. Lydia Parkins's son who has a good job in a store. He does not figure in the story.

PARKINS. In "Told in the Tavern," he is the mysterious stranger who visits the Byfleet cemetery, finds his own name on a tombstone, and enters the tavern owned by Timothy Hall. Parkins hears gossip there about himself and Abby Sands, identifies himself as her lost fiancé, and goes to her after an absence of thirty years. Parkins left Byfleet during the Civil War, went west, and wrote Abby; but her mother, Mrs. Sands, disliked him and evidently intercepted his last letters and let Abby regard him as gone forever. She erected his tombstone.

PARKINS, DR. In "The Two Browns" he is the person whose patent medicine Checkley failed to sell. Checkley was going to call a portrait of Parkins that of John B. Brown in advertising Brown and Checkley's electric potato planter, until Grandison quietly bought the planter.

PARKINS, MRS. LYDIA. In "Mrs. Parkins's Christmas Eve," she is a wealthy but tight-fisted farm widow living alone in Holton. Her husband was Nathan Parkins. Their two sons are grown and gone. Mrs. Parkins resists being either hospitable or generous to anyone near her. When, however, she is rescued from freezing to death in a snowstorm by Mr. Lane, the town minister, his family's hospitality and spirituality reform Mrs. Parkins, who then becomes unselfish.

PARKINS, NATHAN. In "Mrs. Parkins's Christmas Eve," he was Mrs. Lydia Parkins's husband, now deceased.

PARLET, RUTH BASCOM. In "Fair Day," she is Mercy Bascom's hard-working sister-in-law. The two women have quarreled "half a lifetime." At long last, Mercy wants to forget their differences and make up. So does Ruth, according to Mercy's son, Tobias Bascom, who happens to talk with Ruth at the fair.

PARLEY, MR. In "A Visit Next Door," he is the new minister of the village of Dundalk. Mrs. Granger likes him. Her neighbor, Mrs. Filmore, does not. When Mr. Parley and his wife call at Mrs. Granger's home for tea during Mrs. Filmore's visit there, Mrs. Filmore begins to like both Parleys.

PARLEY, MRS. In "A Visit Next Door," she is the new Dundalk minister's wife. When Mrs. Filmore meets her in Mrs. Granger's home, Mrs. Filmore is happy Mrs. Parley agrees to give music lessons to Nelly Filmore, her talented daughter.

PARLOW. In "A Landlocked Sailor," he was the U.S. Navy nurse, foul-mouthed but gentle, who tended Mike Dillon after his shipboard injury and treatment by Dr. John Hallett, the assistant surgeon.

PARSER, AUNT. In *A Country Doctor*, she is Daniel Thacher's aunt and is a witch-like teller of ghost stories.

"THE PARSHLEY CELEBRATION" (1899). Short story. (Characters: Ames, Binney, Asa Binney, David Binney, Martha Binney, Mrs. Binney, John Foster, Mrs. Foster, John, Mrs. Paterson, Storer, Eben Taft, Mrs. Tasker, the Reverend Mr. Tasker, Mary Ann Winn.) At church in Parshley, a small community near Walton, Martha Binney, Asa Binney's second wife, hears once too often that "they" are planning nothing for Decoration Day, now approaching. Asking who "they" are, she challenges the little group—including Mary Ann Winn, who would have married David Binney, Asa's brother, but for his being killed in the Civil War—to join with her in doing something. Plans are made. On the big day, Asa, his son, and their young hired man drive a wagon trimmed with tree boughs and pulled by four horses to a place near the church. John Foster, a storekeeper, locks up and brings a bunch of flags. More farmers follow with their wagons. At the head is proud old Eben Taft, the only living veteran, in his blue uniform. The marchers stop at the home of Mrs. Paterson, whose son was a war casualty, give provisions to the poor old lady, go on to the parents of a fallen son named John, and praise his courage. The marchers decorate veterans' graves and sing anthems. Back in the Binney home, Mary Ann, invited to stay overnight, praises the fine day "we" had. Martha smiles and agrees "they" may soon celebrate the Fourth of July appropriately. Jewett states the moral: A veterans' parade should "thrill the old with remembrance, and the young with a sudden waking of patriotism." "The Parshley Celebration" recasts some of the action presented in "Decoration Day."

PARSONS. In "The Becket Girls' Tree," he is the father of Jess Parsons and John Parsons. The elder Parsons is a farmer-fisherman living near Eastport.

PARSONS. In "A Landless Farmer," she is Asa Parson's pretty daughter. She seems to like Parker Jenkins.

PARSONS, ASA. In "A Landless Farmer," he is a friend of Ezra Allen and Henry Wallis. The three are disgusted at Serena Nudd's mistreatment of her father, Jerry Jenkins. Asa and his wife are delighted when Parker Jenkins returns and sets everything right. When their daughter smiles encouragingly at well-to-do Parker, they are also pleased.

PARSONS, BECKY ("REBECCY," "R'BECKY"). (Real name: Rebecca Parsons.) In "Miss Becky's Pilgrimage," Becky is the unmarried sister of the

Reverend Mr. Joseph Parsons, an unmarried Congregationalist minister. She was his proud housekeeper for forty years before his death in Devonport, New York. As she is returning for a visit to her old hometown of Brookfield, Maine, she meets an old friend named Mahaly Parker on the train out of Boston. In Brookfield, she stays with her cousin, Sophia Annis, is entertained at a tea party by Mahaly's sister, Phebe Littlefield, and meets a widowered minister named Beacham there. Soon the two get married.

PARSONS, ELIZA (" 'LIZA"). In "The Only Rose," she is Mrs. Bickford's sister and the mother of John Parsons and Tommy Parsons. 'Liza sent Mrs. Bickford the three pots of flowers, including "the only rose."

PARSONS, JESS ("JESSIE"). In "The Becket Girls' Tree," she is the little girl who, with her brother, John Parsons, decorates a Christmas tree for Ann Becket and Lydia Becket, their neighbors. The child also gives the grateful old women presents and receive presents from them.

PARSONS, JOHN. In "The Only Rose," he is Mrs. Bickford's handsome nephew. He escorts her to the cemetery; when she leaves to him the decision as to which pot of flowers to put on the grave of each of her three husbands, he keeps "the only rose" to give to his fiancée, Mary Lizzie Gifford. Noting his resemblance to her first husband, Albert Fraley, Mrs. Bickford approves.

PARSONS, JOHN ("JOHNNY"). In "The Becket Girls' Tree," he is the young boy who, with his sister, Jess Parsons, surprises Ann Becket and Lydia Becket with a Christmas tree and accompanying presents. In turn, he receives presents from the grateful old women.

PARSONS, MRS. In "The Becket Girls' Tree," she is the mother of Jess Parsons and John Parsons. She and her husband, Mr. Parsons, are briefly called away from their farmhome near Eastport when she learns that Sarah Ann, the wife of her brother, Henry, is seriously ill in Gloucester.

PARSONS, MRS. ASA. In "A Landless Farmer," she agrees it is nice that their daughter seems to like Parker Jenkins.

PARSONS, THE REVEREND MR. JOSEPH. In "Miss Becky's Pilgrimage," he was Becky Parsons's unmarried brother. Parson Parsons was a fine Congregationalist minister who preached for forty years, twenty-seven or twenty-eight of them in Devonport, New York, before his death.

PARSONS, THEOPHILUS (1797–1882). Professor and Swedenborgian. He was the son of Elizabeth Greenleaf and Theophilus Parsons, who was chief justice of the Massachusetts Supreme Court. The younger Parsons was born in

Newburyport, Massachusetts, graduated from Harvard College, read for the law, and practiced law and was an editor, first in Taunton and then in Boston. In 1823 he became an avid Swedenborgian and also married Catherine Amory Chandler; they had three sons and four daughters. In 1848 Parsons became a knowledgeable, popular Harvard Law School professor. Parsons wrote several outstanding legal works. At the outbreak of the Civil War, he wrote a book titled *The Constitution* (1861), in which he reasoned that the Constitution, though precious, was less vital to the United States than the preservation of "our nationality." During the Civil War, one of his sons served in the Union Army and one daughter was a nurse. Parsons also wrote *Deus Homo* (1867), *The Infinite and the Finite* (1872), and *Outlines of the Religion and Philosophy of Swedenborg* (1875). He was one of Jewett's most valued friends. His Christian faith strengthened her, and she wrote him many spiritually intimate letters. *Bibliography*: Josephine Donovan, "Jewett and Swedenborg," *American Literature* 65 (December 1993): 731–50; Matthiessen.

PARSONS, TOMMY. In "The Only Rose," he is Mrs. Bickford's pleasant nephew. He delivers the three pots of flowers to her.

PARTOUT, JULIE. In "Mère Pochette," she is one of Mère Pochette's gossipy neighbors.

"THE PASSING OF SISTER BARSETT" (1892). Short story. (Characters: Dr. Bangs, Sister Barsett, Betsy, Crane, Mercy Crane, Nancy Deckett, Mrs. Doubleday, Sarah Ellen Dow, Elder French, Aunt Nancy, Mrs. Peak, Tremlett.) Sitting in her doorway one late summer afternoon, Mercy Crane, a widowed and reclusive woman, welcomes Sarah Ellen Dow, who reports the death of Sister Barsett, whom she tended in her many illnesses. The two gossip about Sister Barsett's untidiness, her poor canning ability, and especially her quarrelsome sisters, Nancy Deckett and Mrs. Peak. That pair descended on the dying woman, sat at her bedside while Sarah waited in the kitchen, seemed mostly concerned about what was going to be willed to them, and were incapable of making funeral arrangements. Promising to "watch to-night" with the body, Sarah left in a huff and is happy to have tea and shortcake with Mercy. When she hints that she hopes to be cared for by others the nice way she did for Sister Barsett, Mercy is gently responsive. A neighbor, coming up with a wagon, shouts that Sister Barsett is alive and needs help from Sarah. She solemnly departs in the wagon, and Mercy enjoys a good laugh.

PATERSON, MRS. In "The Parshley Celebration," she is an old woman whose son was a Civil War casualty. He left a wife and children, now all scattered. The marchers during the celebration stop and give Mrs. Paterson some provisions.

PATEY, BEN. In *Deephaven*, he was a thieving man whose praying bothered Mrs. Bonny.

PATRICK. In "A Sorrowful Guest," he is a servant in the home of John Ainslie and his sister, Helen Ainslie, in Boston.

PATTON, JACK ("JIM"). In *Deephaven*, he was the husband of Judith Toggerson Patton, better known as Widow Jim. He was shiftless, alcoholic, and abusive to her.

PATTON, JUDITH TOGGERSON. *See* Jim, Widow.

PATTON, MRS. In "The Green Bowl," she is the mysterious cleaning lady of the church in the woods. She sees Katie Montague and Frances Kent spend the night in the church, takes them next morning to her nearby house for a sumptuous breakfast, and tells Katie the secret of her two green bowls. Mrs. Patton thus makes Katie her "companion" in their evident ability to foresee the future.

PAUL. In *The Tory Lover*, he is a neighbor of a demented female patient treated by Dr. Ezra Green near Portsmouth. She tried to auction Paul.

PEACHAM, LYDIA ANN ("LYDDY ANN"). In "Sister Peacham's Turn," she is Pamela Fellows's hypochondriacal younger sister, described as "thin and precise." Both are old widows. When Pamela challenges Lydia Ann to prepare Thanksgiving Dinner this year for a change, Lydia rises to the occasion, includes the Reverend Mr. Downer and his wife as well as Pamela, afterwards boasts a bit, and feels silently better for making tardy amends.

PEACH-TREE JOE. In "Peach-tree Joe," he is the girlish teen-age soldier who, during the Civil War, fears combat, suddenly is inspired to charge, and is killed by a stray bullet in the summer of 1861 in Virginia. His nickname derives from his loving attention to a peach tree near camp.

"PEACH-TREE JOE" (1893). Short story. (Characters: John, Peach-tree Joe, Sheila.) The narrator listens as John, her family's "master-of-horse," while tending Sheila, her old chestnut, reminisces about soldiering in the Civil War. A peach tree is in bloom beside the stable, and this reminds John of a certain teen-age soldier. Men in the company called him Peach-tree Joe because he lovingly tended a peach tree in front of their "A" tent that first summer down in Virginia. Joe was "a girl-faced fellow" who mended their clothes, sang sweetly, but was in constant terror at the thought of combat. John was chatting with him one day when the bugle sounded. Joe jumped up, shouted that he was no longer afraid, ran on ahead, and was killed by a stray bullet. Jewett punctuates this short piece with several apt comments about the senselessness of war. *Bibliography*: Roman.

PEAK, MRS. In "The News from Petersham," she is Martha's aunt. Mrs. Peak visits her in Petersham, the town in which Mrs. Peak grew up and near which she now lives alone. She hears that Daniel Johnson, her friend from childhood, has a cold. Returning home, Mrs. Peak repeats and exaggerates the story, which leads to the rumor that the old man has died. She is chagrined when she returns to Petersham to attend his funeral, only to learn from Martha that he is well again. Her friends, Mrs. Rogers, Mrs. Smith, and Mrs. West, participate in rumor mongering.

PEAK, MRS. In "The Passing of Sister Barsett," she is one of Sister Barsett's selfish, inept sisters. Nancy Deckett is the other.

PEAK, MRS. In "A Winter Courtship," she is a North Kilby church member who Jefferson Briley says mends clothes for him and would like to marry him. He calls her Sister Peak.

PEASE, MRS. In "The Green Bonnet," rumor has it that she and her sister, Mrs. Folsom, both of Walsingham, will be wearing new spring bonnets on Easter Sunday.

PEASE, SQUIRE. In "The Foreigner," he was a Dunnet Landing squire who, according to Lorenzo Bowden, handled Mrs. John Tolland's will. Almira Todd, who narrates the story, calls him "Square Pease."

PECK, COLONEL TOM. In "Miss Peck's Promotion," he was Eliza Peck's brother, the husband of Harriet White Peck (*see* Pigley, Harriet White Peck), and the father of their three children, including young Tom Peck. Colonel Peck, who was killed in the war, said unselfish Eliza deserved a promotion more than he ever did.

PECK, ELIZA ("ELIZY," "LIZY"). In "Miss Peck's Promotion," she, forty, wanted to be a schoolteacher, lives on the Vermont family farm she has inherited, and adores her young nephew Tom ("Tommy") Peck. She reveres the memory of her brother, Colonel Tom Peck, killed in the war, but dislikes his widow, Harriet, now Mrs. Noah Pigley (*see* Pigley, Harriet White Peck). Eliza assiduously cares for the Rev. Mr. Wilbur Elbury's parsonage and his infant daughter for a year following his wife's death. Eliza's "quailing side" wants to marry Elbury, but her stronger side is relieved when he marries someone else and she can return to her farm and rear Tommy. So she is promoted not into marriage but into sturdy New England spinsterhood. *Bibliography*: Cary, *Jewett*;

Barbara A. Johns, " 'Mateless and Appealing': Growing into Spinsterhood in Sarah Orne Jewett,'' in Nagel, pp. 147–65.

PECK, HARRIET WHITE. In "Miss Peck's Promotion." *See* Pigley, Harriet White Peck.

PECK, MISS. In "The Courting of Sister Wisby,'' according to Mrs. Goodsoe, she was a daughter of Widow Peck and was "forsook'' by " 'a rovin' creatur'.'' Her sister married Jim Heron.

PECK, TOM ("TOMMY"). In "Miss Peck's Promotion,'' he is the red-headed son of the deceased Colonel Tom Peck. Tommy is the nephew of Eliza Peck, who adores him, finally gets permission to rear him on her farm, and plans to will the place to him.

PECK, WIDOW. In "The Courting of Sister Wisby,'' she is mentioned by Mrs. Goodsoe as over-doctored by women ignorant of the best herbal treatment. One of her daughters was forsaken by a man; another married Jim Heron.

PECKER, MISS. In "Miss Debby's Neighbors." *See* Ashby, Mrs. John.

PECKER, MISS. In "A Spring Sunday,'' she is the owner of a house Alonzo Hallett and Mary Ann Hallett pass on their way beyond the church.

PECKHAM. In "A New Parishioner,'' he is the Walton parson who is deceived by Henry Stroud in the hope of having Stroud finance improvements in the church.

PEET. In "The Spur of the Moment,'' he was Miss Peet's father, now deceased. He and Walton, who was younger, were business partners. Only Walton recovered from the crash of 1857. After Peet's death, Walton habitually sent Miss Peet a Christmas check.

PEET, ISAIAH ("IS'IAH"). In "Going to Shrewsbury,'' he is Josh Peet's son and Mrs. Peet's money-lending nephew. He cheated her out of her property when she was widowed. People think he looks like a fox, as did his mother.

PEET, JIM. In "Jim's Little Woman,'' he is Jim's shipmate on the *Dawn of Day*. Jim reported seeing Martha's husband Jim's funeral in Kingston, Jamaica. The innocent report was false.

PEET, JOSH. In "Going to Shrewsbury,'' he is Isaiah Peet's father. Mrs. Peet says her husband's sister married Josh.

PEET, MISS. In "The Spur of the Moment," she is the pessimistic, selfish daughter of Peet, the former business partner, now deceased, of Walton. When Walton dies, Miss Peet mourns the likely loss of Christmas checks he regularly sent her. Circumstances enable her to attend Walton's funeral. Her grief impresses his daughter, Mrs. Ashton, who resolves to continue financial aid to her. The entire event makes Miss Peet reassess her way of looking at life. Jewett, who almost never uses symbolically significant names, does place Miss Peet, surely a withered soul, on Blight Street.

PEET, MRS. In "Going to Shrewsbury," she is a proud, work-worn farm widow, seventy-six. Her nephew, Isaiah Peet, having cheated her out of her property, Mrs. Peet goes to Shrewsbury to live with and be useful to Isabella, her niece. She enjoys some cultural activities in Shrewsbury but dies the following spring.

PEGGY. In "Mr. Bruce," she is the black cook of Tennant and his family. When confided in concerning Kitty Tennant's plan to impersonate a serving-maid, Peggy has a great laugh and cooperates fully.

PEGGY. In *The Tory Lover*, she is Colonel Jonathan Hamilton's pink-faced cook. She sings well. Caesar and Susan are her friends. Peggy may accompany Mary Hamilton to Bristol.

"PEG'S LITTLE CHAIR" (1891). Short story. (Characters: Baptist, Benning, Hannah Benning, Jonas Benning, Margaret Benning, Margaret Benning, General Dunn, Judge Forrester, Henderson, Mrs. Henderson, General Lafayette, Pomeroy, Sally.) Margaret ("Peg") Benning, about seventy but bright-eyed and peppy, shows the narrator her sturdy little chair, which she has owned from childhood and still treasures. It once belonged to a great-aunt and then to Peg's mother. Long ago, Peg's father sailed with his father-in-law but was lost at sea before Peg ever saw him. The grandfather helped his daughter, also named Margaret Benning, widowed and responsible for Peg and her four older siblings. The busy woman set up a public house on the high road from Boston. Her accommodations became famous, not least her well-provisioned table in the thirty-six-foot dining room. Little Peg, her sister, Hannah Benning, their grandmother, Hannah Henderson, and Sally, their black cook, all helped. One day General Dunn and his friend, Pomeroy, announced that General Lafayette was planning to travel the road and would stop at Mrs. Benning's public house. He was to be greeted with well-wishers along the route, a fife-and-drum parade, evergreen boughs, paper flowers, and a banner saying "Welcome, Lafayette, the Nation's Guest." Peg and other children were rehearsed to sing "The Fathers in Glory shall sleep" when the great French hero would appear. Peg, then tiny and frail, constantly dragged her little chair with her; occasionally her busy mother boxed her ears for doing so and for getting in the way. But when Lafayette arrived lame and having difficulty descending from his carriage, Peg placed her little chair for him as a footstool. Lafayette was grateful and gracious, patted Peg on the head, gave her a silver ninepence, and kissed her. Peg, grown old but remembering, takes the precious coin from a little box on her table and shows the narrator.

Jewett derived part of this story from Elizabeth Cushing, an old Berwick resident who remembered that when she was a child Lafayette stopped to visit her mother. The fantasy about the little chair recalls Jewett's memory of a tiny chair belonging to her grandmother or great-grandmother. This story probably also owes something to *Grandfather's Chair: A History for Youth* by Nathaniel Hawthorne. *Bibliography*: Blanchard.

PENDELL. In "A Financial Failure," he is the treasurer of the County Savings Bank in Dartford. His clerks are Downs, Jonas Dyer, and Hathaway. He hired Dyer because Dyer's uncle, also named Jonas Dyer, asked him to do so.

PENDEXTER, ABBY. In "Aunt Cynthy Dallett," she was Aunt Cynthy Dallett's sister and the mother of Cynthy's niece, also named Abby Pendexter. Aunt Cynthy fondly remembers their happy, if restricted, childhood.

PENDEXTER, ABBY. In "Aunt Cynthy Dallett," she is Aunt Cynthy Dallett's poor, aging niece. When Abby Pendexter asks Aunt Cynthy to move down the mountain to her, Cynthy counters by getting Abby to come live with her. Abby will inherit Cynthy's possessions in time.

PENDEXTER, MISS ABBY. In "The Only Rose," she is Mrs. Bickford's neighbor. Abby calls on her, listens sympathetically as the old woman describes her three husbands, and reveals her own unrequited love.

PEN NAMES. Between January 1868 and May 1871, Jewett signed seven of her first eight published works A. C. Eliot, Alice Eliot, Sarah O. Sweet, or S. O. J. Her sixth publication she signed Sarah Jewett. (Sweet may have been a misreading of Jewett's oddly handwritten "Jewett.") In a letter to her (21 May 1870), Horace E. Scudder* advised her to quit using pseudonyms.

PENNELL, JABEZ ("JABE"). In "The King of Folly Island," he is the postmaster of John's Island and a tight-fisted merchant there as well. He delivers mail with inconsiderate slowness to islanders, including George Quint of Folly Island. When George was not named postmaster, he determined to live on his island for the remainder of his life. The two men have been antagonistic ever since.

PENNELL, MISS AUGUSTA. In *The Country of the Pointed Firs*, she is Mrs. Blackett's neighbor and lives on nearby Burnt Island.

PENNELL, MONROE. In *The Country of the Pointed Firs*, he owns a lobster smack, now at the wharf. He catches a boy asleep on duty and throws him overboard.

PENNELL, MRS. JABEZ. In "The King of Folly Island," she is the lonely, unhappy wife of the postmaster of John's Island.

PEPPER. In *Betty Leicester*, he is Dr. Prince's horse.

PEPPERRELL. In *The Tory Lover*, this is the name of some people who came from London to visit Madam Wallingford in Bristol.

PERRIN, NELLY. In "An Every-Day Girl," she is the young telegraph operator Mary Fleming wakes up to learn details about the fire in Dolton, Mary's hometown.

PERRY, ABIGAIL GILMAN (1789–1860). Jewett's maternal grandmother. The daughter of Nathaniel Gilman, the wife of William Perry,* and the mother of Caroline Frances Perry Jewett* (Jewett's mother), she was a fine-mannered, intelligent woman Jewett remembered fondly. (*See also* Gilman, Nicholas.) *Bibliography*: Blanchard.

PERRY, BLISS (1860–1934). Man of letters and educator. Perry was born in Williamstown, Massachusetts. He was well educated at Williams (A.B., 1881, and M.A., 1883), and by study abroad. He married Annie L. Bliss in 1888; they had three children. Perry taught English at Williams (1886–1893), Princeton (1893–1900), and Harvard (1907–1930). He succeeded Horace Scudder* as editor of the *Atlantic Monthly* (1899–1909). Perry edited works on American and English literature, wrote novels, poetry, biographies of Walt Whitman (1906) and John Greenleaf Whittier* (1907), informal essays, and an autobiography, *And Gladly Teach* (1935). Perry was too conservative and bound by tradition to appeal to modern taste. Through her extended connection with the *Atlantic Monthly*, Jewett knew Perry, undoubtedly socialized with him and his wife at the home of Annie Adams Fields* in Boston, and defined him in an undated letter to a friend as "a delightful man with true enthusiasm for the best things." Perry greatly admired Jewett's fiction. *Bibliography*: M. A. DeWolfe Howe, "Bliss Perry," in Edward W. Forbes and John H. Finley, Jr., eds., *The Saturday Club: A Century Completed, 1920–1956* (Boston: Houghton Mifflin, 1958), pp. 131–36.

PERRY, WILLIAM (1788–1887). Jewett's maternal grandfather. A farm lad in Rehoboth, Massachusetts, he earned an M.D. from Harvard in 1814 and began to practice medicine in Exeter, New Hampshire. He married Abigail Gilman, daughter of Nathaniel Gilman, in 1818. Dr. Perry became a highly respected physician and surgeon, testified as an expert witness in court cases, and helped alleviate the suffering of the mentally ill. He declined a professorship at Bowdoin Medical School. He developed a potato starch, built a mill to produce it, and sold it as sizing to regional textile mills. But he neglected to patent his process, and a person in New York state did so and made a fortune. Dr. Perry was a Congregational deacon for sixty years. Late in life he gave over much of his medical practice to his son, Dr. William Gilman Perry (1823–1910), but continued to be active, performing three operations in his eighties and a final one at ninety-one. Theodore Herman Jewett,* Jewett's father, practiced medicine in Exeter with Dr. Perry, met Caroline Frances Perry, one of his five children, and married her in 1842. She became Caroline Frances Perry Jewett,* Jewett's mother. Dr. Perry's other children were Abigail Gilman Perry (1824–1868), Nathaniel Gilman Perry (1826–1855), and John Taylor Perry (1832–1909). Jewett revered her old grandfather, William Perry, who gave her books and asked her to report on them, lectured her on the active moral life, imparted his love of horses to her, and took her occasionally to New York and Boston and once to Cincinnati (winter 1868–1869). Crusty old churchgoers in Jewett's fiction sometimes bear a resemblance to old Dr. Perry. Jewett also wrote an unpublished essay titled "Recollections of Dr. William Perry of Exeter." Jewett also knew her Uncle William Gilman Perry, his first wife, Augusta Maria Willard Rice Perry (1819–1857), his second wife, Lucretia Fisk Perry (1826–1896), and their daughter Frances Fiske Perry (1861–1953), and enjoyed hearing Uncle William and Aunt Lucretia reminisce. In 1868–1869 Jewett visited John Perry, also her uncle, and his wife, Sarah Chandler Perry (1833–1897), in Cincinnati, where he was editor of the *Cincinnati Gazette*. *Bibliography*: Blanchard; Cary, *Letters*; Frost; Silverthorne.

PETER. In "The Mistress of Sydenham Plantation," he was a slave of Mistress Sydenham. Twenty years after his emancipation, he is her only remaining servant, loyally takes her to her ruined plantation on St. Helena's Island and next day, Easter Sunday, escorts her to church.

PETER. In *The Tory Lover*, he is George Fairfax's Virginia-born butler.

PETERBECK, CAPTAIN. In *A Country Doctor*, he was an old friend of Nancy Prince's father.

PETERS. In "Sister Peacham's Turn," he is the Reverend Mr. Downer's friend. Mrs. Peters, his wife, is friendly with both Pamela Fellows and Lydia Ann Peacham.

PETERS, JONAS. In "Miss Manning's Minister," he is described as Miss Narcissa Manning's "factotum." He helps care for the Reverend Edward Taylor following his stroke. The townspeople think Peters, experienced in nursing, may be a deserter from an English regiment once stationed in Canada.

PETERS, MRS. In "The Becket Girls' Tree," she is a lugubrious woman, "both deaf and cross," whose arrival at their home for Thanksgiving dinner Jess Parsons and John Parsons are unhappy about but tolerate.

PETERS, MRS. In "Sister Peacham's Turn," she is friendly with Pamela Fellows and Lydia Ann Peacham. Pamela tells Mrs. Peters she will maneuver Lydia into preparing Thanksgiving dinner this year. Lydia rises to the occasion with great spirit.

PETERS, MRS. WALTON. In "A Bit of Shore Life," she was a person at whose "vandoo" Mrs. Wallis bought a pitcher. At Mrs. Wallis's auction, it was found to be broken.

PHEBE. In "Paper Roses," she is mentioned as the eldest sister of the old woman who buys the paper roses from Ellinor and Kate. The old woman says Phebe used to make similar paper flowers.

PHIL. In "Hallowell's Pretty Sister," he is a Harvard junior. His college friends include Dick Hallowell and Jack Spenser. Dick invites Phil and Jack home for a holiday weekend, during which Dick has his brother, Tom Hallowell, impersonate his pretty sister, Alice Hallowell. Fooled, as Jack is, Phil feels neglected when Jack domineers "Alice," until the real Alice appears.

PHILIPPE. In "Mère Pochette," he is Mère Pochette's gardener.

PHILLIPS, ANDREW ("ANDRER"). In "Andrew's Fortune," he is the likable, bookish, indolent nephew of Stephen Dennett's deceased wife. When Stephen's will, which would have bequeathed Andrew everything, is missing, Andrew loses out, is dumped by his girlfriend, Susan Mathes, but is befriended by Dunning, Stephen's successful Boston friend. Unsuited for farming, Andrew prospers in a Boston tea-importing firm, marries happily, later finds the missing will, but burns it and realizes he has made his own fortune.

PHILLIPS, BILL. In "The Honey Tree," he is Johnny Hopper's school chum. Bill Phillips is described as "inelegant" for sticking his tongue out at Dunn, their disliked school teacher.

PHILLIPS, MRS. In "Good Luck," she is Mrs. Leslie's friend and writes her from Baltimore of the mortal illness of Mrs. Anderson, who was an old friend of Mrs. Leslie's mother.

PHILLIPS, MRS. ANDREW. In "Andrew's Fortune," she is the orphaned niece of a business associate of Andrew, who marries her and is happy.

PHILPOT. In *The Tory Lover*, he is an old boatman who happens to be near the canoe Mary Hamilton uses. Philpot and his friends talk about politics and society.

PHIPPS. In "A New Parishioner," she is Jonas Phipps's orphaned niece, lives with him and his mother, and is called "the Phipps child." Henry Stroud buys some clothes for her.

PHIPPS, JONAS. In "A New Parishioner," he is a Walton handyman, sixty-one, often works for Miss Lydia Dunn, and is a conduit of village gossip. Shrewd and quick, he professes to be more lame than he is.

PHIPPS, MRS. In "A New Parishioner," she is the poor mother of Jonas Phipps, who provides for her as best he can.

PHOEBE. In *A Country Doctor*, she is one of Nancy Prince's servants.

PHOEBE. In *The Tory Lover*, she is Nancy Haggens's slave handmaiden. She may be Phebe Hodgdon. *See also* Hodgdon, Phebe.

PICKETT, MISS CYNTHIA ("CYNTHY"). In "The Guests of Mrs. Timms," she is a timid friend of supercilious Mrs. Persis Flagg, who demeans her. The two take the stage from Woodville to Baxter to visit well-to-do Mrs. Timms, with whom they talked at a county conference and who, they feel, was sincere when she invited them to visit. But they are rebuffed. Miss Pickett gets revenge on Mrs. Flagg when she persuades Mrs. Flagg to visit Miss Nancy Fell, whom Miss Pickett knew when they both lived in Baxter and who treats both unexpected guests most hospitably.

PICKNELL. In *Betty Leicester*, he is the man near whose farm outside Tideshead a French and Indian War battle was fought.

PICKNELL, JULIA. In *Betty Leicester*, she and her sister, Mary Picknell, are friends of Betty Leicester.

PICKNELL, MARY. In *Betty Leicester*, she and her sister, Julia Picknell, are friends of Betty Leicester. Mary has a talent for drawing.

PICKNELL, MRS. In *Betty Leicester*, she is a farm wife and the mother of Julia Picknell and Mary Picknell. She is the area's best housekeeper.

PICTOU, CHARLES. In "Mère Pochette," he is Manon's handsome young lover. Raised as an orphan by an aunt, he leaves Bonaventure for the States to earn money for marriage. When he writes to Manon, her grandmother, Mère Pochette, intercepts and burns the letters. Later, however, he returns home, and the couple marry, with Mère Pochette's blessings, and soon go to the States.

PIERCE, JIM. In "Andrew's Fortune," he is Stephen Dennett's neighbor and is described by gossipy women as rather useless.

PIERRE, FATHER. In "Mère Pochette," he is good Father David's mean and conceited replacement in Bonaventure. He regards himself as too good for the place. He and Mère Pochette intercept, laugh at, and destroy Charles Pictou's letters to Manon, her granddaughter. Father Pierre's replacement is kind Father Henri, in whose presence Mère Pochette repents.

PIGLEY, HARRIET WHITE PECK. In "Miss Peck's Promotion," she is the sister-in-law of Eliza Peck. Harriet is the wife and then the widow of Colonel Tom Peck, the mother of his three children, including young Tom Peck, and then the wife of Noah Pigley. Eliza regards "Harri't" as uppity.

PIGLEY, NOAH. In "Miss Peck's Promotion," he is the second husband of Harriet White Peck (*see* Pigley, Harriet White Peck) and is a businessman.

PIKE, PARSON. In *The Tory Lover*, he is a parson who helps rescue Madam Wallingford from the "patriot" mob.

"A PINCH OF SALT" (1897). Short story. (Characters: Brayton, John Brayton, Mrs. Brayton, Nelly Catesby, Aunt Deborah, Lawyer Dunn, Fisher, Dorcas Snow, Strafford.) On Halloween day, Hannah Dalton, who has been teaching school for years in the Winfield district, returns toward the home of her Aunt Deborah, where Hannah lives. On the way, some children ask her about Halloween legends. She tells them one: If you have only a pinch of salt for supper and drink at a spring where three men's properties join, you will meet the one you love best. That evening her aunt has gone visiting and by mistake Hannah while preparing tea tastes salt instead of sugar from a bowl and goes for a drink to the spring between her aunt's land and that of deaf old Brayton. He is the father of John Brayton, of whom she has been fond ever since he left ten years ago. There is John, just returned from successful mine work in the West to care for his aging parents. He explains that he bought a pasture west of the spring that morning. When she tells John about the salt and the spring water, he seems indifferent; but he returns to her later that evening. They soon get married.

PINKHAM, ABEL. In "Fame's Little Day," he is a successful farmer, sixty, from Wetherford, Vermont. He visits New York City, which he has seen before, with his wife, Mary Ann Pinkham, who has not. Pinkham compliments Mary Ann most kindly. He is paid by Joe Fitch for a consignment of maple sugar.

The Pinkhams feel out of place in the big city and have no fun at all until they see exaggerated notices of their arrival in newspapers, written to gull them. But they enjoy their brief fame and are happy when they leave town.

PINKHAM, DEACON ABEL. In "An Autumn Holiday," he was a friend of the Gunn family. Pinkham had tea with Captain Daniel Gunn and Cousin Statiry (Miss Polly Marsh's cousin). Then Gunn, who imagined at times he was his own sister, wondered which woman Deacon Pinkham had come specifically to see. Perhaps Gunn? Deacon Pinkham may have been related to Ichabod Pinkham.

PINKHAM, ICHABOD. In "An Autumn Holiday," he became the father-in-law of the boy assigned to keep Captain Daniel Gunn away from church while his nephew, Jacob Gunn, and Miss Polly Marsh went there. He may have been related to Deacon Abel Pinkham.

PINKHAM, MARY ANN. In "Fame's Little Day," she is Abel Pinkham's wife and accompanies him to New York City, which she has never seen before. They plan to have a respite from dour Vermont farm life. When they read in the New York papers exaggerated accounts of their arrival, they brighten up and have a pleasant time. Their daughter, Sarah, is a widow; she and her young son, Abel, live with them.

PINKHAM, MRS. OLIVER. In *Deephaven*, she is a person whose extrasensory experience Captain Jacob Lant, after being interrupted, never got around to summarizing.

PINKHAM, SISTER HANNAH JANE. In "The Quest of Mr. Teaby," she lives near East Wilby, likes thrice-widowered Elder Fry but not his plan to quit preaching and go into the butter business, and may now lean toward Teaby, the itinerant peddler, although she is older than he is.

PIQUÉ, LA MOT. In *The Tory Lover*, he is a French rear admiral, who commands a ship that Captain John Paul Jones sights at Quiberon.

PLAISTED. In *The Tory Lover*, this is the name of a Berwick family active in the French and Indian War. Plaisted was the maiden name of Hetty Goodwin.

PLAY DAYS: A BOOK OF STORIES FOR CHILDREN (1878). In "The Water Dolly," Priscilla ("Prissy") Starbird helps her father gather kelp one August morning near Portsmouth and finds a doll with a china face and a silk dress washed ashore. Locating its owner at the hotel nearby, Prissy is allowed to keep it. "Prissy's Visit": Prissy visits her cousin, Rosy, inland, near Conway. They sell berries and birch-bark baskets to passers-by, and Prissy makes $2.04

in two weeks. "My Friend the Housekeeper": While Nelly Ashford is visiting Aunt Bessie in Boston, her father builds an elaborate little house for her in their garden. Nelly returns with Aunt Bessie, is delighted with the house, and gives parties for her friends in it. "Marigold House": Aunt Bessie fools Nelly and her guests in Nelly's "Marigold House" by calling on them disguised as an Irish beggar. She tells the girls about a bad Irish son killed by a giant and a good Irish son who killed the giant and returned to his mother with the giant's treasure. (Bessie's grotesque "Irish" speech includes "I don't slape at me wor-ruk.") "Nancy's Doll": Lame Nancy lives with her old Aunt Nancy in a Boston tenement and is too poor to buy a desired doll. Angelic Miss Helen visits Nancy's neighbor across the street, buys Nancy the doll, and takes her to a hospital where her foot is mended. "The Best China Saucer": Against her mother's orders, Nelly Willis plays with naughty Jane Simmons by having a doll tea party. Jane disgusts her by showing her a necklace she made out of flies strung together. When Jane's tag-along brother breaks a creamer and the fine saucer on which Nelly brought out some pudding, Nelly orders the two away and hides the broken pieces. She dreams about the saucer's funeral and next morning reveals all to her forgiving mother. "The Desert Islanders": Three siblings, Agatha, Mary, and Roger, are inspired by *The Swiss Family Robinson* by Johann Rudolf Wyss to build a shelter of birch trees and hemlock branches on Spring Island, near their home. They disobey orders, stay overnight, are scared during a storm, and are rescued by Alex, their older brother. "Half-Done Polly": Polly Oliver, eight, has such a habit of only half completing various tasks, whether dressing her favorite doll, tidying her room, or weeding her garden patch, that one day her mother tells her she is apt to become an unpopular adult. Polly dreams everything is only half-done, whether it is doing one's school lessons or drowning kittens. She wakes up and thoroughly reforms. "Woodchucks": Their father pays Joe Abbott and Nelly Abbott, his sister, 10¢ for each garden-marauding woodchuck they catch. They proudly kill one, trap and kill another, and put one in a cage. When a neighbor's dog kills it, they sadly conclude that woodchucks, dogs, boys, and girls cannot help being just what they are. "The Kitten's Ghost": Kitty and Jack, the narrator's younger siblings, welcome a stray kitten, soon named Kiesie by Elsie, their Swedish servant. But she steals foods and breaks some china; so the children's mother orders her drowned. One night Jack is scared by Kiesie's ghost in his dark bedroom—until Elsie explains that Kiesie escaped. The kitten soon dies of over-eating. (Jewett's rendition of the Swedish servant's speech lacks verisimilitude, as in "I think it are time she [Kiesie] die.") "The Pepper-Owl": One night soon after Patty, the youngest of three sisters, has gone to bed, she is visited by the silver pepper shaker, in the form of an owl, and the stuffed owl Patty has just seen at the museum. They reduce Patty's size by pulling her down; then all three can enter Patty's doll house for a nocturnal meeting. "The Shipwrecked Buttons": Jack and Kitty, vacationing friends, construct a sailboat of a shingle and handkerchief, make a crew of four buttons, launch it in a tide pool, and forget it. Meanwhile, the boat's pearl-button captain, his French-button wife, and a bone-button sailor reminisce about their peregrinations—until a wave casts them ashore and sinks both boat and sail. (First published in 1870, "The Ship-wrecked Buttons" was the first of Jewett's many stories for children.) "The Yellow Kitten": One afternoon the sleepy narrator is visited by a yellow kitten, who tells her about a "spool-party" he observed in which some feisty spools of wood and one of ivory, wound with silk and cotton thread, talk about trying to get to "Spool-land" after their usefulness is ended. "Patty's Dull Christ-mas": Young Patty Redington is invited to visit Aunt Janet and Aunt Katharine, her father's aged unmarried sisters, a little distance outside her Boston home for Christmas. She reluctantly accepts, fearing her vacation will be dull. But she gives the old pair such great joy that she has a pleasant time as well. (This story is unusually full of direct Christian references.) "Beyond the Toll-Gate": Bar-bara Snow, about four, moves with her parents to a nice neighborhood. Permitted by her mother to walk past the toll-gate, she is soon welcomed to the home of kind old twins, Rhody Brown and Ruthy Brown. Jewett closes by hoping many gates will open to other joys for "dear little dreaming Barbara."

Play Days was designed for readers age eight to twelve. Following *Deephaven* as Jewett's second book, it combines humor, pathos, and occasional heavy-handed moralizing, to extol the virtues of self-reliance and obedience, hard work and reconciliation, and good deeds. In the collection, Nancy of "Nancy's Doll" is the saddest child, Jane Simmons the meanest, and Patty Redington the kindest. Upsetting to some readers is Jewett's implied hostility in *Play Days* toward authoritarian adults, usually female, for trying to squeeze little girls into tradi-tional modes of behavior. *Bibliography*: Donovan; Roman.

PLUNKETT. In *Betty Leicester*, he is a deaf old man aboard the Riverport-to-Tideshead packet. He is the skipper's father.

POCHETTE, JEANNE. In "Mère Pochette," she is Mère Pochette's daughter. Jeanne marries, leaves Bonaventure with her engineer husband for a home in the West, has a baby, Manon by name, and dies. Her husband returns home with Manon, soon dies, and leaves Mère Pochette with the responsibility of raising her grandchild.

POCHETTE, JOSEPH. In "Mère Pochette," he is Mère Pochette's husband. They leave Quebec to live in Bonaventure, where he soon dies.

POCHETTE, MÈRE. In "Mère Pochette," she goes with her husband from Quebec to Bonaventure, where he has bought land. She runs a shop in their home. After his death, she profitably sells some of her land to the railroad company and raises Manon, her deceased daughter Jeanne's child, in a tyran-nical, dictatorial manner. She opposes Manon's love affair with Charles Pictou. She connives with Father Pierre to prevent Manon from receiving Charles's letters. She repents when Manon becomes ill and upon Charles's return gives the couple her blessing. Mère Pochette's first name is also Manon.

POLLY. In "The Hare and the Tortoise," she is Anne Duncan's snappish parrot. Polly bites Mrs. Temple's gloved finger.

POMEROY. In "Peg's Little Chair," he is Margaret Benning's friend. He and General Dunn tell her that General Lafayette will be stopping at her public house.

POND, MRS. In *Betty Leicester*, she is Seth Pond's mother. A former nurse, she is now supported by Seth.

POND, SETH. In *Betty Leicester*, he works for Barbara Leicester and Mary Leicester as an apprentice under Jonathan. He plays the violin and would like to be able to take lessons.

PORLEY, MISS ESTHER ("EASTER"). In "Miss Esther's Guest," she is a Daleham seamstress, lonely in her old house since her beloved mother's death three years earlier. Miss Esther agrees to accept Mr. Rill, an old bachelor from Boston, as her guest for a week. They like each other and may make their friendship permanent.

PORTER, ADDIE. In "The Life of Nancy," she was the "village belle" of East Rodney, Maine. She danced with Tom Aldis, perhaps too amiably. He is relieved when Nancy Gale tells him that Addie merely wanted to make the other girls jealous and is marrying someone else.

POTTER, ABEL. In "A Born Farmer," Jacob Gaines tells his son, Jacob ("Jakey") Gaines, that soft life in Boston is making Jacob as fat as Abel Potter, Jakey's uncle.

POTTERBY, DR. ASA. (Full name: Asa Potterby, A.M., M.D.) In "The New Methuselah," he is a wealthy, scientist single-mindedly focused on his plan to prolong human life beyond the normal span. About sixty now, he experiments with Thomas, an orphan infant, whom he adopts and nurtures scientifically but who eats a hard green apple and dies. Dr. Potterby also finances Masters, the impractical physical scientist.

POTTERBY, MADAM. In "The New Methuselah," she was Dr. Asa Potterby's mother. Now deceased, Madam Potterby hired Mrs. Ann Yard, who in time became Dr. Potterby's housekeeper.

POULETTE, JUSTIN. In "Mère Pochette," he is a person in Bonaventure to whom Mère Pochett sells some of her woodland. She later makes money selling more of her land to the railroad company.

POWDER. In "Law Lane," he is the deceased husband of Mrs. Harriet Powder, who says he served on a jury trying to settle the land dispute between Ezra Barnet and Crosby. Later Powder spoke with the judge.

POWDER, MRS. HARRIET ("HARRI'T). In "Law Lane," she is the progressive, sensible neighbor of Ezra Barnet, Crosby, and their families, all involved in a land dispute. She favors the Crosbys. Her gossip to Miss Lyddy Bangs that young Ezra Barnet and Ruth Crosby are in love is spread by Joel Smith. This endangers the lovers' future until Mrs. Powder makes the slightly injured Jane Barnet think she is dying. The woman repents, and all is soon well.

POWERS, MADAM. In "The New Methuselah," she is mentioned by Mrs. Ann Yard as an old nurse who visited Madam Potterby. Mrs. Yard gave her favorite "pa'sley" greens to Madam Powers, who preferred mustard greens, which she gave Mrs. Yard.

PRENDER, MRS. In "An Empty Purse," she is a tired young widow with two daughters, Nelly Prender and Susy Prender. Miss Debby Gaines calls on them, babysits for Nelly, who has a cold, lets Mrs. Prender go with Susy to visit Mrs. Prender's mother, and does her ironing for her.

PRENDER, NELLY. In "An Empty Purse," she is Mrs. Prender's daughter, has a cold, and stays at home while Miss Debby Gaines babysits and lets Mrs. Prender and her other daughter, Susy Prender, go visit Mrs. Prender's mother.

PRENDER, SUSY. In "An Empty Purse," she is Mrs. Prender's daughter and goes with her to visit Mrs. Prender's mother while Miss Debby Gaines stays with Susy's sister, Nelly Prender, who has a cold.

PRESCOTT. In "Miss Becky's Pilgrimage," he was a person Becky Parsons's old friend, Adaline Emery, married.

PRESCOTT. In "Miss Becky's Pilgrimage," he is the conductor on the railroad train that Becky Parsons takes to Brookfield. She thinks he resembles her old friend Adaline Emery Prescott's husband.

PRESCOTT, ADALINE EMERY. In "Miss Becky's Pilgrimage," she was Becky Parsons's old Brookfield friend who moved to Portland. Becky thinks the Boston-to-Brookfield railroad conductor resembles Adaline's husband.

PRESTON, HARRIET WATERS (1836–1911). Author and translator. She was born in Danvers, Massachusetts, was educated at home, and lived abroad for many years. Beginning in 1868 she translated much literature from the original French and Latin, the most important being *Mirèio* (1872) by Frédéric Mistral, the Provençal poet. Marie Thérèse de Solms Blanc* introduced Jewett to Mistral in Provence in 1898. Preston wrote on Provençal literature for *The Library of the World's Best Literature* (1897), assembled by Charles Dudley Warner.* She wrote five novels cast in New England; they reminded some early critics of Jewett's "regionalism." She coedited a volume of Elizabeth Barrett Browning's poetry (1900). She spent many later years at Keene, New Hampshire, and died in Cambridge, Massachusetts. Jewett and Preston met in 1877 and spent two weeks or so together that summer at York. When Jewett's father, Theodore Herman Jewett,* died, Preston wrote a letter expressing sympathy and praising the man. Something caused the two women to become unfriendly, and they remained so when they chanced to meet in Florence in 1882. *Bibliography*: Blanchard.

PRESTON, MRS. In "An Every-Day Girl," she is the housekeeper at the summer hotel near the village of Dolton. Mary Arley is able to obtain jobs for herself and her friend, Mary Fleming, at the hotel because Mary Arley's mother is Mrs. Preston's cousin. Mrs. Preston is so pleased with Mary Fleming's work, especially during Mrs. Preston's brief illness, that she recommends her to Mr. Dennis, the hotel owner.

PRICE, DEACON JOHN. In "An Only Son," he is a farmer, church deacon, and selectman in Dalton, sixty-seven and twice widowered. His only surviving offspring, Warren Price, is inept at farming and prefers to tinker with an invention of his. When Deacon Price's wallet containing $735 in tax collections is mislaid, he wrongly suspects his son of theft, obtains $800 from fellow-selectman Captain Abel Stone against a proposed land sale to cover the loss, and deposits the proper sum. Later his niece, Eliza Storrow, retrieves the wallet, and Price is reconciled with his son, whose invention proves successful. John returns the money to Stone.

PRICE, MRS. In "The Coon Dog," she is a skinny old farm woman who is a habitual borrower, indulgently laughed at by John York and Isaac Brown. The latter calls her an "old chirpin' cricket." When her daughter, 'Liza Jane Topliff, gains possession of her deceased husband Abijah Topliff's coon dog, Tiger, they rent it to Brown and York. The women hope to sell Tiger for $50, unaware that it is worthless as a hunter.

PRICE, MRS. JOHN. In "An Only Son," she was Deacon John Price's first wife, "a plain, hard-worked woman," now deceased.

PRICE, MRS. JOHN. In "An Only Son," she was Deacon John Price's second wife, "a pale and delicate school-teacher." Also deceased, she was Warren Price's mother. When Warren reappears, Deacon Price prays gratefully at her grave in his family burial plot.

PRICE, WARREN. In "An Only Son," he is Deacon John Price's only son, inept at farming and hence a disappointment to his critical father. When production of Warren's invention is underwritten by an impressed Lowell mechanic, the two Prices are reconciled.

PRIME, MRS. In "The Honey Tree," she is Ann Sarah Hopper's mother and Johnny Hopper's grandmother. Spry old Mrs. Prime insists on climbing the hill with the others to visit the site of the honey tree. She is pleased to share the find with neighbors.

PRINCE, ADELINE ("ADDY," "AD'LINE") THACHER. In *A Country Doctor*, she is the daughter of Mrs. Thacher of Oldfields, John Thacher's sister, Jack Prince's widow, and Nan Prince's mother. To avoid farm work, she got a job in the Lowell mills. During a bad two-year marriage, she became a consumptive alcoholic and now returns to Oldfields to drown herself and her child. Instead, she makes her way to her mother's home, where, after persuading Dr. John Leslie to become Nan's guardian, she immediately dies. Jewett's handling of Adeline Prince may have owed something to her knowledge of a wild South Berwick woman's suicide by drowning. *Bibliography*: Blanchard.

PRINCE, CAPTAIN JACK. In *A Country Doctor*, he was the father of young Jack Prince and Nancy Prince. He went to sea and in time became Dunport's best shipmaster.

PRINCE, DR. In *Betty Leicester*, he is the Tideshead physician. He saves Lizzie Edwards but is unable to save Foster.

PRINCE, DR. In "Miss Tempy's Watchers," he is a physician whose comments on the willingness of the terminally ill to die is mentioned by Sarah Ann Binson in conversation with Mrs. Daniel Crowe.

PRINCE, JACK. In *A Country Doctor*, he was Nancy Prince's brother, Adeline Prince's husband, and Nan Prince's father. He studied medicine, was an assistant surgeon with Dr. Ferris at sea, and died after two years of marriage.

PRINCE, NAN ("ANNA," "NANNY"). In *A Country Doctor*, she is the daughter of Adeline Prince and Jack Prince. Adeline leaves Nan with Adeline's own mother, Mrs. Thacher, and dies. When Mrs. Thacher grows old, she follows Adeline's request and lets Dr. John Leslie of Oldfields become the girl's guardian and informal tutor. Nan regards him as a surrogate father. In her early twenties, Nan visits her rich aunt, Nancy Prince, in Dunport, is asked by George Gerry to marry him there, but prefers to continue her medical studies and become a country doctor in Oldfields like Leslie. Jewett stresses how Nan combines her mother's wild traits and her father's intellectual, aristocratic traits. Her personality and ambition owe much to Jewett's own adolescent behavior. *Bibliography*: Blanchard; Jean Carwile Masteller, "The Women Doctors of Howells, Phelps, and Jewett: The Conflict of Marriage and Career," in Nagel, pp. 135–47.

PRINCE, NANCY ("ANNA"). In *A Country Doctor*, she is the daughter of the deceased Dunport shipmaster Captain Jack Prince, the sister of the deceased young Jack Prince, and, hence, Nan Prince's aunt. Nancy lost, "for a whim," a chance at love and is now a prominent social leader and a rich Episcopalian. She offers to bequeath her fine mansion to Nan if she will marry George Gerry, her protégé. Nan prefers to become a country doctor back in Oldfields.

PRISCILLA. In *A Country Doctor*, she is Nancy Prince's chief servant. Standoffish and depressed, she speaks in an odd, old-fashioned way.

PROCTER, MRS. In *Betty Leicester's English Xmas*, she is a friend of Lady Mary Danesley, who recalls Mrs. Procter's advice never to explain because no one cares. The reference is to Anne Benson Skepper Procter (1798–1888), brilliant society matron and wife, then widow, of Barry Waller Procter (1787–1874), the author using Barry Cornwall as his pen name. Jewett met Mrs. Procter in England in 1882. *Bibliography*: Blanchard.

PROUDFIT, CAPTAIN ELI. In "All My Sad Captains," he is a Longport shipmaster. Though mentioned, he does not figure in the action.

PYNE, MISS HARRIET. In "Martha's Lady," she is the owner and resident of the Pyne house in Ashford. When she is thirty-five, she welcomes her younger cousin Miss Helena Vernon (*see* Dysart, Helena Vernon) for a summer visit. Harriet remains prissy and unimaginative, in contrast to peppy, considerate Helena, who is kind to Harriet's servant, Martha. When Helena, married to Jack Dysart and then widowed, revisits Ashford forty years later, Harriet still cannot understand the permanent, beneficent effect Helena has had on Martha. *Bibliography*: Roman.

PYNE, JUDGE. In "Martha's Lady," he was Miss Harriet Pyne's father, now deceased. He left her a residence and material comforts.

Q

"THE QUEEN'S TWIN" (1898). Short story. (Characters: Mrs. Blackett, William Blackett, Asa Bowden, Mrs. Elder Caplin, Horace, Abby Martin, Albert Martin, Albert Edward Martin, Alfred Martin, Alice Martin, Victoria Martin, Almira Todd.) One September day, Almira Todd takes the narrator, her summer tenant at Dunnet's Landing, for a walk through pastures and woods, along an Indian trail, up and down a hill commanding a sea view, and past a field—to the modest hill home of Abby Martin. Mrs. Todd has explained that her widowed friend, Abby, was born the same day and hour as Queen Victoria, has always felt a special kinship with her, and in many ways has regulated her life because of this "birthright." The narrator listens sympathetically as Abby, a dignified old lady, bent but still beautiful, tells how she voyaged to England as a cook in the 1840s with her husband, Albert Martin, and her brother Horace, a sailing master, and when free rushed with the ship's carpenter to Buckingham Palace just in time to see the queen in her carriage and *her* husband, also named Albert. Abby's children include Victoria, and then Albert Edward, Alfred, and Alice; these names parallel those of some of the queen's children. All of Abby's children, except for deceased Alice, are grown and gone. Abby, feeling a unique "bond" to the queen, says she reads about her, has pictures of her and clippings about her in her "best room," imagines walking hand in hand with her, and communes with and is advised by her. She even dreams about her—and hopes the queen dreams about Abby. She once prepared a special dinner in the fond hope that the queen would be visiting; when a demented cousin turned up instead, Abby served her as a kind of queen's emissary. Upon leaving Abby, Mrs. Todd tells the narrator it is not as though the old woman is alone. Mrs. Todd voices a poignant line when she asks Abby, "Don't it show that for folks that have any fancy in 'em, such beautiful dreams is the real part o' life?"

After "The Queen's Twin" was republished in *Cornhill*, a British magazine, Jewett learned with delight that Queen Victoria, as well as many other Britishers, read and liked it. "The Queen's Twin," along with "A Dunnet Shepherdess," "The Foreigner," and "William's Wedding," continues the story of *The Country of the Pointed Firs*. *Bibliography*: Matthiessen; Sherman; Silverthorne.

"THE QUEST OF MR. TEABY" (1890). Short story. (Characters: Asa Briggs, Abel Dean, Mrs. Abel Dean, Elder Fry, Hart, Ann Maria Hart, Sister Hannah Jane Pinkham, Teaby.) While the narrator is waiting at the East Wilby railroad depot for a slow train one fall day, she overhears the conversation of thin Teaby, an itinerant medicine man, dressed for summer, and plump Sister Hannah Jane Pinkham, dressed for winter. They are friends but met there only by accident. Saying he recently thought about Sister Pinkham, Teaby discusses his route, his nostrums, and his hope to marry, old though he is. When he half-proposes, she says she prefers Elder Fry, except that he has damaged his voice by loud preaching and now plans to get into the arduous butter business. When Teaby walks away, Sister Pinkham notes that he left his torn umbrella; she repairs it on the spot with a few swift stitches and tells the depot master to tell Teaby he can call on her to retrieve it. Jewett was inspired to write this story by seeing a peddler named Teaby on a rural railroad platform. Quests are occasionally so important in Jewett's fiction that Teaby's quest seems a trivializing of the quest motif. Yet Teaby, though hardly of heroic stature, is a good fellow, helps others, is looking for a nice woman, and is optimistically dressed. While Jewett was in Athens in 1900, she was pleased to learn that a dramatized version of "The Quest of Mr. Teaby" was presented by a club in South Berwick. *Bibliography*: Cary, *Letters*; Sherman.

QUIN, BRIDGET ("BIDDY"). In "Where's Nora?", she is the wife of Patrick Quin, who is Nora's uncle.

QUIN, PATRICK ("UNCLE PATSY"). In "Where's Nora?", he is the brother of Mary, who is Nora's mother; hence he is Nora's uncle. Patrick Quin left Dunkenny, Ireland, thirty-five or forty years ago, worked conscientiously on the railroads in America, was injured, and is now lame and pensioned. His sister, Mary Ann, is Michael Duffy's wife. "Uncle Patsy" welcomes Nora.

QUINT, GEORGE ("KING GEORGE"). In "The King of Folly Island," he is the egocentric fisherman who, when he lost his bid to be postmaster of John's Island bought Folly Island, vowed never to set foot on another person's land, and moved his wife and daughter, Phebe, there. His wife died, and Phebe has developed a lung condition. George lets John Frankfort vacation on his island briefly and suggests that he marry Phebe—to no avail.

QUINT, MRS. GEORGE. In "The King of Folly Island," she was George Quint's wife and Phebe Quint's mother. Mrs. George died on Folly Island, evidently in part because of loneliness and separation from her own family.

QUINT, PHEBE. In "The King of Folly Island," she is George Quint's lonely but submissive daughter. The two live on Folly Island. When John Frankfort visits the island briefly, she is attracted to him. He neglects to help her until it is too late. But her selflessness tardily inspires him to be less egocentric. Jewett named this sweet creature Phebe after the niece of John Greenleaf Whittier,* to whom she dedicated *The King of Folly Island and Other People*.

R

RADCLIFFE, CHARLES. In *The Tory Lover*, he was a young Shakespearean actor the teacher Sullivan saw in London. Charles Radcliffe was Lord Newburgh's father and Lord Darwentwater's brother.

RAND. In "A Late Supper," he is a storekeeper who tells Katy Dunning's aunt that Miss Catherine Spring may wish to employ Katy.

RAY, HIRAM. In "A Born Farmer," he is a neighboring farmer who drives Jacob Gaines to the train taking him to Boston. Hiram Ray's son is John Ray.

RAY, JOHN. In "A Born Farmer," he is Hiram Ray's son. They are neighbors of Jacob Gaines and his family. When Jacob and his wife, Adeline Gaines, return from Boston, their daughter, Mary Ellen Gaines, and John Ray are at the station to wagon them home to their old farm. John and Mary Ellen are likely to get married.

RAY, MRS. In "A Born Farmer," she is Hiram Ray's wife and John Ray's mother. When Adeline Gaines, home from Boston, asks Mary Ellen Gaines, her daughter, to go borrow some rye meal from Mrs. Ray, Mary Ellen is happy to comply, because she likes Mrs. Ray's son, John Ray.

RAYNOR. In "Miss Manning's Minister," he was the minister of the First Congregational church in Rinston, Connecticut. When he died after forty-one years of service, he was replaced by the Reverend Edward Taylor, whom Miss Narcissa Manning admires at once.

READING, JEWETT'S FAVORITE. From her earliest years, Jewett was an avid reader. In this she was encouraged by many family members, most effectively by her father, Theodore Herman Jewett.* She read standard eighteenth- and nineteenth-century novelists and poets, and much else. She especially enjoyed Jane Austen, Elizabeth Barrett Browning, Charles Dickens, George Eliot, Henry Fielding, Elizabeth Gaskell, Charles Kingsley, Margaret Oliphant, Tobias Smollett, Laurence Sterne, Harriet Beecher Stowe,* Alfred, Lord Tennyson,* and William Wordsworth. Also to be named are Louisa May Alcott, Hans Christian Andersen, *The Arabian Nights*, Saavedra Miguel de Cervantes, François de Salignac de La Mothe-Fénelon, Gustave Flaubert, Christina Rossetti, and Izaac Walton. Jewett also kept up with current journal, magazine, and periodical publications. Of unique importance to her was Flaubert's statement, which she pinned at the front of her desk: *Écrire la vie ordinaire comme on écrit l'histoire"* ("To write about common life as one writes history").

REBECCA. In "A Christmas Guest," she was Mrs. Norris's daughter, Eben Norris's sister, and the mother, now deceased, of little Rebecca.

REBECCA (" 'BECCA"). In "A Christmas Guest," she is the orphaned daughter of Rebecca, whose mother, Mrs. Norris, cares for the child, now twelve, in her farmhome, shared with Eben Norris, who is her son and Rebecca's uncle. When Mrs. Norris gets sick during the morning before Christmas Day and Eben goes for help, Rebecca is left in charge. On Christmas Eve, during a snowstorm, General _____ enters the house, and Rebecca welcomes the stranger. Next morning he is gone on to Washington during the war, leaving a message of thanks and $10. Little Rebecca is partly a curious biblical figure, to whom General _____ quotes from Matthew 25:35 about a stranger made welcome.

REID, PARSON. In *Deephaven*, he is a minister whose sermons Mrs. Bonny finds inferior to Parson Padelford's.

REILLY, JAMES. In "A Little Captive Maid," he is one of John Balfour's servants. Reilly recommends Nora Connelly to be Balfour's maid. After Balfour's death, Reilly is bequeathed money, will marry the widowed Mrs. Nash, another of Balfour's servants, and will go with her to her farm.

RHETT. In "The Mistress of Sydenham Plantation," he was the owner of a summer home Mistress Sydenham thinks about. His family was ruined during the Civil War.

RICHÉ, MADAME. In "Mr. Bruce," she is the person in whose Boston finishing school Kitty Tennant and Miss Alice Thornton study until they graduate.

RICKER, CORPORAL JOHN. In *The Tory Lover*, he was a handsome soldier reported as killed by the British.

RIDLEY, MRS. In "An Autumn Holiday," she was Parson Ridley's wife and the niece of Parson Croden, Ridley's superior in the church.

RIDLEY, PARSON. In "An Autumn Holiday," he was evidently Parson Croden's assistant.

RILL, MR. In "Miss Esther's Guest," he is a clean old bachelor, from England, and now a retired seal engraver in Boston. He is sent to Daleham to be a guest for a week in Miss Esther Porley's home. The two take to each other. He leaves his caged bullfinch with her as an indication of the likely permanence of their affection.

RISPÉ. In "Mère Pochette," he is the person from whom Joseph Pochette buys a house and some land in Bonaventure. The land proves valuable to Pochette's widow, Mère Pochette.

"RIVER DRIFTWOOD" (1881). Essay. As Jewett boats along the Piscataqua River, she thinks about its history, wishes "human-kind" could communicate better with other forms of life, and wonders whether the food chain—for example, grass to beef to people—may evolve from people to angels, just as brooks and streams feed rivers and so the water goes on to the sea. Jewett touches on fish and flowers and birds, the weather, old wharf buildings and shipyards, houses (including the Hamilton and Wallingford mansions), ministers living nearby, and ancestors (including her paternal grandparents [Theodore Furber Jewett* and Sarah Orne ("Sally") Jewett*]). Her Emersonian conclusion? "How many men have lived and died on its banks, but the river is always young."

RIVERS. In "An Empty Purse," he is the husband of Mrs. Rivers, who complains to Miss Debby Gaines that he is "very particular about everything."

RIVERS, MRS. In "An Empty Purse," she is a well-to-do lady who complains to Miss Debby Gaines shortly before Christmas about buying presents at a crowded store, about her big house, and about her fussy husband. Chagrined by Debby's comments about nonmaterial Christmas gifts, Mrs. Rivers sends her some of her own valued items and a complimentary note.

ROBB, MARY ANN. In "The Night before Thanksgiving," she is a sick old widow who generously helped others but now has almost nothing. About to lose her farm to John Mander, who has cheated her, she waits in her cold kitchen the night before Thanksgiving to be taken by townspeople to the poorhouse. Suddenly Johnny Harris, whom she cared for years ago, keeps his word and returns to her. He brings food and fuel, and promises her a comfortable future.

RODNEY. In *The Tory Lover*, he is Madam Wallingford's faithful old black servant.

ROGERS. In "A Dark Night," he is a bank clerk in western England. He has deceived his employer for six or eight years, during which time he has set up victims for a small group of robbers. He tries but fails to rob Weymouth near Bristol, later does rob his employer, and is last heard of on his way to France.

ROGERS. In *The Tory Lover*, he is one of Major Tilly Haggens's old Portsmouth neighbors.

ROGERS, MRS. In "The News from Petersham," she is Mrs. Peak's neighbor and participates with Mrs. Peak, Mrs. Smith, and Mrs. West in rumor mongering.

ROLLINS. In *The Tory Lover*, he is Parson Pike's chief parishioner. Rollins helps Pike rescue Madame Wallingford from the "patriot" mob.

ROSS, FATHER. In "Where's Nora?", he is mentioned by Mary Ann Duffy as preaching against materialistic desires.

ROSS, JOHNNY. In "Aunt Cynthy Dallett." *See* Foss, Johnny.

ROVER. In "The Coon Dog," it is Isaac Brown's coon dog, so old and pampered that it is regarded as worthless. But during the coon hunt, it and not Tiger trees the coon.

ROWLEY. In "The Two Browns," he is a member of the law firm of Jenks and Rowley. Thinking they are old, Grandison retains John Benedict Brown instead, thus unwittingly enabling Brown to avoid detection.

RUSH, CYNTHY. In "Miss Becky's Pilgrimage," she is an old churchgoer in Brookfield who Sophia Annis says has uselessly set her cap for Beacham, the widowered minister.

RUSSELL. In *The Tory Lover*, he is a friend Madam Wallingford can report to for aid in Bristol.

RYAN, FATHER. In "Between Mass and Vespers," he is an Irish priest, born in Kerry and having served in a New England village for forty-five years. One of his altar boys was Dan Nolan, whose seminary studies he helped finance. But Dan quit, went west, and became a swindler. Learning of Dan's return home, Father Ryan asks Dennis Call to drive him to a forest rendezvous with the young man. Although Dan hits Father Ryan and must be subdued by Dennis, Father

Ryan forgives Dan and persuades him to repent. Father Ryan always regarded Dan as God's replacement for Father Ryan's little brother, drowned long ago in Ireland.

RYAN, JERRY. In "Where's Nora?", he is a railroad switchman and later a water-tank boss. Nora lives with Ryan and his wife when Nora first starts her baking business.

RYAN, JULIA. In "Where's Nora?", she is the dark-haired daughter of Jerry Ryan and his wife.

RYAN, MRS. JERRY. In "Where's Nora?", she is the railroad worker's pleasant wife. She wishes Johnny O'Callahan would become friendly with their daughter, Julia, but knows he prefers Nora.

RYDER, CAPTAIN JABEZ. In "The Mate of the Daylight," he is Captain Joseph Ryder's partially deaf cousin and part owner with him of a schooner. Both are retired sea captains. Jabez shares Joseph's distrust of Dan Lewis but visits Joseph with his wife to calm him down. In a cute aside, Jewett remarks that many deaf people hear all they need to hear and often more than their associates think they do.

RYDER, CAPTAIN JOSEPH ("CAP'N JOE"). In "The Mate of the Daylight," he is a retired sea captain, Melinda Ryder's father, Susan Ryder's grandfather and guardian. He and his cousin, Captain Jabez Ryder, are part owners of a schooner. He is said to have $9,000 or more in savings. Joseph dislikes Dan Lewis, Susan's boyfriend; but when Dan begins to succeed, Joseph helps the couple financially.

RYDER, MELINDA. In "The Mate of the Daylight," she is Captain Joseph Ryder's daughter and Susan Ryder's aunt. Melinda was engaged to Captain Joseph Sewall, but he was lost at sea. While indulging in gloomy reminiscences, she remembers her married sisters and her one brother, Susan's father—all dead.

RYDER, MRS. JABEZ. In "The Mate of the Daylight," she goes with her husband to visit Captain Joseph Ryder, who is Captain Jabez Ryder's husband's upset cousin. She appreciates her husband's considerate behavior.

RYDER, SUSAN. In "The Mate of the Daylight," she is the granddaughter and ward of Captain Joseph Ryder, whose one son, now deceased, was her father. Her aunt is Melinda Ryder. Susan loves Dan Lewis, whose improvident ways Joseph deplores; but when Dan becomes master of the *Daylight*, the two are helped financially by Joseph and get married.

S

SALLY. In "A Dark Carpet," she is the old servant of Mrs. Weston and her family.

SALLY. In "Peg's Little Chair," she is the black cook working for Margaret Benning in her public house. Sally is especially skilled in killing and preparing chickens.

SAND. In "The Mate of the Daylight," he is the owner of a wharf.

SANDS. In *Deephaven*, he was Sands's grandfather, who told the boy about the boy's father Matthew Sands's telepathic experience. The grandfather was once captured by Algerine pirates. His son's second wife made the old man feel useless.

SANDS. In "Law Lane." *See* Barnet, Jane.

SANDS. In "Miss Becky's Pilgrimage," he was Mahaly Parker's first husband. He died after three years of marriage.

SANDS. In "Told in the Tavern," he was a shipmaster and Abby Sands's father. Early in his life he was lost at sea.

SANDS, ABBY. In "Told in the Tavern," she is Parkins's beloved. When he left Byfleet for the West during the Civil War, he wrote to her; but her mother, who disliked him, intercepted his last letters and let Abby regard him as lost. She erected a tombstone in his honor, which, as a fine gardener, she kept planted with flowers. Thirty years later, Parkins returns to Byfleet, and the two are joyfully reunited.

SANDS, CAPTAIN. In *Deephaven*, he is a retired sea captain who first went to sea at fifteen. He owns a cluttered Deephaven warehouse. He shares sixty years of memories with Kate Lancaster and Helen Denis, with whom he also once goes cunner fishing.

SANDS, HANNAH. In *Deephaven*, she is Captain Sands's sister.

SANDS, JO. In *Deephaven*, he owns a trawl with 'Bijah Mauley.

SANDS, JOHN. In ''The Becket Girls' Tree,'' he is the man who delivers to Parsons the letter from Henry, Mrs. Parsons's brother, saying Henry's wife, Sarah Ann, is gravely ill.

SANDS, MATTHEW. In *Deephaven*, he was Captain Sands's father. Matthew was named after an irascible uncle who ordered the boy to put cherries into a barrel of rum. By mistake, the boy put cherries into a barrel of gin, thus spoiling the gin. He ran away to sea for four years. His mother accurately dreamed of his return. He married twice.

SANDS, MRS. In ''A Bit of Shore Life,'' she attends the auction of goods owned by her friend, Mrs. Wallis.

SANDS, MRS. In *Deephaven*, she was the retired Captain Sands's grandmother. Four years after her son, Matthew Sands, ran off to sea, she accurately dreamed of his return.

SANDS, MRS. In *Deephaven*, she is Captain Sands's wife. She wants him to clear the accumulated junk out of his warehouse.

SANDS, MRS. In ''Told in the Tavern,'' she was Abby Sands's mother, long widowed and now deceased. Disliking Parkins, Abby's fiancé, Mrs. Sands intercepted letters from him to Abby and let her regard him as gone forever.

SANDS, MRS. MATTHEW. In *Deephaven*, she was the retired Captain Sands's mother.

SANDS, MRS. MATTHEW. In *Deephaven*, she was the retired Captain Sands's aggressive stepmother. She made her husband's father feel useless.

SANDS, MRS. WILLIAM. "An Autumn Holiday," she was the person in whose home a female missionary society meeting was held. Captain Daniel Gunn disrupted it by seeking to attend it dressed in his deceased sister Patience Gunn's clothes.

SANFORD, JOHN. In "The First Sunday in June," Miss Lydia Bent is happy to notice that he, his wife, and his family attend church on the first Sunday in June.

SANFORD, MRS. In "The First Sunday in June," she is John Sanford's wife. They, with their family, attend church on the first Sunday in June.

SARAH. In *Betty Leicester*, she is Serena's lame sister. She lives up country, makes rag rugs, and reads a geography book. Her talk about royalty prefigures "The Queen's Twin."

SARAH. In "Fame's Little Day," she is the widowed daughter of Mary Ann Pinkham and Abel Pinkham. She and her young son, Abel, live with her parents in their farmhome in Wetherford, Vermont. The Pinkhams mail her a clipping of the dishonest but flattering New York *Tribune* account of their arrival in the big city, knowing it will please her.

SARAH. In "In a Country Practice," she is the faithful old servant of Mrs. Ashurst and her daughters, Lizzie Ashurst and Nelly Ashurst. They are afraid they will have to let her go, but then they inherit $50,000.

SARAH ANN. In "The Becket Girls' Tree," she is the wife of Henry, Mrs. Parsons's brother. The report of Sarah Ann's illness calls Mrs. Parsons away from the Eastport region to Gloucester. Sarah Ann quickly regains her health.

SARAH, AUNT. In "The Green Bonnet," she is the woman in Boston who gave Sarah McFarland, her niece, the ugly green velvet bonnet with ostrich feathers. Young Sarah hates it but feels she must wear it on Easter Sunday.

SARGENT. In *The Tory Lover*, he is a *Ranger* sailor in league with Dickson and First Lieutenant Simpson against Captain John Paul Jones and Roger Wallingford.

SAYWARD. In *The Tory Lover*, this is the family name of guests from York at Mary Hamilton's wedding.

SCUDDER, HORACE (1838–1902). (Full name: Horace Elisha Scudder.) Author and editor. He was born in Boston, graduated from Williams in 1858, and after teaching private pupils in New York for three years published *Seven Little People and Their Friends* anonymously (1862). He returned to Boston, where he edited the *Riverside Magazine for Young People* (1867–1870), was a valued editor for the publishing house of Houghton Mifflin (1870–1890), and succeeded the easygoing Thomas Bailey Aldrich* as the hard-working editor of the *Atlantic Monthly* (1890–1898). Scudder married Grace Owen in 1873 and with her had twin daughters, one dying in infancy. He wrote several biographies, including those of Noah Webster (1882); the travel writer Bayard Taylor (1884); and Scudder's friend James Russell Lowell* (1901). Jewett had a long and generally fruitful relationship with Scudder, beginning with his acceptance of "The Ship-wrecked Buttons" and "The Girl with the Cannon Dresses" for the *Riverside Magazine* and continuing with his acceptance of several of her pieces for the *Atlantic*. Many of her letters to Scudder have survived; dated from 1869 and 1901, they are always courteous, modest, grateful, and flattering. Trouble inter-vened briefly when in 1884 Annie Adams Fields* discovered that Scudder, while at Houghton, Mifflin, was paying her less for her writings than he paid Jewett, who came loyally to her hostess-companion's defense. In 1899 Scudder evi-dently encouraged Jewett to follow the suggestion of Charles Dudley Warner* that she write a historical novel. *The Tory Lover* was the result. Annie Fields evidently remained inimical to Scudder, since she included no letters to him in her 1911 edition of Jewett's letters. *Bibliography*: Blanchard; Cary, *Letters*; Helen McMahon, *Criticism of Fiction: A Study of Trends in the Atlantic Monthly 1857–1898* (New York: Bookman Associates, 1952); Judith A. Roman, *Annie Adams Fields: The Spirit of Charles Street* (Bloomington and Indianapolis: Indiana University Press, 1990); Ellery Sedgwick, "Horace Scudder and Sarah Orne Jewett: Market Forces in Publishing in the 1890s," *American Periodicals: A Journal of History, Criticism, and Bibliography* 2 (1992): 79–88; Thorp.

SCUDDER, JACK. In *Deephaven*, he is Danny's friend. The two find a family of cats in a barrel at Captain Manning's warehouse.

SCUDDER, SKIPPER. In *Deephaven*, he successfully fishes with Jim Tog-gerson.

SEACLIFFE, THE EARL OF. In *Betty Leicester's English Xmas*, he is one of Lady Mary Danesley's guests.

"A SECOND SPRING" (1893). Short story. (Characters: Mrs. Chellis, Dean, Susan Louisa Dean, Durrant, Johnny Durrant, Maria Durrant, Mrs. Durrant, Israel Haydon, Marilla Haydon, Martha Haydon, William Haydon, Martin, Abby Martin, Mrs. Nash, Polly Norris, Miss Smith, Miss Stevens, Mrs. Stevens, Thomas, Elder Wall.) Martha Haydon, Israel Haydon's wonderful wife, has just died, in early May, after forty years of marriage and a hard life on their suc-cessful farm outside Atfield. The funeral guests have left by their many wagons.

Israel, numb with grief, is hardly assuaged by the brief ministrations of his sister, Abby Martin, and his deceased wife's sister, Mrs. Stevens. His son, William Haydon, a prosperous farmer nearby, suggests that Israel come live for a while with him and his wife, Marilla, or else that Maria Durrant, Marilla's able cousin, become Israel's housekeeper. But gruff Israel rejects both ideas. By June he has made a mess of his place by poor housekeeping; so when William invites him over to dinner and he meets Maria there, he agrees to let the considerate, decent woman become his live-in "housemate." All goes well until next May, when Polly Nash, the local gossip, calls on Maria, who has faithfully cleaned, cooked, and sewed for Israel. Polly, while mooching pie and cast-off clothes, tells Maria that folks say she is setting her cap for Israel. Israel returns later, to find Maria in tears and announcing she must depart. Understanding, the stalwart man, after mentioning his continued reverence for Martha, mumbles a heartfelt proposal to her. Once they are married, Maria attends church with him, and one day she meets Mrs. Chellis there. At Maria's suggestion, they invite Mrs. Chellis, a friend of Martha's, to tea, nicely prepared by Maria. Mrs. Chellis reminisces about Martha but also compliments Maria, who that evening tells Israel that Martha was a good wife for him. After some hesitation, he awkwardly replies that he has a good wife now. Jewett describes Israel's grief with great poignancy. The story is livened by comic touches. Curiously, three woman are named Maria, Marilla, and Martha.

SELKIRK, THE DUCHESS OF. In *The Tory Lover*, she is a Britisher who, according to Captain John Paul Jones, regards Americans as "savages."

SELKIRK, LORD. In *The Tory Lover*, he is described by Captain John Paul Jones as a minimal but effective conversationalist.

SERENA ("MISS SERENA," "SERENY"). In *Betty Leicester*, she is the faithful servant of Barbara Leicester and Mary Leicester. At seventeen, almost forty years ago, she began to work for Madam Leicester. She happily visits her up-country sister, Sarah. In *Betty Leicester's English Xmas*, Betty fondly remembers Serena, as well as Letty, Serena's fellow servant.

SERGEANT. In *A Country Doctor*, he is George Gerry's senior partner in their Dunport law firm.

SERGEANT. In *A Country Doctor*, she is mentioned as attorney Sergeant's deceased daughter, who evinced legal talent.

SEWALL. In *The Tory Lover*, this is the name of Loyalists, who are now refugees in Bristol.

SEWALL, CAPTAIN JOSEPH. In "The Mate of the Daylight," he was Melinda Ryder's fiancé, who was lost at sea shortly before they planned to marry. Melinda laments beside a slate slab with his name on it in the family burying ground.

SHACKLEY, ELDER. In *The Tory Lover*, he is a churchman living near Colonel Jonathan Hamilton.

SHARPE, POLLY. In "Miss Sydney's Flowers," she is Becky Marley's lame, rheumatic, rather deaf old sister. They live together in a cramped apartment. Becky sells the molasses candy Polly makes. When Miss Sydney sees Becky at a street stand near Miss Sydney's greenhouse, where she hopes sales will be better, she befriends Becky and thus helps Polly as well.

SHAW, CAPTAIN ASA. In "All My Sad Captains," he is a well-to-do retired shipmaster in Longport. Widowed, he lives with his four unruly children and some carping sisters-in-law. Along with Captain Crowe and Captain John Witherspoon, he woos Maria Lunn but is brusquely rejected.

SHEFFIELD, GEORGE. In "A Sorrowful Guest," he is the cousin of John Ainslie and his sister Helen Ainslie. Sheffield survived combat duty in the Civil War and is now a lawyer in Boston. His cousins call him "the judge." He is the Ainslies's dinner guest, as is Whiston. Sheffield theorizes that Whiston is crazy, whereas John, a surgeon, says he suffers from monomania.

SHEILA. In "An October Ride," she is Jewett's bright, trustworthy horse. Her name is pronounced "Shyla," "because she occasionally "shies." It has been ingeniously suggested that Sheila's shy movements may be analogous to Jewett's writing progress. In "Peach-tree Joe," Sheila is the narrator's old chestnut. While combing Sheila, John the stableman reminisces about one of his experiences during the Civil War. *Bibliography*: Renza, Silverthorne.

SHEPLEY. In "Andrew's Fortune," her name is mentioned when Mrs. Jonas Beedle says the mother of Aunt Hitty, Mrs. Beedle's aunt, was a Shepley.

SHERBURNE. In *The Tory Lover*, this is the name of Madam Wallingford's Boston friends. Nancy Haggens will write them and ask them to comfort Madam Wallingford.

SHERBURNE. In *The Tory Lover*, he is an old Portsmouth sailor on the *Ranger*.

"THE SHORE HOUSE" (1873). *See Deephaven.*

SIBYL. In "The Mistress of Sydenham Plantation," she is an old ex-slave, formerly owned by Mistress Sydenham, who bought her from Middleton. Both women are now demented. Sibyl says that, as infants, she and Middleton nursed at the same breast.

SILAS. In "A New Parishioner," he is a stingy old member of the Walton church who sees no need for a building program.

SIMMONS, JOEL. In "The Honey Tree," he is the Hillborough storekeeper at whose establishment a group of men discuss Johnny Hopper's find of the honey tree with its fifty pounds of honey. Johnny calls Simmons "a real good man" and wants him to have some honey.

SIMMS, BILL. In *A Marsh Island*, he is a man whose extravagant wife forced him to build an unnecessary addition to their house, according to Allen and Jenks, Israel Owen's hired hands.

SIMMS, MARY ANN. In *Deephaven*, she is named as a dressmaker who aided Widow Jim.

SIMMS, MRS. In *A Marsh Island*, she is a subject of the gossip of Allen and Jenks, Israel's hired hands. They identify her as Bill Simms's extravagant wife. She forced him to build an unneeded addition to their house. She is "a homely creatur' enough," says Allen; from "Seabrook way," Jenks adds.

SIMMS, TOMMY. In "Miss Debby's Neighbors," he is a neighbor remembered by Miss Debby as conceited because he had $4,000 in the bank.

SIMPSON, FIRST LIEUTENANT. In *The Tory Lover*, he is a *Ranger* officer. Formerly a Portsmouth shipmaster, he is the brother-in-law of Major John Langdon. Simpson and Dickson wish to dishonor Captain John Paul Jones. Dr. Ezra Green is rightly suspicious of Simpson, who drops out of the story.

SIMPSON, JACK. In *The Tory Lover*, he was a horse-trader and the subject of a Scottish joke McIntire told Captain John Paul Jones.

SINGER, ASA. In "A New Parishioner," he is Miss Lydia Dunn's neighbor, for whom Jonas Phipps works. When Henry Stroud returns to Walton, he visits the Singers. Later, Asa and Jonas enjoy some cider together.

SINGER, MARY ANN. In "A New Parishioner," she is Miss Lydia Dunn's neighbor, borrows some yeast from her, and is probably Asa's daughter. Lydia tells Mary Ann that Ben Stroud cheated Lydia's grandfather.

"SISTER PEACHAM'S TURN" (1902). Short story. (Characters: Mrs. Downer, the Reverend Mr. Downer, Pamela Fellows, Lydia Ann Peacham, Peters, Mrs. Peters.) Pamela Fellows calls on her younger sister, Lydia Ann Peacham. The two are old widows and live separately. Pamela determines to maneuver Lydia Ann, a chronic hypochondriac, into preparing Thanksgiving dinner this year, for a change. Pamela boldly asks Lydia about her plans this time; just as Lydia fibs and says she might ask the Reverend Mr. Downer and his wife for Thanksgiving, Pamela sees Mr. Downer walking outside. She raps with a thimble on the window, and he enters. When Pamela says her sister is hoping to include the Downers with them for Thanksgiving, Lydia jumps in with an invitation and seems to feel peppier at once. Before the big day, Pamela tells some church friends that parishioners should be more hospitable to the Downers and plans to shop for a turkey personally. After the big day, Pamela lets Lydia take full credit and praises her for exerting herself admirably. The following Sunday, while the minister is preaching on "the beauties of hospitality," Lydia silently reproaches herself for having been too self-centered.

SLATER, CAPTAIN. In *A Country Doctor*, he is mentioned as Captain Walter Parish's old friend, now near death.

SMITH. In "The Dulham Ladies," he is evidently a Dulham minister who took the place of the Reverend Edward Dobin when he died.

SMITH, DR. In "In a Country Practice," he is a student Dr. Best describes as adequate—as are Dr. Duncan Grafton and Dr. Grafton—to take up a country practice.

SMITH, JOEL. In "Law Lane," he is a peppy little boy who runs errands for Mrs. Harriet Powder, hears her gossip to Miss Lyddy Bangs about the love affair of young Ezra Barnet and Ruth Crosby, and tells his mother the news.

SMITH, MISS. In "A Second Spring," she is an old woman Israel Haydon tells his son, William Haydon, he does not want as a housekeeper, since she is "an old grenadier."

SMITH, MRS. In "Law Lane," she is the mother of Joel Smith, whose gossip about young Ezra Barnet and Ruth Crosby she spreads.

SMITH, MRS. In "The News from Petersham," she is a church member who converts the rumor of Daniel Johnson's illness into his death.

SMITH, SABRINA. In *Deephaven*, she warned Tom Kew's wife about Tom.

SNOW, ABBY. In "The Life of Nancy," she is the cousin of Mrs. Gale, who is Nancy Gale's mother. Abby Snow lives in Boston. While in Boston, Nancy stays briefly with her.

SNOW, DORCAS. In "A Pinch of Salt," she is Aunt Deborah's cousin. Deborah crosses the pastures and goes down "the other road" to visit Dorcas Snow.

SNOW, MRS. In "An Autumn Holiday," she is Miss Polly Marsh's widowed sister. Elizabeth, the narrator, visits both women and enjoys their gossip about real and imaginary invalids and then about Captain Daniel Gunn, who attended church dressed in his deceased sister Patience Gunn's clothes. Mrs. Snow tells Elizabeth that Gunn's nephew Jacob Gunn liked Polly Marsh.

SO-AND-SO, MRS. In "The Courting of Sister Wisby," she is mentioned by Mrs. Goodsoe as a person whose youngest child might, according to foolish neighborhood talk, become demented.

SOMEBODY, MADAM. In "The Dulham Ladies," she is a Bostonian whose "unusual head-gear" Harriet Dobin recalls when her own thinning hair is ridiculed.

SOPHIA. In *Deephaven*, she is a child who helps Miss Sally Chauncey.

"A SORROWFUL GUEST" (1879). Short story. (Characters: Helen Ainslie, John Ainslie, Atherton, Aunt Alice, Duncan, Henry Dunster, Fred Hathaway, Aunt Marion, Patrick, George Sheffield, Whiston.) On 2 August 1877, John Ainslie, an unmarried Boston physician, invites his unmarried sister Helen, who has been living for years in Florence with their Aunt Alice, recently deceased, to come and try living with him. Happily agreeing, she arrives that October, and they enjoy a pleasant life together. One December afternoon, John invites George Sheffield and Whiston home for dinner. Sheffield, their cousin, is now a lawyer. With John at Harvard, the rich and generous Whiston roomed with his sneaky cousin, Henry Dunster, and later served in the Civil War, as John, George, and Dunster all did. Since then, Whiston has wandered in South America and Europe. At dinner, John and George reminisce about the horrors of war and mention that Dunster had been wounded, left for dead, and subsequently reported as missing in action. Whiston, who also served but was mustered out early, is well mannered at dinner but has a hunted, haunted look and seems to stare as though at a ghost. Before he leaves, John, sensing Whiston is using opium, offers to give him medical advice; later John says Whiston has monomania, while George defines him as insane. Next afternoon, Whiston brings Helen flowers, stays for dinner, and reports that Dunster reappeared to him on a boat off Rio in South America. He says he is leaving America at once by boat and expects to perish soon. A few weeks later, John happens to find Whiston in a local hospital, where the haunted man soon dies. Months later, John goes to the marine hospital in Chelsea to observe a surgical procedure and happens upon Dunster, there because of an injurious fall. When John presses him, Dunster confesses that when he was wounded he went to the rear, drifted out of the army and, turning to drink, wandered to South America, where indeed he did see Whiston at least once. Helen dilates on the effects of sin and crime but concludes that God pities all souls, whether healthy or blighted. Jewett's moralizing recalls Nathaniel Hawthorne, one of her favorite authors.

SPARKS, ANN. In *Betty Leicester*, she is Sarah's neighbor, whom Sarah's sister, Serena, says Sarah must call for help.

SPARKS, CAPTAIN. In "The Taking of Captain Ball," he was Widow Sparks's husband. He died aboard his ship after a drunken fall.

SPARKS, DEACON. In "Miss Esther's Guest," he was Miss Esther Porley's last male guest when fifteen years ago he and his wife, both from East Wilby, attended a county conference and stayed with Miss Esther and her mother, Mrs. Porley.

SPARKS, MRS. In "Miss Esther's Guest," she and her husband Deacon Sparks were Miss Esther Porley's houseguests fifteen years earlier.

SPARKS, WIDOW. In "The Taking of Captain Ball," she lives on Ropewalk Lane, was kind to Ann Ball, and would like to be Captain Ball's housekeeper after Ann's death. Ball rejects her advances.

SPEED, IRA. In "The Hiltons' Holiday," he is a sharp but honest local merchant at whose store John Hilton plans not to buy a new hoe. But when he forgets to buy one at Topham Corners, he decides to let Ira sell him one.

SPEED, MARY. In "The Hiltons' Holiday," she and her sister, Sarah Speed, visit the teacher at the home of Mrs. Becker when Susan Ellen Hilton, Katy Hilton, and the Grover boys are also there.

SPEED, SARAH. In "The Hiltons' Holiday," she and her sister, Mary Speed, visit the place where their teacher lives and while there also see Susan Ellen Hilton, Katy Hilton, and the Grover boys.

SPENCE, MRS. In "Miss Peck's Promotion," she and Maria Corbell watch over the corpse of the first Mrs. Wilbur Elbury at the parsonage.

SPENCER. In *The Tory Lover*, this is a Berwick family mentioned as active in the French and Indian War.

SPENCER, JOHNNY. In "A Native of Winby," he is one of Marilla Hender's pupils. While she repeats the story of Joseph K. Laneway to the class, Johnny draws a cartoon of the illustrious man.

SPENSER, JACK. In "Hallowell's Pretty Sister," he is the friend of Dick Hallowell and Phil. The three are juniors at Harvard together. Jack Spenser has grown so snobbish that when Dick invites Jack and Phil to his family mansion Dick gets his young brother, Tom Hallowell, to impersonate their beautiful sister, Alice Hallowell, to fool Jack. Tom is so effective that Jack tries to make a conquest of "her," until the real Alice arrives. Ultimately, Jack and Alice get married. Jack later graduates from law school.

SPILLANE, JOHANNA. In "A Little Captive Maid," she is the person who purchased a hen from Mrs. Connelly, Nora Connelly's mother, according to the story Nora relates to John Balfour concerning her childhood.

SPOFFORD, HARRIET ELIZABETH PRESCOTT (1835–1921). Author. She was born in Calais, Maine. When her father went west alone in 1849 to seek a fortune for his large family, they moved to Newburyport, Massachusetts, then Derry, New Hampshire. Harriet attended good schools in both places. Her father returned penniless and paralyzed, after which she helped support both sick parents by writing. Her "In the Cellar" (*Atlantic Monthly* [1859]) began her professional success in Boston. Several romantic novels followed. In 1865 she married Richard Smith Spofford, Jr., a successful lawyer. Their one child died in 1867. The Spoffords lived briefly in Washington, D.C. From 1874 on, Harriet Spofford wrote on Deer Island, in the Merrimac River near Newburyport; her husband had purchased the island and a house on it. For decades she was a popular fiction writer, best when featuring distinctive regional types, as in *New-England Legends* (1871) and *The Elder's People* (1920). She vainly hoped to excel as a poet. In *A Little Book of Friends* (1916), Spofford published her essays on ten women acquaintances, including Annie Adams Fields* and Jewett. Much earlier, Jewett wrote Spofford two fine letters (17 February [1889], 9 June 1897) to praise her works, especially her sensitive verse; Jewett also helped Annie Fields entertain Harriet Spofford as their guest, and visited her home with Annie Fields in 1888. *Bibliography*: Blanchard, Cary, *Letters*; Thelma J. Shinn, "Harriet Prescott Spofford: A Reconsideration," *Turn-of-the-Century Women* 1 (Summer 1984):36–45.

SPOONER, EZRA. In "Little French Mary," he is one of the old men in Dulham who are charmed by French Mary and who miss her when she leaves. He is Captain Weathers's devoted friend.

SPRING, JOSEPH. In "A Late Supper," he is Miss Catherine Spring's nephew. He depresses her by telling her that her niece, Mary, will not need her help. When Miss Spring offers tea to him, his wife, Martha, and their friend, Miss Stanby, but then disappears, Joseph becomes terribly agitated.

SPRING, MARTHA. In "A Late Supper," she is the wife of Miss Catherine Spring's nephew, Joseph Spring.

SPRING, MISS CATHERINE. In "A Late Supper," she is the aging Brookton woman whose finances are so depleted she must advertise to rent rooms to summer guests. Her need to borrow cream for tea for her nephew, Joseph Spring, his wife, Martha Spring, and their friend, Miss Stanby, results in her meeting a pair of future tenants, Miss Ashton and her niece Alice West, on a train aboard which Miss Spring is caught briefly.

"A SPRING SUNDAY" (1904). Short story. (Characters: Dougherty, Addie Hallett, Alonzo Hallett, Joseph Hallett, Mary Ann Hallett, Oliver Hallett, Nora, Miss Pecker.) Alonzo Hallett and his wife, Mary Ann Hallett, have been married sixty-two years. They decide to skip church and take the trolley car ten miles out of their "wide-awake little city" to Miller Falls, a village where they lived until twenty years ago. Alonzo moved from his store there into the city and became a successful businessman. They pack a lunch and head out, but get to talking sadly about their little daughter, Addie Hallett, who died at Miller Falls. Once in the "straggling village," they spot their old house, a familiar grove of beeches, and a foot bridge they used to take to cross the river. They sense the presence of their healthy children, all grown, married, and with families. Before returning home, the tenderly loving old couple enjoy a picnic and seem suddenly like teen-agers again, bathed by the spicy spring air.

"THE SPUR OF THE MOMENT" (1902). Short story. (Characters: Mrs. Ashton, Mrs. Dartmouth, Mrs. Douglas, Dumphy, Duncan, Duncan, Fallon, Haines, Jenks, Peet, Miss Peet, Wallis, Walton.) One snowy, rainy winter day Mrs. Dartmouth is bored in her nice house. She looks into the street at an old carriage with an old horse and his freezing driver, who is hoping to pick up a fare. On the spur of the moment, she sends her servant to him with money and orders to go to the home of tight Miss Peet in case she needs a carriage for an hour. Meanwhile, Miss Peet is annoyed no one has sent a carriage for her to go to the funeral of Walton, her kind old friend. Each year he provided her with a Christmas check, now surely ended. She goes in the old carriage, as provided, to the funeral, where cabmen with fine coaches wait to return their employers home again after the funeral. A big coachman, unnamed, recognizes the driver of the old carriage. He calls the shivering man by name—Fallon—and confirms the fact that Fallon was once a clever gardener for Mrs. Douglas. Fallon says he went west, broke his arm, returned home, and is driving briefly for Dumphy, a sick friend the big coachman also knows. Fallon adds that his wife is sick and that he is desperate. At the funeral Miss Peet feels remorseful for not being kinder to Walton, long an invalid. Her face seems so touchingly sympathetic to Mrs. Ashton, Walton's daughter, that she arranges for Miss Peet to continue to get her allowance. Mrs. Dartmouth is surprised to receive flowers regularly delivered from Mrs. Douglas's garden by Fallon, who well remembers the "handsome" lady who rapped on her window and sent money out to him that bitter night.

STACY, JOHN. In "An Only Son," he was a Dalton resident whose fate, like that of Job, Mrs. Starbird comments on. She recalls that Stacy's wife and three children all died, his house burned down, and a bank failure left him destitute. But he sprang "right up again, like a bent withe."

"THE STAGE TAVERN" (1900). Short story. (Characters: Solomon Dunn, John Harris, Lizzie Harris, Major Tom Harris, Mrs. Harris, Squire Harris, General Jack Norton.) In early spring, Lizzie Harris expertly drives General Jack Norton from the railroad station at Burnside, Maine, to the Stage Tavern near Westford. While in college decades ago, Norton stayed briefly at the tavern, run then by Squire Harris, the father of Norton's college chum, Tom Harris. Both Norton and Tom Harris enlisted during their junior year, fought in the Civil War in Virginia in 1862, and were wounded. They have not seen each other since. Harris became a major, but his head wound later caused him to go blind. Norton stayed in the army, served in the West, was "damaged" by Indians, retired, and made a fortune in Arizona mining. He plans to surprise Harris, still at the tavern, but is surprised in turn to learn that pretty Lizzie is Tom's daughter. The two ex-soldiers have a mellow reunion in the attractive tavern, which presents a challenge to Lizzie, a recent Radcliffe graduate. She wants to manage the tavern herself. Lizzie's delicate mother has recently died, she has a young brother, John Harris, to educate, and the family needs money. Norton finds Lizzie charmingly fresh, would like to do something for her, and after he leaves persuades tourists to stop at the tavern. He and Lizzie exchange letters. In the fall, Lizzie again drives Norton to the tavern. Their talk seems strained. She tells him John is now in college. Norton says he remembers the tavern as a kind of home. She says taverns should be that way for travelers. He says he cannot leave her again but feels too old for her. She says he does not seem old at all to her. The two enter the tavern with happy hearts. "The Stage Tavern" begins beautifully, with marvelously nuanced wording. The ending, however, is hasty, especially when, with insufficient groundwork, Jewett calls Norton and Lizzie blushing "lovers."

STANBY, MISS. In "A Late Supper," she is a friend of Joseph Spring and Martha Spring. The three pay a surprise visit to Miss Catherine Spring, Joseph's aunt. She graciously invites the three to supper.

STANDISH. In *Betty Leicester*, she is evidently Mary Duncan's servant, with the Duncans in Switzerland.

STAPLES, HENRY. In "Little French Mary," he is one of the old men in Dulham who are charmed by French Mary and who miss her when she leaves. He is the local storekeeper and postmaster.

STAPLES, SIMON. In *The Tory Lover*, he is a *Ranger* sailor, was once a logger, and has a sense of humor.

STARBIRD, AUNT HANNAH. In *Deephaven*, she was Captain Sands's aunt from East Parish. She raised his sister, Hannah Sands, because the girl was named after her.

STARBIRD, MRS. In "An Only Son," she is Deacon John Price's cousin. She goes with his niece, Eliza Storrow, to a golden wedding celebration in Somerset and is away with her two nights. After she comments on the fate of an acquaintance named John Stacy—losing his family, his house, and his money—she adds that John should have roughly pushed his son Warren Price away from farm work, which he disliked, and into some other line of work. Warren stays on the farm and invents a profitable machine. Would he have done so if his father had been harsh?

STARBUCK. In *The Tory Lover*, he is a *Ranger* sailor, once beaten up by Captain John Paul Jones. Jewett may have borrowed this unusual name from Captain Ahab's chief mate aboard the *Pequod* in Herman Melville's *Moby Dick*.

STARK, MRS. In "The Mate of the Daylight," she is a sea captain's widow about whose welfare Captain Joseph Ryder inquires.

STATIRY, COUSIN. In "An Autumn Holiday," she is mentioned by Miss Polly Marsh as her cousin. The two, with Jacob Gunn, attended the church service that Captain Daniel Gunn disrupted by appearing in his sister's clothes.

STEVENS, MISS. In "A Second Spring," she is the invalid daughter of Mrs. Stevens, who is Israel Haydon's sister-in-law.

STEVENS, MRS. In "A Second Spring," she is Israel Haydon's sister-in-law. When Israel's wife, Martha Haydon, dies, Mrs. Stevens comes to his home for a brief time to render what help she can.

STILES. In "A Bit of Shore Life," she is Mrs. Wallis's sister. She gave many items to Stiles, who the day before helped Mrs. Wallis get ready to auction many of her belongings.

STINCE. In ''Stolen Pleasures,'' she is the overdressed little daughter of Jim Stince and Nell Stince.

STINCE, JIM. In ''Stolen Pleasures,'' he is Nell Stince's easy-come, easy-go husband.

STINCE, NELL. In ''Stolen Pleasures,'' she is Jim Stince's wife. She is Hattie Webber's materialistic, mean-minded friend and would like to see Hattie have trouble with her husband, John Webber.

"STOLEN PLEASURES" (c. 1880). Short story. (Characters: Jones, Stince, Jim Stince, Nell Stince, Webber, Austin Webber, Hattie Webber, John Webber, Mrs. Webber.) After work at a machine shop one hot evening in August, John Webber declines an offer to spend Sunday boating on the beach with some fellow employees. He has planned to surprise his nagging wife, Hattie Webber, by taking her and their baby to the beach at Harborside. At home he finds only a critical note from Hattie. She and the baby have gone with Nell Stince, Jim Stince, and their baby to a beach house at Harborside for a few days. Nell and Jim are spendthrifts and regard John as foolishly frugal; Hattie tends to agree. Crushed, John next morning takes a train to his old Vermont farmhome and explains the situation to his widowed mother. She is happy to see him, says he should have let Hattie anticipate a vacation instead of seeking to surprise her, and tells him to go get Nell. Having had a bad time with the Stinces, Nell is happy to spend a couple of weeks with John and his mother, shows her the baby, and invites her to come visit later.

STONE, CAPTAIN ABEL. In ''An Only Son,'' he is a former sea captain, retired for fifteen years and with substantial savings. He bought a poor farm but enjoys experimenting with crops on it. He is a Dalton selectman, along with John Kendall and Deacon John Price. When Price needs $800 to replace missing tax money entrusted to his care, Stone readily loans him the sum against his planned land sale. The missing money turns up and Price repays Stone, who uses the cash to buy ''a few planks'' of Otis's three-masted schooner.

STORER. In ''The Parshley Celebration,'' he is an old churchgoer who complains to Martha Binney that the ''public spirit'' of Parshley is not what it used to be when he was a boy.

STORROW, ELIZA (" 'LIZA"). In ''An Only Son,'' she is Deacon John Price's niece and housekeeper. She misplaces his wallet, goes away two nights with Mrs. Starbird to attend a golden wedding celebration at Somerset, and hence causes him terrible grief. On her return, she finds the wallet in her calico work dress, lightly hands it to him, thinks he should not have worried, and never learns the whole truth.

THE STORY OF THE NORMANS, TOLD CHIEFLY IN RELATION TO THEIR CONQUEST OF ENGLAND (1887). History book. Jewett narrates the activities of Rolf, first duke of the Normans, who ruled from 911 to 927, his son William "Longsword" (ruled 927–943), his son Richard "the Fearless" (r. 943–996), his son Richard "the Good" (r. 996–1016), and his sons Richard III (r. 1026–1028) and Robert "the Magnificent" (r. 1028–1035). The high point of *The Story of the Normans* comes when Jewett delves into the story of William the Conqueror (r. 1035–1087), the illegitimate son of Robert the Magnificent, now known as Robert the Devil. Jewett calls William "one of the great men and great rulers of the world," and says he combined "the opposing elements of Christian knighthood, and the fighting spirit of the viking blood," and led "a pure life in a most unbridled and immoral age." The gory "twist . . . [ing] and twin . . . [ing]" of Norman and English corpses, resulting in William's victory at Hastings in 1066, symbolizes to Jewett a beneficent "mix in government, in blood, in brotherhood, and in ownership of England while England stands." The remainder of *The Story of the Normans* quickly sketches some of William's descendants. Jewett's conclusion is that "[t]he English are strongest, but the Normans are quickest. The battle has been given to Progress, and the Norman, not the Saxon, had the right to lead the way." Normans were mainly superior with respect to government, the arts, social customs, and "vitality."

G. P. Putnam's Sons, New York and London publishers, asked Jewett to write *The Story of the Normans*, as part of their "The Story of the Nations" series for juvenile readers. In 1881 she began research in the Boston Public Library, turned to other work, and resumed the task in 1885. She was conscientious but unscholarly. She relied mainly on Edward Augustus Freeman's *The History of the Norman Conquest* (6 vols., 1867–1879), now regarded as often informative, but anachronistic in approach and sometimes inaccurate. Her book was reprinted in 1889, 1898, and 1901, published in London in 1898, and reprinted twice or more. Appealing to theorists of her era, she postulates that, while heredity affects individual behavior, climate partly dictates social customs; she also evinces a Darwinist attitude toward war. Criticizing *The Story of the Normans*, modern scholars note that Jewett conflates historical fact and romantic legend and also fictionalizes dialogue. Worse is her racial bias favoring the Norman race and her occasional degrading of women—too often depicted as patient, uncomplaining, sewing well, weeping, and even resembling puppets. *Bibliography*: Blanchard; Cary, *Jewett*; Jack Lindsay, *The Normans and Their World* (London: Hart-Davis, MacGibbon, 1974); Roman; Silverthorne; Ann Williams, *The English and the Norman Conquest* (Woodbridge, UK: Boydell Press, 1995).

STOVER. In "Decoration Day," he was John Stover's brother, killed in the Wilderness during the Civil War.

STOVER. In "The Taking of Captain Ball," he is a storekeeper who, according to Mrs. Captain Topliff, sold her some inferior dress material.

STOVER, JOHN. In "Decoration Day," he was a first lieutenant during the Civil War and, with Asa Brown and Henry Merrill, plans the holiday parade. Stover and Merrill discuss the sad life of their deceased comrade, Eben Munson, and also the suggestion of Elder Dallas that surviving veterans ought to gather war information of historical value.

STOVER, MA'AM. In "By the Morning Boat," she is an invalid pauper who proudly retains some authority over neighbors and friends. She gives Elisha a watch when he leaves their coastal town in Maine for Boston.

STOWE, HARRIET BEECHER (1811–1896). Author. She was born Harriet Elizabeth Beecher in Litchfield, Connecticut. Her mother died in 1815, leaving eight young children and a Calvinist preacher husband, Lyman Beecher, who remarried and sired three more children. Harriet Beecher was privately educated in Litchfield, attended and taught at the Hartford Female Seminary, and moved with her family to Cincinnati in 1832. She taught at the Western Female Institute in Cincinnati and married Calvin Ellis Stowe, who taught biblical literature at Cincinnati's Lane Theological Seminary, where her father was president. When Calvin Stowe began teaching at Bowden College, New Brunswick, Maine, Mrs. Stowe and their six surviving children moved there too. Having seen African-American slaves mistreated in Kentucky and critical of the 1850 Fugitive Slave Law, Mrs. Stowe joined the abolitionist movement and wrote *Uncle Tom's Cabin; or, Life Among the Lowly* (1852). It was a bestseller, earned her $10,000 quickly and more later, was dramatized without her consent, and even sold a million copies in a British pirated edition. She made her home in Andover, Massachusetts, when her husband began teaching at the Andover Theological Seminary from 1852. She published *A Key to Uncle Tom's Cabin* . . . (1853); *Sunny Memories of Foreign Lands* (2 vols., 1854), following the first of several tours abroad; and *Dred: A Tale of the Great Dismal Swamp* (1856), which sold phenomenally well but is downgraded by modern critics. She moved to Hartford, Connecticut, in 1864 with her husband, by then retired. Mrs. Stowe's later career is marked by much fine local-color writing (*The Minister's Wooing* [1859], *The Pearl of Orr's Island* [1862], *Oldtown Folks* [1869], *Sam Lawson's Oldtown Fireside Stories* [1872], and *Poganuc People* [1878]), but also numerous potboilers. She met and admired Anna Isabella, Lady Byron, Lord Byron's wife, and was sympathetic when Lady Byron told her about Byron's incest with his half-sister. When Teresa Guiccioli, his Italian mistress, published her recollections of Byron in 1869 and criticized Lady Byron, Mrs. Stowe wrote *Lady Byron Vindicated* . . . (1870). This was of a piece with Mrs. Stowe's steady advocacy of women's rights; but the upshot was a decline in her popularity, for presenting Lady Byron as an example of a Victorian woman too pure to be hurt by an indiscreet man and yet hurt. Readers in a society dominated by men ridiculed Mrs. Stowe. Nor was her name improved by the 1874 lawsuit against her preacher brother, Henry Ward Beecher, for adultery. Family tragedies, senility, and mental collapse followed for Mrs. Stowe, now remembered as the author of the best of all nineteenth-century bestsellers.

Jewett often acknowledged the indebtedness of her *Deephaven* to Mrs. Stowe's *Pearl of Orr's Island*, which also depicts Maine country folks and their dialect, and which Jewett read at thirteen or fourteen. She also visited Orr's Island, near Brunswick, Maine. She met Mrs. Stowe in 1878 at the home of Mary Claflin,* their mutual friend. In the home of Annie Adams Fields,* perhaps before and certainly after the death of her publisher husband, James T. Fields, the two writers also met. James Fields serialized much of Mrs. Stowe's work in the *Atlantic Monthly*, of which he was editor (1861–1871). During their visit in 1884 to Charles Dudley Warner* and his wife in Hartford, Jewett and Annie Fields called on Mrs. Stowe, then a near neighbor; Jewett gave her a copy of *A Country Doctor*, which in a letter to Annie Fields (24 September 1884) Mrs. Stowe praised as interesting, strong, bright, and earnest. In 1894, visiting the Warners again, Annie Fields and Jewett again called on Mrs. Stowe, who by then was senile and whose funeral in Hartford they attended two years later. Annie Fields nicknamed Jewett "Pinny Lawson," partly after Sam Lawson, Mrs. Stowe's fictive storyteller. ("Pinny" was owing to Jewett's being tall, slender, and with a supposedly small head.) *Bibliography*: Blanchard; Joan D. Hedrick, *Harriet Beecher Stowe: A Life* (New York: Oxford University Press, 1994); Sherman; Silverthorne.

STRAFFORD. In "A Pinch of Salt," this is the name of one or more of Hannah Dalton's pupils.

STRAFFORD, KATY. In "The Flight of Betsey Lane," she is the granddaughter of General Thornton and Mrs. Thornton, for whom Betsey Lane worked long ago. Mrs. Strafford lives in London, voyages for health reasons to America for a brief time, and visits Betsey. In gratitude for her loyal service to her grandmother, Katy Strafford gives Betsey a present of $100.

STROUD, BEN. In "A New Parishioner," he was Henry Stroud's father; he cheated Miss Lydia Dunn's grandfather, Parson Dunn, forty or so years ago. Lydia holds this fact against Ben's memory. Ben has a son younger than Henry, but nothing is mentioned about him.

STROUD, HENRY. In "A New Parishioner," he is Ben Stroud's son. Miss Lydia Dunn liked him before he left Walton at sixteen or seventeen. Jonas Phipps tells Lydia he and Henry are now sixty-one. Reputed to have made a great deal of money in South America, Henry returns from New Orleans to Walton, becomes the "new parishioner," prays beautifully aloud in church, and is lavish with small gifts and notes for big purchases. He fools all the townspeople except Lydia and even momentarily disarms her with an offer to give her $6,000 because his father cheated her grandfather, Parson Dunn. When

Henry Stroud is arrested for fraud and dies in Walpole on his way to New York, Lydia is praised for her acuity.

STROUD, MRS. BEN. In "A New Parisioner," she was Ben Stroud's wife, now deceased and remembered by Miss Lydia Dunn as a better church member than Ben ever was.

STROUD, MRS. HENRY. In "A New Parishioner," she is the wife of fraudulent Henry Stroud, who hints that she is dead; in reality, she left him.

SULLIVAN. In "The Gray Mills of Farley," he is a worker at the mills whom Dan tells Ellen Carroll he will help.

SULLIVAN. In *The Tory Lover*, he is the master teacher at Berwick. Now over eighty, he is Margery Sullivan's husband and the father of James Sullivan and General John Sullivan. Mary Hamilton adores him. He hints of his rebellious Irish and French background. His mysterious letter to Lord Newburgh startles that man into trying to have Roger Wallingford pardoned and released from the Mill Prison.

SULLIVAN, CORNY ("TIMBERTOES"). In "The Luck of the Bogans," he is a veteran wounded while serving in the British army at Sebastopol. He lost a leg there, hence his nickname. His drinking crony at Mike Bogan's saloon is Jerry Bogan (no relation to Mike).

SULLIVAN, DAN. In "A Little Captive Maid," he is the one who, according to Nora Connelly, gave her cousin, Johnny Donahue, the fife she hears him play outside John Balfour's house.

SULLIVAN, EBEN. In *The Tory Lover*, he is mentioned as commanding Berwick soldiers against the British.

SULLIVAN, GENERAL JOHN. In *The Tory Lover*, he is the son of the teacher Sullivan and his wife Margery Sullivan, and is James Sullivan's brother. General John Sullivan was with General George Washington on Long Island. General Sullivan helps Mary Hamilton get to the ship that is to carry her to Bristol.

SULLIVAN, JAMES ("JAMIE"). In *The Tory Lover*, he is the lame, scholarly son of the teacher Sullivan and his wife Margery Sullivan, and is General John Sullivan's brother. James is a judge who praised John Hancock.

SULLIVAN, MARGERY. In *The Tory Lover*, she is the teacher Sullivan's wife. His beloved if "unequal companion," she is the mother of James Sullivan and General John Sullivan. She met her future husband of more than fifty years aboard the ship carrying them both to America.

SULLIVAN, MARY. In "Between Mass and Vespers," she is a deceased person whose wake Father Ryan, though busy, has been asked to conduct.

SUSAN. In *A Country Doctor*, she is Miss Eunice Fraley's married sister. Their mother, the redoubtable Mrs. Fraley, eagerly lets Susan and her children visit Dunport occasionally but soon tires of them.

SUSAN. In "Tom's Husband," she is a young servant working faithfully for Tom Wilson and Alice Dunn Wilson. Her aunt, Catherine, also works for them. When Susan gets married and leaves the Wilsons's home Tom is inconvenienced.

SUSAN. In *The Tory Lover*, she is the sister of Cooper, the sailor, and is Madam Wallingford's "ancient countrywoman" servant. It is decided Susan will not accompany Madam Wallingford to Bristol.

SUSAN. In "A Visit Next Door," she works for Mrs. Granger and has cousins "up country."

SUSAN ELLEN. In "A Winter Courtship," she is one of Fanny Tobin's two daughters. The other is Adeline. Evidently both are comfortably married. Their widowed mother is traveling with Jefferson Briley in his wagon from Sanscrit Pond to North Kilby to stay with Susan Ellen when Briley proposes marriage to her.

SYDENHAM, MISTRESS. In "The Mistress of Sydenham Plantation," she is a "daft" old woman, formerly the lady presiding over a Southern plantation on St. Helena's Island. Her husband and sons were killed in the Civil War. Twenty years later, the mansion long ruined and the land distributed to the freed slaves, she orders Peter, her one remaining servant, to take her from Beaufort to the island, where she looks at the plantation once more and imagines that all is as it used to be.

SYDNEY, MISS. In "Miss Sydney's Flowers," she is the wealthy, reclusive old woman with a greenhouse full of flowers. When a new street is built near it and passers-by delight in viewing her blooms, Miss Sydney is drawn out of her shell, becomes unselfish and caring, and begins to make friends again, including Becky Marley, Polly Sharpe, and Bessie Thorne.

SYKES, JOHN. In "By the Morning Boat," he is a neighbor who wagons Elisha from his farmhome in Maine to catch the Boston steamer.

SYLVIA ("SYLVY"). In "A White Heron," she is a sensitive, nature-loving girl, nine. Her grandmother, Mrs. Tilley, a lonely farm widow, informally adopted her a year earlier, taking her from crowded city life with the old woman's daughter and Sylvia's too numerous siblings. The girl, who intimately knows the nearby woods, would love to tell a handsome young ornithologist who suddenly appears the location of the nest of a white heron he wants to kill and stuff. But she finally displays more veneration of the bird and what it represents than "loyalty" to the scientist, lovable though he could be.

T

TAFT, EBEN. In ''The Parshley Celebration,'' he is the only Civil War veteran left in Parshley. He is said to be well off. He dons his blue uniform and marches as the flag bearer at the head of the procession celebrating Decoration Day.

"THE TAKING OF CAPTAIN BALL" (1889). Short story. (Characters: Captain Allister, Ann Ball, Captain Ball, Miss Calvinn, Mr. Calvinn, Mrs. Calvinn, Captain Dunn, Mrs. Ann French, Miss Miranda Hull, Silas Jenkins, Captain Sparks, Widow Sparks, Stover, Captain Topliff, Mrs. Captain Topliff.) Ann Ball, the quietly adoring older sister of Captain Ball, a retired, rheumatic, bachelor shipmaster, was his frugal housekeeper in his tidewater home for years. She has just died. His great-niece, also named Ann Ball, sends word that she wants to come from New York state, evidently with members of her family, and take over. Resisting, Captain Ball hires aggressive but seemingly compliant Mrs. French from Massachusetts instead. She says she heard about the position through relatives of Mr. Calvinn, the town minister. Mrs. French makes a tasty chowder.

The scene now shifts. The widowed Mrs. Captain Topliff, pushing seventy, and her dressmaker, Miss Miranda Hull, sew and gossip about Mrs. French, Ball, his money-saving late sister, and Widow Sparks, who also wanted to be Ball's housekeeper. So did Mrs. Topliff and Miss Hull, if the truth were revealed. Mrs. Topliff confides that Mrs. French got Ball to rebuff his great-niece, wonders who Mrs. French is, and compares her to a ''carr' on bird.''

Two months pass. While their wives are away in September, Captain Allister and Captain Dunn are invited to Ball's place for some chowder and Madeira. Allister's asking where Mrs. French is from angers defensive Ball. Mrs. French persuades Ball to invite his great-niece to visit, at least briefly. She turns out to be Ball's great-niece, when Mrs. Ann French, long widowed, identifies herself. Mr. Calvinn and his family were in on the stratagem. The gossipers are discomfited when Ball professes that he knew everything all along. Ann happily remains. Ball secretly laments the fact that Anne is not a pretty girl dressed in pink, as he always pictured her; she would have brightened his house more. Feminists take umbrage at Captain Ball's treatment of the socially constricted New England women around him. *Bibliography*: Roman.

TALCOT. In *A Country Doctor*, he is evidently the Oldfields minister, reportedly ill at one point.

TALCOT. In *The Country of the Pointed Firs*, he owned the farm near Dunnet Landing that a family from St. George has taken over. Almira Todd, Mrs. Blackett, and the narrator get nice doughnuts there.

TANNER, ANN'LIZA. In *Deephaven*, she is Seth Tanner's wife. At the Denby circus, Ann'Liza says the elephant "ain't got no animation." Mrs. Tom Kew says Ann'Liza is the laziest person she knows.

TANNER, JOHN. In "The Green Bonnet," he is the Walsingham blacksmith. At sixteen he inherited the shop from his father, lives with his mother, is respected as "almost a man of genius," and is now twenty-four or -five. He sings at the Easter Sunday church service and likes Sarah McFarland, with or without a bonnet.

TANNER, MRS. In "The Green Bonnet," she is John Tanner's widowed mother. They make their home in Walsingham, across the street from the church and his blacksmith shop.

TANNER, SETH. In *Deephaven*, he is Ann'Liza Tanner's husband.

TARBELL. In "The Mate of the Daylight," he is the owner of a tavern Captain Peter Downs says he saw Captain Joseph Ryder visit for a "nipper."

TARROW, LADY. In "Jenny Garrow's Lovers," she is the aristocratic wife of Sir John Tarrow of Tarrow, England.

TARROW, SIR JOHN. In "Jenny Garrow's Lovers," he is the ruling aristocrat at Tarrow, England. One of his guests praised Jenny Garrow as "the fairest maid mine eyes have looked upon."

TASKER, MRS. In "The Parshley Celebration," she is the Reverend Mrs. Tasker's wife. The two participate in the Decoration Day march.

TASKER, THE REVEREND MR. In "The Parshley Celebration," he is the enthusiastic minister of the Parshley church. He and his wife participate in the Decoration Day march.

TAYLOR, THE REVEREND EDWARD. In "Miss Manning's Minister," he is the minister of the First Congregational church at Rinston, Connecticut. In his late forties, he came to Rinston following long service as a missionary in India. Soon after his arrival in Rinston, he suffers a severe stroke. Miss Narcissa Manning, who has admired him from the start, takes him into her home, cooks for and reads to him, and finds meaning for her life in doing so. After his partial recovery, Taylor accepts an assignment elsewhere but soon returns to Miss Manning, saying he cannot be happy without her. They get married.

TEABY. In "The Quest of Mr. Teaby," he is an odd-gaited, thin, tiny, helpful peddler of nostrums. Some call him Uncle Teaby. Never married, he half-proposes to Sister Hannah Jane Pinkham at the East Wilby railroad depot. Although Sister Pinkham says she likes Elder Fry, she seems to be inclining toward Teaby. Jewett was inspired to write "The Quest of Mr. Teaby" after seeing an essence peddler named Teaby at a rural depot platform. *Bibliography*: Fields, *Letters*.

TEMPLE, HENRY. In "The Hare and the Tortoise," he is the admirable but stolid and slow suitor for Mary Chester's hand in Boston. Henry loses out to the more dashing Richard Dean.

TEMPLE, MRS. In "The Hare and the Tortoise," she is Henry Temple's mother. The respectable, "not . . . brilliant" Mrs. Temple is from "a noble Salem family," and is friendly with Anne Duncan, Sophia Duncan, and Mary Chester. Mrs. Temple wants her son Henry to wed Mary.

TENNANT. In "Mr. Bruce," he is the father of Kitty Tennant and Miss Margaret Tennant. A Boston businessman, he and his wife have a dinner party for four men, including Philip Bruce. Kitty pretends to be a serving-maid at the party, which causes Tennant much laughter but almost fatally delays what becomes her love affair with and marriage to Bruce. Tennant's sister is Kate Hunter, Robert Hunter's wife.

TENNANT, KITTY. In "Mr. Bruce." *See* Bruce, Kitty.

TENNANT, MISS MARGARET. In *Deephaven*, she tells ghost stories when she visits Kate Lancaster and Helen Denis in Deephaven. In "Mr. Bruce,"

Margaret Tennant ("Maggie," Margie," "Meg") is the daughter of Boston businessman Tennant, the sister of Kitty Tennant (three years younger than Margaret), and the friend of Aunt Mary and Anne Langdon. Margaret, when fifty and living in her fine old Boston house, tells Mary and Anne the story of Kitty's rocky friendship with Philip Bruce, who finally marries her.

TENNANT, MRS. In "Mr. Bruce," she is the Boston businessman Tennant's wife and the mother of Kitty Tennant and Miss Margaret Tennant. When Mrs. Tennant's servants are temporarily unavailable, Kitty acts as the serving-maid at a dinner party; this delays Kitty's friendship with and marriage to Philip Bruce, one of the dinner guests.

TENNYSON, ALFRED, LORD (1809–1892). English poet. Born in Somersby and educated at Trinity College, Cambridge, Tennyson began publishing in 1827 but did not gain distinction until the 1830s. The two-volume 1842 edition of his poems contains much of his finest work. Tennyson succeeded William Wordsworth as poet laureate in 1850; married Emily Sellwood that year; and in 1854 established a residence with her at Farringford, on the Isle of Wight, where he continued to write steadily. James T. Fields, the husband of Annie Adams Fields,* had published Tennyson in the United States; the Fieldses occasionally visited Tennyson in England, beginning in 1859. In June 1892, Annie Fields and Jewett called at the home of the Tennysons at Farringford. The two visited the Tennysons again later that summer at their home in Surrey; on this occasion the poet, though frail and soon to die, recited some of his poetry, admired Jewett's Japanese crystal and silver lavaliere (a gift from Sarah Wyman Whitman*), and asked if she found story plots in its depths. Jewett regarded Tennyson as the greatest man she had ever seen. *Bibliography*: Blanchard; Cary, *Letters*; Silverthorne.

THACHER. In *A Country Doctor*, he was Adeline Thacher Prince's feisty, firm-minded great-grandfather.

THACHER, DANIEL ("DAN'L). In *A Country Doctor*, he was the father of Adeline Thacher Prince and John Thacher. Daniel was crippled in an accident while lumbering. His widow cares for Adeline's daughter, Nan Prince.

THACHER, JOHN. In *A Country Doctor*, he is Adeline Thacher Prince's brother, four years her senior. Soon after Adeline returns home and dies, he also dies.

THACHER, MRS. DANIEL. In *A Country Doctor*, she is Adeline Thacher Prince's mother and Nan Prince's grandmother. Mrs. Thacher cares for Nan until she is too old to do so, after which she happily lets Dr. John Leslie become the girl's guardian.

THAXTER, CELIA LAIGHTON (1835–1894). Writer. Born Celia Laighton in Portsmouth, New Hampshire, she was the daughter of Thomas B. Laighton and Eliza Rymes Laighton. Celia's father dealt in lumber and West Indies goods, edited the *New-Hampshire Gazette*, and was a state legislator. Failing to become governor of New Hampshire, he got himself appointed keeper of the Isles of Shoals lighthouse. In 1839 he moved with his family to White Island, where Celia and her two younger brothers were tutored by their parents, temporary visitors, and Levi Lincoln Thaxter, a bright, unstable Harvard graduate. In 1848 Laighton built a resort hotel, with Thaxter's help, on nearby Hog Island, which Laighton renamed Appledore Island. Summer visitors to the hotel included Ralph Waldo Emerson, Annie Adams Fields,* Childe Hassam (who painted several pictures of Celia's Appledore garden), Nathaniel Hawthorne, James Russell Lowell,* Herman Melville, Henry David Thoreau, Mark Twain,* and John Greenleaf Whittier.* Marrying in 1851, Celia and Thaxter had three sons. (One became a professor of botany at Harvard; another was mentally retarded.) In 1860 or so, the Thaxters moved to Newtonville, Massachusetts, and their marital troubles worsened. In 1861 Celia's "Land-Locked," a poem about homesickness for the sea, appeared in the *Atlantic Monthly*. Without her permission, it was published by Lowell, then the *Atlantic* editor. When her father died in 1866, Celia returned to Appledore to nurse her mother. After her mother's death in 1877, Celia attempted to communicate with her through formal séances. In 1880 Celia and her family moved to Kittery Point, Maine. In 1884 her husband died. Celia often contributed to periodicals; her best books include *Poems* (1871), *Among the Isles of Shoals* (1873, prose sketches), *Poems for Children* (1884), and *An Island Garden* (1894, prose sketches, illustrated by Hassam). Her works describe nature as beautiful but cruel, and her naturalistic philosophy is often bitter. Celia was an accomplished watercolorist and an avid gardener on Appledore. Sales of her poems and her paintings on china supported her family. After Celia died and was buried on Appledore, Annie Fields coedited *Letters of Celia Thaxter* (1895).

Jewett and Celia were close friends. Jewett affectionately called her "Sandpiper," while she called Jewett "Owl" and "Owlet." Jewett appreciated Celia's horticultural efforts and sympathized with her beliefs in spiritualism. Much of the descriptive power Jewett displays in *The Country of the Pointed Firs* is owing to her being shown around the Isles of Shoals by Celia. Jewett's "The Foreigner" echoes Celia's belief that she communicated with her deceased mother's spirit. The title, if nothing else, of Jewett's "A Landlocked Sailor" echoes Celia's "Land-Locked." Jewett edited Celia's *Poems* (1896). *Bibliography*: David Park Curry, *Childe Hassam: An Island Garden Revisited* (Denver Art Museum and W. W. Norton, 1990); Oscar Laighton, *Ninety Years at the Isles of Shoals* (Andover, Mass.: Andover Press, 1929); Rosamond Thaxter, *The Life and Letters of Celia Thaxter* (Francestown, N.H.: Marshall Jones, 1963); Perry D. Westbrook, *Acres of Flint: Writers of Rural New England, 1870–1900* (Washington, D.C.: Scarecrow Press, 1951).

THOMAS. In "The New Methuselah," he is the sleepy little orphan adopted by Dr. Asa Potterby, who wants to experiment on him so as to enable Thomas to live at least to age 150. But Thomas, at nineteen months, eats a hard green apple and dies. Otherwise, he might have become "the new Methuselah."

THOMAS. In "A Second Spring," he is a clumsy lad who briefly helps Israel Haydon with farm work but is notable mainly for his huge appetite.

THOMAS, MARILLA. In *A Country Doctor*, she is Dr. John Leslie's officious, complaining, but essentially kind housekeeper.

THOMAS, MISS. In "The Becket Girls' Tree," she was the Sunday School teacher who briefly substituted for Ann Donnell, whom Jess Parsons and John Parsons preferred, and from whom they learned more. Miss Thomas later sends each of the two children a book as a Christmas present.

THOMPSON, BENJAMIN ("BEN"). In *The Tory Lover*, he is said to have been unfairly driven from Rumford, without his family, to seek Tory protection. He is described by Dickson as toadying to the Wentworths.

THOMPSON, MRS. In "Andrew's Fortune," she is mentioned as one who will help with arrangements, as will Mrs. Ash, following Mrs. Towner's sudden death.

THOMSON, MRS. In "The Girl with the Cannon Dresses," she is mentioned as Mrs. Bunt's friend. Mrs. Thomson lives at the Corners. Dulcidora Bunt dislikes sewing and therefore "hate[s]" Mrs. Thomson when she asks pointedly about the progress of her needlework.

THORNDIKE, ABEL. In "A Village Patriot," he is an old, widowered carpenter. On the Fourth of July, he reads a chapter of a biography of George Washington and sets off fireworks, to the delight of spectators, including his daughter, Phebe Thorndike, and her boyfriend, Charley Burrill, who works with Abel Thorndike and boards with the Thorndikes.

THORNDIKE, PHEBE. In "A Village Patriot," she is Abel Thorndike's daughter and the girlfriend of Charley Burrill, who works with her father and boards with both Thorndikes.

THORNE, BESSIE. In "Miss Sydney's Flowers," she is a young woman who observes Miss Sydney, pities her for her loneliness, visits her, and is graciously welcomed. When Jack, Bessie's uncle, tells her about a job opening in a museum, she tells Miss Sydney about it, whereupon Miss Sydney recommends Becky Marley.

THORNE, MRS. In "Miss Sydney's Flowers," she is a former acquaintance of Miss Sydney, but the two have drifted apart. Mrs. Thorne encourages her daughter, Bessie, to call on Miss Sydney.

THORNIFORD, MRS. In *Deephaven*, she is Kate Lancaster'a aunt. She visits Kate and Helen Denis by yacht at Deephaven.

THORNTON. In "Mr. Bruce," he is a widowered Baltimore businessman. His daughter, Miss Alice Thornton, invites Kitty Tennant to be a guest. During her stay, Kitty encounters Philip Bruce at a whist party in the Thornton home. She does not recognize him, although she saw him earlier in Boston.

THORNTON. In *The Tory Lover*, he is a confederate of Dickson, who rendezvoused with him at Nantes. Thornton is a spy for Arthur Lee.

THORNTON, GENERAL. In "The Flight of Betsey Lane," he was a man in whose home Betsey Lane was a loyal worker.

THORNTON, MISS ALICE. In "Mr. Bruce," she is a fellow student with Kitty Tennant at Madame Riché's Boston finishing school. Later, Alice invites Kitty to be a guest in the Baltimore home she manages for her widowered father. While there, Kitty encounters Philip Bruce again.

THORNTON, MRS. In "The Flight of Betsey Lane," she was the grandmother of Katy Strafford, who calls Betsey Lane "her gran'ma's right hand." Katy Strafford, while on a visit home from her residence in London, calls on Betsey at the Byfleet Poor-house and in gratitude gives her $100. Betsey spends it on a visit to the Centennial in Philadelphia.

TIGER. In "A Born Farmer," he is the "little old" dog belonging to Jacob Gaines. Tiger goes to Boston with Gaines and his family and returns with them to their farmhome on Pine Hills.

TIGER. In "The Coon Dog," it is the coon dog bequeathed by Abijah Topliff to his wife, 'Liza Jane Topliff. She and her mother, Mrs. Price, regard Tiger as worth at least $50. Isaac Brown and John York rent Tiger for 50¢, but during the coon hunt it is not Tiger but Rover, Brown's old coon dog, that trees the coon. Mrs. Price still hopes to sell Tiger for a good sum.

TIGHE. In "Decoration Day," he is Martin Tighe's older son. The young man is useful on the family farm.

TIGHE. In "Decoration Day," he is Martin Tighe's younger son. The lad plays the fife during the veterans' parade.

TIGHE, JOHN. In "Decoration Day," he was a Civil War veteran, now deceased. The veterans decorate his pauper's grave during the parade.

TIGHE, MARTIN. In "Decoration Day," he is a Civil War veteran, with a left hand crippled by a war wound. He lives in Barlow Plains, has been criticized by the citizens for needing town charity, but is cheered when he rides on a wagon during the veterans' parade.

TILLEY. In "A White Heron," he was the husband, now deceased, of Mrs. Tilley and the father of their son, Dan Tilley, and their daughter, who was Sylvia's mother, and four other children. Mrs. Tilley tells the ornithologist that her husband and her son "didn't hitch" and that after they had argued and the son had left, the father "never held up his head ag'in."

TILLEY, ALVA. In *The Country of the Pointed Firs*, she is a person whose folks are going to the Bowden reunion.

TILLEY, CAPTAIN ELIJAH (" 'LIJAH"). In *The Country of the Pointed Firs*, he is an old sailor, whose wife, Sarah, has been dead almost eight years. He dreadfully misses his "poor dear," with whom he had a miraculously tender marriage. He fishes, knits well, and mends fish nets. The narrator visits his tidy little house and sympathetically responds to his reminiscences. Almira Todd, whom he has known since childhood, strangely calls him "plodding." In "The Foreigner," Elijah Tilley told the narrator that Johnny Bowden and Jonathan Bowden were safe on Green Island the night of the storm. She relayed the news to Almira Todd. In "William's Wedding," Elijah Tilley is mentioned by the narrator as someone she would like to visit. Tilley is modeled closely on Dan Butland, an old sailor Jewett met on the beach at Wells, Maine, in June 1885. *Bibliography*: Blanchard; Silverthorne.

TILLEY, DAN. In "A White Heron," he is or was Mrs. Tilley's son. Dan argued with his father, went to California, "was no hand to write letters," and is now perhaps dead.

TILLEY, MRS. In "A White Heron," she is a kind old woman, of limited means but hospitable. She is the widowed grandmother of Sylvia, whom she has informally adopted and who loves life on her farm near the woods. Sylvia's mother is perhaps the only living child Mrs. Tilley has left. She tells the ornithologist that she "buried four children."

TILLEY, SARAH. In *The Country of the Pointed Firs*, she was Elijah Tilley's evidently sweet and caring wife. She was a tidy homemaker, and at her death almost eight years ago he was "sore stricken." Almira Todd remembers Sarah as a unique friend.

TIMMS, CAPTAIN ("CAP'N"). In "The Guests of Mrs. Timms," he is the deceased husband of the insincere Mrs. Timms.

TIMMS, JOHN. In "The Honey Tree," he is an old Hillborough man. John Timms is so deaf that at the gathering in the store of Joel Simmons, John Wells has to shout news of the honey tree into his ear.

TIMMS, MRS. In "The Guests of Mrs. Timms," she is the well-to-do widow of Captain Timms of Longport. She inherited a house in Baxter from her aunt, a woman named Bascoms. While at a county conference, Mrs. Timms saw Mrs. Persis Flagg, a former resident of Longport now living in Woodville. She invited Mrs. Flagg to visit her in Baxter, and to bring along her friend, Miss Cynthia Pickett. But when the two "guests" arrive unexpectedly, Mrs. Timms rebuffs them with scant, insincere, and tardy hospitality.

TITCOMB. In *The Tory Lover*, he is an inmate of the Mill Prison, taken recently off an American man-of-war.

TOBIAS. In *Deephaven*, he was Captain Sands's uncle, with whom Sands's grandfather once lived. His wife may be named Melinda.

TOBIN. In "A Winter Courtship," he was Fanny Tobin's husband, now deceased, and the father of Adeline and Susan Ellen. Mrs. Tobin boasts of his handiness with his fists to encourage Jefferson Briley to contend that he too could raise his fists in a good cause.

TOBIN, FANNY. In "A Winter Courtship," she is an elderly widow and the mother of Adeline and Susan Ellen. Mrs. Tobin plans to visit Susan Ellen for a while. On the road in the wagon of Jefferson Briley, who carries mail and passengers between Sanscrit Pond and North Kilby, Mrs. Tobin by flattery, coy hesitations, and "an amiable simper" maneuvers "Jeff'son" into a proposal, silently wondering all the while how much money he has saved. Since she lives in a lonely farmhouse and he is a homeless old bachelor, their agreed-on marriage is more for comfort and economy than for passion. *Bibliography*: Roman.

TOBY. In *Betty Leicester's English Xmas*, he is Betty Leicester's new dog, in London.

TODD. In *The Country of the Pointed Firs*, he was the father of Joanna Todd and Edward Todd. He owned Shell-heap Island, built a house on its thirty acres, dug clams there, and sold them profitably in Portland.

TODD, ALMIRA ("ALMIRY"). In *The Country of the Pointed Firs*, she is the narrator's quietly hospitable hostess. She was born on Green Island. Her mother is Mrs. Blackett, and her brother is William Blackett. Now sixty-seven, she expertly collects and dispenses herbs. She is described as massive, statuesque, sibylline. She is profoundly, though quietly, emotional. She tells the narrator she loved elsewhere but married Nathan Todd, now deceased. They had no children. Almira and the narrator share much in conversation and by going places together. In "The Queen's Twin," Almira takes the narrator to meet Abby Martin, who regards herself as Queen Victoria's "twin." In "The Dunnet Shepherdess," Almira smears her brother William Blackett's face with an herbal mixture to ward off mosquitoes before he goes trout fishing. In "The Foreigner," Almira tells our narrator the story of Captain John Tolland's French wife. Almira reluctantly befriended the foreign woman in Dunnet Landing, was with her as she lay dying, and saw as she did the ghost of the dying woman's mother. In "William's Wedding," Almira greets the visiting narrator testily but soon warms up and is quietly delighted when William marries Esther Hight. Almira serves the newlyweds cakes and wine. In appearance and behavior, Almira is partly based on Rosilla Bachelder, who lived in Martinsville, Maine, and whom Jewett and Annie Adams Fields* met when they vacationed there for a month in 1895. *Bibliography*: Blanchard.

TODD, EDWARD. In *The Country of the Pointed Firs*, he is Almira Todd's cousin and Joanna Todd's married brother. When she was tragically jilted, Joanna turned over her half of their farm to him. He reluctantly accepted the gift and was always kind to her.

TODD, JOANNA. In *The Country of the Pointed Firs*, she was Almira Todd's cousin by marriage and a little older than Almira. When Joanna was tragically "crossed in love," she gave her brother, Edward Todd, her half of the house they owned and became a hermit on Shell-heap Island. She felt she had committed an unpardonable sin, part of which was being briefly wrathful toward God. On the island she lived in a house her father had built; she farmed and fished, was aided by sad friends with little gifts, but died and was buried on her island twenty-two years earlier.

TODD, MRS. In *The Country of the Pointed Firs*, she was the mother of Joanna Todd and Edward Todd. She had a "grim streak," according to Almira Todd, and never knew how to be happy. In her sorrow, Joanna began to resemble her mother.

TODD, MRS. EDWARD In *The Country of the Pointed Firs*, she was the decent wife of Joanna Todd's brother and tried to persuade Joanna not to give him her half of their farm.

TODD, NATHAN. In *The Country of the Pointed Firs*, he was Almira Todd's seafaring husband. She let him know that she had loved someone else, but she was mutedly happy with him. He brought a pin from the Mediterranean region for his cousin, Joanna Todd. He drowned between the Squaw Islands.

TOGGERSON. In *Deephaven. See* Jim, Widow.

TOGGERSON, JIM. In *Deephaven*, he successfully fishes with Skipper Scudder.

TOGGERSON, JOSEPH. In *Deephaven*, he was Widow Jim's grandfather.

"TOLD IN THE TAVERN" (1894). Short story. (Characters: John Bean, John Dimmock, Capt. Asa Fitch, Mrs. Fitch, Timothy Hall, Jackson, Parkins, Sands, Abby Sands, Mrs. Sands.) A stranger gets off the last train into Byfleet one chilly spring night. He goes to the village cemetery, looks around for some tombstones, and sees one with his own name on it! Meanwhile, several men are chatting by the fire at Timothy Hall's tavern. Some cattle drovers and a well-dressed stranger enter. Gossip turns to the subject of Abby Sands, Byfleet's much-praised gardener. She was engaged to a controversial fellow named Parkins, who combined ambition and conceit, they say. At the start of the Civil War he went west, maybe got into mining, and perhaps was killed by Indians. He wrote Abby for a while, but then his letters stopped. Did her mother, long widowed and disliking Parkins, intercept them? Anyway, Abby spent $67 on a headstone for him and planted flowers around it. When the talk breaks up and the men either leave or nap, the stranger identifies himself as Parkins, says he has heard both truth and lies this night, was driven far away and made lonely by the fault of others, has money now, and will return to the lonely Abby and make her happy.

TOLLAND. In "The Foreigner," he is a young sailor from Dunnet Landing whose good name is enough to recommend him to Boston shippers.

TOLLAND, CAPTAIN JOHN. In "The Foreigner," he was a sea captain who helped rescue a French singer and dancer in Kingston, Jamaica, took her to Portland, married her, and lived with her in Dunnet Landing. Later he was lost at sea in the Straits of Malacca.

TOLLAND, ELIZA. In "The Foreigner," she was John Tolland's sister, who inherited and shared a family home with him. When she could not get along with his wife, he bought her out, and she moved away. Eliza did not attend Mrs. Tolland's funeral.

TOLLAND, ELLEN. In "The Foreigner," she is mentioned by Almira Todd as her mother Mrs. Blackett's close friend, long dead and still mourned.

TOLLAND, MRS. In "The Foreigner," she is mentioned as Captain John Tolland's deceased mother. She left many chairs in her best room, which John's widow did not rearrange.

TOLLAND, MRS. JOHN. In "The Foreigner," she was the foreign woman, born in France. Her first husband, perhaps Portuguese, and their children died of yellow fever in Kingston, Jamaica, after which she sang and danced for tips before rowdy men. Captain John Tolland helped rescue her in Jamaica and then married her. They lived in Dunnet Landing until he was lost at sea. She was never fully accepted by the townspeople, because she spoke mostly French and was Catholic. Reluctant at first, Almira Todd befriended Mrs. Tolland, who taught her much about herbs and cooking and at whose deathbed both women saw the foreigner's mother's spirit. In one of her most arresting images, Jewett has Almira depict the foreign woman's "fixed smile, that wa'n't a smile; there wa'n't no light behind it, same's a lamp can't shine if it ain't lit." She is sometimes called "Mis' Cap'n Tolland."

TOM. In "The Orchard's Grandmother," he is mentioned as Mary ("Polly") Brenton's favorite cousin. After his visit, Polly misses him "sadly."

"TOM'S HUSBAND" (1882). Short story. (Characters: Alice Wilson Ashton, Captain Ashton, Catherine, Dunn, Jackson, Susan, Jack Towne, Mary Dunn Wilson, Mrs. Wilson, Tom Wilson.) Tom Wilson, after a blissful enough engagement to Mary Dunn, marries her. Slight troubles soon start. His widowered father, once rich, married an asthmatic woman, died, and left his idle textile mill in financial disarray. Tom's stepmother, Mrs. Wilson, moved to Philadelphia and left him the family house. Tom's sister, Alice Wilson Ashton, the wife of Captain Ashton, an officer in the navy, is with her husband and their two sons in Nagasaki, Japan. Alice entertains a good deal and complains of insufficient funds from the family estate. Tom, having left college during his junior year because of weak eyesight, is now an idler who collects old coins. Since Mary dislikes housework and Tom enjoys supervising their servants, she proposes that he manage the house and she reopen the mill and try to turn a profit. Instead of arguing, Tom agrees with a sincere laugh. With the help of old mill hands, Mary does so well that after three years the company pays substantial dividends, their share of which pleases the faraway Ashtons. Gradually, Mary becomes absorbed in her successful commercial venture and indifferent to Tom, who begins to sink into a feeling of uselessness. He suddenly realizes that many women must feel similarly bypassed by life. His stepmother, Mrs. Wilson, visits one dim November day and commends him for being an excellent housekeeper. This causes Tom to snap; he rebels against boredom and frustration, and practically orders Mary to let others run the mill and to vacation with him for six months in Europe. A look on his normally calm face makes her acquiesce.

The combination of Tom's initially jocular passivity and Mary's steady commercial success makes her unprepared-for final surrender seem more farcical than serious. But when reread, "Tom's Husband" is seen to reflect Jewett's combined discontent with the traditional "contracted sphere of women," as she phrases it here, and criticism of flaccid men in the New England of her time. Jewett includes remarks about Irishmen moving west and being replaced by French-Canadian factory laborers in New England. Lynn and Boston are mentioned as cities near the action. "Tom's Husband" anticipates Dorothy Canfield Fisher's novel *The Home-Maker* (1924), in which a wife who hates housework embarks on a successful career while her husband, hurt in an accident, happily does the chores at home. *Bibliography*: Cary, *Jewett*; Thomas A. Maik, "Reclaiming Paradise: Role Reversal as Liberation in Sarah Orne Jewett's 'Tom's Husband,' " *Legacy* 7 (Spring 1990): 223–37; Roman; Judith Roman, "A Closer Look at the Jewett-Fields Relationship," in Nagel, pp. 119–34; Silverthorne.

TOMSON, PARSON. In *The Tory Lover*, he is a guest at Colonel Jonathan Hamilton's dinner party. Tomson attended Harvard.

TOPHAM. In *The Country of the Pointed Firs*, this is the name of the aunt of Almira Todd, who stayed inland with the older woman to go to school.

TOPLIFF, ABIJAH (" 'BIJAH"). In "The Coon Dog," he is 'Liza Jane Topliff's husband. Evidently estranged from her, he died in Connecticut and left her his allegedly fine coon dog, Tiger.

TOPLIFF, CAPTAIN. In "The Taking of Captain Ball," he was the husband of Mrs. Captain Topliff, now widowed. Although she remembers him as "pleasant-tempered," others call him "most trying."

TOPLIFF, 'LIZA JANE (" 'LIZY"). In "The Coon Dog," she is the recently widowed farm wife of Abijah Topliff, whose supposedly valuable coon dog, Tiger, she inherits. She and her mother rent Tiger to Isaac Brown and John York for 50¢. Even after the dog proves worthless, the ignorant women still hope to sell it for a good sum.

TOPLIFF, MRS. In "Law Lane," she injured herself in a fall and died the following day. When Jane Barnet asks Mrs. Harriet Powder if Jane's fall is equally serious, Mrs. Powder pretends it is, to get Jane to repent and end the land dispute before she dies.

TOPLIFF, MRS. CAPTAIN. In "The Taking of Captain Ball," she is Captain Topliff's widow, who remembers him as "pleasant-tempered." She gossips with Miss Miranda Hull about Mrs. Ann French.

TORBY. In "Mary and Martha," he is a merchant in the village in whose shop Martha Dean and Mary Dean can sell their nicely sewn products.

TORBY, DEACON. In "All My Sad Captains," he is a Longport church functionary who learns that the Reverend Mr. Farley will be the new minister.

THE TORY LOVER (1900–1901). Novel. (Characters: John Adams, Samuel Adams, Ajax, Apollo, Praise-God Barebones, Barrington, Abbé de Beaumont, Betsey, Blunt, Duke de Boufflers, Boutineau, Caesar, Judge Chadbourne, the Duchess of Chartres, the Duke of Chartres, James Chase, Le Ray de Chaumont, Cooper, Cuffee, Sam Curwen, Lord Darwentwater, John Davis, Mrs. John Davis, Deane, Delane, Dickson, Mrs. Dickson, John Dougall, Johnny Downes, Duke, Earl, William Earl, Lord Mount Edgecumbe, George Fairfax, Mrs. George Fairfax, Falls, Faneuil, Joseph Fernald, Ford, Benjamin Franklin, Gardner, Nicholas Gilman, General Goodwin, Hetty Goodwin, Lord Gormanstown, Grant, Thankful Grant, Gray, Dr. Ezra Green, Grosvenor, Hackett, Major Tilly Haggens, Nancy Haggens, Lieutenant Hall, Colonel Jonathan Hamilton, Mary Hamilton, Hammet, John Hancock, Hanscom, David Hartley, Charles Herbert, Hertel, Hight, Hill, Hill, Martha Hill, Hodgdon, Humphrey Hodgdon, Phebe Hodgdon, Howth, Solomon Hutchings, Governor Thomas Hutchinson, Jack, Jenkins, Captain John Paul Jones, Keay, Kersainte, Hate-Evil Kilgore, Major John Langdon, Arthur Lee, Lejay, Lightfoot, Lord, Billy Lord, Cato Lord, Humphry Lord, Ichabod Lord, John Lord, Nathan Lord, Lyman, Jean MacDuff, McIntire, John Marr, Matthew, Moody, Robert Morris, Captain Moulton, Mrs. Mullet, Nancy, Hannah Neal, Lord Newburgh, Paul, Peggy, Pepperrell, Peter, Philpot, Phoebe, Parson Pike, La Mot Piqué, Plaisted, Charles Radcliffe, Corporal John Ricker, Rodney, Rogers, Rollins, Russell, Sargent, Sayward, the Countess of Selkirk, Lord Selkirk, Sewall, Elder Shackley, Sherburne, Sherburne, First Lieutenant Simpson, Jack Simpson, Spencer, Simon Staples, Starbuck, Sullivan, Eben Sullivan, General John Sullivan, James Sullivan, Margery Sullivan, Susan, Benjamin Thompson, Thornton, Titcomb, Parson Tomson, Trimlestown, Judge Wallingford, Madam Wallingford, Roger Wallingford, Warner, Gideon Warren, Hitty Warren, Wentworth, Wyat, Elizabeth Wyat, William Young.)

On 31 October 1777, Colonel Jonathan Hamilton and his sister, Mary Hamilton, welcome dinner guests to his Berwick home, including the pro-British Judge Chadbourne and the fiery Captain John Paul Jones, whose *Ranger* is docked nearby. They talk about the war, troops, money, loyalty, and Tories. Mary chats with Elizabeth Wyat, who says a mob suspects Roger Wallingford, Mary's close friend, of being a Tory sympathizer, and will demand his vow of rebellion or burn down his mother Madam Wallingford's mansion. In the garden, Roger tells Mary he has a commission to sail with Jones; however, Jones may doubt his patriotism and refuse him. After they part, Mary dances with Jones, who is falling in love with her; but she asks him to accept Roger. Jones agrees, mainly to keep the rascal away from her. Given a ring from her in gratitude, Jones assembles his crew and sets sail for Portsmouth.

Next morning, Roger reports to Jones and is insulted by him as they start for France. Jonathan visits Major Tilly Haggens and his sister, Nancy Haggens; they worry about events. At Berwick, Mary cheers up Jonathan, learns that Roger's lonely, pro-Tory mother is heartbroken, and next afternoon goes upriver to the Wallingford home to comfort her. Aboard the *Ranger* a group of sailors gossip, joke, and argue, after which an officer named Dickson, formerly dishonest in business against the Wallingfords, goes to the ship's loyal surgeon, Dr. Ezra Green, to fret about Jones. Near the French coast, Jones entertains Roger in his cabin. Speaking frankly, they agree that Dickson, who wants to seize British vessels for quick profit, would like First Lieutenant Simpson to supplant Jones. Roger pledges loyalty to the cause but suddenly sees Mary's ring on his rival's hand. The *Ranger* seizes two British prize vessels, and Roger tosses overboard letters he planned to send home. One December day, Mary visits Sullivan, her old teacher; they discuss the war, and he reminisces about his rebellious student days in France and comments on Roger and Jones. The *Ranger* casts anchor at Nantes. To his face, Roger threatens to kill Dickson for gossiping against Jones, who goes to Paris only to be denied by the American commissioners a command of *L'Indien*, as promised. When he returns, he orders Roger to explain his obvious misery and, when answered, says Mary's ring was only for friendship. Roger, delighted, accompanies Jones to confer with canny Benjamin Franklin at Passy, outside Paris. Franklin listens to Jones's hope for patriotic action, asks Roger about his mother, and gives him letters from her and from Mary.

Weeks pass. At Quiberon Jones fires a salute from the *Ranger* to a French frigate and is saluted in return. The *Ranger* leaves Brest on 10 April 1778 and sneaks into Whitehaven; members of Jones's crew burn several British ships. Since someone—later proved to have been Dickson—tampered with the fire-providing candles, damage is minimal. Roger does not return from the town, and Dickson says Roger alerted the town and then remained behind. Jones mistrusts Dickson but has no contrary evidence. In truth, Roger saw Dickson rush into the town allegedly to reconnoiter; Roger followed and caught him alerting the enemy but was stabbed by him. Roger is taken to the Mill Prison near Plymouth.

At the Hamilton mansion in May, Phebe Hodgdon is supervising some spinning by fellow servants when news comes of casualties and the capture and treachery of Roger. Mary shouts that the report is an insulting lie and in the evening visits Madam Wallingford to help her. A mob arrives, intent on forcing her out and sacking the place; but Chadbourne, Haggens, and other friends drive the gang away. In the morning, Chadbourne fails to persuade Madam Wallingford to sign a loyalty oath. Instead, the old woman, carrying secret letters from old Sullivan, sets sail for Bristol on a vessel she owns. She is accompanied by

Mary. At sea for some weeks, they talk about old times in "Barvick," disagree about politics, but comfort each other. Meanwhile, Roger meets up with friends from Berwick, among other Americans, at the Mill Prison.

Madam Wallingford and Mary are welcomed in Bristol by the old lady's cousin, Mrs. John Davis, wife of an anti-American merchant and alderman. Davis debates politics with Mary, admires her spunk and beauty, and next morning goes by horseback with her to Bath to meet George Fairfax, a Virginia tobacco merchant, and through him Lord Newburgh—to whom Mary delivers a letter from Sullivan. It concerns secret material about Newburgh's father, who was Charles Radcliffe, and about Charles's brother, Lord Darwentwater. Newburgh gets influential Lord Mount Edgecumbe to order the Mill Prison governor to release Roger. But when Mary and Davis arrive there, they learn that Roger has escaped but may have been shot. Some time after they return to Bristol, Mary is pining away at the abbey church one summer day when Captain Jones, disguised as a Spanish sailor, enters and is astonished to see her. He tells her he is on some errands while his *Ranger* is at Brest, learns details of Mary's actions, and says Roger was a spy and Dickson proved it. She persuades him of Dickson's villainy and fears her beloved Roger may now be dead on the moors. That night Jones whispers beneath Mary's window to go to the Old Passage Inn outside Bristol next night for news he has just learned concerning Roger. She and Davis report there. Roger, who has worked for a farmer in the region, also arrives, secretly. So does Jones, who has deceived Dickson into thinking Dickson can sell some battle plans from the *Ranger* to certain men at the inn. Dickson gets drunk, betrays himself, and is taken away by Jones's men. Roger embraces Mary. In October, the pair, with his hearty old mother, sail to Berwick for a glorious wedding.

The Tory Lover was largely an ambitious, even lovable, mistake from the beginning. In 1894 Jewett first thought of writing a melodramatic historical novel featuring Captain John Paul Jones, was encouraged to turn to it in earnest by Horace Scudder* and Charles Dudley Warner,* and worked steadily on it for more than a year. The publication of *Hugh Wynne: Free Quaker* (1897), a fine American Revolutionary War novel, also helped motivate Jewett. Its author was S. Weir Mitchell, the distinguished but controversial Philadelphia physician-novelist whom she knew and informally consulted concerning her ailments. Jewett had almost no ability to write a big historical novel. Few of the more than 150 characters seem real. Jones visited Berwick, and his *Ranger* was built on an island in the Piscataqua River, to be sure; but almost nothing is made of this fact nor of Jones's professional activities in the immediate region. Dickson should have been hanged but never gets his comeuppance. Old Sullivan, the master-teacher, is a Hawthornean bookworm in a cloud of dead reminiscence; his wife, however, is engagingly peppy. Jewett's style is wooden, her diction often falsely archaic. Her "not un-" usage is ludicrous, as, for example, when she has Jones tell Mary, "I was not unknown in Bristol." Jewett's metaphors and similes are vapid, with one exception: When caught, Dickson's "face was like a handful of dirty wool." The best thing about *The Tory Lover* is Jewett's depiction of Berwick.

Jewett follows history when she pleases but takes several permissible liberties. Some of Jones's recruits from Berwick are accurately named, and his first mate was a real scoundrel named Dickson. In real life, Nicholas Gilman* was Jewett's great-great-grandfather and had a son also named Nicholas, while Charlotte Gilman, Jewett's great-great-aunt, married Jonathan Hamilton. Jewett's Judge Chadbourne is based on Judge Benjamin Chadbourne, a York jurist who saved from a mob the Tory great-grandfather of Elizabeth and Mary Barrell, elderly York spinsters Jewett knew. A Hetty Goodwin was really abducted by Indians. Tilly Haggens is based on John Haggins (or Higgins), who in 1774 built and first occupied what became the Jewett house in South Berwick. Mary Hamilton was real-life Colonel Jonathan Hamilton's first wife and not his sister. Hamilton House, now a South Berwick preserved antiquity, was built in 1787–1788. Roger Plaisted was killed with his sons by Indians in 1675, and Elizabeth Wiatt died, at age eighteen, in 1713; Jewett saw both names in the Wallingford family cemetery in Berwick. The teacher Sullivan was based on real-life John Sullivan, an Irish scholar exiled as a Jacobite to France; he migrated to York, Maine Territory, about 1723, married an Irish peasant, moved to Berwick, and became a teacher and father of a general and a jurist. The loyalty to the colonies of real-life Benjamin Thompson was irrationally questioned, and he was driven to England, where he became Count Rumford; Jewett's characterization of Roger Wallingford's political vacillation is based on Thompson's perplexity, and she wrote an essay (now lost) on his wife, Countess Rumford. Parson Tomson is modeled on Parson John Thompson, who, however, did not preach in Berwick until 1783. Lieutenant Roger Wallingford aboard Jones's *Ranger* was really Samuel Richard Wallingford, who died at sea.

The Tory Lover sold well, was reprinted four times in three months, and remains Jewett's most popular work. It was translated into French by H. Doüesnel as *Le Roman d'Un Loyaliste* (1905). However, it was criticized by several friends, most notably by Henry James,* whose letter to Jewett (5 October 1901) begins with "the mere twaddle of graciousness," includes criticism of her "misguided" and even " 'cheap' " attempt to depict bygone consciousnesses, and ends by urging Jewett to return to familiar subjects treated so well in *The Country of the Pointed Firs*. *Bibliography*: Blanchard; Rebecca Wall Nail, " 'Where Every Prospect Pleases': Sarah Orne Jewett, South Berwick, and the Importance of Place," in Nagel, pp. 185–98; Silverthorne; Thorp.

TOWNE, JACK. In "Tom's Husband," he is the former mill supervisor of Tom Wilson's deceased father. Although Towne is retired, married, and financially secure, Mary Dunn Wilson rehires him and values his assistance.

TOWNER, MRS. In "Andrew's Fortune," she is an old, weak-sighted neighbor who helps Betsey Morris tidy up Stephen Dennett's home after he dies. She puts his will in a book resembling the Bible, out of which it accidentally fell. Her sudden death frustrates the attempts of others to locate the will. Mrs. Towner is said to own a wood lot on Kimball's tract.

"THE TOWN POOR" (1890). Short story. (Characters: Miss Ann Bray, Deacon Bray, Mandana Bray, Ellen, Janes, Abel Janes, Mrs. Abel Janes, the Reverend Daniel Longbrother, William Trimble, Mrs. William Trimble, Asa Wright, Miss Rebecca Wright.) The widowed Mrs. William Trimble, who has a comfortable farm, and her friend, Miss Rebecca Wright, are returning to Hampton by wagon from a church installation. They decide to visit Miss Ann Bray and her younger sister, Mandana ("Mandy") Bray, both so impoverished since the death of their father, Deacon Bray, that the town selectmen have auctioned their possessions and paid Abel Janes and his wife $5 a month to give them room and board. Mrs. Janes opens her chilly house to the visitors and lets them go upstairs to see the Bray sisters. Their parched existence in a miserably cramped back room—the two serve their guests leftover tea—so moves Mrs. Trimble that she vows to speak to the selectmen and arrange finances to enable the pair to return to their own house.

Auctioning off poor people, who would be sent to the lowest bidder, was evidently practiced in South Berwick in the time of Jewett, who felt it was better to do so, or to send the indigent to town-financed farms, than to warehouse them in county farms. *Bibliography*: Blanchard.

TOWNSEND, JACK. In "A Landless Farmer," he lives in Harlow's Mills and is a customer of Ezra Allen, who invites Jerry Jenkins to wagon over with him to see Townsend.

TREMLETT. In "The Passing of Sister Barsett," this is the name of a family Sarah Ellen Dow says she sat with at church.

TREVOR, LIZZIE. In "Miss Tempy's Watchers," she is a teacher Temperance ("Tempy") Dent quietly helped. Lizzie "taught [at] the Corners school," repaid her student loans, and though seriously fatigued was too poor to rest by visiting "Niagary Falls" and then an uncle in Chicago. Tempy gave her $60 to do so. Lizzie later married well in upstate New York

TRILBY, MRS. In "A Visit Next Door," she is a poor woman living with her family across the street from Mrs. Filmore and Mrs. Granger. Jewett's 1884 use of the unusual name "Trilby" preceded the publication in 1894 of *Trilby* by George du Maurier,* whom Jewett met in 1892.

TRIMBLE, MRS. WILLIAM. In "The Town Poor," she is William Trimble's widow. She now runs the farm, is active in business, and is generous—and more capable than her husband ever was. After visiting poor Miss Ann Bray and her sister, Mandana Bray, Mrs. Trimble vows to mitigate their plight.

TRIMBLE, WILLIAM. In "The Town Poor," he is Mrs. William Trimble's deceased husband.

TRIMLESTOWN, LORD. In *The Tory Lover*, he was a well-dressed aristocrat the teacher Sullivan remembers seeing in Dublin.

TUFTS, WASHINGTON. In "A Landless Farmer," he is a farmhand who wagons Jerry Jenkins from Serena Nudd's house to Mary Lydia Bryan's house.

TULLY, WIDOW. In *Deephaven*, she has been Captain Manning's respected housekeeper for forty years. In reality she may never have been married and may have been a Connecticut toll-bridge keeper.

TURNER, SALLY. In *A Country Doctor*, she is a person Susan Martin makes silk bonnets for. Miss Betsy Milman also wears Susan's bonnets. Dr. John Leslie says Betsy and Sally mend his clothes. The two may be sisters.

TUTTLE, CAPTAIN. In *The Country of the Pointed Firs*, he was a sea captain who, according to Littlepage, knew a great deal about bees.

TWAIN, MARK (1835–1910). Author. Born Samuel Langhorne Clemens in Florida, Missouri, he moved in 1839 with his family to Hannibal, Missouri, and grew up on the banks of his beloved Mississippi River. After a varied boyhood and youth—as a printer's apprentice, a steamboat pilot, and a journalist—he gained fame as the author of "The Celebrated Jumping Frog of Calaveras County" (1865). He followed with *The Innocents Abroad* (1869) about his tour of the Holy Land and adjacent regions, married Olivia Langdon (1870), and added to his popularity with the regionalist classic, *Roughing It* (1872). He coauthored *The Gilded Age: A Tale of To-Day* (1873) with Charles Dudley Warner.* Following in quick succession were *The Adventures of Tom Sawyer* (1876), *The Prince and the Pauper* (1882), the nostalgic *Life on the Mississippi* (1883), *Adventures of Huckleberry Finn* (1884), and *A Connecticut Yankee in King Arthur's Court* (1889). In the 1890s and later, Twain's bitterness, always evident in his savagely satirical thrusts, became more open and pervasive. An investment in an unsuccessful typesetting machine drove him to near-bankruptcy, he went on a rollicking but enervating lecture tour around the world, and the first of multiple deaths struck his family. Ultimately, his wife and two of his three daughters predeceased him. His increasing pessimism manifested itself in *The Tragedy of Pudd'nhead Wilson* (1894), "The Man That Corrupted Hadleyburg" (1900), *Christian Science* (1907), *The Mysterious Stranger* (1910), and much else.

Twain's intimate friend, William Dean Howells,* while editor of the *Atlantic Monthly* encouraged his regional writing precisely as he did Jewett's. Through Howells in the Boston area, or through Warner in Hartford, Jewett may have first encountered Twain, who was often a guest of both men. In 1887, when Jewett was helping establish a memorial fund for Henry Wadsworth Longfellow, she successfully appealed to Twain to lecture at a Boston fund-raiser. During their trip to Europe in 1892, Jewett and Annie Adams Fields* met Twain and his wife in Venice by chance. According to an anecdote, Twain said the Old Masters should have labeled fruits in their still lifes so we would not mistake pears for turnips. When Olivia rebuked him for not considering the taste and feelings of others, Jewett said, "Now, you've been spoke to!" When Twain was in Boston lecturing for charity in 1894, Annie Fields invited him to have dinner at her home with Oliver Wendell Holmes.* Jewett was also present. Jewett once said that every time she saw Twain she liked him better. *Bibliography*: Blanchard; Albert Bigelow Payne, *Mark Twain: A Biography . . . ,* 3 vols. (New York: Harper and Brothers, 1912).

"THE TWO BROWNS" (1886). Short story. (Characters: Bob, Brown, John Benedict Brown, John Benedict Brown, Lucy Brown, Checkley, Gales, Grandison.) Lucy Brown persuades her husband, John Benedict Brown, to go to his office despite the snowy weather. She wants to supervise the servants' house-cleaning. After playing with their baby daughter a minute, off he goes—a fourth-generation lawyer, rather aristocratic, but wishing his father had let him study engineering. He stops at an office to renew Lucy's subscription to a church newspaper; while there he bumps into Checkley, a fast-talking prep-school class-mate. He takes Checkley to his own office, where he allows himself to be persuaded to invest in a secret scheme—to the tune of $10,000 from one of his inheritances. A year later, Brown regrets trusting Checkley; but after another year J. Benedict Brown appears to be doing so well that Lucy dreams of his becoming a chief justice. Meanwhile another Brown is developing—John B. Brown of nearby Jersey City, partner and legal representative of Brown and Checkley's Planter Company. Checkley has devised and is selling an electric potato-planter. Brown, whose wife has just had a baby boy—another John Benedict Brown—regularly goes to his modest headquarters with Checkley on a side street near his law office. He occasionally fears exposure, but profits are reassuringly solid. One day Grandison, a successful old inventor who knew and respected Brown's father, asks Brown to be his attorney and represent him. Grandison suspects the cog-wheel device of his steam harrow has been infringed by "a couple of jackasses" in a nearby office. He would like to sue them "all to pieces" or else buy them out with "a handsome sum." Alarmed, Brown returns to Checkley, who cheekily says since their luck may turn bad they must sell to Grandison at once. Brown confesses his dual life to Lucy, who is happy one Brown made money for another. A defect of the story is the remarkable superficiality of the Browns's marriage. *Bibliography*: Roman.

TYLER, MRS. In "Jenny Garrow's Lovers," she is the mother of Richard Tyler and William Tyler. Not long after William goes to sea, she dies.

TYLER, RICHARD ("DICK"). In "Jenny Garrow's Lovers," he is William ("Bill") Tyler's tall, dark, odd, quiet brother. The two are rivals for Jenny Garrow's affections. Jenny lets Bill escort her to the wedding of her friend, Phebe Haiton; but once there, she declines his proposal of marriage because she suddenly prefers Dick. He does not know this, however; and when Bill disappears, Dick is convicted of Bill's murder. Although Bill returns home after five years, Jenny has since died and Dick has been ruined by his long incarceration.

TYLER, WILLIAM ("BILL"). In "Jenny Garrow's Lovers," he is Richard ("Dick") Tyler's ruddy, fair, graceful brother. The two are in love with Jenny Garrow. When she declines Bill's proposal of marriage, Bill runs off to sea so quickly that Dick is convicted of killing him. Bill returns home five years later to find nothing but family ruination.

V

VERNON, MISS HELENA. In "Martha's Lady." *See* Dysart, Helena Vernon.

VERNON, MRS. In "Martha's Lady," she is the high-society mother of Miss Helena Vernon (*see* Dysart, Helena Vernon). The two live in Boston. After visiting her cousin, Miss Harriet Pyne, in Ashford, Helena goes with her family to spend August in the White Hills.

VERSES (1916). Collection of nineteen posthumously published poems. In them, Jewett often strikes gloomy tones in a minor key. They mostly concern loss, stoic melancholy, spiritual resilience, and love of nature. Two poems titled "To My Father" celebrate her relationship with her "angel[ic]" father, whose thoughts still reach her and who will lead her to heavenly peace. "Assurance" says we can sweetly meet deceased, worry-free friends without the need of words. "The Gloucester Mother" contains perhaps Jewett's most poignant poetic lines:

> God bless them all who die at sea!
> If they must sleep in restless waves,
> God make them dream they are ashore
> With grass above their graves!

In "Flowers in the Dark" the poet leaves a noisy, brightly lit room to walk in a fragrant garden. "Boat Song" expresses the hope that the poet's friend will drift with her under the stars. From a broad space in "Top of the Hill" one November day the poet observes post-summer bees, flowers, trees, and water under fading light. "At Home from Church" tells of seeing bees, lilacs, and trees and hearing a Sabbath stillness broken by church bells; celestial music would be preferable. In "Together" the poet senses the presence of a friend now absent. The canary in "A Caged Bird" is trapped, as we are in life; neither it nor we know what lies outside, ahead, and above. "Star Island," once a landmark, is now desolate but for its Gosport church and "forgotten" graveyard. The subject of "The Widows' House (at Bethlehem, Pennsylvania)" is a quaint Moravian residence for old women remembering vernal joys and longing to be reunited with their "mates." Once-proud "Dunluce Castle" is now empty of victors and captives alike. "Discontent" explains that the robin, not envious of swallows, tells the buttercup not to envy "trig" daisies. "A Four-Leaved Clo-ver" is something Polly will find if she diligently searches the hayfield. "A Child's Grave" imagines the departure from merriment a century ago of nine-year-old Polly Townsend and her entrance into rest until Judgment Day. "The Spendthrift Doll" tells of children who foolishly bought gifts for a doll sitting in a fancy carriage instead of practical presents for more needy, deserving dolls. In "The Little Doll That Lied," nine good dolls are sad because a tenth doll, owned by Polly, must be chastized for fibbing. "The Fallen Oak" explains that the loss of an oak made possible a road open to a fine vista. These poems, often in simple quatrains, display conventional prosody. For example, "Dunluce Cas-tle" is in galloping fourteeners, while "Discontent" has skillful feminine rhymes.

Jewett also wrote a number of love poems—as yet incompletely published—addressed to Annie Adams Fields* and other female friends, in what may be construed as revelatory of a lesbian nature. Jewett also wrote lyrics to at least one fine song, titled "Boat Song." *Bibliography*: Josephine Donovan, "The Unpub-lished Love Poetry of Sarah Orne Jewett," in Nagel, pp. 107–17; John Austin Parker, "Sarah Orne's Jewett's 'Boat Song,' " *American Literature* 23 (March 1951): 133–36.

"A VILLAGE PATRIOT" (1896). Short story. (Characters: Allison, Charley Burrill, Jim Fisher, Abel Thorndike, Phebe Thorndike.) Six men are shingling part of a country house owned by a man in Boston. They have permission to knock off work early on the third of July. Four go to Boston to celebrate the Fourth. But Abel Thorndike, the oldest and now a widower, goes to his home in the village, where he lives with his daughter, Phebe Thorndike. Charley Bur-rill, a brisk young shingler from Boston, has boarded with the Thorndikes all spring, and he and Phebe have fallen in love. After dinner on the Fourth, the two take a little buggy ride. That night Thorndike, whose favorite reading is a biography of George Washington, goes to the riverbank and sets off some fireworks he has bought despite his normal frugality. The display delights many spectators. Next morning Charley tells his fellow workers this was his best Fourth ever.

"A VILLAGE SHOP" (1888). Short story. (Characters: Betty, Mary Dustin, John Grant, Nelly Grant, Jaffrey, Esther Jaffrey, Judge Jaffrey, Leonard Jaffrey, Madam Jaffrey, Marlborough Jaffrey.) Leonard Jaffrey is the last male of the once-illustrious Jaffrey family, which boasts a wealthy colonial merchant, a jurist, and a clergyman (Leonard's deceased father). Leonard has quit Harvard, returned through fear of failure to the depleted Jaffrey mansion in the tide-river town of Grafton, and becomes an indolent bookworm. Soon after their mother dies, his older sister, Esther Jaffrey, opens a shop in their house and sells thread, needles, buttons, whalebone, edgings, tapes, collars, and the like needed by "home-keeping women." Criticized at first by townspeople, Esther is soon sympathized with, even as Leonard continues to be admired as an awesomely wise compendium of knowledge because of his constant, if unproductive, reading. Years pass. Leonard never marries, although Esther would like him to do so. Summer tourists improve the town's finances. Construction of a public library is begun. Just as Esther thinks of selling some fine old mahogany chairs for desperately needed cash, John Grant, a rich farmer and town selectman widowered a dozen years, enters the shop and persuades Esther to let Nelly Grant, his daughter, room and board with her; the sweet young girl, a senior at the local academy, can thus absorb some of her ladylike ways. Soon Leonard, whom Esther venerates for his "vast learning," gives Latin and philosophy lessons to Nelly, whom he admires with a gamey eye even as he peps up. By spring the two are taking walks together. One warm May evening, Esther catches the two in an embrace in the garden. She tries to rebuke them, although Leonard says they plan to wed. In the morning, Grant arrives at the head of an official delegation to offer Leonard the position as town librarian at $1,000 a year. All pomposity, smiles, and an air of forgiveness, Leonard tells Esther she "must" quit the shop, to which the pale woman, though lighthearted, says "*Never!*"

Jewett disarms critics by saying, early in this story, that "Esther Jaffrey, like Hawthorne's Miss [Hepzibah] Pyncheon [in *The House of the Seven Gables*], had become reduced to the keeping of a shop." Jewett then need not add that Hawthorne's Pyncheon family tree has two men named Jaffrey (one a judge), that pasty Leonard resembles Clifford Pyncheon, and that Nelly is like Hawthorne's Phoebe, though less admirable. Noteworthy is Jewett's use of several apt similes and metaphors—best when Leonard is compared to a barnacle. Jewett plants foreshadowing hints that cleverly come to naught: Leonard should have been crowned by the heavy book dangerously tilted from a shelf over his bed; he did not pawn the family silver tea urn, as perhaps expected; and John Grant—who almost invites Esther to visit New York and Washington with him—does not propose to her in the end.

"A VISIT NEXT DOOR" (1884). Short story. (Characters: Mrs. Brien, Downing, George Filmore, Jack Filmore, Mrs. George Filmore, Nelly Filmore, Dick Granger, Henry Granger, Mary Granger, Mrs. Henry Granger, Mr. Parley, Mrs.

Parley, Susan, Mrs. Trilby.) Mrs. Henry Granger and her next-door neighbor, Mrs. George Filmore, used to be more friendly than they are now. Henry Granger is more successful as a businessman in the small town of Dundalk than George Filmore, who has no "go-a-head." Mary Granger, the Grangers's daughter, now fifteen, has a piano but a poor singing voice. Nelly Filmore, the Filmores's daughter, also fifteen and Mary's friend, has a fine voice but no piano. When Mrs. Filmore seems unusually tired, Mary suggests that Mrs. Granger invite the woman to pack up as though taking a week's vacation, visit the Grangers, stay in their guest room, and be cared for. The idea catches on and is followed up, and the estranged women renew their old friendship. Mr. Parley, the minister, and his wife, a talented musician, call at the Granger home for tea. Mrs. Parley and Mary both play the piano well; and Mrs. Filmore, moved to tears, commends them and wishes Nelly could improve her ability by practice. Mrs. Parley offers to give Nelly lessons, and Mrs. Granger offers Nelly the use of their piano. Jewett closes by moralizing on friendships and hopes that Nelly, later perhaps a music teacher herself, will invite Mrs. Trilby, a poor neighbor living across the street, to spend a week with her.

W

WADE, JO. In "Decoration Day," he is a crippled Civil War veteran living in Barlow Plains. Using a crutch, he marches in the parade. His friend, Henry Merrill, describes Wade as "amazin' spry for a short distance."

WALKER. In "A Change of Heart," Mrs. Bascom tells her friend, Sally Martin, that Sally has inherited the "narrow stubbedness" of Sally's "Gran'ther Walker." Sally agrees she has his "setness."

WALKINTWO, MRS. In "Mr. Bruce," she is the teacher in whose Boston boarding school Kitty Tennant and Miss Margaret Tennant are placed as teenagers.

WALL, CAPTAIN. In *Deephaven*, he is a sea captain whom Captain Sands once knew.

WALL, ELDER. In "A Second Spring," he is the Atfield minister whose sermon at Martha Haydon's funeral is praised by her grief-stricken husband, Israel Haydon.

WALL, MRS. In "Farmer Finch," she is a feeble old neighbor who calls on John Finch when he is sick. Polly Finch treats her courteously and is happy when she implicitly praises Polly by explaining how well her cousin, Serena Allen, took to farming to support her children. Polly is sad, however, to think she may one day resemble Mrs. Wall, now old and bent.

WALLINGFORD, JUDGE. In *The Tory Lover*, he was Madam Wallingford's husband and Roger Wallingford's father. Mary Hamilton attended his funeral in 1771. John Davis says Wallingford was a colonel.

WALLINGFORD, MADAM. In *The Tory Lover*, she is a proud old Tory widow. She is sad when her son, Roger Wallingford, joins the rebel cause and ships out with Captain John Paul Jones. She refuses to sign the rebels' oath. She is comforted by Mary Hamilton, who accompanies her to Bristol, where Madam Wallingford visits her cousin, Mrs. John Davis. Madam Wallingford hopes Davis can help free Roger from prison. The Wallingford mansion is mentioned in "River Driftwood."

WALLINGFORD, ROGER. In *The Tory Lover*, he loves Mary Hamilton, obtains a commission to sail aboard the *Ranger* with Captain John Paul Jones to raid British ships, is betrayed by Dickson at Whitehaven, and is jailed at the Mill Prison near Plymouth. He escapes and meets Mary at an inn near Bristol. They return home and will get married. Roger Wallingford was probably a lieutenant.

WALLIS. In "A Bit of Shore Life," he was Mrs. Wallis's son, lost at sea.

WALLIS. In "The Only Rose," he was Mrs. Bickford's second husband. She remembers him as a good conversationalist, possessed of an inventive mind, but impractical in marketing his ideas.

WALLIS. In "The Spur of the Moment," the big coachman says that after he worked as Duncan's coachman twenty-two years, he has been Wallis's coachman twelve years.

WALLIS, HENRY. In "A Landless Farmer," he is a friend of Ezra Allen and Asa Parsons. The three are disgusted at Serena Nudd's heartless treatment of her father, Jerry Jenkins, who is Ezra's uncle.

WALLIS, JOHN. In "A Bit of Shore Life," he is Mrs. Wallis's married son, about thirty and a successful inventor living in Boston. He persuades his mother to auction her household effects and come live with him and his wife. He may mean well, but he is crassly materialistic and is blind to his mother's emotions. *Bibliography*: Roman.

WALLIS, MIRANDA. In "A Bit of Shore Life," she is Mrs. Wallis's deceased daughter. Miranda's brother, John, put up a fine monument at her grave.

WALLIS, MRS. In "A Bit of Shore Life," she is the old widow whose son, John, persuaded her to auction her household effects and come live with him and his wife in Boston. Mrs. Willis does so reluctantly. Although her home is shabby, the reader should be quietly horrified when she is uprooted from it. The narrator is impressed by Mrs. Willis's pitiable statement that this is "a world o' change and loss."

WALLIS, MRS. In "An Empty Purse," she is an evidently well-to-do woman. She has a manservant named Johnson. She misses her granddaughters for Christmas dinner but is cheered when Miss Debby Gaines pays her a pleasant visit.

WALLIS, MRS. JOHN. In "A Bit of Shore Life," she is Mrs. Wallis's daughter-in-law in Boston. Will she treat the old woman nicely?

WALTER. In "A Business Man," he is a person in John Craven's business office. Walter looks after Craven's real-estate investments. He may be, like Jack Craven, John Craven's son. (Jewett seems unclear here.)

WALTON. In "The Spur of the Moment," he was the business partner of Peet, the father of Miss Peet. Walton survived the crash of 1857, regularly sent Miss Peet a Christmas check, and, after a long invalidism, has just died. Miss Peet is able to attend his funeral, during which her grief so impresses his daughter, Mrs. Ashton, that she resolves to continue financial aid to Miss Peet.

WARBURTON, MISTRESS HONOR. In "Lady Ferry," she was, according to a passage about Boston in Thomas Highward's book, "cursed, and doomed to live in this world forever." It is hinted that she may be Lady Ferry. *See also* Ferry, Lady.

WARD, MRS. HUMPHRY (1851–1920). English novelist. Born Mary Augusta Arnold in Tasmania, she was the niece of Matthew Arnold (1822–1888), the poet and critic. She grew up in Oxford, England, where she married an Oxford don. The Wards moved to London, where her husband became an editor and she wrote voluminously. Her most significant novel was *Robert Elsmere* (1888), arguing that Christian social responsibility is more important than miraculous aspects of Christian doctrine—a point Jewett agreed with. Arnold, one of Jewett's favorite authors, was a friend of the publisher James T. Fields and his wife, Annie Adams Fields.* Through Annie Fields, Jewett met Arnold and his wife in Boston during his 1883–1884 American lecture tour. In London in 1892 and again in 1898, Jewett and Annie Fields called on Mrs. Ward, whom Jewett described in a letter to Sarah Wyman Whitman* (20 August 1892) as "very clear and shining in her young mind, brilliant and full of charm, and with a lovely simplicity and sincerity of manner." For some weeks in 1902, Jewett entertained Dorothy Ward, Mrs. Ward's daughter, at South Berwick. *Bibliography*: Blanchard; Fields, *Letters*; Silverthorne.

"A WAR DEBT" (1895). Short story. (Characters: Colonel Bellamy, Madam Bellamy, Miss Bellamy, Margaret Burton, Thomas Burton, Thomas Burton, Thomas Burton, Clendennin, Dennis, Henry, Milton.) When Thomas ("Tom") Burton, a neat Bostonian, visits his frail old grandmother, Margaret Burton, one nice October day, she shows him a silver cup her son (Tom's father, also named Thomas Burton), pilfered during the Civil War from a Virginia plantation shortly before he was killed in combat. She wants Tom to return it; he agrees, wanting to go shooting down in Virginia anyway. The inscription on the delicate cup— "Je vous en prie / Bel-ami"—leads him indirectly by train and horse to Fairford, the war-ruined Virginia estate of Colonel Bellamy, who attended Harvard with Tom's grandfather (also named Thomas Burton). When reminded of those days of his youth, the old colonel remembers his college friend well. The impoverished Bellamys graciously invite Tom to a sparse dinner and to stay overnight. He sleeps in the room of their granddaughter, absent on a brief visit. The old couple are thrilled to have their cup back, since it once belonged to the colonel's grandfather. As Tom leaves, a Bellamy portrait on the wall reminds him of an impressively charming girl he saw on the train. Madam Bellamy tells him that her granddaughter was on that train and that the portrait is that of the girl's great-grandmother. The story ends abruptly with Tom promising the colonel to return for some Christmas hunting.

Jewett wrote "A War Debt" before visiting Virginia and yet chooses to elevate the charm of rural Fairford in the South over that of urban Boston in the North. She says Tom, who is "straight and trim, like a Frenchman," sizes up the Bellamys's granddaughter on the train as a "new . . . fine . . . Norman among Saxons" and compares her to a thoroughbred horse. Jewett stereotypically demeans freed blacks, depicting them as irresponsibly unworthy of freedom and having one "boy" speak thus: "Yas, 'tis Mars Bell'my shore, an' 's gun." These and other loaded passages have raised the hackles of several critics, two of whom, however, go too far: One too presciently says that Tom "courts" the granddaughter; another, that the girl's "fate" is sealed simply because Tom is attracted to her. Death permeates "A War Debt": Tom's grandfather, father, and mother are dead; Colonel Bellamy's four sons were killed in the war, and his two daughters are dead. *Bibliography*: Cary, *Jewett*; Donovan; Roman; Silverthorne.

WARE, MRS. In *Deephaven*, she and her sister, Miss Exper'ence Hull, attend church together in Deephaven.

WARFORD. In *Betty Leicester's English Xmas*, he is Lady Mary Danesley's nephew and the heir to her Danesley House. He is fifteen, a tall, shy pupil at Eton. He visits his aunt for Christmas, meets Betty Leicester, and because of her thoughtful friendliness has a fine time.

WARNER. In *The Tory Lover*, he is a Portsmouth resident. When Roger Wallingford was a child, Roger and his father, Judge Wallingford, visited Warner and met Benjamin Franklin there.

WARNER, CHARLES DUDLEY (1829–1900). Author and editor. Warner, who was born in Plainfield, Massachusetts, became the ward of an uncle in Cazenovia, New York, when his father died. He graduated from Hamilton College (1851), was a railroad surveyor in Missouri (1853–1854), and earned a law degree from the University of Pennsylvania (1856). He married Susan Lee (1858). They had no children. Disliking law work in Chicago (1858–1860), he became associate editor of the Republican *Hartford Evening Press* (from 1860). Seven years later he became part-owner and editor of the *Hartford Courant*, when it absorbed the *Evening Press*. He gathered his Charles Lamb–like essays—inspired by his rural home (later dubbed Nook Farm) outside Hartford—into *My Summer in a Garden* (1871); his *Courant* travel dispatches, the result of a long vacation with his wife in England and Europe, became *Saunterings* (1872). He and Mark Twain,* his famous Nook Farm neighbor, collaborated on *The Gilded Age: A Tale of To-Day* (1873), on which Warner's fame now largely rests. Another friendly neighbor was Harriet Beecher Stowe,* author of *Uncle Tom's Cabin; or, Life Among the Lowly*, while a welcome visitor was the Boston editor, William Dean Howells.* For decades Warner poured out popular, though often bland, books: books about travel abroad and in the United States; the autobiographical *Being a Boy* (1877), combining reminiscence of childhood fun and homespun moralizing; studies of Captain John Smith, Washington Irving, and Helen Hunt Jackson; three novels criticizing ruthless capitalists; and earnest efforts at literary criticism. Warner was a popular circuit lecturer, promoting education, labor-law, prison, and copyright reforms, and also African-American suffrage. Two works he coedited are the superficial *Biographical Dictionary and Synopsis of Books Ancient and Modern* (1896) and *A Library of the World's Best Literature* (30 vols., 1896–1897), which was superb and earned him $10,000.

If not earlier, Jewett met Warner on 3 December 1879 at the reception given Oliver Wendell Holmes* by the *Atlantic Monthly*. Warner, who encouraged many women writers, was Jewett's constant advocate. Warner and his wife often visited Annie Adams Fields† in Boston and saw Jewett there. In September 1884, she and Annie Fields visited the Warners in Hartford for several days. On 20 June 1894, Warner addressed the Berwick Academy gathering when the Fogg Memorial project, including the Jewett Civil War memorial window, was dedicated. In the mid-1890s, Warner visited Jewett at South Berwick and perhaps encouraged her then (and certainly did so later) to write the novel about Captain John Paul Jones that became *The Tory Lover*. *Bibliography*: Blanchard; Annie Fields, *Charles Dudley Warner* (New York: McClure, Phillips, 1904); Silverthorne.

WARREN, GIDEON. In *The Tory Lover*, he is an American sailor from Berwick who has been in the Mill Prison for seven months. He knows Roger Wallingford.

WARREN, HITTY. In *The Tory Lover*, she is a servant in Colonel Jonathan Hamilton's home.

WASHINGTON, GENERAL GEORGE (1732–1799). The American Revolutionary War leader and later the first president of the United States. In *The Tory Lover*, he is mentioned.

WASH'N'TON. In "The King of Folly Island," he is named by Dan'el as a relative from Castine, perhaps ill or otherwise in need of help.

WATERS. In "A Financial Failure," he is the middle-aged widower who, according to Downs, is "well off" and is "paying attention" to Love Hayland. When Jonas Dyer, who loves Love, hears this, he successfully ratchets up his courtship of the girl.

WAYLAND, DR. In *A Country Doctor*, he was Dr. John Leslie's predecessor in Oldfields.

WAYLAND, MRS. In "Going to Shrewsbury," she is the sister of Mrs. Peet, who is going to stay with Isabella, Mrs. Wayland's daughter, now comfortably married in Shrewsbury.

"A WAY STATION" (1890). Short story. (Characters: none named.) On December 24, a refined-looking old lady walks from her big house down a hill to meet a passenger as a train arrives at a crowded branch-line station. Some passengers arrive and are greeted, while others board and depart. When no one arrives for the old lady, she sadly returns home. The station master explains to the narrator, a stranger passing through, that the old lady's son was killed in an accident. Soon after she attended his funeral, her mind failed and she now still hopes to greet him.

WAYTON. In "Miss Esther's Guest," he is the young son of Mr. Wayton, the Daleham minister, and his wife. Miss Esther Porley mends the boy's clothes.

WAYTON, MR. In "Miss Esther's Guest," he is the rather recently appointed minister at Daleham.

WAYTON, MRS. In "Miss Esther's Guest," she is the wife of Mr. Wayton, the Daleham minister. Mrs. Wayton befriends Miss Esther Porley and generously hires her to mend her little boy's clothes, although she herself could easily do so.

WEATHERS, CAPTAIN. In "Little French Mary," he is one of the old men in Dulham who are charmed by French Mary and miss her when she leaves. He knows a few French words, from having sailed to Le Havre and Bordeaux. He praises the work of Alexis, French Mary's father.

WEBBER. In "Stolen Pleasures," he is the infant son of John Webber and Hattie Webber. When Hattie takes him to the beach with her friends, Nell Stince and Jim Stince, the baby catches cold.

WEBBER, AUSTIN. In "Stolen Pleasures," he is evidently John Webber's older brother. Mrs. Webber, their mother, explains that Austin is busy with his family.

WEBBER, HATTIE. In "Stolen Pleasures," she is John Webber's nagging, critical wife. She takes their baby boy to the beach with her friends, Nell Stince and Jim Stince, does not enjoy her brief time there, and is happy to accompany John to visit his mother.

WEBBER, JOHN ("JOHHNY"). In "Stolen Pleasures," he is a hard-working, frugal employee in a machine company. His plan to surprise his wife, Hattie Webber, by taking her and their baby boy to the beach, is frustrated when he finds she has gone to the beach without him. When John visits his mother in Vermont, she persuades him to go get his family and bring them to Vermont. He does so, and all is well.

WEBBER, MRS. In "Stolen Pleasures," she is John Webber's widowed mother. When he visits her for the first time in three years at her Vermont farmhome, she persuades him to bring his wife, Hattie Webber, to the farm so she can see her grandchild for the first time.

WELCH, MRS. In "Miss Sydney's Flowers," she is a hard-working washerwoman who lives in the same apartment building where Becky Marley and Polly Sharpe live. She gives Becky and Polly an apple pie.

WELLS, MARTIN. In "The Honey Tree," he is a Hillborough resident who learns at the store of Joe Simmons that Johnny Hopper found the honey tree. He participates in the recovery of the honey.

WELLS, MRS. MARTIN. In "The Honey Tree," she is the kind housewife who was comforted by the Reverend Mr. Dennett when her little daughter died.

In gratitude, Mrs. Martin generously supplies Mrs. Dennett, who Mrs. Wells says "ain't no gre't of a housekeeper," with her own fine baked goods.

WELSH, EZRY. In "The Courting of Sister Wisby," he used his "hoss-cart," according to Mrs. Goodsoe, to take Silas Brimblecom away when Eliza Wisby ejected him from her home during their trial marriage.

WENDELL, MARY. In *Deephaven*, she works in a Boston store and visits the Deephaven lighthouse. When she sees Kate Lancaster there, she offers to get her a job in her store.

WENTWORTH. In *The Tory Lover*, he is a guest at Colonel Jonathan Hamilton's dinner party. Wentworth brings up the unpleasant subject of Tories. His mansion is at Little Harbor, in Maine Territory.

WESCOTT, MRS. SAM. In "The Failure of David Berry," she is Sam's wife. Sam tells David she buys and likes ready-made shoes, including slightly damaged ones.

WESCOTT, SAM. In "The Failure of David Berry," he is a successful poultry merchant who persuades David Berry to sell him the wooden shop in which David makes shoes, to rent a shop in the village, to accept Sam's loan of $50, and to put in a line of ready-made shoes. When Sam demands repayment, David, whose business is doing poorly, loses his shop and soon dies.

WEST. In "A Bit of Shore Life," he was Andrew West's father, now deceased. Andrew's sister, Cynthia West, and Andrew's son, Georgie, were afraid of him; Hannah West, Andrew's and Cynthia's sister, was not.

WEST. In "A New Parishioner," he and his wife are the present owners of the farm formerly belonging to Ben Stroud. Ben's son, Henry Stroud, rents a room there and tidies up the Stroud family burying ground.

WEST, ALICE. In "A Late Supper," she is Miss Ashton's niece. The two meet Miss Catherine Spring on the train going north from Brookton for a summer vacation, learn that she rents rooms, and find their lodgings in the mountains unsatisfactory. So Alice writes to engage rooms of Miss Spring.

WEST, ANDREW ("ANDRER"). In "A Bit of Shore Life," he is Georgie West's fisherman father, sadly, wordlessly widowed. A visit by his sister, Hannah West, results in the narrator's seeing Hannah's farmhome. Andrew West, as well as Danny in *Deephaven*, is based on George Hatch, whom Jewett knew and fished with at Wells, Maine. *Bibliography*: Blanchard, Silverthorne.

WEST, CYNTHIA ("CYNTHY"). In "A Bit of Shore Life," she is the sister of Andrew West and Hannah West. Over fifty, she is younger than Hannah, is shy, loves her riotous garden, and sells honey from her beehives. The narrator is moved to tears by Cynthia's isolation and loneliness.

WEST, GEORGIE. In "A Bit of Shore Life," he is Andrew West's son, a serious and mature twelve-year-old. He fishes with the narrator and goes with her to visit Cynthia West and Hannah West, his aunts, who live six miles inland.

WEST, HANNAH. In "A Bit of Shore Life," she is Andrew West's sister and also timid Cynthia West's older sister. Hannah is described as "a master smart woman" and "a regular driver." She taught school when only seventeen and then became a tailor. She loved a sailor but returned home to care for their father when he fell ill, and never married. Unlike the younger Cynthia, Hannah was never afraid of their father, now deceased. She presently manages affairs at the farmhome she shares with Cynthia. Hannah graciously welcomes her nephew, Georgie West, and the narrator when they visit.

WEST, MISS. In "An Autumn Holiday," she is mentioned by Miss Polly Marsh as one who had "lung fever" last spring and whom Polly cared for.

WEST, MR. In "The Green Bonnet," he is the Walsingham township minister. His Easter Sunday sermon, about planting and growing a grain of wheat, impresses his parishioners.

WEST, MRS. In "A Bit of Shore Life," she was the mother of Andrew West, Cynthia West, and Hannah West. She was Mrs. Wallis's schoolmate. A fall severely injured Mrs. West, and she died last spring after a series of strokes.

WEST, MRS. In "A Garden Story," she is an official who decides to send the orphan, Peggy McAllister, from the hospital on Blank Street in Boston to Miss Ann Dunning in Littletown, so Peggy can have a country week. Miss Dunning soon arranges to make the stay permanent.

WEST, MRS. In "A New Parishioner," she and her husband own the former Stroud property. When Henry Stroud returns to Walton, she rents him a room. Miss Lydia Dunn is critical of Mrs. West's cooking.

WEST, MRS. In "The News from Petersham," she is Mrs. Peak's neighbor and participates with Mrs. Peak, Mrs. Rogers, and Mrs. West in rumor mongering.

WESTON, EZRA. In "Miss Peck's Promotion," he is a neighbor who tells Eliza Peck that Mrs. Wilbur Elbury has died in childbirth and that Eliza is urgently needed at the parsonage.

WESTON, JACK. In "A Dark Carpet," he is Mrs. Weston's son. Jack is still in school, criticizes the dark carpet, but improves its general looks by making a set of shelves for the parlor it is placed in.

WESTON, MARY. In "A Dark Carpet," she is Mrs. Weston's older daughter. Having a headache, Mary does not help select the dark carpet. She is critical of it but improves its looks by making a colorful pillow for the sofa in the parlor it is placed in.

WESTON, NELLY ("NELL"). In "A Dark Carpet," she is Mrs. Weston's younger daughter. She and her brother, Tom Weston, buy the dark carpet. They are criticized for their selection, but she improves its looks by making some colorful covers for chairs in the parlor it is placed in.

WESTON, MRS. In "A Dark Carpet," she is the widowed mother of Jack Weston, Mary Weston, Nelly Weston, and Tom Weston. She is critical of the dark carpet but is relieved when her children cooperate to brighten the parlor it is placed in.

WESTON, TOM. In "A Dark Carpet," he is Mrs. Weston's older son. When his father died, Tom, only fifteen, assumed the role of head of the household and went to work. He and his sister, Nelly Weston, buy the dark carpet, are criticized for it, but join their siblings, Jack Weston and Mary Weston, in brightening the parlor it is placed in.

WEYMOUTH. In "A Dark Night," he delivers to Bristol gold and bank notes for a squire, whom he knows in western England. He is almost robbed by Rogers but is saved by Elizabeth Brent, whom Weymouth loves. Although she is part of the group of robbers, Weymouth follows her to America. Once she is reformed, they get married.

"WHERE'S NORA?" (1897). Short story. (Characters: Father Daley, Corny Donahoe, Dan Donahoe, Mary Donahoe, Mary Ann Duffy, Michael Duffy, Mickey Dunn, Ellen, John Flaherty, Tom Flaherty, McLoughlin, Mary, Mary, Peter Murphy, O'Callahan, Johnny O'Callahan, Nora O'Callahan, Bridget Quin, Patrick Quin, Father Ross, Jerry Ryan, Julia Ryan, Mrs. Jerry Ryan.) Last night Nora arrived from Dunkenny, County Kerry, Ireland, and reported to the home of Michael ("Mike") Duffy and his wife, Mary Duffy, in an American mill town. Mary is the sister of Nora's mother, also named Mary. Mike tells Patrick Quin, the brother of Nora's mother and hence Mike's brother-in-law, that Nora is out walking to satisfy her curiosity a bit about "Americky." Patrick, injured working on the railroad, now lame and pensioned, and his wife, Bridget Quin, want the "gerrl" to come for dinner and tell them all the news from Ireland, which Patrick left thirty-five or forty years earlier. Nora suddenly skips up, delights her "Uncle Patsy," says she wants a job not in the mills but on the railroad, and reveals that she has just met a handsome young brakeman named Johnny O'Callahan. Patrick knows and likes him. At Johnny's suggestion, Nora begins to work at Birch Plains, a nearby rail junction, making marvelous buns and biscuits for sale to passengers. Three months pass, and Johnny half-persuades Nora, by now a great success, to marry him. One morning a railroad executive, impressed by Nora, hires her to open and manage a lunch counter at a new station. She and Johnny get married, and he helps her extend her counter shop to board some friends. The following summer they have a baby boy. Nora, her son, and old Patrick sail for Cork, make their way to Dunkenny, and arrive one fine May morning at the little white-walled home of Nora's mother, for a tearful welcome. This sentimental story, overburdened with Irish dialogue, is unified by the often-repeated refrain, "Where's Nora?", which both ties its parts together and tries to follow red-haired Nora's lively movements. *Bibliography*: Morgan and Renza.

WHINN, TOM. In "The Luck of the Bogans," he is Peggy Muldoon's drinking crony in Bantry. Once an active sailor, he now has no legs and propels himself in a cart by using two sticks.

WHISTON. In "A Sorrowful Guest," he is the dinner guest of John Ainslie and his sister, Helen Ainslie, in Boston. Rich and generous, Whiston roomed at Harvard with his sponging cousin, Henry Dunster. The two were in combat during the Civil War and agreed that if one were killed he would try to communicate with the survivor. Dunster was wounded and thought dead. Whiston had a fever, was mustered out early, did well in business in South America, but then began to see Dunster. After Whiston tells his story to John and dies soon thereafter, John finds Dunster alive and gets him to admit that Whiston did see him once near Rio.

WHITE, CHESTER. In *Deephaven*, he is a man some farmers at the Denby circus discuss a pig with.

WHITEFIELD, JOHN. In "Mary and Martha," he is the aging cousin of Martha Dean and Mary Dean, whose longstanding family argument with him is assuaged when they invite him to Thanksgiving dinner. In gratitude, he promises to give them the sewing machine of his deceased wife, Maria Whitefield.

WHITEFIELD, MARIA. In "Mary and Martha," she is John Whitefield's deceased wife. Her well-to-do brother, Josiah, gave her a sewing machine, which John promises to give his cousins, Martha Dean and Mary Dean.

"A WHITE HERON" (1886). Short story. (Characters: Moolly, Sylvia, Tilley, Dan Tilley, Mrs. Tilley.) During a pleasant June evening, Sylvia is bringing home Moolly, the cow belonging to her grandmother, Mrs. Tilley, from the woods. Mrs. Tilley, old and widowed, helped her burdened daughter a year earlier by taking shy Sylvia, to her secluded farm, away from cramped city life and too many siblings. Sylvia loves the place, the trees, and the birds all around her. Suddenly a handsome young ornithologist accosts her on the road, accompanies her to Mrs. Tilley's house, and accepts that kind woman's hospitality for a couple of days. He is seeking a specimen of white heron to kill, stuff, and add to his collection. He offers Sylvia $10 if she can lead him to the nest of such a heron, which he has seen but missed. A fruitless day passes, during which Sylvia searches with the young scientist in the woods and he shoots a few birds. Though troubled by this, she admires him, for "the woman's heart, asleep in the child, was vaguely thrilled by a dream of love." She would be as loyal to him as a dog to its master and wants to help. She is restless the second night, creeps out before dawn, enters the woods, and climbs a shaggy hemlock. Its upper branches lead her to branches of a tall dead pine, which she ascends until, as dawn breaks, she can see villages, church spires, the sea itself—and a proud, graceful white heron's nest. She returns to the young man, who senses something in the girl; but she simply "cannot tell the heron's secret and give its life away."

Most critics regard "A White Heron" as Jewett's finest story. It is a masterpiece revealing a sensitive child's overpowering, Wordsworthian love of and loyalty to nature. *Bibliography*: Terry Heller, "The Rhetoric of Communion in Jewett's 'A White Heron,' " *Colby College Quarterly* 26 (September 1990): 182–94; Karen K. Moreno, " 'A White Heron': Sylvia's Lonely Journey," *Connecticut Review* 13 (Spring 1991): 81–85; Renza; Sherman.

WHITEHOUSE. In "A New Parishioner," he is the owner of a Walton tavern. When Henry Stroud returns to town, he stops there first.

"THE WHITE ROSE ROAD" (1889). Essay. (Characters: Becky, John, Katy). One pleasant June day, the narrator and friends take a horse-drawn carriage, driven by John, along a road near the fishing village of Ogunquit. The adjacent woods are an arbor for animals. Women are in the fields. White roses are planted at the doorway of each farmhouse. Lovers have picked some of the roses, while the sick have held others in "pale hands." The narrator sees a widowered farmer; he used to haul timber to the shipyards and was once the head of a big family. His orphaned grandchild returns from school; she is like a bird, like a flower. Work is hard here for young people. The narrator sees columbines, mulleins, rudbeckias, sweet williams, pasture grass, and the New Hampshire hills beyond. The narrator recalls a woman famous for planting rose bushes far and wide down in Virginia. Her deserted garden is probably all trampled by this time. The carriage passes a spring bordering Berwick, York, and Wells. Fewer people live hereabouts now, and farmlands are surrendering to encroaching trees. Riding past a rural funeral, the narrator observes a solemn old woman, mourning "with a kind of primitive majesty." All the same, the day is cheerful and glorious. The narrator steps along an Indian path and sees brooks once full of fish polluted by waste from tanneries and factories. If one is city-bound, it is right to remember "the possibilities of rural life," including the road dotted by white roses. Jewett here praises not only nature but also Indians over "white settlers." Strangely, although "The White Rose Road" describes a walk Jewett and her mother, Caroline Perry Jewett,* once took up into the hills past Berwick, she omits all mention of her mother. *Bibliography*: Blanchard; Cary, *Jewett*; Sherman.

WHITMAN, SARAH WYMAN (1842–1904). (Full name: Sarah Wyman de St. Prex Whitman.) Painter, designer, and illustrator. She was born in Massachusetts, moved to Baltimore, and in 1866 married Boston wool merchant Henry Whitman. Mrs. Whitman and her husband never had children. She studied art under Thomas Couture in Paris and William Morris Hunt in Boston. She was active in teaching Bible classes in Boston and elsewhere, taught at the Museum of Fine Arts in Boston, helped found what became Radcliffe College, and was a trustee there. Her friends included Oliver Wendell Holmes, Jr., William James, and Samuel Eliot Morison. Mrs. Whitman exhibited her work widely and won several medals. She designed the stained-glass windows in Memorial Hall, Cambridge, Massachusetts, and in the Episcopal Church in Andover, Massachusetts; the Houghton Mifflin building at the World's Columbia Exposition in Chicago; and the interior of the Fogg Memorial at Berwick Academy. She also designed stained-glass panes for the windows in the library of the Cambridge home of Annie Adams Fields.* Mrs. Whitman was Jewett's closest friend after Annie Fields. Jewett and Mrs. Whitman met in the 1880s. Jewett admired her, welcomed her comments on fiction she wrote, attended adult Bible classes led by Mrs. Whitman at the Trinity Church in Boston, and in 1903 commissioned her to design a memorial window for her father, Theodore Herman Jewett,* in Memorial Hall (now Pickard Theater) at Bowdoin College. Mrs. Whitman designed the covers of *The King of Folly Island, Strangers and Wayfarers, Betty Leicester*, and *The Queen's Twin and Other Stories*. Among many other designs for book covers, she also designed the cover of *An Island Garden* (1894) by Celia Laighton Thaxter.* Though incapacitated toward the end of her life, Jewett in 1907 nominally edited *Letters of Sarah Wyman Whitman* (the selections being made by another) and provided an unsigned preface for it. *Bibliography*: Clara Erskine Clement, *Women in the Fine Arts from the Seventh Century B.C. to the Twentieth Century A.D.* (New York: Hacker Art Books, 1974; orig., 1904).

WHITTIER, JOHN GREENLEAF (1807–1892). Poet. He was born near Haverhill, Massachusetts, in a family homestead built in 1688. He read widely, especially loved the poetry of Robert Burns, and was a staunch, hard-working Quaker farm lad. He entered Haverhill Academy in 1827, taught school, became an antislavery advocate, and was an editor in and near Boston, in Hartford, Connecticut, and elsewhere until 1844. From 1836 he principally resided in Amesbury, Massachusetts. He was a contributing editor for the *National Era* (1847–1860). Most famous of his poems in the decade before the Civil War are "Ichabod," "Maud Miller," "The Barefoot Boy," "The Gift of Tritemius" (in the first issue of the *Atlantic Monthly* [November 1857]), "Skipper Ireson's Ride," and "Telling the Bees." During the war Whittier supported the Union cause with intense but not always artistic verse. "Barbara Frietchie," for example, is moving but historically ludicrous. "Laus Deo" (1865) extols the constitutional amendment abolishing slavery. His most famous poem, "Snow-Bound: A Winter Idyl" (1866), combines homely description and sincere sentiment. It earned $10,000 in a few months; *The Tent on the Beach* (1867), partly recycling earlier works, made so much money that Whittier wrote James T. Fields, his publisher, in genuine embarrassment. In the last decades of his life, Whittier was increasingly revered for expressing rural New England values, including his calm religious faith. The last of his more than forty books was a collection of verse titled *At Sundown* (1890).

Jewett, who delighted in his homespun poetry from childhood, met Whittier in the office of publisher James R. Osgood in 1877, socialized with him in the home of Mary Bucklin Davenport Claflin* and William Claflin* later that year, and sent Whittier a copy of *Deephaven*. Although in a letter (24 July 1877) he praised it encouragingly, he shyly declined her invitation to visit her in Berwick. They became such close friends that she called herself his honorary daughter. In the 1880s she and Annie Adams Fields* visited Whittier in Amesbury and elsewhere. At least once Jewett rode horseback thirty miles from Berwick to Amesbury for a confab. They often compared illnesses and alleged remedies. In 1882 Jewett wrote Whittier about spiritualism, which he considered sympathetically with their mutual friend, Celia Laighton Thaxter,* among others, but later repudiated. On the eve of the departure of Annie Fields and Jewett for Europe in 1882, Whittier wrote "Godspeed," a sonnet in which he described Jewett as one "for whom New England's by-ways bloom,/Who walks among us welcome as the Spring,/Calling up blossoms where her light feet stray." In 1885 Whittier accepted, then declined, an invitation to make a prolonged visit to Annie Fields and Jewett in the former's Boston home; he felt he would be more of a literary lion there than suited him. He suggested the idea for Jewett's "The Courtship of Sister Wisby." He said he was able to "travel by proxy" when she, and Annie Fields as well, wrote him from abroad. Jewett sent the last letter she ever addressed to him, from London (9 September 1892), two days after he had died. In "A Bit of Shore Life" Jewett has the narrator and Cynthia West, a beekeeper, mention Whittier's "Telling the Bees." In 1891

Jewett wrote "A Tribute to John Greenleaf Whittier on His Eighty-Fourth Birthday." *Bibliography*: Blanchard; Richard Cary, ed., " 'Yours Always Lovingly': Sarah Orne Jewett to John Greenleaf Whittier," *Essex Institute Historical Collection* 107 (1971): 412–50; Matthiessen; John A. Pollard, *John Greenleaf Whittier: Friend of Man* (Boston: Houghton Mifflin, 1969); Sherman.

WILLET, MRS. In *A Country Doctor*, she is one of Dr. John Leslie's patients.

"WILLIAM'S WEDDING" (1910). Short story, unfinished. (Characters: Mrs. Beggs, Mrs. Blackett, William Blackett, Johnny Bowden, Mrs. Bowden, Mrs. Caplin, Captain Denton, Maria Harris, Esther Hight, Mrs. Thankful Hight, Captain Littlepage, Elijah Tilley, Almira Todd.) The narrator, after an alienating hiatus, happily revisits Almira Todd at Dunnet Landing, in May, before going to France for the summer. She learns that William Blackett, Almira's brother, is going to marry Esther Hight, whom he has courted for forty years; the death of Mrs. Thankful Hight, her mother, has freed her to do so. Esther has made arrangements for her land and sheep. The next day, a warm Sunday, neighbors, both welcome and otherwise, call on tight-lipped Almira for news. Johnny Bowden brings Esther to the unnamed minister's little white home. William has sailed his dory straight across the bay. Soon he and his bride emerge hitched, come to his sister's home for cakes and wine, are treated with restrained tenderness, and leave for his island home. The winter-blighted grass seems greener. Esther has brought a motherless lamb with her; William makes a nest for the creature in their dory and pins his blushing companion's shawl over her shoulders. "William's Wedding," along with "A Dunnet Shepherdess," "The Foreigner," and "The Queen's Twin," continues the story of *The Country of the Pointed Firs*. *Bibliography*: Rebecca Wall Nail, " 'Where Every Prospect Pleases': Sarah Orne Jewett, South Berwick, and the Importance of Place," in Nagel, pp. 185–98; Roman; Sherman.

WILLIS, MR. In "The Becket Girls' Tree," he is the young Eastport minister. When he was teaching Sunday School, Jess Parsons and John Parsons saw their first Christmas tree in his church.

WILLS. In *A Country Doctor*, he is mentioned by George Gerry and Captain Walter Parish as a man qualified to testify in connection with a ship collision.

WILSON, MARY DUNN ("POLLY"). In "Tom's Husband," she is Tom Wilson's wife. She has such "executive ability" that, when permitted, she turns the formerly idle Wilson mill into a profitable concern. She is an example of Jewett's female characters discontent with restrictions placed on women in the New England of her era. Tom calls her Polly.

WILSON, MRS. In "Tom's Husband," she is Tom Wilson's asthmatic step-mother. She approves of his marriage and lets Tom and his wife, Mary Dunn Wilson, live in the family house while she moves to Philadelphia.

WILSON, TOM. In "Tom's Husband," he is an idler. He was hurt in a mill accident, left college in his junior year because of weak eyes, married Mary Dunn (*see* Wilson, Mary Dunn), collects coins, and soon "laughingly" feels "old-womanish." He happily lets her run the formerly idle family mill while he supervises their servants; but he gradually feels left out of her life, suddenly rebels, and successfully demands that they both take a long European vacation. He is a typical example of Jewett's inept male characters.

WINCHESTER, MRS. SUSAN. In *A Marsh Island*, she is the wealthy, su-percilious aunt of Richard ("Dick") Dale, who became her ward after his mother's death when he was ten. She accidentally drops in on Dick when he is summering at the farmhome of Israel Owen and his family. Susan urges Dick not to marry Doris Owen and is undoubtedly relieved when he does not.

WINN. In "A Native of Winby," this is the name of a Winby family whose features Joseph K. Laneway recognizes in one of Marilla Hender's pupils.

WINN, MARY ANN. In "The Parshley Celebration," she would have married David Binney but for his death during the Civil War. Remaining in Parshley, she has turned into a lonely, timid, defensive, and critical woman. When Martha Binney, the wife of David's brother, Asa Binney, suggests a Decoration Day march, Mary Ann joins in and becomes more amiable.

WINN, MRS. In "Going to Shrewsbury," she is a sister of Mrs. Peet, who does not plan to stay with Mrs. Winn's four unmarried daughters in Shrewsbury because they work in the mill and lack the means to provide for her. The narrator later learns that the nieces saved money, planned to leave the mill, and wanted to buy Mrs. Peet's farm back and live with her there. The old woman, however, soon preferred city life but then quickly died.

WINNIS, PHEBE. In "Jenny Garrow's Lovers," she is Stephen Winnis's bride. Margery Blake, Jenny Garrow, Richard Tyler, and William Tyler attend her wedding. Phebe is John Haiton's daughter.

WINNIS, STEPHEN. In "Jenny Garrow's Lovers," he is the bridegroom of Phebe, who is John Haiton's daughter. Stephen later dies of fever.

WINSLOW, LO'ISA. In *Deephaven*, she is Captain Sands's daughter. The captain says she is married and living in nearby Riverport.

"A WINTER COURTSHIP" (1889). Short story. (Characters: Adeline, Mrs. Ash, Elder Bickers, Jefferson Briley, Mrs. Peak, Susan Ellen, Tobin, Fanny Tobin.) For eighteen years Jefferson Briley, an old bachelor, has driven a horse-drawn covered wagon on the seven-mile road between North Kilby and Sanscrit Pond. He handles mail and passengers. One cold December day, widowed Fanny Tobin, who owns a farmhouse, climbs into the wagon with much baggage. She is heading for North Kilby to stay part of the winter with her daughter, Susan Ellen. Briley persuades Mrs. Tobin to sit up front with him under his two buffalo robes to guard against the cold. Briley, who reads about Wild West outlaws, says he is packing a pistol in case of robbery along the way. He also hints that Mrs. Ash, of Sanscrit Pond, and Mrs. Peak, of North Kilby, with both of whom he occasionally boards, would like to snare him. In her turn, Mrs. Tobin commends her late husband for his handy fists but also responds to Briley's boasts "with an amiable simper," much coyness, and a come-on suggestion that he ought to have a home to call his own. He boldly says that he and Mrs. Tobin "covet" each other. She pauses, agrees to wed him, and lets him have "a good smack" (that is, a kiss) as she alights at her daughter's door. Jewett's final comment, that Briley was "taken on the road" despite his pistol, is another good smack. The attractiveness of "A Winter Courtship" lies in the local-color dialogue of the two as they cautiously reveal normally guarded feelings. *Bibliography*: Blanchard; Cary, *Jewett*.

"A WINTER DRIVE" (1881). Essay. (Character: John.) Jewett says a road in winter looks different from the same road in summer. Nature in winter is at the mercy of rough weather. Yet she prefers trees leafless in winter to gloriously leafy ones in summer—unless the ones in winter are dead. Winter drives get one to places and are invigorating both to the horse and to the driver, in this case her friend, John. Mountains, hills, forests, and farmhouses stand out in winter. Seeing a man with a wagon of firewood reminds Jewett that she increasingly dislikes seeing trees cut down; she inveighs against "the wholesale slaughter of the American forests" and calls for tree laws similar to game laws. Trees have character, good and bad, just as people do, and the varying progress of trees—or lack thereof—is also comparable to that of humans. Jewett heads toward a landmark hill called Agamenticus, over a frozen pond, and into an eerie forest. She sympathizes with lonely, crooked elms snubbed by "a herd" of nearby white pines. Some trees, however—notably apple trees—do not mind solitude. She sees a sick, lonely old lilac and some cocky pitch pines. Exchanging news with some woodchoppers, she wonders if their noisy acts scare the trees still left standing. Stumps of felled trees seem like their own monuments. Returning to the pond, she remembers as a child seeing witch hazel blooming in the snow. Back on the road in the twilight, she encounters a clam man on his sled. She goes on home to her fireplace. In an epiphanic moment, Jewett approvingly mentions "Hylozoism, . . . the doctrine that life and matter are one." "A Winter Drive" relates to Jewett's later "A Neighbor's Landmark." *Bibliography*: Robert D. Rhode, "Sarah Orne Jewett and 'The Palpable Present Intimate,' " *Colby Library Quarterly* 8 (September 1968): 146–55.

WINTERFORD. In "The Hare and the Tortoise," this is the name of a family known to Mrs. Temple and her son, Henry Temple. Henry uses one of the Winterfords's tickets to go to the concert in Boston that Mary Chester also attends.

WINTER, MISS. In *Betty Leicester*, she was Betty Leicester's governess on the Isle of Wight and is soon to join Mary Duncan in Switzerland.

WISBY, ELIZA ("LIZY," "SISTER"). In "The Courting of Sister Wisby," she is the well-to-do woman who is the subject of Mrs. Goodsoe's main story. Mostly as a joke, church members asked Eliza to give room and board to Silas Brimblecom, a visiting preacher, during a church meeting of some duration. She was courted by, but mainly courted, Silas. After a stormy trial marriage, they wed; subsequently, Eliza welcomed his daughter, Phebe Brimblecom, into her farmhome and eventually willed her the bulk of her estate.

WITHERSPOON, CAPTAIN JOHN. In "All My Sad Captains," he is a tiny, feisty retired shipmaster in Longport. He has never married, has little money, and lives with a deaf, widowed cousin. Captain Witherspoon, along with Captain Crowe and Captain Asa Shaw, courts the widowed Maria Lunn. Witherspoon, the most gallant and romantic, wins.

WOLFE, HARRIET. In "Mr. Bruce," she was Mrs. Tennant's deaf friend, now deceased. While acting as the Tennant family servant, Kitty Tennant delivers to her mother what she says is a letter from Miss Wolfe, so as to have fun and probably also to see Philip Bruce once more. Mrs. Tennant experiences "a perfect convulsion of laughter."

WOOLDEN, MRS. In "The Dulham Ladies," she is a Dulham woman Harriet Dobin regards as obnoxious. When Mrs. Woolden sees Harriet and her sister, Lucinda Dobin, with their false bangs, she says they look like poodles.

WRIGHT, ASA. In "The Town Poor," he is Miss Rebecca Wright's brother. The two were once neighbors of Miss Ann Bray and her sister, Mandana Bray.

WRIGHT, MISS REBECCA (" 'BECCA"). In "The Town Poor," she is Mrs. William Trimble's friend. The two visit Miss Ann Bray and her sister, Mandana

Bray, who are friends from Miss Rebecca Wright's childhood and who are now housed in the home of Abel Janes and his family.

WYAT. In *The Tory Lover*, he is Elizabeth Wyat's patriot father.

WYAT, ELIZABETH ("BETSEY"). In *The Tory Lover*, she is Mary Hamilton's close friend. Elizabeth Wyat is a guest at Colonel Jonathan Hamilton's dinner party.

Y

YARD, MRS. ANN. In "The New Methuselah," she was Madam Potterby's young, quiet servant and is now Dr. Asa Potterby's talkative old housekeeper. Mrs. Yard resents everything about Masters, Dr. Potterby's friend, and Masters's housekeeper, Nancy Bland. Long ago, Mrs. Yard gave her favorite "pa'sley" greens to Madam Powers, who was a nurse visiting Madam Potterby and who preferred mustard greens, which she gave Mrs. Yard.

YORK. In "The Coon Dog," he is any of John York's sons. They accompany their father and Isaac Brown and his sons on the coon hunt.

YORK, JOHN. In "The Coon Dog," he is Isaac Brown's friend. The two men and their sons go on the coon hunt during which Brown's dog, Rover, trees the coon.

YORK, MRS. JOHN. In "The Coon Dog," she is John York's wife and the mother of his sons.

YOUNG, WILLIAM. In *The Tory Lover*, he is a *Ranger* sailor, from Dover.

SELECTED BIBLIOGRAPHY

Abbott, John S. *A History of Maine*, rev. by Edward L. Elwell. Augusta, Maine: Brown Thurston, 1892.

Auchincloss, Louis. "Sarah Orne Jewett" in *Pioneers and Caretakers*. Minneapolis: University of Minnesota Press, 1965.

Blanchard, Paula. *Sarah Orne Jewett: Her World and Her Work*. Reading, Mass.: Addison-Wesley, 1994.

Brooks, Van Wyck. *New England: Indian Summer (1865–1915)*. New York: E. P. Dutton, 1940.

Carter, Everett. *Howells and the Age of Realism*. New York: J. B. Lippincott, 1954.

Cary, Richard, ed. *Appreciation of Sarah Orne Jewett: 29 Interpretive Essays*. Waterville, Maine: Colby College Press, 1973.

———. *Sarah Orne Jewett*. New York: Twayne, 1962.

———, ed. *Sarah Orne Jewett Letters*. Waterville, Maine: Colby College Press, 1956; enl., rev. ed.; Waterville, Maine.: Colby College Press, 1967.

Cather, Willa. *Not Under Forty*. New York: Alfred A. Knopf, 1953.

Donovan, Josephine. *Sarah Orne Jewett*. New York: Frederick Ungar, 1980.

Faderman, Lillian. *Surpassing the Love of Man: Romantic Friendship Between Women from the Renaissance to the Present*. New York: William Morrow, 1981.

Fields, Annie, ed. *Letters of Sarah Orne Jewett*. Boston and New York: Houghton Mifflin, 1911.

Frost, John Eldridge. *Sarah Orne Jewett*. Kittery Point, Maine: Gundalow Club, 1960.

Keyworth, Cynthia. *Master Smart Women: A Portrait of Sarah Orne Jewett* (based on film by Jane Morrison and Peter Namuth). Unity, Maine: North Country Press, 1988.

Matthiessen, F. O. *Sarah Orne Jewett*. Boston and New York: Houghton Mifflin, 1929.

Nagel, Gwen L. " 'This prim corner of land where she was queen': Sarah Orne Jewett's New England Gardens," *Colby Library Quarterly* 22 (March 1986): 43–62.

————, ed. *Critical Essays on Sarah Orne Jewett.* Boston: G. K. Hall, 1984.

Nagel, Gwen L., and James Nagel, comps. *Sarah Orne Jewett: A Reference Guide.* Boston: G. K. Hall, 1978.

Rhode, Robert D. *Setting in the American Short Story of Local Color 1865–1900.* The Hague and Paris: Mouton, 1975.

Roman, Margaret. *Sarah Orne Jewett: Reconstructing Gender.* Tuscaloosa and London: University of Alabama Press, 1992.

Rowe, William Hutchinson. *The Maritime History of Maine: Three Centuries of Ship-building and Seafaring.* New York: W. W. Norton, 1948.

Sherman, Sarah Way. *Sarah Orne Jewett: An American Persephone.* Hanover, N.H., and London: University Press of New England, 1989.

Silverthorne, Elizabeth. *Sarah Orne Jewett: A Writer's Life.* Woodstock, N.Y.: Overlook Press, 1993.

Sougnac, Jean. *Sarah Orne Jewett.* Paris: Jouve et Cie., 1937.

Spofford, Harriet Prescott. *A Little Book of Friends.* Boston: Little, Brown, 1916.

Thorp, Margaret F. *Sarah Orne Jewett.* Minneapolis: University of Minnesota Press, 1966.

Weber, Clara Carter, and Carl J. Weber. *A Bibliography of the Published Writings of Sarah Orne Jewett.* Waterville, Maine: Colby College Press, 1949.

Westbrook, Perry D. *A Literary History of New England.* Bethlehem: Lehigh University Press, 1988.

Of special value are the bibliographies included in the books cited above by Paula Blanchard, Josephine Donovan, Margaret Roman, Sarah Way Sherman, Elizabeth Silverthorne, and Margaret Ferrand Thorp. See also *American Literary Scholarship: An Annual/ 1963* and later, ed. James Woodress et al., Durham, N.C.: Duke University Press; bibliographies published annually by the Modern Language Association of America; and standard dictionaries, encyclopedias, and reference books.

INDEX

Note: Peripheral and incidental references, including nonsubstantive ones to titles of works that did not evidently influence Jewett, are omitted. Page references to main entries are in **boldfaced** type.

About the Author

ROBERT L. GALE is Professor Emeritus of American Literature at the University of Pittsburgh. His previous books include *An F. Scott Fitzgerald Encyclopedia* (1998), *A Herman Melville Encyclopedia* (1995), *A Nathaniel Hawthorne Encyclopedia* (1991), *A Henry James Encyclopedia* (1989), *The Gay Nineties in America: A Cultural Dictionary of the 1890s* (1992) and *A Cultural Encyclopedia of the 1850s in America* (1993), all available from Greenwood Press.